The retreat of social democracy

Political Analyses

Series editors: Bill Jones and Michael Moran

Roland Axtmann
Liberal democracy into the twenty-first century: globalization, integration and the nation-state

John Burton
Violence explained: the sources of conflict, violence and crime and their prevention

Stuart Croft
Strategies of arms control: a history and typology

Stuart Croft, John Redmond, G. Wyn Rees and Mark Webber
The enlargement of Europe

E. Franklin Dukes
Resolving public conflict: transforming community and governance

Brendan Evans and Andrew Taylor
From Salisbury to Major: continuity and change in Conservative politics

Michael Foley
The politics of the British constitution

Michael Foley and John E. Owens
Congress and the Presidency: institutional politics in a separated system

Nick Moon
Opinion polls: history, theory and practice

Michael Moran
Governing the health care state: a comparative study of the United Kingdom, the United States and Germany

John Turner
The Tories and Europe

The retreat of social democracy

John Callaghan

Manchester University Press
Manchester and New York

distributed exclusively in the USA by St. Martin's Press

Published by Manchester University Press
Oxford Road, Manchester M13 9NR, UK
and Room 400, 175 Fifth Avenue, New York, NY 10010, USA
http://www.man.ac.uk/mup

Distributed exclusively in the USA by
St. Martin's Press, Inc., 175 Fifth Avenue, New York,
NY 10010, USA

Distributed exclusively in Canada by
UBC Press, University of British Columbia, 6344 Memorial Road,
Vancouver, BC, Canada V6T 1Z2

British Library Cataloguing-in-Publication Data
A catalogue record for this book is available from the British Library

Library of Congress Cataloging-in-Publication Data applied for

ISBN 0 7190 5031 6 *hardback*
0 7190 5032 4 *paperback*

First published 2000

07 06 05 04 03 02 01 00 10 9 8 7 6 5 4 3 2 1

Typeset
by Helen Skelton Publishing, London
Printed in Great Britain
by Biddles Ltd, Guildford and King's Lynn

Contents

List of tables

Series editors' foreword

The *Politics Today* series has been running successfully since the late 1970s, aimed mainly at an undergraduate audience. After over a decade in which a dozen or more titles had been produced, some of which have run to several new editions, MUP thought it time to launch a new politics series, aimed at a different audience and a different need.

The *Politics Analyses* series was prompted by a relative dearth of research-based political science series which persists despite the fecund source of publication ideas provided by current political developments. In the UK we observe, for example: the rapid evolution of Labour politics as the party seeks to find a reliable electoral base; the continuing development of the post-Thatcher Conservative Party; the growth of pressure group activity and lobbying in modern British politics; and the irresistibe moves towards constitutional reform of an arguably outdated state.

Abroad, there are even more themes upon which to draw, for example: the ending of the Thatcher–Reagan axis; the parallel collapse of communism in Europe and Russia; and the gradual retreat of socialism from the former heartlands in Western Europe.

The series seeks to explore some of these new ideas to a depth beyond the scope of the *Politics Today* series – while maintaining a similar direct and accessible style – and to serve an audience of academics, practitioners and the well-informed reader as well as undergraduates.

Acknowledgements

I would like to thank my editors at Manchester University Press, the anonymous readers who commented on the manuscript in the summer of 1999 and Sean Tunney, who helped me with the research. I owe an obvious debt to the numerous authors cited in the text, but absolve them of responsibility for any errors that may be found within it.

John Callaghan

Preface

Social democratic parties in Western Europe generally encountered more difficult economic circumstances after 1970 than they had experienced in the boom years after the Second World War. This was particularly apparent in Britain where the Labour Party was excluded from government for all but five of the twenty-seven years leading up to the 'New Labour' victory of May 1997. Britain returned to a level of unemployment and a growth of poverty and inequality reminiscent of the inter-war years. Yet in order to get elected the Labour Party had to abandon most of what it believed in before 1983. By 1997 the Labour leader was a convinced proponent of flexible labour markets, keen to export the 'Anglo-American model' of capitalism to the rest of the European Union, where governments were perceived to be somewhat behind Britain in the fight against excessive welfare budgets, onerous regulatory regimes that cramp 'the market', old fashioned corporatism, 'tax and spend' policies inimical to enterprise, and so on. The crusade in question was launched well before Tony Blair's government was formed.[1]

A number of observations can be made about this which help to explain the objectives of this book. First to be explained is how the Labour Party arrived at policies which place it to the right of conservatives such as Jacques Chirac and Helmut Kohl. If Labour proselytises on behalf of policies which were implemented by the British Conservative Party under Mrs Thatcher, it does so to signal both its acceptance of the Thatcher 'settlement' and as evidence of its determination to resist the import of 'Eurosclerosis' into Britain via the European Union. This suggests that there are forces at work inside the European Union which do not accept the obsolescence of 'old' social democracy as identified by New Labour. My enquiry is accordingly concerned to see how other social democratic parties have coped with the end of the 'golden age' – especially those in France, Sweden and Germany – on the assumption that they have coped with it differently. Though there has been no public debate in the Labour Party on the subject of 'globalisation', and no analyses of it in any of its publications, New Labour leaders nevertheless routinely invoke the term as part of the rationale for their repudiation of 'old' social democracy, which sought to subordinate economic rationality – largely through the mechanisms of the state – to social and cultural goals such as the alleviation of poverty, a degree of economic equality, a concern for social solidarity, economic stability and so on.

What is meant by globalisation and how it affects social democracy are questions taken up throughout this book. It will simply be noted here that the internationalisation of capital and its implications for social democratic governance was a problem which the left addressed from the late 1960s. During the 1970s, as I show in chapter three, various policies were devised to combat the growing power of capital. These still presumed that the nation state was the appropriate site for such a struggle. The rapid pace of economic integration proved this presumption false. The question that now arises is whether such policies – or new policies – could achieve the desired effect of bringing capital to heel if they were made operable at a transnational level. What interest has social democracy shown in such a project? The evidence from Britain suggests very little, but elsewhere there has been at least some debate and various initiatives have sought to move it on, as I will show in chapters seven and eight. New Labour actually makes a virtue of globalisation which it depicts as an ineluctable, technologically driven force, sweeping all before it. Globalisation is thus the force of modernity, and it is because the Thatcher scorched-earth policy is believed to have 'modernised' Britain that New Labour is happy to accept much of the *status quo* it found upon taking office. It follows that if the European Union is to successfully coexist with globalisation it too must 'modernise' in the same way. Indeed, such logic leads to the conclusion that the other states of the European Union must travel down the 'Anglo-American' road.

The choice of perspective and issues in this book is certainly Anglo-centric but it should already be evident that in making the British Labour Party the point of comparison I am in important respects taking what its leaders claim about the world as my point of departure. For what is to be examined is said to be an international experience. Objectively, as it were, international economic developments determine that only certain policies are relevant in the modern world and that most of the social democratic policies of old are redundant. A degree of direct coercive transfer of policy, deriving from these structural forces, might be expected in the light of this, leading to policy diffusion and a measure of policy convergence. Subjectively, politicians learn from each other and some are proactive in exporting the received wisdom of the hour. This has always been the case, but is much more pronounced today in an age of regional economic integration, transnational political institutions, and rapid communications. There are also ideological reasons of current salience for 'spreading the message' which will be examined throughout this book. Here I will note only that New Labour has assiduously proselytised for both the 'third way' and a host of specific policies associated with it. 'First we must build support for the third way in Europe', Tony Blair told his audience at the launch of the British Presidency of the EU.[2] 'This means education not regulation, skills and technology, not costs on business, and open competition and markets, not protectionism.'

Gordon Brown made similar observations at the British-American Chamber of Commerce where he said that Britain wanted to learn 'from the entrepreneurial and flexible labour markets of the American economy' and adopt a 'new way [which] rejects the old European model, which stifled job creation with over-regulation and inflexibility'.[3] Peter Mandelson further explicated the message at the European University Institute in Florence by warning that the European social model was jeopardised by both 'the electorate's unwillingness to pay high taxes to finance the welfare state' and by 'limitations on the capacity of European business to finance high non-wage social costs'.[4] A few weeks later Tony Blair announced that 'We need to reform the European social model, not play around with it'.[5] He pointed out that 'welfare systems need reform to curb spiralling costs and make work the most attractive option'. While 'old-style tax and spend' was no longer an option, efficiency was best promoted 'through competition, liberalisation and open markets'. Governments 'can best improve economic performance by addressing supply-side weaknesses – quickening the pace of change and equipping people to cope positively with its consequences'. As he informed the French Assembly, 'There is no right or left politics in economic management today. There is good and bad'.[6]

The sweeping claims made in these confident assertions chime in with a broader debate on the 'death of socialism' and the 'end of social democracy'. The British experience may well warrant such claims. It remains to be seen if the rest of Western Europe will follow suit.

Notes

1 An example is the lecture Tony Blair delivered to the City of London in April 1997. See chapter eight.

2 Speech delivered at Waterloo Station, 5 December 1997, on the launch of the British Presidency of the European Union.

3 Speech at the British–American Chamber of Commerce, New York, 5 December.

4 Speech to the European University Institute in Florence, 30 January 1998.

5 Speech at The Hague, 20 January 1998.

6 Speech to the French National Assembly, 24 March 1998.

List of abbreviations

ACAS	Advisory, Conciliation and Arbitration Service (UK)
AES	Alternative Economic Strategy (UK)
AfA	Arbeitsgeneinschaft fur Arbeitnehmerfragen (German SPD party circle dealing with work-related questions)
APO	Ausserparlamentarische Opposition ('extra-parliamentary opposition', Germany)
BDA	Bundesvereinigung der Deutschen Arbeitgeberverbände (German confederation of employers' federations)
BDI	Bundesverband der Deutschen Industrie (German employers' federation)
CBI	Confederation of British Industry
CCD	Campaigns and Communications Directorate
CDA	Christen Democratisch Appèl (Christian Democratic Appeal, Netherlands)
CERES	Centre d'Études, de Recherches et d'Éducation Socialistes (Centre for Socialist Study, Research and Education, France)
CDU/CSU	Christlich Demokratische Union (Christian Democratic Party, Germany)/Christlich-Soziale Union (Christian-Social Union, Bavaria)
CFDT	Confédération Française Démocratique du Travail (French trade union federation)
CGIL	Confederazione Generale Italiana del Lavoro (Italian trade union confederation)
CGPME	Confederation Generale des Petites et Moyennes Enterprises (French confederation of small and medium firms)
CGT	Confédération Générale du Travail (French trade union federation)
CLPD	Campaign for Labour Party Democracy (UK)

CNPF	Conseil National du Patronat Français (French employers' organisation)
DDR	Deutsche Demokratische Rebublik (German Democratic republic)
DGB	Deutscher Gewerkschaftsbund (German trade union federation)
DNA	Der Norske Arbeiderparti (Labour Party, Norway)
ECOFIN	European Council of Finance Ministers
EDA	Eniaia Dimokratiki Aristera (Unified Democratic Left, Greece)
EEC	European Economic Community
EMS	European Monetary System
EMU	Economic and Monetary Union
ENI	Ente Nazionale Idrocarburi (Italian state holding company)
ETUC	European Trade Union Confederation
EU	European Union
FDP	Freie Demokratische Partei (Free Democratic Party, Germany)
FGDS	Fédération de la Gauche Démocratique et Socialiste (French federation of socialist groups)
GDP	Gross Domestic Product
ILO	International Labour Organisation
IMF	International Monetary Fund
IRI	Istituto per la Ricostruzione Industriale (Italian state holding company)
KKE	Kommounistiko Komma Elladas (Communist Party, Greece)
LO	Landorganisationen (Swedish trade union confederation)
LO	Landsorganisasjonen (Norwegian trade union confederation)
MNCs	Multinational companies
MPG	Miljöpartiet De Gröna (Green Party, Sweden)
NATO	North Atlantic Treaty Organisation
NEC	National Executive Committee (of the Labour Party, UK)
NVV	(Dutch trade union federation
OECD	Organisation for Economic Cooperation and Development
ÖGB	Österreichischer Gewerkschaftsbund (Austrian federation of trade unions)
OMOV	one member one vote
OPEC	Organization of Petroleum Exporting Countries
ÖVP	Österreichs Volkspartei (People's Party, Austria)
PASOK	Panellinio Sosialistiko Kinima (Panhellenic Socialist Movement, Greece)
PCE	Partida Communista de España (Communist Party, Spain)
PCF	Parti Communiste Français (Communist Party, France)
PCI	Partito Comunista Italiano (Communist Party, Italy)
PDS	Partei Demokratisches Socialisms (Party of Democratic Socialism, Germany)

PES	Party of European Socialists
PLP	Parliamentary Labour Party (UK)
PS	Parti Socialiste (Socialist Party, France; also in French-speaking Belgium)
PSDI	Partito Social Democratico Italiano (Social Democratic Party, Italy)
PSI	Partito Socialista Italiano (Socialist Party, Italy)
PSIUP	Partito Socialista Italiano de Unità Proletaria (Independent Socialist Party of the Proletarian Unity, Italy)
PSOE	Partido Socialista Obrero Español (Socialist Workers Party, Spain)
PvdA	Partij van de Arbeid (Labour Party, Netherlands)
SACO	Sveriges Akademikers Centralorganisation (Central Organisation of Professional Employees, Sweden *or* Confederation of Professional Associations, Sweden)
SAF	Svenska Arbetsgivareföreningen (Swedish employers' association)
SAP	Socialdemokratiska Arbetarepartiet (Social Democratic Party, Sweden)
SD	Social Demokratiet (Social Democratic Party, Denmark)
SDP	Social Democratic Party (UK)
SDS	Sozialistsche Deutsche Studentbund (Socialist Student Union, Germany)
SFIO	Section Française de l'Internationale Ouvrière (Socialist Party, France)
SIC	Socialist International Council
SIF	(Swedish white-collar union)
SKAF	(Swedish municipal workers' union)
SP	Socialistische Partij (Socialist Party, Flemish-speaking Belgium)
SPD	Sozialdemokratische Partei Deutschlands (Social Democratic Party, Germany)
SPÖ	Sozialistische Partei Österreichs (Socialist Party, Austria)
TCO	Tjänstemännens Centralorganisation (Swedish confederation of professional employees)
TUC	Trades Union Congress (UK)
UGT	Unión General de Trabajadores (Spanish trade union federation)
UN	United Nations
UNICE	Union of Industrial and Employers' Confederations of Europe
VKP	Vänsterpartietwere (Left Party Communists, Sweden)
VNO-NCW	(Dutch employers' association)
Vp	Vänsterpartiet (Left Party, Sweden)
VVD	Volksparztij voor Vrijheid en Democratie (People's Party for Freedom and Democracy, Netherlands)
WTO	World Trade Organisation

1

The golden age of social democracy

This chapter, which is intended to set the scene for what follows, considers the nature of social democracy in its 'golden age' when its more hubristic advocates believed that it could achieve anything (it had mastered capitalism, could eliminate poverty, maintain full employment and so on). This seems a necessary prelude to the more prolonged examination of the period since 1970 which follows in the rest of the book – a period when some of its leaders and erstwhile supporters sometimes suggested that social democracy could do nothing (for example, about mass unemployment, poverty, global capitalism). My intention here is to show that social democracy's achievements were real but limited. The 'golden age' was not so golden after all and when it began to fade social democracy was beset by forces that had only recently been supposed obsolete – capitalism, and those who demanded its transformation.

The early evolution of social democracy

By the middle of the twentieth century social democracy in Western Europe was associated with the creation and further extension of welfare-state capitalism, in the name of equality and social justice. Many of the policies deemed relevant to this project had been formulated as early as the 1890s and it was at the end of that decade that Eduard Bernstein, Friedrich Engels' executor and a leader of the German Social Democratic Party (SPD), called for a revision of the party's Marxist programme to take account of new realities. Doctrinal emphasis on class polarisation and class conflict, economic catastrophism and breakdown, was wrong and should be displaced by formal recognition of democratic gradualism – such was Bernstein's message.[1] In practical terms those Western European parties of the Second International (1889–1914) that formally subscribed to revolutionary change were already moving away from it as Bernstein published his famous thesis; adaptation to their own national conditions saw to that, in particular, the disciplines of the electoral struggle and the interests of the trade unions. By end of 1914 Lenin had concluded that the social democratic parties had already abandoned socialism and that those who continued to believe in the Marxist analysis of capitalism needed to form a separate party and a new International. In the subsequent evolution of the parties of the old Second International, however, long periods of failure in electoral competition proved to be a constant stimulus to the 'revisionist' impulse. Looked at in the round, the parties of Western European social democracy became increasingly pragmatic about what could be achieved at any given stage of the contest with liberal and conservative forces. At the same time they continued to draw moral strength, inspiration and distinction from the struggle against poverty, inequality and the other irrationalities of the market, and the language of socialism remained dominant in party discourse.

In the inter-war years the communist parties became the rival foci for militancy as the social democrats championed a gradual, democratic and parliamentary road to socialism. It was easy to depict this endeavour as a story of failure. In Germany and France , moreover, the party loyalists were generally the older, skilled workers – the younger activist elements were drawn to left-wing socialism or communism.[2] The war had created conditions for bitterness, betrayal and disillusionment, the Bolshevik Revolution and the world economic crisis preserved them and added some more. For all its pragmatic tendencies social democracy was led by men with a socialist vision, or a vision of a moralised society, but with little idea of its relation to the demands of the hour – Kautsky and Hilferding in Germany, Otto Bauer in Austria, MacDonald and Snowden in Britain, Compere-Morel and Blum in France. Beyond the leadership echelons, advocates of planning, nationalisation, 'encroachment' on managerial prerogatives and the 'living wage' advanced practical programmes of reform which sought to address the concerns of the social democratic constituency. In industrialised Britain and Germany the parties drew their main strength from the industrial centres and from the ranks of the blue-collar workers. Even in less industrialised France the socialists depended on the urban centres for half their seats in the Assembly in the 1920s, although here the Communist Party gained the upper hand in heavy industry and the socialists' heartland moved south.[3]

But the decisive stimulus for the creation of welfare states across Western Europe in the ten years following the Second World War was the war itself and the cold war division of the continent that followed it. Prior to the war, the Victorian formula of 'relief within a framework of repression'[4] continued to prevail, though increasingly accompanied by piecemeal reforms that could be justified in terms of greater social stability and some future profit. The dysfunctions of the largely unregulated capitalist economies of the late nineteenth century, and the increasing quantity of reactive legislation required to cope with them, had so impressed some observers – liberal, as well as socialist – that it became possible to believe in the gradual, but historically determined, extension of the state's regulatory and protective functions. Fabian socialists in Britain envisaged 'housekeeping on a national scale' as the eventual outcome of this process with collectivism – 'the economic obverse of democracy' – sweeping *laissez-faire* individualism aside.

Some conservatives had seen the danger which the rising 'social question' portended, but also an opportunity for containing it with a dose of the Fabian medicine – whether it was the 'ransom' which Joseph Chamberlain thought the propertied would have to pay to protect their interests, or the Kaiser's insight that the healing of social ills 'cannot be achieved exclusively by way of repressing socialistic excesses but must be sought simultaneously through the positive promotion of the workers' welfare'.[5] Perhaps these adjustments had the desired effect of providing the safety valve that prevented an explosion, though there are many other reasons to explain the failure of the revolution that never came. Even reformists were to be disappointed in that there never was the straightforward paradigm shift from individualism to collectivism – a sort of scientific revolution – which many of them expected.[6] To a considerable extent the old habit of constructing the poverty-stricken working class as the authors of their own misfortune persisted, and has persisted to this day. This bourgeois tendency to moralise and individualise problems that were really systemic in nature conveniently focused attention on the improvident, immoral and feckless character of the poor and the problem of sorting the 'deserving' from the 'undeserving' among them. Concentrations of the latter had become known as the 'underclass', 'abyss' or 'residuum' in the late nineteenth and early twentieth centuries and were characterised by their criminal and depraved tendencies which derived from cultures – even genetics – of degeneration.[7] Sorting this parasitical mass from the deserving poor was long regarded as best left to charities; good character might then be rescued, the demands of conscience assuaged, good money saved from following bad, and the structure of inequality, withal, preserved intact. Despite a veritable explosion of charitable activity in Victorian England, however, the heyday of 'good works' evangelism passed without making a noticeable difference to the scale of the problem.

Numerous forces exerted pressure to challenge the common sense of the day and reconstruct 'the facts' in such a way that the socioeconomic sources of 'the social question' could be acknowledged to some extent, and action taken through the state to address them.[8] The appearance in virtually every European country of a social democratic party in the period 1870–1914, many of them Marxist, and of increasingly powerful trade unions[9] with close connections to such parties, must be considered as of cardinal importance in this process. Here was an important lobby for 'the right to work', free education, old-age pensions, restricted hours of labour, national insurance, workmen's compensation, the minimum wage, a national health service, family allowances and the rest.[10] To be sure, business interests eventually played a part in making welfare legislation acceptable to the established order; Rimlinger argues that the development of modern welfare 'is at least in part a response to the rising productivity and increasing scarcity of labour [which arose] in the course of economic development';[11] in short, at least some employers realised that it was in everyone's benefit if society made a social investment in labour. But this realisation was a function of conflict between the classes as well as of economic development and such related issues as the growth of rationality and scientific analysis. A 'mountain of unreason' had been built on property rights and had to be shifted, it could not be shifted by persuasion alone.[12] The amount of social investment required to reach desirable heights of business profitability is in any case not a subject of precise measurement. Employers came up with different answers to this question at different times and juggled with other considerations that were thought to affect the workers' efficiency – such as the discipline instilled by poverty and unemployment.[13]

Spending on social policy increased between the wars but the 'social service state', as Asa Briggs has termed it – a state providing only limited services for targeted sections of the population – was the norm, not the welfare state. For most of this time, for example, 'Britain had no coherent social policy', though socialism 'was the catalyst' of such social policies as there were, if only because of the threat that it represented.[14] The employers, as Hobsbawm observes, 'counter-attacked with much effect' between 1921 and 1934, restoring the actuarially sound basis of unemployment benefit only at the cost of much human misery. 'Yet the main result of the hard-faced inter-war decades was to alienate a solid core of millions of citizens permanently (it is safe to say) from any party which [did] not promise socialism'.[15] Relief within the framework of repression persisted throughout the inter-war years in most Western European countries.[16]

Social democratic government was a short-lived rarity in this period and one chiefly confined to crisis conditions, though this did not prevent the enactment of important reforms by the Popular Front government in France in 1936–38[17] or the Social Democratic Party (SAP) in Sweden. The coalition government dominated by the social democrats in Sweden from 1932 introduced state-subsidised unemployment insurance within two years of its formation. The SAP also strengthened itself with this measure by choosing a form of unemployment insurance which supported its trade union ally, the *Landorganisationen* (LO); henceforward the unemployment funds set up and administered by the unions were to be supported with public money. This gave an added incentive to workers to join trade unions and it is no coincidence that the Ghent system of unemployment insurance, as it is known, was adopted in all five nations with the highest degree of unionisation – Sweden, Denmark, Finland, Iceland and Belgium.[18] Swedish social democracy is nevertheless unique in laying the foundations of its future hegemony in the 1930s, though the Labour government in New Zealand also made strides towards a welfare state when it introduced new pensions benefits and health services in the Social Security Act of 1938. After the Second World War most European systems of welfare were in need of such basic reform that it amounted to a new start. The pressure to bring this about had never been greater. In France 'a complete plan of social security' was demanded by the Resistance, which envisaged the setting up of 'a true economic and social democracy';[19] in Germany the '*sozialer Rechstaat*' was 'the central concept embodied into the 1949 Constitution of the Federal Republic'.[20] Against the theorists of the right, the International Labour Organisation (ILO) noted in 1950, the 'quest for universality' was to be found everywhere in Western Europe.[21]

The post-war welfare state

It is clear with hindsight that the welfare state was neither an unqualified success for the working class nor a device that was simply functional to the needs of capital; it was a compromise made possible by a particular conjuncture. The system of social policies implemented by the British Labour Party were in some respects more the product of liberal hard-headedness than socialist 'New Jerusalemism'.[22] Keynes saw that the Beveridge proposals were 'the cheapest alternative open to us' and there is no doubt that Beveridge's definition of subsistence conformed to a 'very basic spartan minimum'.[23] But the National Health Service introduced in 1948 was genuinely universal, even if the system of social security was not. The reforms instituted in Britain by the Labour government of 1945–50 allegedly made her 'the envy of the world', yet Britain was spending less on social security by the late 1950s than all her major European industrial rivals and most of the smaller ones too.[24] This underlines the fact that whether it was Adenauer's Christian Democratic Germany, Christian Democratic Italy, politically volatile France or stable Social Democratic Sweden, welfare states had emerged by the mid-1950s. Furthermore, a conservative like Adenauer was prepared in 1957 to go much further than had been thought possible by the social democrats of 1945 – to tie certain welfare entitlements to rising living standards – such was the confidence by then that the costs of social investment were affordable as well as necessary.

Immediately after the war the left had a major say in Western European politics. Communist parties emerged as the dominant party of the left in France and Italy and the radical mood generated by the war was signified by the fact that communists entered the coalition governments of Italy, France, Austria, Belgium, Norway, and Denmark. Social democratic parties also came out of the war stronger and leaning further to the left than they had been when it began. Unity or close collaboration between socialists and communists was looked upon sympathetically in some countries, especially in Italy where Pietro Nenni's socialists experienced splits and divisions over the alliance well into the 1960s.[25] In Germany the pre-war left had been shattered by the Nazi dictatorship, yet the Social Democratic Party secured 29.2 per cent of the vote in the first elections to the *Bundestag* in 1949 – despite losing a large proportion of its electorate in the partition of the country – this being just 400,000 votes short of the share obtained by the Christian Democrat/Christian Social Union (CDU/CSU). In the Scandinavian countries the Social Democrats were the major party of government. In Britain the party of reform governed alone immediately after the war and liked to think of itself as the standard-bearer for the middle way between communism and American capitalism. Armed intervention kept socialists and communists at bay in Greece which was plunged into civil war at the end of 1944. Spain and Portugal survived as the region's right-wing dictatorships. Elsewhere the right saw the need to come to terms with the socialists. De Gaulle lifted much of his agenda for government from the programme of the Resistance and proceeded to nationalise banks, insurance companies and the major utilities, also approving Jean Monnet's scheme for economic modernisation and indicative planning by December 1945. De Gaulle had to contend with a situation in which the combined socialist and communist vote represented 51 per cent of the poll. In Germany, there was no electoral information to go on until the municipal elections of September 1946, but when the emerging Christian Democrats assembled at Bad Godesberg in December 1945 'the popular appeal of the socialist programme' was clearly visible in resolutions employing the vocabulary of 'economic control', 'nationalisation', 'socialism based on Christian responsibility', and 'involvement of the workforce in controlling the economy'.[26]

Cold war

But the high-water mark of the Western European left soon passed when the Cold War took over as the dominant theme from the summer of 1947. This proved to be one of the main reasons for the longevity of the Axis-assisted dictatorship in Spain. Even in some of the democracies – notably Italy and France with their unacceptably large communist parties, but also West Germany on the front line of the conflict – the cold war was a major factor underpinning the dominance of the right-wing parties and the exclusion of the left. The post-war settlement included – to name but a few of its seedy features – systemic corruption and Mafia influence in Christian Democratic Italy; the survival in public office of thousands of former Nazi officials in West Germany; colonial wars in Indo-China, Malaysia, North Africa, Madagascar and elsewhere (waged by governments that involved socialists in France, Belgium, Holland and Britain); a more systematic exploitation of colonial dependencies (for example by the 1945 Labour government); and alliances with ruthless dictatorships sporting anti-communist credentials.[27]

It would be as well to remind ourselves of some of the other limitations on the social democratic success in its golden age – a period which is apt to look increasingly gilded the further we move away from it. None of the social democratic parties ever commanded 50 per cent of the votes of eligible electors and only the Swedish and Austrian parties obtained over 50 per cent of the votes actually cast. Even in these countries such success happened rarely and only at the end of the golden age – 1968 in Sweden (50.1 per cent) and 1971 and 1979 in Austria (50 and 51 per cent respectively). The British Labour Party obtained over 48 per cent of the votes in 1945, 1950, 1951 and 1966, as did the Panhellenic Socialist Movement (PASOK) in Greece in 1981; but only the parties of Austria, Norway, Sweden and the UK could average between 40 and 50 per cent of the vote in the years 1945–70.[28] Between 1945 and 1973 the social democratic parties that spent most years in government were those of Sweden, Norway, Denmark, Austria and Britain – in that order. But while the SAP in Sweden was in power continuously, the British Labour Party was in office for just twelve of the twenty-eight years in question, despite ranking fifth in this particular league table. In other words, with the exception of the Scandinavian countries and the singular case of neutral Austria, where the Socialist Party (SPÖ) was in virtually continuous coalition, the golden age is not synonymous with the governmental dominance of social democracy in Western Europe and even in Sweden social democratic government often required support from other parties in the *Riksdag* (notably the Communists).

As we have observed, in some of the countries of Western Europe the social democrats were unable even to test their electoral strength. In Portugal the Salazar dictatorship held sway until 1974. In Spain General Franco remained in control until his death in 1975 and during most of the post-war era 'the years of state terror between 1936 and 1944' were thought to have 'paid off handsomely in mass political apathy'.[29] Immediately after the war, however, the exiled leaders of the Spanish left had been persuaded that the *caudillo's* days were numbered; after all a Labour government had been elected in the UK, shortly after the founding conference of the United Nations had approved by acclamation a Mexican resolution aimed at the exclusion of fascist Spain. But British Labour's foreign policy in 1945–51 would contemplate nothing that might offer opportunities to the communist parties and the world simply looked on as the Franco regime crushed the communist-led guerrilla war which threatened it in those years. Before long the fascist state in Spain came to be looked on as part of the Free West.

In Greece the West went one better when the British intervened militarily in 1944 to forestall the formation of a communist–socialist government. As in the case of Spain, the formation of a Labour government did nothing to challenge the continuity of (conservative) policy. When the US took over the British interventionist role in 1947 it did so because British imperialism was overloaded. After a civil war in which 158,000 Greeks died,[30] the country was reduced to the status of a client regime of the USA in the 1950s and 1960s. Its democratic credentials were correspondingly thin. 'Emergency regulations' remained in place and periodic waves of repression were directed against the left which fought under the umbrella organisation of the Unified Democratic Left (EDA) from September 1951. The banned Communist Party (KKE) attempted to contest elections through the EDA but even with 9.6 per cent of the vote in 1952 it was unable to gain seats in parliament, such was the disproportional representation secured by the electoral system which the country adopted on American 'advice'. When the EDA gained 25 per cent of the vote in 1958 a new anti-Communist campaign was unleashed, particularly in the countryside. The democratic credentials of the regime can also be gauged from the fact that the military coup of 1967 was brought about because the colonels objected to the halting attempts of Georgios Papandreou's government to introduce parliamentary accountability to the affairs of the Ministry of Defence. Only when the Junta collapsed in 1974 was the KKE legalised, but by that time it had been divided into parties of the Exterior (Moscow-oriented) and Interior (Eurocommunist) for six years. The non-communist left regrouped in 1974 when the PASOK was formed by Andreas Papandreou. In the November general election the PASOK won 13.6 per cent of the vote, while the combined communist vote was just under 10 per cent – about the level that it had been before its long period of illegality.

While the Greek left had been directly crippled by the cold war, the left in Italy and France was placed in a similar position by the fact that it was dominated by the communist parties. In France the Communist Party (PCF) obtained over 26 per cent of the poll in 1945 and held this quarter of the voters until the late 1950s when support fell to around 20 per cent – a position retained until May 1981. During the heyday of social democracy the French Socialist Party (SFIO) never succeeded in overtaking the PCF. In 1951 the French socialists secured only 14.5 per cent of the vote and though this rose to just over 20 per cent ten years later, the socialist vote was still only around one-fifth of the poll in 1973. Similarly in Italy, the Socialist Party (PSI) consistently lagged behind the Communist Party (PCI). While the PSI had to settle for less than 15 per cent of the vote, the PCI held at least one-fifth of the poll and continued to increase their share until 1976 when it peaked at 34.4 per cent. In both countries the communists commanded superior organisational resources in membership, publications and trade union influence. But after May 1947, when they were expelled from the first post-war governments, communists were kept out of central government, left coalitions failed to materialise and socialists only featured as very junior partners in bourgeois governments, when they featured in government at all. This ensured that both the SFIO and the PSI were associated with some very reactionary policies. In Italy the PSI freed themselves from alliance with the Communists – a process that began after the Soviet invasion of Hungary in 1956 – and between 1963 and 1972 the PSI entered into coalition with the Christian Democrats, the chief bulwark of the cold war *status quo* in the country. In France, socialist ministers were implicated in such policies as the military suppression of the miners' strike of 1948, the colonial wars in Indo-China and Algeria and the Anglo-French invasion of Egypt in 1956.

The left thus remained deeply divided during the golden age and excluded from power not only in the countries of Southern Europe, but also in France and West Germany (where the social democrats had to wait until 1966 before entering a Grand Coalition with their principal rivals). To differing degrees the main reformist parties were divided internally. Foreign policy arguments produced serious and persistent divisions as the social democratic leaders came to accept – some much faster than others – American leadership through NATO. The cold war and the related threat of nuclear catastrophe ensured that these divisions were never far from the surface and in Denmark and Norway the dissident wings actually broke away to form socialist people's parties. The enforced retreat from empire in countries such as France, Holland and Britain also generated controversy – violence and destabilisation in the French case. Britain notably held aloof from the process of European integration which led to the formation of the Common Market in 1957 chiefly because its world role remained bound up with the remnants of Empire. The continued drift towards doctrinal 'revisionism' also caused factional problems for the parties affected.

The social democratic settlement

And yet elements of the social democratic programme became a permanent feature of the new post-war social settlement surviving the impact of the cold war and the return to power of conservative parties. In Germany, for example, the Christian Democrats' Ahlen Programme of 1947, closely associated with the firm anti-socialist Konrad Adenauer, mixed liberal and Christian socialist ideas while Ludwig Erhard's 'social market economy' was already seen as an attractive alternative to the state socialism advocated by Kurt Schumacher's SPD before the *Bundesrepublik* was formally established. The defence of capitalist democracy seemed to require acceptance of many social democratic ideas as well as a propaganda war against the command economies of the East and all those who gave them credence in the West. Fear of the left certainly contributed to this 'post-war settlement' immediately after the war, when great uncertainty surrounded the question of whether the 'mixed economy' would work for very long. But it was the post-war boom which sustained the right's commitment to the new order. Capitalism not only tolerated much higher levels of public expenditure, public ownership and state intervention for purposes of economic management, it seemed to thrive on these measures.

The Western economies entered a period of sustained full employment and economic growth. By the mid-1950s a revolution in economic thinking associated with the pre-war ideas of J. M. Keynes was widely believed to have made this possible, though few noticed that in its heyday Keynesianism was only really tested in slowing down booms rather than confronting serious recession.

The Swedish Social Democratic Party (SAP) could nevertheless claim that they had been the first to successfully try out the new thinking in the 1930s by addressing the unemployment problem with government-financed investment schemes and by funding public-works programmes at market rates of pay. In 1933 Ernest Wigforss wrote *Can We Afford To Work?*, which specifically argued that such state intervention would set in motion a 'multiplier' effect.[31] By contrast, the British Labour Party was relatively slow to adopt Keynes' ideas.[32] Nevertheless the generation of parliamentary leaders which came to the fore in the 1950s were Keynesian through-and-through. Anthony Crosland, their most gifted theorist, was persuaded that the full employment, mixed economy – under the direction of Keynesian ministers and disinterested civil servants – represented a radical break with the capitalism of old. In 1952 he was already convinced that 'capitalism is undergoing a metamorphosis into a quite different system and ... is rendering academic most of the traditional socialist analysis'.[33] The latter had allegedly underestimated a number of transformative tendencies including the impact of political democracy and the growth of the state; pressure from business itself to eliminate the trade cycle; the separation of ownership and control in modern business and the associated rise of a class of professional managers interested in long-run economic growth and stability; finally, the variegated nature of the modern class structure which told against the Marxist prophecy of class polarisation and proletarian revolution. The state power, purportedly 'dominating the economic life of the country' and removing the insecurity of yesteryear, had grown to such an extent that in Crosland's estimation 'this one change alone would justify the statement that the capitalist era has now passed into history'.[34]

According to Crosland, the recurrence of chronic, mass unemployment was now 'most unlikely' because governments knew how to spend their way out of economic depression and any government failing to use this power could not survive above a year in office if it permitted the unemployment levels previously regarded as normal. A huge ideological shift had apparently taken place both reinforcing and reflecting a shift in the balance of power towards the state, the professional managers and the trade unions. In the 1950s the Keynesian social democrats were inclined to assume that the government of the day could achieve such economic targets as it chose to set. Crosland thought that 'the national shift to the left with all its implications for the balance of power may be accepted as permanent'.[35] The new dispensation allegedly gave more power to the trade unions under a Conservative government than business enjoyed under Labour, in part, so it was said, because full employment was the least vulnerable gain of the post-war years to political reaction. The idea that full employment might have had more to do with exogenous factors rather than state management of the economy did not commend itself to the Keynesian social democrat. Douglas Jay expressed the common sense of the day when he said that it was 'perverse' to resist the 'rational and cheering inference that the application of the remedy has had something to do with the cure of the disease'.[36]

Notwithstanding all this emphasis on the efficacy of Keynesian management of macroeconomic variables, the essential assumption of revisionism was that capitalism worked. This belief, as Sassoon observes in his massive study of the West European left, 'was shared by all socialist revisionists throughout Europe in the 1950s, and was a necessary part of their new vision',[37] whether they were Keynesians or not. Social democracy now saw its mission as the quest for social justice in the context of an expanding, full-employment economy, which its own 'intellectual victory' had made possible. For Jay there was 'no doubt' that 'by far the most effective method' of achieving this social justice was 'progressive direct taxation and centrally financed public services', indeed it was 'almost true to say that progressive direct taxation can transform society'. By the early 1960s it seemed to Jay that most of the success in eliminating poverty 'has been due to deliberate redistribution through public finance, particularly social services and progressive taxation'.[38] Crosland was confident that poverty could be made to disappear 'within a decade' if the rate of economic growth experienced in the mid-1950s could be maintained. The strong assumption in these circles was that only the incompetence of state managers could prevent such an outcome.

The issue of who actually owned industry was considered irrelevant by the Keynesians because they believed that they had all the indirect controls they needed without going to the unnecessary expense and bureaucratic trouble of state ownership. The trade cycle had been 'scotched if not killed' and inflation was so little troubling that the greater danger might well prove to be deflation, in Douglas Jay's view of 1962.[39] Britain seemed to stand on 'the threshold of mass abundance', but it had been apparent to Crosland since the mid-1950s that 'a rapid rate of growth ... so far from being inconsistent with socialist ideals [had become] a precondition for their attainment'.[40] Revisionism was addicted to the accumulation of capital. Economic growth generated the fiscal revenues to fund social reform and dissolved distributional conflicts that might otherwise arise in the pursuit of equality;[41] in short, it made everyone a winner. A rosy glow suffused much of the propaganda of the period in consequence of the assumption that full employment and economic growth were sustainable. The post-war boom years were widely seen as a period of consent and support for the central institutions of government, the mixed economy and even authority in general. Halsey found evidence in Britain of the progress of liberty, equality and fraternity, via full employment, upward mobility, enlarged educational opportunities and 'slowly burgeoning mass affluence'.[42] Almond and Verba's multinational comparative study, *The Civic Culture*, identified a strong sense of deference to political authority and attitudes of trust and confidence in government as the sources of democratic strength in Britain; such virtues were believed to derive at least in part from the commitment to social and economic reform in the political system.[43]

The Swedish model

Nowhere was more admired by social democrats than Sweden, where the SAP governed continuously in the years 1932–76 and the vision of social citizenship[44] was closer to realisation than anywhere else. Here the social democrats and their sympathisers were said to pervade the state apparatus at all levels, such was their hegemony.[45] Here too was to be found that harmonious rationality in state-employer-employee relations which many social democrats attributed to secular trends transforming industrial society. The bitter industrial relations of the 1920s had receded from view after the highly centralised federation of blue-collar unions, the LO, had signed a Basic Agreement with the equally comprehensive and centralised employers' association, the SAF, at Saltsjobaden in 1938. On this occasion apparently permanent procedures for mediation and national collective bargaining were adopted in return for the LO's recognition of managerial prerogatives.[46] Unofficial strikes and lockouts, once the scourge of industry, soon became a rarity as the LO effectively policed its side of the deal, and acquired the power to veto strikes by affiliated unions in 1941. Though the government was not directly involved in centralised bargaining – it being even a matter of pride that the LO–SAF negotiations were conducted independently of such interference, in a spirit of reason and responsibility – collective bargaining agreements were made legally enforceable. The continuous presence of social democratic governments, with which the LO had an organizational and ideological affiliation, obviously helped to remind the employers of the prevailing values in Swedish society, and a form of corporatism – a form of institutionalised wage restraint – became entrenched.

In practical terms the Swedish advance was helped by the country's official neutrality during the Second World War and its ability to find export markets in the immediate aftermath when so many other countries suffered economic collapse or dislocation. Social democratic hegemony rested to an important degree on the divisions which plagued the political right. But social democrats were tempted to emphasise the enlightened leadership of the SAP when searching for the secrets of Sweden's success. The moral authority of the party might be said to derive from its successful Keynesian strategy of the 1930s, following its earlier championing of universal suffrage. By the 1940s it was credible to equate social democratic government and social democratic values with the 'People's Home' – or Swedish national identity itself. The leaders of the SAP might be said to have skilfully used state policy to reinforce and spread, if not actually create, a social democratic culture.[47] The Ghent system of social insurance did this, as we have seen, by encouraging trade union membership which embraced a growing proportion of the workforce – rising to 85 per cent. The fact that SAP governments successfully pursued economic growth, generous and universal public service provision and income distribution was thought to encourage social solidarity – and hence greater support for social democracy. But by the end of the boom years it was also observed that the percentage of gross national product (GNP) devoted to collective services and welfare was everywhere related to the strength of trade unions, pressure from below, and various indices of social democratic strength.[48]

The SAP had looked long and hard at the question of public ownership between 1920 and 1935 when its Socialisation Committee considered the matter. Though state ownership had its champions in the party such as Hjalmar Branting, even they were careful to link the issue to increased productivity and not to regard it as intrinsically desirable. Others – such as Nils Karleby and Rickard Sandler – frankly concluded that the market was more efficient than state socialism, which they saw, at the Soviet extreme, as a form of mercantilism that was incompatible with freedom. For these social democrats, state socialism in Soviet Russia assumed fixity where there was none – in consumption needs for example – and could not produce prosperity. Sandler and Karleby concluded well before the war that the role of government was best defined as helping markets to work better.[49] Later, the SAP's 1944 *Post-War Programme*, written at a time when the relevance of government controls could hardly be denied, admittedly talked about 'socialism', public ownership, and state planning – much to the chagrin of the SAF which energetically campaigned to save private ownership and 'freedom'. But full employment and economic growth were achieved without the need for such measures and they were not heard of again.[50] The Karleby-Sandler position triumphed. Far more pressing than physical control planning in the thoughts of post-war SAP governments was the problem of inflation in the actual context of a sustained boom. Once again Sweden seemed to show the way forward with an active labour policy and a form of wage bargaining which in combination discriminated against inefficient branches of the economy and channelled resources to the dynamic and productive.[51]

This was achieved by insisting on both measures to create employment and increased labour mobility – the active labour policy – and the principle that wages be determined by the nature of the job, rather than the employer's ability to pay. The latter principle would force the less efficient firms to change for the better or face bankruptcy, while the active labour policy would retrain workers from such sectors and channel them into the more efficient and dynamic sectors of the economy. Pay rises would be linked to productivity increases. In this way, according to the thinking of the trade union economists who devised the scheme, full employment could be reconciled with both price stability and a measure of wage compression as the pay of the low paid increased and workers in the more efficient firms or sectors were subject to a measure of wage restraint. By the 1960s and 1970s a significant compression of differentials among blue-collar workers was actually in evidence and the difference between the best- and worst-paid workers continued to narrow until 1980. Firms in the dynamic sectors of the Swedish economy also benefited both from high profits and a supply of retrained workers. During the boom years this Rehn-Meidner model was thought of as the most sophisticated device for combining capitalist growth and social democratic objectives. It was not possible to adopt such a scheme everywhere, but all reformist socialists were essentially concerned to achieve the same happy outcome – social justice combined with capitalist growth.

From the mid-1950s social democratic parties everywhere were led by politicians who saw the sense in this standpoint and who themselves stressed the efficacy of macroeconomic management of largely private economies, combined with such social democratic adjustment measures as redistribution, the provision of educational opportunity, free health care and a comprehensive array of social services. In time the right began to argue that the very success of the measures taken rendered any further social democratic incursions against 'the market' superfluous to requirements. The mid- to late 1950s saw a great deal of discussion concerning the emergence of an 'affluent society'. But it was one marked by 'public squalor' as well as private plenty and it was not difficult for social democrats in most countries to make a case for devoting a greater proportion of the national income to social purposes such as education, health and housing in pursuit of improved standards, as well as equality. In Sweden, where the greatest distance had been covered towards the realisation of both private affluence and generosity of public services, the right argued that the time was ripe for the individual to make private provision in areas hitherto covered by the state, so that they could enjoy the benefits of a 'property owning democracy'.[52] But the SAP answered the point by stressing that prosperity itself generated demands on society and these demands required social action in such fields as transport, the environment, education, health and housing. Leading Social Democrats such as Olof Palme and Tage Erlander saw 'the discontent of rising expectations' and realised that the rising complexity of wants and the growing need for long-term perspectives made the public sector an aid to progress rather than the hindrance which the right depicted.[53]

Planning

By the beginning of the 1960s almost everyone accepted that effective planning was both feasible and necessary to the prosperity of modern economies. Similar industries and services had been brought into public ownership across Western Europe. Except in France and Italy, nationalisation – regardless of the government enacting it – was confined to basic industries and basic services. Control over the business cycle was seen as being 'one of the decisive factors in establishing the dynamic and prosperous capitalism of the postwar era' even in countries which had ignored the Keynesian argument.[54] Indeed, the combination of full employment, high rates of economic growth and international competitiveness in France, Italy, Austria and Germany was by the early 1960s all the more impressive for the absence of Keynesian social democratic government. In different ways, what all these countries were supposed to have in common was public authority management of the economy, supported by rising social welfare expenditure, increasing regulation of competition and long-range national planning. Economic planning seemed to be 'the most characteristic expression of the new capitalism'.[55] In France, where there was an ancient statist tradition going back to Colbert, indicative planning was centred on the Commissariat du Plan – the one de Gaulle initiated in December 1945 – and the web of large state-owned and private companies which were connected to it and managed by men trained in the same elite universities as the planners. The development of French planning in the 1950s seemed not to be hindered at all either by the *immobilisme* of the Fourth Republic, with its unstable coalition governments, or the hegemony of the Gaullist right which the Fifth Republic established after 1958. The very fact that it revolved around the collaboration of officials and managers with a similar technocratic leaning seemed to vindicate those who insisted on the shared interest in stable economic growth of modern big firms and the new managerial state, both of which were said to suffer from an aversion to uncertainty and risk.

Italy and Austria maintained even bigger public sectors than France. In Italy much of the nationalised economy was the legacy of Mussolini's fascist regime. As in France, the Italian state-owned enterprises included much of the banking industry and, though the left had never formed a majority government, the Italian state seemed to possess that control over the direction of investment which Bevanites in Britain vainly argued for within the Labour Party. In Austria the fascist experience also explained much of the public enterprise extant in the 1950s, but the Russian post-war occupation, which only ended in 1955, also bequeathed diverse and substantial state-owned concerns. Around one-quarter of the country's industrial output and exports derived from this sector. Its management mirrored the seemingly permanent coalition in national government between the two main parties – the social democrats (SPÖ) and the Austrian People's Party (ÖVP). All public bodies in Austria were run on the basis of the representation of these two parties in direct proportion to their support in general elections (which was in fact very similar). Since Austrian society was also characterised by a high degree of interest group membership, with many associations linked to the political parties, this was a form of corporatism which might predictably put party clientele before economic efficiency. Yet Austria, like Italy, was regarded as 'outstandingly successful in the postwar world' in economic terms and these singular arrangements in the management of the state sector were even thought to have helped.[56] Nor was this merely the opinion of social democrats. Though few would have wanted consciously to copy the Austrian and Italian public sectors, it was the apparent relationship between planning and economic growth which these idiosyncratic arrangements served to underline by their very oddity. By the early 1960s planning and economic growth seemed to be causally related and interested almost everyone including such capitalist institutions as the Organisation for Economic Cooperation and Development (OECD), the CIA, the British Conservative Party and the president of the USA.[57]

Bad Godesberg

What planning entailed, however, had changed markedly for most social democrats, as we can see in the case of the German SPD. When the West German state was created in 1949 it was initially regarded by the SPD as a restoration of capitalism and as such an insecure basis for democracy. Kurt Schumacher's[58] conviction, like that of his contemporary Nye Bevan, the leader of the Labour Party left in Britain, was that democracy was only assured under a system of state ownership of the major means of production.[59] Both leaders mixed Marxism and reformism, but it should be remembered that at this time even the CDU/CSU and the British Conservative Party supported nationalisation, and all parties talked about planning. The case for state ownership naturally had many supporters in the social democratic parties while this mood lasted.[60] Schumacher's militancy also derived from his own and his party's sufferings at the hands of the Nazis and the related conviction that the worker's party would eventually triumph as reason prevailed and the sins of capitalism, conservatism and Catholicism were seen for what they were.

As elsewhere, it was sustained economic growth and the gradual emergence of a welfare state which contributed to the SPD's retreat from this anti-capitalist posture – coupled with an inability to win federal elections. After Schumacher's death in 1952, the SPD began to modify its policies. In 1954 it announced that it saw itself as a people's party rather than a party of the working class. A programme commission was set up in 1955 which eventually produced the draft for the new statement of principles approved at Bad Godesberg in November 1959, which dropped the party's formal commitment to Marxism.[61] Democratic socialism in Europe, it asserted, was 'rooted in

Christian ethics, humanism and classical philosophy'. The goal of the party's economic policy had become 'the constant growth of prosperity and a just share for all in the national product'. This in turn entailed full employment, a stable currency and increased productivity. The idea that the party's ultimate goal might be socialism and the elimination of capitalism was formally dropped.

The SPD had in fact symbolically acknowledged that the majority of West Germans were content with the social market economy created by Adenauer and Erhard; the Bad Godesberg Programme was all about public relations and the party's brand image. State ownership was downgraded and the party's economic position was summed up by the formula 'as much competition as possible – as much planning as necessary'. The party programme did refer to the problem of big business and the need to prevent its abuse of power, and public ownership was mentioned as a legitimate device with which to tackle this issue. But it was studiously vague on these subjects and careful to stress that 'private ownership of the means of production can claim protection by society as long as it does not hinder the establishment of social justice'.

Similarly, the SPD was forced to modify its stance on certain foreign policy questions on which it found itself a minority voice in the late 1940s and early1950s.[62] Schumacher was determined that the SPD would not be branded as the unpatriotic party and believed that the division of Germany had to be healed if war in Europe was to be avoided. For both of these reasons the SPD refused to accept the country's partition and was critical of the Atlanticist foreign policy of Konrad Adenauer, especially the priority accorded to Western European integration, German rearmament and membership of NATO – in short, those aspects of policy which seemed to consolidate the cold war *status quo*. The fact that the SPD lost its former strongholds to the German Democratic Republic (DDR) was another reason why the SPD would not accept the logic of the cold war – an estimated 50 per cent of its Weimar electorate was in the Eastern part of the country.[63] Its difficulty, however, was that Adenauer's pro-Western, pro-capitalist and anti-communist stance commanded wide support and while the SPD vote climbed from 6.9 million in 1949 to 11.4 million in 1961, the CDU/CSU vote rose from 7.3 to 15 million by 1957.

Change within the SPD was encouraged by revisionists such as Carlo Schmid, Herbert Wehner and Fritz Erler and came with the emergence of men such as Willy Brandt, the strongly pro-NATO, anti-communist mayor of Berlin and the SPD's chancellor candidate in 1961 and 1965. NATO membership was accepted by the party in 1960 and bipartisanship in defence policy became possible for the first time so that a broad party consensus came to reign here as in domestic policy. The Bad Godesberg Programme had referred to the party's commitment to German unity and its settled conviction that 'the division of Germany is a threat to peace', but in practice the SPD had moved so far from its initial refusal to accept the partition of Germany during the 1960s that the need for coexistence with the DDR came to be seen as permanent by the end of the decade. Brandt's celebrated *Ostpolitik* actually entailed a policy of peaceful coexistence with the DDR and full cooperation short of formal recognition.

Apart from references to equality of rights for women and a voice, via co-determination, for workers, the SPD's imagination regarding social justice was exhausted by the commitment to prosperity and full employment in the Bad Godesberg Programme, combined with the affirmation of welfare measures of the sort which the Christian Democrats largely adhered to.[64] This was much the same situation prevailing in the other major social democratic parties, though there was often resistance to explicit doctrinal revision as the Labour Party demonstrated when Hugh Gaitskell failed to remove Clause IV from its constitution in 1959. The SFIO persisted in using a Marxist vocabulary, but as in the case of the PSI – which entered coalitions with the right from 1963 – such rhetoric had no bearing on its policies for government. The social democratic vision rarely extended beyond parliamentary democracy, rising living standards and state-provided welfare – in Germany or anywhere else. Nevertheless the social democratic parties were distinct from their conservative rivals in generally taking a stronger view of the merits of state ownership, state planning, income redistribution and welfare state spending. If the socialist, even Marxist, rhetoric which some of them indulged in was for the benefit of their own militants, this at least tells us that such parties still attracted activists who wanted to transform capitalism altogether. Leftist governments were actually observed to create greater income equalization, spend more on education and health, and expand the public sector faster than right-wing administrations. Their core constituencies, moreover, favoured this approach and were thought to benefit most from its results.[65] It is true that by the 1960s revisionism offered nothing new in radical thinking, but was rather preoccupied with jettisoning old ideas which it considered obsolete and detrimental to its image. But then this was an age when affluence had apparently undermined the allure of socialism for all but the intransigent minority, and state ownership of the means of production seemed superfluous to requirements. The social democratic position on planning and income redistribution became increasingly modest and it was possible to perceive ideological convergence in the party systems of Western Europe rather than an 'end of ideology' as such.

Problems of social democracy

The 'conservative socialism'[66] of the early 1960s was soon subject to an ideological challenge, but it did not come from within the social democratic parties themselves. Whether it was advances in feminism, political economy, new ideas on democracy, or the whole range of broadly cultural and environmental issues, new ideas on the left in the late 1960s came from somewhere else. By the following decade there was apparent evidence of a shift in values within the generation born into post-war affluence. Inglehart[67] has theorised this as a process of value change from materialist to post-materialist values, linking it to the unprecedented prosperity of post-war Western Europe, rising levels of education, changes in the occupational structure and the emergence of effective mass communications. People place a high value on whatever needs are in short supply, it is argued, and tend to retain the value priorities that were established in their formative years. Those Western Europeans brought up since 1945, who experienced the unprecedented prosperity of the 1950s and 1960s, attached increasing importance to expressive or 'post-materialist' values according to Inglehart. Surveys conducted in 1970 and 1971 provided empirical support for these arguments and acquired added force from the fact that the left was visibly fracturing in some countries as Inglehart wrote.

In the countries that were most affluent, Inglehart expected the value shift to translate into a declining support for the social democratic programme of managed economic growth and a more generous welfare system. In Western Europe, countries such as Denmark, Sweden, Norway and West Germany, rather than Greece, Portugal and Ireland, would be the ones where a post-materialist challenge to social democracy would occur, for these were the countries where diminishing returns already attended the old social democratic policies, at least for the middle class and the better paid wage earners. Inglehart was clear that this derived from the success of the mixed economy/welfare state in those countries and that any return to *laissez-faire* would only lead to a resurgence of class conflict on the old basis. Further surveys of opinion in 1979, 1981 and 1983 provided support for Inglehart's hypotheses.[68] The main prediction that concerns us is the idea that the left in the affluent countries would change and become more divided consequent upon the rise of post-materialist values among the young. By the time the later surveys were conducted, it was a settled conviction that new divisions had emerged on the left. Since progress towards the institutionalisation of the new values involved radical changes – to promote participatory democracy, sex equality, environmental progress and so on – their advocates eventually turned to the established left parties which were increasingly torn between old and new goals. Middle-class activists brought the new agenda into the social democratic milieu but it was always possible that the left's traditional working-class supporters would be alienated to the extent of switching to the right, if the old values were sufficiently displaced. In this eventuality class voting would decline as the middle-class post-materialists supported the left and a growing section of the old working-class vote turned to right-wing parties espousing the old materialism. Of course the new values were also embedded in new parties – notably green parties – and in electoral systems where such parties could gain European, parliamentary, or regional representation the social democrats were forced to adapt programmatically.

At the same time as evidence of post-materialist values began to emerge, there was also a revival of interest in Marxism. This is not as paradoxical as it may sound because the Marxism which attracted interest in the late 1960s was far more heterodox than anything that had gone before and far more concerned with the cultural 'superstructure' which the official Marxism of the communist parties had conceived as mere epiphenomena of material forces. Nevertheless, Marxist political economy also came back into vogue as it became increasingly apparent that Keynesian analyses of contemporary capitalism were deficient in their understanding of its dominant trends. The monopoly power of big business grew unnoticed by the social democratic thinkers of the 1950s and 1960s and yet the really big companies were increasingly able to evade government policies and competitive forces. The emergence of increasing numbers of multinational firms, in particular, in the 1960s further enhanced the power of big capital to slip the controls of governments and undermined national authorities in the weaker states of the world. If multinationals could circumvent the capacity of governments to tax, control credit, and affect investment levels, where did this leave revisionist assumptions?[69] If the management of national economies, which lay at the heart of the social democratic project, supposed that the indirect controls at the disposal of government were efficacious and actually responsible for the full employment and growth of the long boom such trends made this open to doubt. Though unpopular with 1950s social democrats it was always arguable that factors not directly responsive to government policy, such as the growth of world trade and levels of investment, had been more important for sustained full employment than government policy.[70] By the late 1960s the thought could arise that there were no national economies left to manage. The growth of multinational companies (MNCs) certainly put this national framework in doubt and the doubts grew in the 1970s.

Sustained full employment also strengthened the bargaining power of organized labour and weakened the disciplinary measures available to management. The likely consequences of such a situation had inspired little speculation and there was no previous experience that could stand as historical precedent. The Polish Marxist Michael Kalecki had been unusual in giving this problem some attention as early as 1943 when he predicted that 'the self-assurance and class consciousness of the working class would grow'. This, he argued, was why the 'class instinct' of employers 'tells them that full employment is unsound from their point of view, and that unemployment is an integral part of the "normal" capitalist system'.[71] Trade union membership grew during the long boom and was beginning to be seen as a problem by the late 1960s, placing strains on the relationship of organised labour and social democracy. An inflationary trend, which varied in intensity from country to country, was present throughout the advanced capitalist world. Growth rates began to fall in the early 1970s. Managing the *status quo* was becoming more difficult and demands for fundamental change became more insistent.

Notes

1 E. Bernstein, *Evolutionary Socialism* (New York, Schocken, [1899] 1961).

2 D. S. White, 'Reconsidering European socialism', *Journal of Contemporary History*, 16 (1981) 254–5.

3 *Ibid.*, p. 261.

4 As Sidney and Beatrice Webb described it.

5 Quoted by G. V. Rimlinger, *Welfare Policy and Industrialization in Europe, America and Russia* (New York, Wiley, 1971), p. 112. See also his 'Welfare policy and economic development: a comparative historical perspective', *Journal of Economic History*, 26 (1966) 566.

6 See on this struggle of ideologies, C. Woodward, 'Reality of social reform: from laissez-faire to the welfare atate', *Yale Law Journal*, 72 (1962) 287–312.

7 There is a massive literature on this. See B. Semmel, *Imperialism and Social Reform* (London, Allen and Unwin, 1960); G. Stedman-Jones, *Outcast London* (Harmondsworth, Peregrine Books, 1976); G. R. Searle, *The Quest For National Efficiency* (Berkeley and Los Angeles, CA, University of California Press, 1971).

8 We could include war, imperial rivalries and crises, empirical studies on 'the condition of the people', a 'social science' lobby and the need for 'national efficiency' among them.

9 F. L. Pryor, *Public Expenditures in Communist and Capitalist Nations* (London, Macmillan, 1968) argues that the only variable significantly related to the origin of social welfare schemes is the extent of trade union organisation in a country. See pp. 444–6. J. R. Hay points out that 'There is a wide measure of agreement among historians and social scientists that political pressure from the working class was one of the main reasons for the origins of social reform'. See his *The Origins of the Liberal Welfare Reforms 1906–1914* (London, Macmillan, 1975), p. 25.

10 See A. Marwick, 'The Labour Party and the welfare state in Britain 1900–1948', *American Historical Review*, 73:2 (1967) 389–99; K. D. Brown, 'The Labour Party and the unemployment question 1906–1910', *Historical Journal*, 14:3 (1971) 599–616; Rimlinger points out that in Germany 'if conditions had ripened by the early 1880s for the institution of new social rights, it was mainly because of pressure from below'. Rimlinger, *Welfare Policy and Industrialization*, p. 112.

11 Rimlinger, 'Welfare policy and economic development', p. 556

12 J. Saville, 'The welfare state: an historical appraisal', *New Reasoner*, 3, Winter (1957–8) 9–10.

13 The employers' perception is covered in J. R. Hay, 'Employers and social policy in Britain: the evolution of welfare legislation 1905–1914', *Social History*, 4 (1977) 435–55; the themes, not surprisingly, are profitability, cost, industrial discipline, and social integration.

14 B. B. Gilbert, *British Social Policy, 1914–1939* (London, Batsford, 1970), p. 305.

15 E. J. Hobsbawm, 'Trends in the British Labour movement', in his *Labouring Men* (London, Wiedenfeld and Nicolson, 1968), p. 330. For some of the detail see R. Lowe, 'The erosion of state intervention in Britain 1917–24', *Economic History Review*, 31 (1978).

16 See on this R. McKibbin, 'The "social psychology" of unemployment in inter-war Britain', in his *Ideologies of Class* (Oxford, Oxford University Press, 1990), pp. 246–52.

17 H. W. Ehrmann, *French Labor From Popular Front to Liberation* (Oxford, Oxford University Press, 1947).

18 B. Rothstein, 'Marxism, institutional analysis, and working-class power: the Swedish case', *Politics and Society*, 18:3 (1990) 335–6.

19 The Resistance Charter of 1944 is reproduced in full in D. Thompson, *Democracy in France Since 1870* (Oxford, Oxford University Press, fifth edition, 1969), pp. 314–16.

20 Rimlinger, *Welfare Policy and Industrialization*, p. 139.

21 Quoted in A. Briggs, 'The welfare state in historical perspective', *Archives de Europeenes de Sociologie*, 2 (1961) 223.

22 The idea that socialist and humanitarian evangelism swept in the British welfare state to create a 'dependency culture' is the thesis advocated by C. Barnett, *The Audit of War* (London, Macmillan, 1986) and in his *The Lost Victory* (London, Macmillan, 1995).

23 Keynes is quoted in J. Harris, 'Social planning in wartime', in J. M. Winter (ed.), *War and Economic Development* (London, Cambridge University Press, 1975), p. 244; see also J. Harris, 'Enterprise and the welfare state: a comparative perspective', in T. Gourvish and A. O'Day (eds), *Britain Since 1945* (London, Macmillan, 1991), p. 49.

24 J. Kohl, 'Trends and problems in postwar public expenditure development in Western Europe and North America', in P. Flora and A. J. Heidenheimer (eds), *The Development of Welfare States in Europe and North America* (New Brunswick, NJ, Transaction Publishers, 1981), pp. 307–44.

25 The PSDI was set up in 1947 in opposition to Nenni's policy and in 1964 the PSIUP broke away after the PSI definitively ended the alliance with the PCI.

26 H.-P. Schwartz, *Konrad Adenauer: Volume One: From the German Empire to the Federal Republic, 1876–1952* (Oxford, Berghahn, 1995), p. 346.

27 On Spain see P. Preston, *Franco* (London, Fontana, 1995), ch. 21; on West Germany's Nazi problem, H. Arendt, *Eichmann in Jerusalem* (Harmondsworth, Penguin, 1965), makes some telling points on pp. 16, 79 and 185; the British Labour government's colonial policies are dealt with in J. Callaghan, *Great Power Complex* (London, Pluto Press, 1997), ch. 5.

28 See A. Przeworski and J. Sprague, *Paper Stones: A History of Electoral Socialism* (Chicago, IL, University of Chicago Press, 1986), p. 30.

29 Preston, *Franco*, p. 731.

30 D. Eudes, *The Kapetanios: Partisans and Civil War in Greece, 1943–49* (London, New Left Books, 1972), p. 354. President Truman's 'containment' speech to Congress on 12 March 1947 referred to the USA's 'unreserved interest in Greece' and demanded $300 million warning that 'without financial aid from America,

Greece will fall under Communist domination within twenty-four hours'. Quoted by Eudes, p. 279.

31 See T. Tilton, 'Why don't the Swedish Social Democrats nationalize industry?', *Scandinavian Studies*, 59 (1987) 142–66 and his *The Political Theory of Swedish Social Democracy* (Oxford, Clarendon Press, 1990).

32 See D. Winch, *Economics and Policy* (London, Hodder and Stoughton, 1969), pp. 282–4. Keynes nevertheless had his Labour advocates such as Douglas Jay, in *The Socialist Case* (London, Faber and Faber, 1937); see on this E. Durbin, *New Jerusalems: The Labour Party and the Economics of Democratic Socialism* (London, Routledge and Kegan Paul, 1985).

33 C. A. R. Crosland, 'The transition From capitalism', in R. H. S. Crossman (ed.), *New Fabian Essays* (London, Turnstile Press, 1952), p. 35.

34 *Ibid.*, p. 39.

35 C. A. R. Crosland, *The Future of Socialism* (London, Cape, 1956), pp. 28–9.

36 D. Jay, *Socialism in the New Society* (London, Longmans, 1962), p. 134

37 D. Sassoon, *One Hundred Years of Socialism: The West European Left in the Twentieth Century* (London, I. B. Tauris, 1996), p. 245.

38 Jay, *Socialism in the New Society*, pp. 147, 178, 181, 206.

39 *Ibid.*, p. 136.

40 Crosland, *Future of Socialism*, pp. 515 and 378–9.

41 'Increased real income provides us with an admirable detour around the rancour anciently associated with efforts to redistribute wealth' as J. K. Galbraith put it in a bestseller of the period. See *The Affluent Society* (Harmondsworth, Pelican, 1958), p. 121.

42 A. H. Halsey, *Change in British Society* (London, Oxford University Press, 1981), pp. 156–7.

43 G. Almond and S. Verba, *The Civic Culture* (Princeton, NJ, Princeton University Press, 1963), pp. 197–8.

44 T. H. Marshall famously argued that the welfare state implicitly ushered in an era in which citizenship was a sufficient condition for social rights, to add to the political and legal rights which had already been won. The argument was notably premature in the British case. See his *Citizenship and Social Class and Other Essays* (London, Cambridge University Press, 1950).

45 F. Castles, *The Social Democratic Image of Society* (London, Sage, 1978), p. 96.

46 See P. Swenson, 'Bringing capital back in, or social democracy reconsidered', *World Politics*, 43:4 (1991), 519.

47 G. Esping-Andersen, *Politics Against Markets* (Princeton, NJ, Princeton University Press, 1985), p. 33.

48 See, C. Hewitt, 'The effect of political democracy and social democracy on equality in industrial societies: a cross-national comparison', *American Sociological Review*, xlii:3 (1977).

49 See Tilton, 'Why don't the Swedish Social Democrats nationalize industry?', pp. 142–66.

50 R. Meidner, 'Why did the Swedish model fail?', in R. Miliband and L. Panitch (eds), *The Socialist Register 1993* (London, Merlin, 1993), p. 212.

51 This known as the Rehn-Meidner policy after the LO economists who devised it.

52 H. Heclo and H. Madsen, *Policy and Politics in Sweden* (Philadelphia, PA, Temple University Press, 1987), p. 145.

53 *Ibid.*

54 A. Shonfield, *Modern Capitalism: The Changing Balance of Public and Private Power* (London, Oxford University Press, 1965), p. 64.

55 *Ibid.*, p. 121.

56 *Ibid.*, p. 192.

57 See P. Krugman, 'The myth of Asia's miracle', *Foreign Affairs*, November–December (1994) 62–6.

58 Schumacher dominated the SPD after the war and its policies. He has been described as 'an heroic and charismatic figure whose devotion to socialism verged on fanaticism'. See W. Carr, 'German social democracy since 1945', in R. Fletcher (ed.), *Bernstein to Brandt: A Short History of German Social Democracy* (London, Edward Arnold, 1987), p. 195.

59 G. Braunthal, *The German Social Democrats Since 1969* (Boulder, CO, Westview Press, 1994), p. 16; Bevan's views were expounded in *Tribune*, during the 1950s, but also in his *In Place of Fear* (London, Quartet, [1952] 1978).

60 The German trade unions, for example, were strong supporters of planning, socialisation and co-determination until the social market economy emerged in the early 1950s. See D. Prowe, 'Ordnungsmacht and mitbestimmung', in D. E. Barclay and E. D. Weitz, *Between Reform and Revolution: German Socialism and Communism from 1840 to 1990* (Oxford, Berghahn, 1998), pp. 397–420.

61 The document is reproduced in English in C. C. Schweitzer, D. Karsten *et al.* (eds), *Politics and Government in the Federal Republic of Germany: Basic Documents* (Leamington Spa, Berg, 1984), pp. 215–18.

62 See, D. Orlow, 'German social democracy and European unification, 1945 to 1955' in Barclay and Weitz, *Between Reform and Revolution*, pp. 467–88.

63 E. Kolinsky, *Parties, Opposition and Society in West Germany* (London, Croom Helm, 1984), p. 18.

64 The first Act regulating co-determination at shop floor level – where it was largely uncontroversial – had already been passed in 1953 by a Christian Democratic government; it was not until 1972 that this law was superseded and not until 1976 that the principle of co-determination was extended to board level in companies employing over 2,000 workers. Even though the Co-determination Act of 1976 was fiercely opposed by the main business organisations, the *Bundestag* voted in favour by a huge majority.

65 See R. Tufte, 'Political parties, social class, and economic policy preferences', *Government and Opposition*, 14:1 (1979) 18–36; F. Castles and R. D. McKinlay, 'Does politics matter? An analysis of the public welfare commitment in advanced democratic states', *European Journal of Political Research*, 7:2 (1979) 169–86.

66 S. M. Lipset, 'The changing class structure and contemporary European politics', in S. Graubard (ed.), *A New Europe?* (Boston, MA, Houghton Mifflin, 1964), p. 362.

67 R. Inglehart, *The Silent Revolution: Changing Values and Political Styles Among Western Publics* (Princeton, NJ, Princeton University Press, 1977), ch. 2.

68 R. Inglehart, 'Value change in industrial societies', *American Political Science Review*, 81:4 (1987) 1289–303.

69 S. Hymer and R. Rowthorn, 'Multinational corporations and international oligopoly: The non-American challenge', in C. P. Kindelberger (ed.), *The International Corporation: A Symposium* (Cambridge, MA, MIT Press, 1970), p. 88.

70 R. C. O. Matthews, 'Why has Britain had full employment since the war?', *Economic Journal*, 78:3 (1968) 555–69.

71 M. Kalecki, 'Political aspects of full employment', in M. Kalecki, *Selected Essays on the Dynamics of the Capitalist Economy, 1933–70* (London, Cambridge University Press, 1971), p. 140.

2

End of the golden age

It now seems clear that the golden age rested on a particular combination of historical factors that can not be easily reproduced. The period began with wages depressed by the world crisis of the 1930s and the austerity of the war. The years of reconstruction that followed the war kept the bargaining power of labour weak in large parts of Western Europe. In Germany, Japan, Italy and other leading countries dictatorial regimes had also persecuted and even destroyed organised labour. It is little wonder that the accumulation of capital proceeded on the basis of very low labour costs well into the 1950s.[1] Full employment could produce tight labour markets in Britain and Sweden, but in general there were ways around the problem. As late as the mid-1950s countries such as Germany, France and Denmark still had as much as one-quarter of their working populations employed in agriculture, while in Ireland, Italy, Greece, Spain and Portugal the proportion was much higher. The growth of industry and services drew on this internal labour pool as labour migrated to the towns and agriculture became more efficient. Cheap and plentiful labour – much of it additionally imported from former colonies – assisted the high growth and low inflation rates of the time.

The US had also emerged from the Second World War as the manufacturer of most of the world's goods, with by far the highest productivity of labour. It was also the world's leading creditor nation. Everyone else wanted American goods in the 1940s and needed the dollars with which to purchase them. The US state occupied a unique position of leadership and was able to establish a capitalist world order under its protective hegemony. Even before the war ended, the international monetary system outlined at Bretton Woods in 1944 had recognised the supremacy of the dollar by anchoring a new regime of fixed exchange rates between the leading national currencies and a fixed rate of exchange between the dollar and gold. The open world economy under US hegemony which American policy makers planned during the war was qualified by a conscious decision not to return to the pre-1931 system. Certain restrictive practices were to be permitted in the interests of stability and so that states had a measure of policy autonomy. Capital controls were permitted and the development of the cold war reinforced the determination of policy makers to prevent speculative and other flows of capital from undermining the interventionist welfare states which developed in Western Europe. In this system of embedded liberalism – as John Ruggie has called it[2] – bankers played second fiddle to the alliance of Keynesians and social democrats who wanted finance as the servant of political economy rather than its master. What made this system unusual was its design by politicians rather than bankers, with political considerations uppermost rather than the profit making objectives of the financiers, upon whose control and interests all previous international monetary systems had been based. World money was no longer to be a by-product of profit-making. As Arrighi points out: 'In the world monetary system established at Bretton Woods ... the "production" of world money was taken over by a network of governmental organizations motivated primarily by considerations of welfare, security, and power ...'[3]

In the short-run at least the liquidity problems of the post-war world were perceived through a political lens as the cold war between the US and the Soviet Union unfolded in the course of 1945–47. By the summer of 1947 – and the announcement of the Marshall Plan – the US was prepared to assist the post-war reconstruction of West European economies in order to buttress these against communism and secure long-term markets for its own goods. The Korean War which began in June 1950 assisted the spread of these principles to Japan and forced up world demand with the assistance of a sort of military Keynesianism. Japanese and German capitalism were thus restored in the interests of the cold war with the help of an enormous transfusion of US capital. The growth of international trade and currency stability were seen as crucial to the prosperity of the US and its anti-communist allies – but so was the political stability of the leading capitalist nations. Principles of liberal political economy were not allowed to get in the way of this; Japan was allowed to protect its own economy, the West Europeans were allowed to have interventionist welfare states. The realisation of social democratic goals thus developed under US protection.[4]

Politics and full employment

Though defence spending played a part in the growth of post-war demand in the context of the cold war, as we have observed, it was not the whole story. Government expenditure, which had averaged 18 per cent of the GDP of OECD countries in 1929, had risen to 27 per cent by the time of the Korean War, and reached an average of 37 per cent by 1973. This reflected the growing importance of the welfare state even in countries – the majority of them – where left government was a rarity. During this period the range of household incomes also became more equal, especially in the US, Japan, Sweden and France, less so in the UK, Germany and the Netherlands.[5] The growth of welfare expenditure was financed by the rise in labour productivity during this period, which exceeded the growth of consumption. Economic growth was powered by the spread of Fordist principles of mass production which combined technical and managerial innovation with production economies of scale and a wage remuneration capable of sustaining mass consumption.[6] Consumer durables industries were notable exemplars of this phenomenon, as rising living standards inaugurated the 'affluent society' in the 1950s. The intensive exploitation of workers that is associated with Fordism also spread to agriculture, primary industries and the service sector.

The unprecedented boom of the post-war years thus arose from the expansion of world trade and the spread of Fordism within an institutional structure – in which the US was the hegemonic power – which controlled international finance and permitted the sustained growth of both military and welfare state expenditures. Such was the success of this system of 'mixed economy' that the goals of social democracy were generally considered to be achievable within its framework. Moreover, according to Glyn, 'the overwhelming proportion of the cost of egalitarian redistribution was met out of wages – redistribution within the working class broadly defined'.[7] Economic growth, based on growing labour productivity, was supported by social reform and seemed to dissolve distributional conflicts between and within the social classes; workers had certain rights and growing living standards, while capitalists made profits and retained the prerogatives of management.

Confidence in the economic powers of central government thus soared upon this basis and welfare coverage was extended in one way or another during the 1950s and 1960s until social expenditure, by the early 1970s, represented around 20 per cent of the GDP of a typical West European state (17–18 per cent in the UK).[8] The unprecedented security which workers enjoyed during these boom years lasted an unprecedented length of time. Expectations began to change, deference was eroded, and the organisations of labour grew stronger. However, despite the massive growth of the welfare state and social democratic confidence in the 'strategy of equality' which it was supposed to represent it became apparent that the problems of poverty and inequality persisted. Indeed, the welfare state was criticised from the left in some countries for its failure to tackle these problems, while at the same time subsidising middle-class incomes.

Some social democrats nevertheless came to believe that the welfare statist society had swung the balance of social power in favour of organised labour. Korpi, for example, writing about the Swedish experience in the 1970s, conceptualised this as a cumulative process, as increasing 'power resources' – full employment, welfare entitlements, trade union organisation and social democratic government – sharpened working-class appetites for further measures of egalitarianism.[9] Korpi stressed that progress in Sweden derived from the class character of the social democratic programme, but he also argued that further steps towards equality were both imperilled and made necessary by the continuing insecurities generated by capitalism. This struck a significantly more guarded note than those who had argued in the 1950s and 60s that Western economies were subject to such a degree of conscious manipulation by politicians that the fundamental goals of socialism had either been realised or were within reach.

Korpi's power resources argument was nevertheless unduly optimistic about the capacity of a labour movement to determine the development of a society, even in a country such as Sweden where the Social Democrats were normally in government. The emergence of increasing numbers of multinational corporations in the 1960s enhanced the power of the big firms to slip the controls of governments and even undermined national authorities in the weaker states. Marxist analysts put the multinational company back in the picture during the 1960s and by the end of the decade there was reason to believe that the capacity of governments to tax, exercise control over credit, and affect investment levels was being circumvented.[10] But as governments lost control of important parts of the national economy, they acquired increasing responsibilities as employers and consumers, as producers of goods and services, and as providers of welfare and full employment. Economic growth enabled governments to harvest the increased tax receipts necessary to finance this growing expenditure but any slackening of the growth rate threatened a fiscal crisis, deficit financing and inflationary consequences.

By the early 1970s, lower growth rates became endemic, as did higher rates of inflation, in the advanced capitalist economies, as Tables 2.1, 2.2 and 2.3 illustrate. One explanation of these falling growth rates centres on the power of organised labour which certainly grew during the 1960s. The absolute number of trade union members increased in all West European states, while the fastest growth occurred among white-collar workers in the public and service sectors. Unemployment averaged less than 3 per cent in the advanced capitalist countries at this time and unions became actively involved as essential components of national economic management. Full employment and partnership with government in the management of the economy together enhanced union power. Labour markets thus deteriorated from a capitalist viewpoint under the combined impact of full employment, growing regulatory controls and more generous and extensive welfare. The growth of real incomes became an annual event, with even the backward sectors of the economy joining in as well as those where productivity increases rarely offset the cost of the exercise, as in much of the public sector. In the stagflationary 1970s it became a commonplace in the weaker capitalist countries such as Britain to suppose that the prosperity of private enterprise was incompatible with strong trade unions. Yet it had been a feature of the more successful

Table 2.1 *Economic growth in Western Europe: annual % rates of change – whole economy*

	1965–73	*1973–81*	*Change*
Spain	6.5	2.1	–4.4
Netherlands	5.1	1.8	–3.3
Italy	5.4	2.4	–3.0
France	5.4	2.5	–2.9
Belgium	4.9	2.0	–2.9
UK	3.1	0.5	–2.6
Germany	4.2	2.0	–2.2
Sweden	3.9	1.5	–2.4
Denmark	3.8	1.4	–2.4
Norway	4.1	4.2	+0.1
Finland	5.0	2.6	–2.4
Greece	7.4	3.0	–4.4
Austria	5.3	2.6	–2.7

Source: OECD, cited in S. Holland (ed.) *Out of the Crisis: A Project for European Recovery* (Nottingham, Spokesman, 1983), pp. 187, 189.

Table 2.2 *Economic growth in Western Europe: annual % rates of change – manufacturing*

	1965–73	*1973–81*	*Change*
Spain	10.0	1.8	–8.2
France	7.6	1.6	–6.0
Belgium	7.1	1.2	–5.9
Netherlands	6.3	1.0	–5.3
UK	3.0	–2.3	–5.3
Italy	7.6	2.9	–4.7
Germany	4.8	1.2	–3.6
Sweden	4.1	–0.2	–4.3
Denmark	4.7	2.0	–2.7
Norway	4.7	0.1	–4.6
Finland	7.1	3.5	–3.6
Greece	11.9	3.1	–8.8
Austria	6.5	2.3	–4.2

Source: OECD, cited in S. Holland (ed.) *Out of the Crisis: A Project for European Recovery* (Nottingham, Spokesman, 1983), pp. 187, 189.

Table 2.3 *Inflation of consumer prices in Western Europe (% per year)*

	1967–73	*1973–80*	*1981*
Italy	5.0	17.0	19.5
Spain	6.8	17.9	14.6
UK	7.0	16.0	11.9
France	5.9	11.1	13.4
Belgium	4.5	8.1	7.6
Netherlands	6.3	7.1	6.7
Germany	4.3	4.8	5.9
Sweden	5.3	10.3	11.0
Denmark	6.7	11.0	9.2
Norway	6.3	9.0	13.3
Finland	6.4	12.5	12.0
Greece	4.7	17.3	24.5
Austria	4.8	6.3	6.8

Source: OECD, cited in S. Holland (ed.) *Out of the Crisis: A Project for European Recovery* (Nottingham, Spokesman, 1983), pp. 187, 189.

social democratic systems – such as in Sweden – that wage restraint in the boom years was based precisely on exceptionally strong trade unions and social democratic government. As long as social democratic goals and capitalist success went together, Scandinavian corporatism was viewed as an asset rather than a liability.

One influential explanation of the end of this harmonious accord traces the root of the problem to the 1960s and worsening cost-push inflation as the growth in real wages in the countries of the OECD began to rise much faster than labour productivity in the context of labour shortages. Over-accumulation of capital in relation to an inelastic supply of labour, in this view, allowed wages to eat into profits. 'Between 1968 and 1973 the share of profits in business output fell by about 15 per cent'.[11] The onset of crisis in the 1970s thus manifested itself as a squeeze on profits, an acceleration in the rate of inflation and the growth of working-class militancy. Increasing competition played a part in this profits squeeze in the manufacturing sector, but since profitability fell just as fast in protected sectors of the economy, it has been argued that labour shortages were the more important contributor.[12] This view naturally appealed to the right, which pointed to the institutional arrangements of the Keynesian welfare state as the critical source of the protection from market discipline that underpinned continuously rising demand in the economy. Labour's power had grown at the expense of capital, so it was said, and to restore profitability it would be necessary to dismantle these arrangements.

Brenner rightly questions whether it was possible for a long-term system-wide downturn of the sort actually experienced between 1965 and 1973 to derive from a profits squeeze based on tight labour markets with workers everywhere advancing their wage claims beyond the level that productivity gains would allow. This would presuppose that labour markets behaved in the same way in all the leading capitalist countries. For there is little doubt that the economic downturn was experienced by all the advanced capitalist economies between 1965 and 1973, and simultaneous recessions followed in 1970–71, 1974–75, 1979–82 and 1990–91. Brenner asks how could this happen in all the leading advanced capitalist countries at the same time, when the strength of national economies and labour movements varied so widely. Such a degree of economic coordination seemed unlikely to result from the behaviour of labour when labour markets were so different. Moreover, he asks, why did the traditional device for curing excessive wage demands – mass unemployment – fail to solve the problem and restore profitability? Brenner argues that it was unable to do so because the profits squeeze did not result from the power of organised labour. Instead he finds the cause of the economic slowdown in the uneven development of the advanced capitalist economies. A 'malign invisible hand' was at work in the tendency of producers to develop the productive forces without regard for existing investments and the rates of return expected from them. The profits of established producers were squeezed as rivals installed increasingly cheap and effective methods of production. Overcapacity and overproduction resulted worldwide as the manufacturers of first one country then another established a competitive edge which helped to drive rates of profit down in various industries.

Over the longer term, according to Brenner, it is the persistence of these problems that has led to falling investment growth, falling output growth, reduced productivity growth and wage growth, and rising unemployment.[13] Germany and Japan captured markets from the US and Britain in the course of the 1960s and forced a major fall in the aggregate profitability of the advanced capitalist economies. The US, which registered its first trade deficit in 1971, was eventually forced to scupper the Bretton Woods arrangements after resorting to a large devaluation of the dollar in the same year in an effort to restore the competitiveness of its exports. It then embarked upon a major wave of new investment and wage cutting in the 1970s. This put pressure on German and Japanese profitability in the context of a general slowing down of international demand. Newly industrialising countries emerging in the 1980s in East Asia helped to prevent the recovery of profitability and to perpetuate the downturn by again driving down prices of manufactured goods. This argument seems to explain much of what was happening to capitalist economies. While leading economists are at a loss to explain the slowdown in productivity growth that was visible from the mid-1960s – declaring, nevertheless, that 'the magic has gone'[14] – Brenner is one of those who denies that it is in any case a cause of the economic crisis; US manufacturing firms raised productivity at a faster rate than at any time during the post-war period in 1979–89, while reducing hourly real wages by about 15 percentage points over the course of 1973–91 – both 'achievements' owing much to the class-war policies of the Reagan years.[15]

End of the Bretton Woods system

The US thus played a notable role in the demise of the international monetary order which it had done so much to create, and this in turn added to the economic problems of the 1970s. In the 1960s it had financed the Vietnam War and domestic reform (President Johnson's Great Society programme) in an inflationary way, rather than through increased taxation. A greater volume of dollars was brought into circulation which the rest of the world was obliged to purchase at fixed rates of exchange. The deterioration of the American balance of payments and its trade balance in particular underlined the weaknesses of its economy. But since the value of the dollar was fixed against gold, the American currency was increasingly overvalued. This transferred both the costs and the inflationary consequences of American overspending to the rest of the world, especially to its major trading partners. These countries resisted American pressure to revalue their currencies against the dollar, while the Americans ignored European pressure to correct its trade imbalances by measures to reduce US consumption. Instead, President Nixon suspended the gold convertibility of the dollar in August 1971 in order to strengthen the US's apparently faltering monetary hegemony and obtain the devaluation of the dollar that would restore the competitiveness of US exports. The world was then awash with devalued, non-convertible dollars. This triggered protectionist measures globally as governments sought to defend growth rates against the perceived selfishness of the US government.

An additional source of world money existed beyond the control of the US government, or indeed of any government. This also played a part in the collapse of the Bretton Woods system and contributed to the increasing volatility of the world economy in the 1970s. Though borrowing and selling currencies outside their country of origin is something that financial institutions had always done, the largest part of this business after 1945 was conducted in dollars in Europe (principally London) and came to be known as the Eurodollar market. The market grew in the 1950s in response to both national restrictions which governments placed on the buying and selling of their currencies and the migration of US companies to Europe.[16] It met a need for short-term credit and allowed the main players to operate as if national regulations and borders did not exist. American banks and companies seeking investment opportunities turned to the Eurodollar market in the 1950s, as the financial institutions of countries such as Britain turned increasingly to dealing in dollars because of restrictions imposed on international transactions in their own currencies. By the end of the 1960s the largest American banks controlled two-thirds of the Eurodollar business, though the market was big enough to breathe new vigour into British overseas banks and the City of London – which is why the British authorities encouraged it. As American multinationals expanded into Europe, so were its banks encouraged to develop beyond national shores, using as they did so an increasing array of financial devices for the creation of short-term credit.

When it was the US's turn to impose restrictions on capital movements in the late 1960s in response to balance of payments problems, 'American multinationals that wanted to make new or supplementary investments abroad either sought capital themselves in London or had their subsidiaries raise money there'.[17] Thus the accumulation of liquidity beyond the regulatory control of governments and central banks in offshore deposits rapidly expanded. Transactions in foreign currencies had become part of the routine business of MNCs and the movement of short-term funds was symptomatic of the new level of world economic integration. By the 1960s, according to Scammell, 'the volume of mobile funds in the international monetary system was now so large that in a speculative confrontation no central bank, no accumulation of exchange reserves, could defend an exchange rate for long if the international financial community considered it to be too high'.[18] National economies became vulnerable to rapid movements of short-term funds. These in turn could be triggered by changes in US policy, though the US itself was less adversely affected than the states of Western Europe and actually reaped certain benefits from the popularity of the Eurodollar.[19] America's worsening balance of payments deficit, for example, one of the causes of the accumulation of dollars in Europe in the 1960s and 1970s, was allowed to persist because of the demand for Eurodollars.

As the importance of the Eurodollar market soared the system of fixed parities between the major currencies created at Bretton Woods began to fall apart, in the general context of worsening inflationary rates. These developments were related. As prices rose at differential rates between national economies there was a diminishing prospect for stability in the rate at which currencies were exchanged. Fixed exchange rates could only be a defence against speculative, mobile, short-term funds if they could be held permanently, but this was impossible. The Bretton Woods system had actually required periodic adjustments of exchange rates to take account of changing economic realities. Each one of these provided opportunities for increasingly damaging speculative disruptions as funds were gambled on future exchange rate changes. After Nixon's unilateral decision to untie the dollar from the price of gold, a regime of floating exchange rates soon supervened. Governments now changed exchange rates and interest rates in an effort to attract or repel offshore funds as circumstances required. But these very measures increased the opportunities for currency speculation by those who held the offshore funds.

A new system of fixed exchange rates was negotiated in the Smithsonian Agreement of December 1971, embodying a 9 per cent devaluation of the dollar. But this was insufficient to correct the American current account deficit and imports of manufactured goods continued to flood into the country. Massive speculation against the dollar eventually led, in March 1973, to a return to floating exchange rates – a move which once again increased the scope for currency speculation. Meanwhile, the US removed all controls on capital exports. Arrighi notes that 'by the mid-1970s the volume of purely monetary transactions carried out in offshore money markets already exceeded the value of world trade many times over ... by 1979 foreign exchange trading amounted to $17.5 trillion, or more than eleven times the total value of world trade ... According to another estimate, yearly transactions in the London Eurodollar market alone were six times the value of world trade in 1979 but about twenty five times seven years later'.[20] Thus the final collapse of the Bretton Woods system brought an end to fixed exchange rates but not to the world role of the dollar. The rapid growth of offshore dollar markets continued to provide the US with access to huge credit markets in its own currency.

The social democratic compromise was thus simultaneously under attack from falling productivity of labour, falling rates of profit and the diminishing potency of national regulatory devices consequent upon the growing internationalisation of markets, production and credit. A third crisis – much of it ideological in character – attacked the legitimacy of social democratic politics directly. From within social democracy and to its left the 1970s witnessed an attack on capitalist prerogatives and other aspects of the post-war consensus. This, and its aftermath, is the focus of the present book. In this chapter we will look at how the economic problems of the age were constructed into a right-wing critique of everything social democracy stood for. The inflationary problem became the key issue in this ideological attack. As productivity gains fell in most areas of industrial activity, increases in real wages continued, as did the costs of fixed capital. Profitability had to fall in these circumstances. The bigger firms passed on their increased costs to the consumer in the form of price rises. If wages continued to rise, inflation had to follow; if they did not purchasing power had to fall.

Political economy of inflation

The rate of inflation in the advanced capitalist countries actually rose from an average of 3 per cent in 1965 to 7.8 per cent in 1973. The leap was fuelled by deficit financing and the growth of credit, as we have seen. Governments adopted expansionary policies in 1971 to get out of the recessionary dip of that year which was synchronised across the capitalist world. Unusually rapid economic growth was widely experienced in 1972 and 1973 and the rate of inflation accelerated. The collapse of the Bretton Woods system affected this process by increasing both the scope for speculation and the volume of cheap credit. At the same time the prices of primary products rose dramatically in real terms and began to feed into consumer prices. The growth of food prices and the price of crude oil (which quadrupled in the winter of 1973–74) had the biggest effect on the general rate of inflation. Inflationary expectations also increased and this affected subsequent wage struggles for years to come. By the time of the oil-price rise, double-digit inflation was already established and the boom in production was over. The Organization of Petroleum Exporting Countries (OPEC) aggravated the already severe problems of the system by transferring an additional $64 billion of purchasing power to its annual income – the equivalent of 1.5 per cent of world capitalist output.[21] Since there was no possibility of the oil-producing countries actually spending this money, world demand fell by a corresponding amount. Between the third quarter of 1974 and the second of 1975 industrial production crashed by 10 per cent.

Share prices and investment collapsed at the same time, while unemployment soared from 8 million in 1973 to 15 million by the spring of 1975, for the advanced capitalist countries as a whole. Yet prices continued to rise at the average rate of 10 per cent. Governments were now caught in the grip of a major fiscal crisis. Public expenditures had to increase because of growing unemployment and inflation, but fiscal revenues fell as the slump reduced taxation yields. Public debt increased markedly – for example in Britain by 250 per cent in two years (1974–76). Governments thus became increasingly dependent on the private institutions which purchased such financial assets, giving them a significant influence over public policy. 'In the group of OECD countries, public debts increased beyond bounds throughout the 1980s (in excess of US$13 trillion in 1995)'.[22] This is the context in which the economist Fred Hirsch referred to the 'politicisation' of the world economy.[23]

In other words, the interests of these financial markets came to hold sway and the ideology of 'sound money' advanced accordingly. Holders of public debt – private banks and companies, many of them foreign – were determined to preserve the value of their liquid assets and ultra-sensitive to any development which they believed likely to increase the rate of inflation and/or devalue the currency in which the debt was denominated. Not only did they pressure governments to cut public expenditure by threatening not to buy long-term public debt unless government complied with their preference for deflationary measures; they were now big enough and powerful enough to be able to bring about the policies they desired. Douglas Wass, the permanent secretary to the Treasury in Britain, pointed to this power in 1978 and highlighted the related 'internationalisation of economic activity' which he described as 'the single most important structural change in the world economy in the second half of the twentieth century'.[24] The independence of national economic management was thus called into question, not simply because of the temporary conjunctural difficulties of the British government, but because of permanent structural changes in the world economy.

The massive fluctuations in the exchange rates of the major industrial countries in the late 1970s underlined doubts about the viability of floating exchange rates as a basis for a new international monetary order. Not only did they cause uncertainty by undermining the profit-and-loss calculations of business, forcing corporations to engage in their own forward currency trading, they had inflationary effects of their own.[25] The volatility of exchange rates adversely affected the finances of governments, particularly in the Third World, as sometimes massive shifts in the value of the dollar affected receipts from exports, the cost of imports and even the size of the national income. From the Latin American debt crisis in the early 1980s to the collapse of financial markets in South East Asia in 1997, extreme turbulence has threatened even worse disasters to come. But a new regulatory authority was not forthcoming and attempts by the Group of Ten (leading industrial nations) to curtail the Eurocurrency market simply led the banks which controlled it to relocate even further away, often in former British colonies (now designated as 'overseas territories'), such as the Bahamas and the Cayman Islands. While the dollar was still the *de facto* world currency, the US economy was no longer so dominant that it could impose rules which everyone, including itself, would observe – nor was the US inclined to do so when its policy makers began to see virtue in the new deregulated arrangements. Governments were thus enjoined to adopt the rules of the financial markets – 'adherence to the principles and practice of sound money'.[26]

For the US government this was intended to restore confidence in the dollar and bring offshore, privately controlled money back to America with the aid of high interest rates and financial deregulation. Meanwhile, the 1970s witnessed an intensification of the 'multinationalisation' of the world economy with the accumulated value of US foreign direct investment doubling between 1970 and 1978 (to $168 billion) and non-US foreign direct investment, mostly European, trebling (to $232 billion) to become 58 per cent of the total. After the revaluation of the yen in 1971 Japanese foreign direct investment surged in an effort to find cheaper labour markets, overwhelmingly in Asia. The major recipients were the so-called Asian Tiger economies of Singapore, Taiwan, South Korea and Malaysia. By the late 1980s a further round of outward expansion of labour-intensive industrial investment centred on China, Vietnam and Thailand, with Japan and the four Tigers supplying the capital.[27] Deregulation of financial markets during the 1980s stimulated further growth of, and innovation within, finance capital. Corporate profits increasingly evaded taxation. Tax revenues were under strain anyway because of the need for more money to service the public debt and fund transfer payments to the unemployed, at a time when unemployment and neo-liberal regressive tax policies cut the supply of government money. Offshore tax havens boomed – the Cayman Islands, for example, became the fifth largest banking centre in the world, measured in deposits, the bulk of which belong to the transnational oil company Shell.[28]

Prospects for the left

At the outset of the economic downturn it was already predicted that tax revolts were on the agenda. With the largest companies and the richest individuals avoiding taxation in a variety of ways, the burden fell increasingly on those unable to opt out – wage and salary earners. Unless governments addressed the issue of tax avoidance systematically, it was predictable that regressive indirect taxes would increase as a proportion of the tax burden and that state spending priorities would be restructured in the context of public spending cuts. Governments had actually gone the other way – increasingly resorting to greater subsidy of the private sector in a vain bid to affect its behaviour by bribery. This merely widened the tax gap for public authorities. Meanwhile the incomes of the mass of state employees were predictably subject to systematic erosion because wages in the state sector could not be offset by productivity gains. In 1973 O'Connor also warned that market-oriented efficiency criteria would be introduced in this sector and undermine professional standards.[29] As state employees became subject to work intensification, users of public services would find a growing gap between their expectations and their actual experiences of the services in question, as the fiscal crisis and inflation imposed a regime of austerity. For all this, the greatest tax revolt came from the rich and the corporations rather than from those who had none of their powers to evade taxation.

Some left observers also noted that 'the international interpenetration of capital' was greatly strengthening its power as that of the nation-state fell. European companies – with the approval of employers' organisations, technocrats and politicians – were already merging to meet the challenge of American multinationals in the 1960s. In 1958 a list was made of the employers' organizations of the six member states of the EEC; it filled 513 pages.[30] The employers were quick to influence the EEC and maintain regular channels of influence. Mandel observed in 1969 that European integration necessarily led to an immediate shift in the balance of forces against wage earners. 'Increasing international interpenetration of capital is bound to weaken the economic leverage of the trade unions, at least on a purely national level ... Once it has reached the stage at which ... the ownership of the principal means of production is spread throughout all the member states of the EEC, the economic power of national trade unions will to a large extent be broken.'[31] That stage had not yet been reached in 1969 but Mandel predicted that 'In the gigantic socio-economic metamorphosis which late capitalism is now experiencing ... sections of the working class could suffer as bitter a fate as they did in the first industrial revolution'.[32] Wages would be pressed down, workers and whole countries would be blackmailed by threats of industrial relocation unless they could follow the lead of the most perceptive among them in demanding international bargaining and international agreements.[33]

At the same time, according to Mandel, 'overwhelming pressure' would build up in favour of a different kind of state in Europe as the material infrastructure for genuinely supranational state organs grew within the EEC.[34] In the next chapter we will see that a consciousness of these internationalising forces informed left analyses within social democratic parties in the 1970s. But the emphasis on the need to break with social democratic policies as hitherto conceived did not include proposals for supranational institutions to regulate international capital. Those social democratic governments faced with rapidly deteriorating economic circumstances in the 1970s responded with crisis management policies and in Britain it was the right that gained the intellectual initiative.

Overloaded government

Though the economic crisis of the early 1970s affected all countries it had its biggest impact in the US and the UK. In these economies the low growth rates and rising inflation of the late 1960s were quickly transformed into the worst stagflationary conditions of the 1970s and both countries witnessed the sharpest political reaction in the form of a demand for a return to neo-liberal economic policies. By the Reagan era this had developed into a broad-ranging, frontal attack on organised and unorganised workers in the US which succeeded so well that by the middle of the decade the top 20 per cent had a greater share of national income than at any time since the Second World War and the bottom 20 per cent had its lowest.[35] In the UK a break with the Keynesian post-war consensus had appeared likely with the election of the Conservative government of 1970–74, under Edward Heath. But Heath's administration retreated from this course in the face of a strike wave of unprecedented proportions. It then contrived to lose its parliamentary majority by calling an early election on the issue of 'who governs?' in February 1974. A second election in October of the same year completed the process of installing a new Labour government with a slender parliamentary majority. Within two years this government also found its economic policies in tatters to the extent of abandoning its manifesto promises of a Keynesian reflation of the economy in favour of monetarist measures to control inflation. By the winter of 1978–79 the Labour government found itself unable to continue the strict wages policy which had spanned, in one form or another, its entire period of office, as low-paid public-sector unions in particular took strike action in the so-called Winter of Discontent. In May 1979 the first Conservative government under Margaret Thatcher's premiership took office as working-class voters deserted Labour on a scale not seen since the war.

The alternation of Labour and Conservative governments unable to realise manifesto commitments, overwhelmed by industrial strife and bedevilled by stagflationary economic conditions proved congenial to the promotion of theories which traced the origins of the crisis to the 'social democratic settlement' of the post-war boom years. These theories require a brief and selective scrutiny at this stage of the present enquiry.[36] They represent an articulate expression of the views of the Thatcher governments in Britain and helped to justify the drift of policy, contributing to what may be regarded as a paradigm shift in the dominant public discourse. Of course, the ideological offensive was by no means confined to Britain and it is notable that one of its intentionally transnational manifestations – the report of the so-called Trilateral Commission – reasoned that a crisis in democracy had been caused by the 'democratic surge' of the late 1960s and early 1970s, a matter we will return to in the next chapter. It will suffice for now to note that the authors reasoned that this 'surge' had grossly increased demands on government, challenged and weakened government authority, generated inflation and placed democracy in jeopardy. Their paradoxical conclusion was that Western governments were suffering from an 'excess of democracy' and that a demobolisation of 'marginal groups' was necessary to set matters aright.[37]

Such theories often presented the problem as one of governmental 'overload' or even of 'ungovernability'. Various mechanisms at work within liberal democracies were identified as the source of growing pressures on the state and rising expectations of public-sector performance. The activity of pressure groups – celebrated in the 1950s and 1960s as the foundation of 'polyarchy' or pluralist democracy[38] – was now being seen as problematic. Mancur Olson put forward a less rosy theory of groups and organisations in 1965 – which became a sensation in the 1970s – based on the observation that since the achievement of any common goal provides a public good for members of the organisation in question – that is a good which all members of the group 'consume' equally – the individual member of an organisation must always be tempted to freeload, since rational calculation reveals that, while he stands to benefit from any improvement won by others, his own efforts have no noticeable effect on outcomes. The larger the group, the less it will further its common interests since on any rational calculation, the benefits are thinly dispersed, while the impact of any one member's contribution (or non-contribution) will be negligible. Small groups, however, Olson argued, operate according to a different logic since any successful prosecution of their case can produce such significant benefits to the individual member that they outweigh the costs of participation and the problem of the 'free-rider' is minimised.[39]

This argument provided one of the bases for regarding welfare states and the corporatist economic arrangements which always accompanied them as fertile ground for effective pressure-group activity at the cost of permanent inflation and rising taxation. The taxpayer corresponded to the member of a large group with little incentive to act; the special cause groups clustered in and around the state, on the other hand, were held to be responsible for his exploitation and, via rising public expenditure, incessant demands and rising expectations. Friedrich von Hayek, a long-standing opponent of the post-war consensus, was quick to promote the thesis[40] and wrote a foreword to the German translation of Olson's book – in a translation which he helped to bring about. Olson himself later applied the theory outlined in *The Logic of Collective Action* to the problem of economies in decline, of which the UK was thought to be the prime example. In *The Rise and Decline of Nations*,[41] he argued that stable democracies were particularly prone to an 'institutional sclerosis' – an inability to modernise – arising from the very fact that special interest groups are so effective in defending their time-honoured perquisites – to the detriment of the nation. Though Olson argued that countries that had suffered major political upheavals were less likely to develop these symptoms, his book generated debate and focused concern in Kiesinger's Germany when the economy faltered in 1966–67. Indeed, a version of Olson's argument continued to adhere to Germany in the journalistic notion, popular in the 1990s, of 'Eurosclerosis' – or the idea that the highly regulated economies of the European Union (EU) – Sweden is another often-cited example – suffer from numerous rigidities as compared with the market-driven economies of the US and the UK. But prior to the upheaval of the 1980s the UK was the acknowledged 'sick man of Europe'. The UK political establishment had identified the trade unions as the main culprit for the country's economic problems since the late 1960s and by the early 1970s influential journalists[42] were raising the prospect of a major crisis of democracy unless something was done about them.

In 1974 Peter Jay, son of the prominent Labour Keynesian Douglas Jay and economics editor of *The Times*, asserted that free collective bargaining, full employment and price stability were incompatible in the long run. The problem though, as he saw it, was that there seemed to be no way that a democratic system could jettison the first two or do without inflation.[43] Samuel Brittan, principal economic commentator of the *Financial Times*, came to similarly negative conclusions, arguing that the 'disruptive effects of the pursuit of group self-interest in the market place' and 'the generation of excessive expectations' together constituted 'two endemic threats to liberal democracy'.[44]

In Brittan's view excessive expectations were generated by the democratic aspects of the system, while the disruptive effects of group activity stemmed from 'elementary economic logic', though there were 'clear interrelations between the two problems' – not least that 'liberal democracy inhibits governments from tackling coercive groups either by abnegation of the full-employment commitment, or by the effective restriction of union monopoly power, or by the enforcement of an "incomes policy"'.[45] The Thatcher governments were later able to refute this proposition by combining electoral success with just such remedies, but that is another matter. In the 1970s, Brittan – no doubt looking back over the whole post-war period – thought that 'the best way to think of politicians ... was neither as ideologues nor as spokesmen, but as entrepreneurs who deal in votes just as oilmen deal in oil'.[46] Voters, however, had little incentive to vote – since on any rational calculation any one vote could make no difference to an electoral outcome; and they had even less incentive to study policies. This combination of entrepreneurial politicians and ignorant electors, according to Brittan, produced a built-in bias towards 'the lack of budget constraint'. Politicians tended to outbid each other for votes, while electorates tended 'to expect too much from government action at too little cost'. Like Hayek, Olson and Jay, Brittan came to the conclusion that the very workings of liberal democracy thus made inflationary finance a convenient 'short-term method of postponing political choice between incompatible objectives'. But the coercive power of trade unions was in Brittan's view the most serious threat to democracy.

The rivalry between unions for shares of the national income, in this account, forces a growing proportion of the public to adopt militant trade union attitudes to defend its own interests. Governments committed to the maintenance of full employment expand the money supply and public debt to prevent rising wage bills translating into unemployment. A spiral is created which produces accelerating inflation. Brittan saw the need for political leaders to coalesce and thus stop the party-political generation of excessive expectations, but felt that the long-term solution lay in the re-education of the public; however the prospects for a statutory reduction of trade union power did not seem good as he composed his essay in 1974. Similarly, the option of removing some of the functions of government from the political system seemed a 'forlorn hope', though a desirable measure, to Anthony King, when he addressed 'the problem of overload' in 1975. King's emphasis was on the growing gap between public demands and the capacities of government in the 1970s, coupled with the growth of governmental responsibilities – an argument that also found an audience in the US, Germany and Switzerland.[47] The experience of incomes policies had demonstrated, according to King, that all incomes policies are voluntary – government did not have the power to enforce them. The failure of such policies, he conceded, was related to 'the failure of economic policy generally', but this only underlined the fact that 'whatever their aims' in this field, with the exception of full employment, 'post-war Governments have failed to achieve them, at least for any sustained period'.[48]

Even the golden age of the long boom had thus become tarnished in this telling of it.

The evidence of 'ungovernability' in Britain was found in the increasing difficulty of parties to fulfil their manifesto commitments; the frequency of governmental U-turns; the perennial problems of crime, Northern Ireland, inflation, and economic underachievement. Yet the responsibilities of government tended to grow even as their powers diminished, it was said. Government was simultaneously locked into a growing number of dependency relationships and the victim of increasing acts of non-compliance by the other participants. King also found politicians increasingly compelled to admit that there were many policy areas where their understanding of the problems was insufficient. The consequences of mass dissatisfaction with this mismatch between the growing responsibilities of government and its fading capacity to deal adequately with any of them, could involve a 'crisis of the regime'. But King also predicted a search for new models of politics if, as 'seems probable ... the state in Britain, and quite possibly in other Western countries, will have become by the late 1970s, to an even greater extent than now, merely one among a number of contenders for wealth, power, and influence, the others including large companies, trade unions and their members, foreign companies, foreign governments, international organisations'.[49] Ten years after this article was published consciousness of globalisation was such that King's list of 'contenders' had grown familiar; significantly, only the inclusion of 'trade unions and their members' could look utterly misplaced.

Other versions of these arguments pointed in the same directions; roll back the state, reduce government responsibilities and thereby depoliticise areas of life that had become dangerously dependent on government action at a time when it was increasingly incompetent or unable to resolve problems. It was necessary to restrict trade unions, reduce the influence of pressure groups, cut back state expenditure and re-educate the voters. By the time the Heath government fell in 1974 some senior civil servants had also come round to the view that Britain was becoming ungovernable and the 'too much democracy' school of thought was becoming popular around Whitehall.[50] Certainly the line of action it recommended would go some way to reducing the influence of vested interests on public policy – by helping to remove pressure groups from the state where they had become embedded – and in scaling down public expectations. Nevertheless such policies would not preclude specific statutory action to reduce the power of trade unions and other interest groups – such as those, for example, clustered around the welfare state. The problem of 'institutional sclerosis' or 'pluralistic stagnation' demanded no less.[51] Such arguments only reinforced the thesis canvassed by pro-business groups such as the Institute of Economic Affairs[52] to prioritise the inflationary problem by resorting to the monetarist policies advocated by Professor Milton Friedman of the University of Chicago and to target welfare benefits and dispense with universalism; others demanded nothing less than the dismantling of the welfare state.[53] Sound money doctrines now passed from the fringe of political life to the leadership of the Conservative Party in the mid-1970s after the election of Margaret Thatcher to the leadership supported by born-again economic liberals such Geoffrey Howe and Sir Keith Joseph.

The most dogmatic of the 'New Right' theorists, such as Hayek and Friedman, regarded the welfare state as an instrument of political repression. They saw equality as inimical to freedom, regarded social justice as a fraud, identified equality of opportunity as a chimera, the commitment to full employment as the cause of the inflationary menace and so on. Britain, with its growing unemployment, rising inflation, incompetent government by both main political parties and a long-standing economic malaise made worse by the circumstances of the 1970s, was ripe for a major assault on the post-war settlement. Pre-war doctrines which 'explained' low growth rates in terms of excessive state expenditure or found the poor to be the authors of their own misfortune came back into public rhetoric. Democracy was found wanting as a system by conservatives who found it subversive of authority and by liberals who saw it as engine of big government and threats to the liberty of the individual.[54] Proposals were made to put control of the money supply beyond its influence, either by administrative or constitutional measures.[55]

Marxist analyses of the crisis shared certain features in common with the neo-conservative theories of ungovernability outlined above, but drew very different conclusions, as we shall see in chapter three. Revisionist social democracy, however, saw nothing fundamentally new in the situation, even though some of the elements of the problem were all too obvious. Crosland's 'programme of radical reform for the 1960s', published in 1962, had argued that the next Labour government should 'increase the proportion of the national income devoted to social purposes'. Although he acknowledged the tax-evading powers of capital and the rich, he believed that the limit of taxable capacity on personal incomes had not been reached. He stood by his contention that 'a determined reforming government can now generally get its way without a change in ownership'; modern corporations, he believed, were 'slaves to their public relations departments' and 'apologetic where their predecessors were haughty'. In practice, he asserted, 'monopoly is ... rather rare' and big firms faced the countervailing powers of the unions and government.[56]

Just over ten years later, Crosland reviewed the intervening period during which Labour had held office for six years (1964–70). One success of this period of government, he noted, was that it had 'raised total public expenditure from 41 to 48 per cent of GDP'.[57] But 'in 1970 unemployment was higher, inflation more rapid and economic growth slower than when the Conservatives left office in 1964'.[58] Low growth, he observed, had 'bedevilled all the efforts and good intentions of the Labour Government'. Moreover, 'for the first time the mass of manual workers found themselves caught in the net of progressive direct taxation. In the 1950s the typical manual worker paid virtually no income tax; even in 1960 his tax and insurance contributions took only 8 per cent of his earnings; but by 1970 they took nearly twenty per cent ... The inevitable result...was more inflation, strikes, and industrial unrest ...'[59] At the end of Labour's period in power, and three years in to the succeeding Conservative administration, Crosland described a situation in which 'extreme class inequalities remain, poverty is far from eliminated, the economy is in a state of semi-permanent crisis and inflation is rampant'.[60]

Despite all of this Crosland asked Marxists in 1973 to take note that 'if one examines the Western world as a whole there are no clear signs of a new and fundamental crisis' and he saw 'no reason to alter the revisionist thesis that government can generally impose its will ... on the private corporation'.[61] While revisionist goals such as the relief of poverty, social equality and the redistribution of wealth thus remained relevant, however, Crosland admitted that none of them 'are within sight of achievement'.[62] This was because of 'slow growth' and the deliberate use of deflation as an instrument of policy, with the latter arising under the previous Labour government because of its 'obsession with a particular parity for sterling'. Slow growth, he admitted, arose in part from the low productivity increases of the UK economy, but he believed that 'nobody can claim to know the answer' to that particular problem.[63] Deflationary policies were another matter. According to Crosland these arose from the political decision to give priority to correcting the balance of payments deficit inherited by the incoming Labour government in 1964. While admitting that 'pressure from the United States and other monetary authorities' had played a part in establishing this priority, Crosland expressed the view that a deflationary policy could be avoided in the future by a combination of more flexible exchange rates and a prices and incomes policy.[64] This proved an underestimation of the problem almost on a par with his view, expressed in the same pamphlet, that 'the greater part of the environmental problem stems not from present or future growth but from past growth'.[65] Croslandite social democracy was as blind to the scale and complexity of the economic crisis as it was unimaginative in perceiving the emerging wider agenda of radical politics.

Social democratic government in the 1970s

In Britain the sense of crisis was heightened by the successive conflicts experienced under the Conservative government of 1970–74 and the manner of its demise, as unemployment and inflation rose to new heights,[66] successive states of emergency were proclaimed, and industrial and political strikes abounded. Labour Party policy swung sharply to the left in these years of opposition, as we will see in chapter three. As the Conservative secretary of state for employment, Robert Carr, announced that Keynesian techniques were of diminishing value in determining the level of employment,[67] his government's Industrial Relations Act (1971) – which sought the introduction of legal restrictions on 'free collective bargaining', and a statutory wages policy in 1972 – forced the unions to find a modus vivendi with the parliamentary leadership of the Labour Party. The result was the Social Contract, an agreement to trade wage restraint for a programme of legislative reforms. In *Economic Policy and the Cost of Living*, published by the Trades Union Congress (TUC)-Labour Party Liaison Committee in February 1973, the agreement was shown to include food subsidies, price and rent controls, the redistribution of income and wealth, industrial investment and repeal of the Conservatives' Industrial Relations Act. The parliamentary leadership was nevertheless very much in the hands of revisionists unsympathetic to the new stress on public ownership and state intervention which swept the party's annual conference and National Executive Committee (NEC). One of the more dramatic signs that the old leadership would determine the party's policies in office, whatever the mass party may have wanted, was Harold Wilson's decision to veto the demand to nationalise twenty-five companies. This had received massive support at the 1973 annual conference and was expected to go in the manifesto with which Labour fought the general election of February 1974.

Both major parties lost votes in the election, but Labour obtained 301 seats against 297 for the Conservatives with minor parties holding the balance. Labour was able to form a government until another general election was held in October of the same year, and this produced an overall Labour majority of just three seats. In between these elections the government set about implementing its Social Contract with the TUC, though one member of the Treasury team noted in his diary that 'we are all anti-Keynesians now' and thus privately signalled the ideological retreat that had already taken place.[68] James Callaghan was elected by the parliamentary party to replace Harold Wilson as leader after the latter's resignation in March 1976. By this time the economic strategy of the government bore little relation to the ideas endorsed by the party in opposition. *Labour's Programme 1973* had envisaged the creation of a National Enterprise Board (NEB) to intervene in the promotion of publicly owned enterprises, as well as job creation, investment, the adoption of new technologies and higher levels of investment. These targets would be spread to the private sector by means of compulsory planning agreements, similar to those practised in France. In the event the NEB was confined to bailing out moribund firms and planning agreements were restricted to feeble voluntary arrangements which the private sector was able to ignore completely. Proposals to introduce industrial democracy were likewise watered down and then killed off in cabinet sub-committee. The government's real and urgent ambition and necessity was to tackle the double-digit inflation largely bequeathed by the previous administration. The growth in public expenditure after 1972 and the mini-boom engineered by the chancellor, Anthony Barber, helped to produce a record balance of trade deficit in 1974 and a rate of inflation which reached around 27 per cent by the summer of 1975.

So within six months of forming a government Labour embarked upon deflationary policies, effectively abandoning the old full-employment commitment as public expenditure was cut and taxes increased in the budget of April 1975. By July, the first of a succession of wages policies was agreed with trade union leaders and over the next year the rate of inflation fell – but only to around 17 per cent. There is no justification for the view expressed in Callaghan's memoirs that 'the country had experienced a remission from the hyper-inflation of earlier years'.[69] Inflation was still ruinously high and according to Treasury estimates – estimates that proved, however, to be wildly inaccurate – the government needed to borrow £12 billion in order to finance its expenditure in the year 1976–77. These figures for inflation and public debt constituted a fertile basis for speculation against sterling and the Bank of England used a large proportion of its reserves between February and May 1976 trying to prevent a collapse of the currency. In June Britain obtained a short-term loan from the Group of Ten industrial nations but speculators were emboldened to continue the run against the pound in the knowledge that the loan had to be repaid by December. Consequently the $5 billion actually raised was used vainly defending the pound. It was at this point that the government became embroiled in the so-called 'IMF crisis'.

A long-term loan was thought to be necessary in view of the Treasury's estimates of the shortfall between public expenditure and revenues in the coming year, coupled with an expected balance of payments deficit of £3 billion for 1977. Callaghan's first appearance before the annual conference as leader of the party took place at the end of September 1976 when the prospect of raising the International Monetary Fund (IMF) loan – with all that that entailed for future economic policy – was already on his mind. The speech, written by Peter Jay – one of the theorists of 'overload' discussed above – was in part an apologia for raising the loan, but it also told the assembled delegates that they had been pricing themselves out of jobs. Continuing the theme, Callaghan said:

> We used to think that you could spend your way out of a recession and increase employment by cutting taxes and boosting Government spending. I tell you in all candour that that option no longer exists, and that if it ever did exist, it only worked on each occasion since the war by injecting a bigger dose of inflation into the economy, followed by a higher level of unemployment as the next step.[70]

A widening gap now opened between the economic policies favoured by the majority of the mass party and those pursued by the government.

Of the social democratic parties that happened to be in government in the 1970s, the British Labour Party had by far the worst experience. In Sweden the government was able to make such important reforms that it is more usefully considered in the next chapter where we consider radical responses to the breakdown of the post-war order. In West Germany, Europe's strongest economy, the social democrats had been part of a Grand Coalition with the Christian Democrats since 1966. They were able to remain in power without their main rivals from September 1969 (with the aid of the Free Democrats) when Willy Brandt became chancellor. Throughout this early period levels of government intervention rose as tripartite planning was adopted and the state tried to directly influence investment decisions. The idea of long-term structural planning in the service of technological modernisation was championed by a new Research and Technology Ministry.[71] Modernisation was also encouraged by the growth of industrial grants and subsidies which were massively channelled into microelectronics, communication technology, computers, energy technology and the like, but also directed at regions and industries imperilled by foreign competition (such as the Saar steel industry). The state took over costs and risks which companies – even large companies – would not bear.[72] By 1974 state-financed industrial assistance represented 5.6 per cent of GNP.[73] Public spending and taxes increased but the economy was growing at 6 per cent per annum when Brandt took over and inflation was under control. Important educational and welfare reforms were also enacted which increased the generosity of pensions, unemployment benefits and family allowances and made more financial support available for students. The social democrats were doing what they believed in – assisting business and financing social reform.

The economic context had deteriorated, however, by the time of the first leap in oil prices in 1973 and when Helmut Schmidt took over from Brandt in 1974 policy was focused on inflation and the elimination of unacceptably high wage rises, while unemployment rose (topping a million by the end of the year). But if we take the period 1969–79 as a whole, state expenditure increased from 37.9 per cent of GDP to 47.3 per cent.[74] By 1981 the state held up to 80 per cent of the shares in 600 firms and utilities, while the public sector accounted for 9.2 per cent of salaried employees and 16 per cent of gross fixed capital formation. Between the first oil shock and the return of boom conditions in 1976 the government did its best to clamp down on wages and stifle inflation, while ignoring trade union demands to tackle rising unemployment.[75] The *Bundesbank* was in charge of economic policy, though it had to share this role with the financial markets after March 1973 when floating exchange rates were adopted.[76] As financial orthodoxy reasserted itself, confidence in the efficacy of planning waned, though the policy of subsidising private firms persisted.

The return of price stability and faster economic growth in 1976 allowed the government to institute a four-year public investment programme to modernise the infrastructure and address the unemployment issue with schemes for early retirement and the raising of the school leaving age. Perhaps the most important reform of this period was the 1976 Codetermination Act, even though it fell short of the original proposals for parity of representation on the supervisory boards of firms employing more than 2,000 people. The main employers' organisation, the BDA, denounced the measure as hostile to the market and undemocratic, offering financial assistance to firms willing to challenge its constitutionality through the courts.[77] The SPD's lack of a majority told against it on this issue because the Free Democrats (FDP) took the employers' view and the measure was passed into law, giving management the upper hand in board representation.

By 1978 Schmidt was aiming for 4.5 per cent growth and was able to cut taxes and improve certain benefits such as maternity leave. But beginning with the second oil-price crisis in 1979 through to the international recession of 1980–82, policy reverted to a renewed offensive against wages and inflation and the government aimed to reduce the budget deficit in the face of growing unemployment – a task which involved cuts in social welfare benefits. The *Bundesbank* imposed the worst credit squeeze in West Germany's post-war history and unemployment reached a record high for the same period. By now the BDA was looking at the Reagan administration's policies with envious eyes, demanding welfare cuts to reduce indirect labour costs. Schmidt dismissed as pure folly the proposal emanating from the recently elected socialist government in France that together they should embark on a coordinated reflation.[78] Instead the Mitterrand government was completely isolated when it went against the grain of prevailing policies after 1981. In 1982, when the SPD-FDP coalition fell apart and the SPD were thrown into opposition, only 10 per cent of top business people favoured the continuation of the government.[79]

Throughout this period in office the SPD had experienced serious problems with its own left, as we shall see in the next chapter. It was also faced with a growing challenge to its left which eventually led to the electoral breakthrough of *Die Grunen* (the Greens), a question we take up in chapter four. These influences were visible in the successive drafts of the party's Basic Values Commission which was established after Brandt pressed for a new basic programme in 1984, no doubt in recognition of the party's identity crisis. Programmatic renewal would probably not have taken place had the SPD remained in government in the 1980s. In any case the most influential programme of the 1980s was written in and promoted by the US and was hostile to many social democratic values. This 'Washington Consensus' – promoted with missionary zeal by the IMF and World Bank, joined later by the OECD and the World Trade Organisation (WTO) – was the gospel of financial- and labour-market deregulation, reduced government spending, privatisation and deflation. It became the hegemonic ideology of the period with the ascendancy of the Reagan, Thatcher and Kohl administrations and was heralded in some quarters as the final demise of socialism.[80]

Notes

1 See E. Mandel, *Late Capitalism* (London, New Left Books, 1975), ch. 5., pp. 146–83.
2 J. Ruggie, 'International regimes, transactions and change: embedded liberalism in the postwar economic order', *International Organisation*, 36 (1982) 379–415.
3 G. Arrighi, *The Long Twentieth Century* (London, Verso, 1994), p. 278.
4 See K. Van der Pilj, *The Making of a Transatlantic Ruling Class* (London, Verso, 1984).
5 A. Glyn, 'Social democracy and full employment', *New Left Review*, 211 (1995) 42.
6 M. Aglietta, *Regulation et Crises* (Brussels, Calman-Levy, 1976); the 'regulationist school' sees a crisis of Fordism from the beginning of the period discussed in this study. See. A. Lipietz, *The Globalisation of the General Crisis of Fordism* (Paris, Cepremap, 1984).
7 Glyn, 'Social democracy', pp. 44–5.
8 P. Armstrong, A. Glyn and J. Harrison, *Capitalism Since World War Two* (London, Fontana, 1984), p. 197.
9 W. Korpi, *The Working Class in Welfare Capitalism* (London, Routledge and Kegan Paul, 1978), p. 323.
10 S. Hymer and R. Rowthorn, 'Multinational corporations and international oligopoly: the non-American challenge', in C. P. Kindelberger (ed.), *The International Corporation: A Symposium* (Cambridge, MA, MIT Press, 1970), 88.
11 Armstrong *et al.*, *Capitalism Since World War Two*, p. 246.
12 *Ibid.*, p. 253.
13 R. Brenner, *The Economics of Global Turbulence*, special issue of *New Left Review*, 229 (1998) 8–9.
14 See for example P. Krugman, *Peddling Prosperity* (New York, Norton, 1994), pp. 3–19.
15 R. Brenner and M. Glick, 'The regulation approach: theory and history', *New Left Review*, 188 (1991) 117.
16 The growth in American foreign direct investment in Europe from the late 1950s eventually prompted a European response, especially from the late 1960s. During the 1970s a boom in foreign direct investment ensued which intensified the trend towards the transnationalisation of capital.
17 H. Van der Wee, *Prosperity and Upheaval: The World Economy 1945–1980* (Harmondsworth, Pelican, 1987), p. 470.
18 W. M. Scammell, *The International Economy Since 1945* (London, Macmillan, 1980), p. 103.
19 S. Strange, *International Monetary Relations* (London, Oxford University Press 1976), p. 187.
20 Arrighi, *Long Twentieth Century*, p. 299. See also F. W. Scharpf, *Crisis and Choice in European Social Democracy* (Ithaca, NY, Cornell University, 1987). Looking back at this period Scharpf concluded that Keynesian full employment was undermined 'by the fact that world market integration, which was economically and institutionally completed in the 1970s, has constrained the scope of national macroeconomic policy permanently and fundamentally. The institutional changes that have made the world market the sole relevant frame of reference for capital

investors seem to be irreversible' (p. 258). My view is that while this may be true in financial markets, it is a wild exaggeration to claim this degree of global economic integration in the 'real' economy.

21 Armstrong *et al.*, *Capitalism Since World War Two*, p. 310.

22 M. Chossudovsky, *The Globalisation of Poverty: Impacts of IMF and World Bank Reforms* (London, Zed Books, 1997), p. 18.

23 F. Hirsch, *Alternatives to World Monetary Disorder* (New York, Random House, 1977).

24 D. Wass, 'The changing problems of economic management', *Economic Trends*, 293 (1978) 98.

25 Van der Wee, *Prosperity and Upheaval*, pp. 507, 509.

26 Arrighi, *Long Twentieth Century*, p. 314.

27 *Ibid.*, pp. 304, 345–7.

28 Chossudovsky, *Globalisation of Poverty*, p. 23.

29 J. O'Connor, *The Fiscal Crisis of the State* (New York, St. Martin's Press, 1973), pp. 241, 221–60.

30 E. Mandel, *Europe versus America* (London, New Left Books, [1968] 1970), p. 109 footnote.

31 *Ibid.*, p. 113.

32 *Ibid.*, p. 116.

33 *Ibid.*, p. 115.

34 *Ibid.*, p. 56.

35 See, J. Cohen and J. Rogers, '"Reaganism" after Reagan', in L. Panitch and R. Miliband (eds), *The Socialist Register 1988* (London, Merlin, 1988), pp. 400–1; K. Moody, 'Reagan, the business agenda and the collapse of labour', in L. Panitch and R. Miliband (eds), *The Socialist Register 1987* (London, Merlin, 1987); F. Fox Piven and R. A. Cloward, *The New Class War: Reagan's Attack on the Welfare State and its Consequences* (New York, Praeger, 1980), p. 8.

36 There had always been critics of the full employment, mixed economies of the post-war years but little attention was paid to them until the 1970s. See for example, F. A. Hayek, *The Road to Serfdom* (London, Routledge and Kegan Paul, [1944] 1976); and M. Friedman, *Capitalism and Freedom* (Chicago, IL, University of Chicago, 1962).

37 M. J. Crozier, S. P. Huntingdon and J. Watanuki, *Crisis of Democracy* (New York, New York University Press, 1975), p. 33.

38 Notably by R. Dahl in such books as *A Preface to Democratic Theory* (Chicago, IL, University of Chicago, 1962); *Polyarchy* (New Haven, CT, Yale University Press, 1971); and *Who Governs?* (New Haven, CT, Yale University Press, 1961).

39 M. Olson, *The Logic of Collective Action: Public Goods and the Theory of Groups* (Cambridge, MA, Harvard University Press, 1965), ch. 1.

40 F. Hayek, *Law, Legislation, and Liberty: A New Statement of the Liberal Principles of Justice and Political Economy* (London, Routledge and Kegan Paul, one-volume edition, 1982), vol. 3, pp. 97, 143.

41 New Haven, CT, Yale University Press, 1982.

42 Such as Patrick Cosgrave, Paul Johnson, Peter Jay and Samuel Brittan.

43 P. Jay, 'How inflations threatens', *The Times*, 1 July 1974.

44 S. Brittan, 'The Economic Contradictions of Democracy', first published in the *British Journal of Political Science*, 5 (1975) 129–59. I will henceforth refer to the shortened version published in A. King (ed.), *Why Is Britain Becoming Harder to Govern?* (London, BBC, 1976), pp. 96–138.
45 *Ibid.*, p. 98.
46 *Ibid.*, p. 101.
47 E. K. Scheuch, *Wird Die Bundesrepublik Unregierbar?* (Cologne, Arbeitgeberverband der Metallindustrie, 1976); *Schweitzer Monatshefte*, symposium, Wird Die Schweiz Unregeirbar? (Is Switzerland Ungovernable?), April 1975.
48 A. King, 'The problem of overload', in *Why Is Britain Becoming Harder To Govern?*, p. 10.
49 *Ibid.*, p. 27.
50 E. Dell, *A Hard Pounding* (Oxford, Oxford University Press, 1991), p. 19.
51 S. H. Beer, *Britain Against Itself* (London, Faber and Faber, 1982); Beer found that the Royal Commission on the Health Service in 1979 heard evidence from no less than 1,224 groups – taken as an indication of the scale of the problem and a source of the army of experts which was seen as the real policy-making power inside the welfare state system.
52 See C. Muller, 'The institute of economic affairs: undermining the post-war consensus', *Contemporary British History*, 10:1 (1996) 88–110.
53 Such as the Adam Smith Institute established in the summer of 1977; see R. Heffernan, 'Blueprint for a revolution? the politics of the Adam Smith Institute', in M. Kandiah (ed.), *Think Tanks in British Politics Vol. 2* (London, Frank Cass, 1996), pp. 73–87.
54 See R. Scruton, *The Meaning of Conservatism* (London, Macmillan, 1980), pp. 53–9, where democracy is a 'contagion' and 'disease'.
55 M. Friedman, *A Programme for Monetary Stability* (New York, Fordham University Press, 1960); P. Jay, *Employment, Inflation and Politics* (London, Institute of Economic Affairs, 1976).
56 C. A. R. Crosland, *The Conservative Enemy: A Programme of Radical Reform for the 1960s* (London, Cape, 1962), pp. 12, 16, 36–43, 56–8.
57 C. A. R. Crosland, Socialism Now and Other Essays (London, Cape, 1974), p. 19. The title essay was first published in 1973.
58 *Ibid.*, p. 18.
59 *Ibid.*, p. 25.
60 *Ibid.*, p. 26.
61 *Ibid.*, pp. 27, 34.
62 C. A. R. Crosland, *A Social Democratic Britain* (London, Fabian Society, tract 404, 1971), p. 1.
63 *Ibid.*, p. 7.
64 *Ibid.*, pp. 7–8.
65 *Ibid.*, p. 6.
66 Unemployment peaked at 929,000 in January 1972, while inflation, which averaged above 8 per cent in the first three years of the government, reached 19 per cent by the end of 1974.
67 In the Commons on 23 November 1971. Cited in Dell, *A Hard Pounding*, p. 5.
68 Dell, *A Hard Pounding*, p. 79.

69 J. Callaghan, *Time and Chance* (London, Collins, 1987), p. 413.
70 *Ibid.*, p. 426.
71 K. H. F. Dyson, 'The politics of economic management in West Germany', *West European Politics*, 2 (1981) 35–6.
72 J. Esser, 'State, business and trade unions in West Germany after the "political wende"', *West European Politics*, 2 (1986) 201.
73 J. Story, 'The Federal Republic – a conservative revisionist', *West European Politics*, 2 (1981) 65.
74 Dyson, 'Politics of economic management', p. 49.
75 R. Compston, 'Union participation in economic policy-making in France, Italy, Germany and Great Britain, 1970–1993', *West European Politics*, 3 (1995) 325. See also A. Martin and G. Ross, 'European trade unions and the economic crisis: perceptions and strategies', *West European Politics*, 1 (1980) 50.
76 J. Leaman, 'Central banking and the crisis of social democracy – a comparative analysis of British and German views', *German Politics*, 3 (1995) 28.
77 J. A. Helm, 'Codetermination in West Germany', *West European Politics*, 1 (1986) 34.
78 This rather vindicated the Socialist Party (PS) perception of the SPD as a right-wing brake on progressive policies when it rebuffed German proposals for a common electoral platform for the first direct elections to the European parliament in 1976. Yet the SPD's European policies in the late 1970s were notably to the left of those it pursued at home, calling for a structural policy to restore full employment, controls on multinational investment, a thirty-five-hour week and greater power for the European parliament.
79 D. Webber, 'Combatting and acquiescing in unemployment? Crisis management in Sweden and West Germany', *West European Politics*, 1 (1983) 75–6.
80 See L. S. Carney, 'Globalisation: the final demise of socialism?', *International Journal of Politics, Culture and Society*, 10:1 (1996–7) 141–73.

3

The turn to the left

At the end of chapter one I pointed out that even before the post-war boom came to an end the prevailing doctrines of social democracy were already subject to a radical left critique. A 'New Left' had emerged signifying both a renaissance of Marxism – a more heterodox and creative Marxism than that which had typified the communist parties in the 1950s – and the emergence of an innovative agenda which was ascribed to new social movments. Though the forces of feminism, environmentalism and Marxism would soon differentiate, and the growing concerns about racism, Western foreign policies, the nuclear arms race and the US war in Vietnam were not necessarily connected to any of them, they were united in posing a challenge to the dominant assumptions of the social democrats. The same could be said about the growth of trade union militancy, which led some commentators to talk of 'the resurgence of class conflict in Western Europe'. Wage militancy in conditions of full employment had inflationary consequences which might ultimately destabilise the weaker economies, as we have noted, but there was more than this in the industrial disputes of the late 1960s. There was also evidence of discontent with the social democratic institutions. The shop-floor militants were critical of the existing representation which their unions and parties afforded. Industrial democracy also moved back into the discussion – after decades of silence – and common cause on this issue brought trade unionists and New Leftists into alliance.

Even in the US, where there was no social democratic party, popular discontent channelled by the civil rights movement and the lobbying of organised labour – which was active in campaigns for housing, education, health and jobs, as well as civil rights – 'created enough political pressure to force a much enlarged flow of benefits from the social welfare program created in the 1930s and ... the creation of new programs too ...'[1] In the years 1965 to 1975 'more than twenty-five major pieces of federal regulatory legislation in the area of consumer and environmental protection, occupational health and safety and personnel policy were enacted by the Federal Government'.[2] Before it became apparent that the boom years were finished, even the US state sought social stability through measures that conflicted with the short-term interests of particular companies and sectors of industry.

Throughout Western Europe, however, factions of social democracy could be found even in the boom years that wanted more than Keynesian management strategies to promote growth and mitigate the inequalities and dysfunctions generated by the market economy. One of these variants of social democracy was broadly concerned to alter the structure of power in society by strengthening the state against private capital and bringing organised labour into the industrial decision-making process. This current began to grow in the 1960s. By the 1970s the vision of a benign welfare state coordinating democratic pressures from below so that rational intervention, equality and harmony gradually displaced the market and its anti-social consequences – the vision of Gunnar Myrdal[3] and Crosland – was shattered. Technocratic planning was unable to prevent the explosion of discontent in France in 1968. In Britain it had failed to get beyond the rhetorical stage reached by Harold Wilson in 1963. In Italy class conflict grew after the country belatedly achieved full employment in the 1960s and industrial unrest peaked in the autumn of 1969 when strikers in both the public and private sectors demanded socialist reforms to challenge the existing state capitalism, as well as improved pay and working conditions.[4] As in post-Franco Spain, where the left was unexpectedly strong in the first stage of the transition to democracy, the Italian left was concerned to democratise the existing public enterprise sector rather than add to it. The growing hegemony of the Italian Communist Party was also perceived as a real threat, at least until its electoral peak in 1976.[5] In Portugal after the regime change of 1974 public ownership spread to industrial companies, banking and insurance. In France it featured prominently in the Common Programme of the left adopted in 1972 and the Socialists and the CFDT trade union federation in particular stressed the goal of workers' self-management, rather than old-style nationalisation. But we will begin with Britain – one of the leaders in the vulnerability of its economy, the shallowness of the social democratic consensus and the ease with which it was finally cast aside.

We examined some aspects of the British crisis in the last chapter when we looked at the 1970s. But much of this had been anticipated in the previous decade during the course of the Labour government which had entered office in October 1964, united behind its leader's vision of planned economic growth. After six years in power no section of the party was content with the meagre results achieved. From the moment Labour took office the government was preoccupied with reducing the £800 million balance of payments deficit bequeathed to it by the previous Conservative administration. The prime minister – who was personally convinced of the continuing viability of

Britain's world role and the maintenance of the sterling area – followed conservative advice by defending the value of the pound, instead of devaluing. This defence of the pound, made difficult by the structural weaknesses of the UK economy and the persistent speculative activities of international finance, led the government to opt for deflationary measures with which to reduce the balance of payments deficit. Labour's programmatic commitments to faster economic growth were thus jettisoned, even though repeated sterling crises finally led to devaluation in November 1967. By this time socialist critics were conscious of the links between maintenance of the sterling exchange rate, the costly military presence which Britain maintained 'East of Suez' and the government's 'special relationship' with the US. To preserve the value of the pound, it was argued, Wilson needed American financial support, but this was incompatible with public criticisms of the US war in Vietnam, let alone defence cuts that would 'weaken the alliance'.[6]

In the eyes of the government's left critics all of these interdependencies had to be removed. The British balance of payments was in fundamental disequilibrium because of chronic underinvestment in domestic manufacturing, decades of relatively slow growth and low productivity. It was argued that the government should have addressed these problems by short-term measures such as devaluation, the introduction of import controls, and substantial cuts in its insupportable overseas defence expenditures, coupled with long-term measures to stimulate investment. A National Plan had been promised in 1964 but had come to nothing. However, belief in the efficacy of planning was still strong and some socialists looked upon the Italian state holding company, IRI, as the model for introducing new public enterprise that would harness modern technology, set standards, pool expertise, channel investment funds and provoke competition. Instead Wilson had been guided by the IMF and an assortment of economic reactionaries, with the result that his administration had remained in the pockets of City speculators.[7] The Labour left journal *Tribune* noted in 1968 that a worsening balance of payments exacerbated by financial speculation was the consequence of any reflationary strategy in Britain unless specific measures were taken to prevent it – such as exchange controls, export directives and import controls. The TUC came to much the same conclusion in its *Economic Review*, which began to set out the case for extending planning to external trade and financial flows in the same year.[8]

An Alternative Economic Strategy (AES) was beginning to emerge, and its advocates were increasingly cognisant of the growing multinational character of capital.[9] Evidence of growing dissent within the Labour Party was visible in the numerous rebellions of the annual conference between 1964 and 1970 when the government's policies were rejected.[10] This was only possible because of the alienation of significant affiliated trade unions whose block votes were now turned against the parliamentary leadership. In part this was because leftists had been elected to leadership positions in some of the biggest unions, itself evidence of the mood of the rank and file, particularly among the growing army of shop stewards. But it was also the result of friction over the government's incomes policy and its tendency to scapegoat the unions for its own economic failures. The climax was reached in 1969 when Wilson proposed new legislation to curb the unions in the White Paper, *In Place of Strife* – a proposal which the unions successfully resisted. The politicisation of the unions continued, however, when the succeeding Conservative government – apparently committed to deflationary policies and the reinvigoration of market forces – introduced an Industrial Relations Act in 1971. Rising inflation and unemployment, coupled with slower economic growth, ensured that the years 1970–74 generated a massive strike wave, numerous states of emergency and a pervasive sense of crisis. Of course this was partly due to international factors, which we will return to in the next chapter, but the polarisation in Britain was real enough and little affected by the Conservatives' celebrated *volte-face* over economic policy in 1972.

In opposition, Labour's policy-making committees were now dominated by the left.[11] With the publication of the consultative document *Programme For Britain* in July 1972 and *Labour's Programme 1973*, which the annual conference approved the following year, the National Executive Committee began its advocacy of an economic policy which dominated left Labour thinking for a decade. By 1976 the AES envisaged a programme of reflation and redistribution of income defended by import controls, and an extended sector of public enterprise, planning agreements and industrial democracy designed to boost investment and productivity. The AES found support, with differing emphases and priorities, from the TUC and trade unions affiliated to the Labour Party, from the Tribune Group of Labour MPs, the constituency Labour parties, various intra-party pressure groups and groups beyond the party, such as the communists, the Institute for Workers' Control and academics associated with the Conference of Socialist Economists and the Cambridge Political Economy Group. Most of these contributors recognised that traditional Keynesian measures were becoming ineffective because of changing power relationships consequent upon the growth of MNCs and the growing permeability of the UK economy. Stuart Holland, a former adviser to Harold Wilson in the 1960s and a major contributor to the work of the NEC's Public Sector Group and Industrial Policy Committee in the 1970s, was responsible for the fullest elaboration of this argument.

In *Labour's Programme 1973* the growing concentration of capital in manufacturing industry was said to justify action at the level of the giant firm itself if the agreed aim of effecting 'a fundamental and irreversible shift in the balance of power and wealth' was to be achieved by a Labour government. The document favoured a Keynesian reflation to deal with unemployment, but the central lever of power was to be economic planning harnessing the energies of the dominant firms. A new state holding company – a National Enterprise

Board – would create new public enterprise by the acquisition of around twenty-five giant companies distributed across the same number of economic sectors.[12] A system of planning agreements would embrace a further hundred of the largest manufacturing firms and all major public enterprise, as well as North Sea oil and shipbuilding. Controls on speculative flows of capital were also envisaged and the programme promised protective measures against countries which sought competitive advantage by subsidising exports or undervaluing their currencies. The main thrust of the argument, however, was that command of the biggest firms would enable the government to affect the level and direction of investment and set standards which the private companies in the oligopolistic sector would be compelled to emulate. The government would seek agreements over prices, profits, investment and industrial relations, but would turn to coercion on these and other matters if necessary and remove directors or purchase companies outright when it thought fit to do so. It would prevent the takeover of British firms by foreign companies and make sure that the government had the right to appoint public directors to the resident subsidiaries of non-resident multinationals, as well as to the main boards of resident multinationals. It would take measures to compel greater disclosure of information from such companies and seek an international agreement to regulate them. At home it would promote industrial democracy.

Crosland, the only member of the party's centre-right leadership who seemed faintly interested in these issues, suggested in 1973 that the multinational trend had peaked.[13] Stuart Holland, by contrast, saw MNCs as a threat to government autonomy in respect of monetary and financial policy, balance of payments policy, regional policy, in the effectiveness of industrial aid and subsidies, and with regard to planning generally. In his view – a view which informed *Labour's Programme 1973* – the trend to monopoly and multinational capital had produced a new mesoeconomic layer impervious to the indirect controls of Keynesianism. The top hundred manufacturing companies already controlled about half of net output by 1970 and were set fair to control two-thirds of it by 1980. These companies increasingly adopted multi-divisional management structures and spread their risks by diversification of product. They competed for market share globally, but not by price cutting. Multinational expansion abroad rendered their cost and profit structures opaque and made them masters of debt and payments transfers that obscured the real level of profit, assisted tax evasion and their avoidance of many macroeconomic policies. Though governments sought to bribe these companies with massive subsidies and extract taxes from them, both had become redundant tools of manipulation. What was really happening, according to Holland, was an inversion of welfare state values as the richest received the lion's share of benefits, subsidies and tax gratuities.[14]

The balance of public and private power was shifting rapidly towards the big companies. Trade had increasingly become intra-company in character and the multinationals controlled a growing volume of the short-term capital flows associated with it. But foreign exchange dealings dwarfed the value of trade in goods and services. A government's exchange rate policy could now be easily undermined by the speculative activities of the big companies and by their ability to time exports, stocks of exports and debt repayments. As the proportion of world trade accounted for by MNCs continued to grow, so did their ability to bring about currency devaluations once they had decided that such an outcome was inevitable. Over time the potential for national economic management was being lost, according to Holland. Multinationals were using their potential power to locate abroad as a bargaining counter to set the terms upon which they would continue to operate in Britain. Indeed the evidence was already visible, according to this analysis, that they were locating labour-intensive industries in less developed countries. The paradox of Britain's poor economic performance, given its high proportion of Europe's MNCs (140 out of the top 500), suggested that they had already written off the country as a main site for expansion. Urgent action was needed to assume control of the strong points of the mesoeconomic sector, including its financial institutions, so that the state could adopt new planning instruments. Unless this imbalance of public and private power was addressed, Holland argued, the state would seek to make the prevailing system work at the expense of the powerless, by employing wage controls, anti-trade union legislation and the suppression of workers' rights.[15]

The Labour government, elected in 1974 with a slender parliamentary majority, effectively ignored the AES. Wilson had vetoed the proposal to nationalise twenty-five top companies from the manifesto, even though the annual conference had supported the idea the previous year. After the left's defeat in the referendum of 1975, by which Britain remained a member of the European Economic Community (EEC), Tony Benn and other advocates of the AES were demoted in the government. The Labour Party outside parliament nevertheless continued to support an alternative economic policy and increasingly favoured constitutional reforms to ensure that the parliamentary leadership observed majority decisions. New Leftists joined the party in the 1970s and began to make an impact in the constituencies and local government. By 1976 the core of the AES consisted of import controls, public ownership of key firms and financial institutions, industrial democracy and planning agreements. But its supporters ranged from those who favoured a modest Keynesian reflation to those who saw it as a first step towards socialism.[16] While private sector unions perceived the AES as a way of diverting resources to manufacturing, public-sector unions stressed expansion of state employment as the best way to create jobs – precisely because the manufacturing sector was shrinking.[17] When the Labour conference voted for nationalisation of the leading financial institutions in 1976, the nine trade unions in this sector registered their misgivings or outright opposition. While some on the radical left argued that the AES was insufficient to address the problems identified by Holland and that Labour would never mobilise the popular forces required to create a real assault on capital,[18] others complained that it was silent on the needs of women, had nothing to say on the environment, and worried that it favoured centralising and bureaucratic remedies as a response to Britain's relative economic decline.[19] Within the coalition that constituted the Labour left, priorities thus varied enormously.

The lack of coherence in the AES can be illustrated by looking at the problem of financial capital more closely. Though Labour conferences had periodically resolved to nationalise the big four clearing banks and the biggest insurance companies since 1971, and both the TUC and NEC had supported such measures, the wider world of finance was neglected. Yet there was a growing conviction that the City of London was both useless as a source of investment in industrial regeneration and a source of instability. This 'cartelized concentration of power',[20] as it was called, preferred short-term investment in bonds and futures, was inclined to blackmail governments pursuing reflationary policies (or insufficiently deflationary policies), could determine the rate of interest and the exchange rate, and was able to turn balance of payments deficits into financial crises. It was obviously a power to be reckoned with and some supporters of the AES could see that 'any government which tries to introduce radical changes in such areas as the distribution of income or the ownership of property will find itself facing bankruptcy as money pours out through the foreign exchanges and multinational firms boycott the economy, shifting their activities elsewhere'.[21] Supporters of the AES saw political motivation in the persistent speculation against sterling after Labour was returned to power in 1974, even though the government pursued a policy of wage restraints and spending cuts, and achieved falling rates of inflation and a narrowing balance of payments deficit.[22] What would be the reaction if a Labour government of the future attempted to implement the AES? Logic suggested that emergency measures designed to prevent a flight of capital – such as the suspension of dealings on foreign exchange markets and the temporary freezing of foreign money banked or invested in Britain – would not be enough. A comprehensive system of controls on short- and long-term capital movements, together with controls on MNCs, was needed. But even these measures could be evaded or sabotaged in the longer term unless other key states implemented them too.

Since this was unlikely in the interim, it was argued that a Labour government would be well advised to run down the City's activities and nationalise the surviving remnant, while nationalising many MNCs too. To prevent retaliation and crippling trade boycotts, the government could requisition the enormous overseas assets of British firms to repay debts incurred by the nationalisation programme. Similarly, the City 'could be eliminated by trading off Britain's financial assets against its financial liabilities', leaving a surplus estimated at £1, 200 million in 1974. The City only accounted for one-tenth of all Britain's invisible earnings – about the same as a fortnight's export earnings or the amount that could be made up by reducing unemployment by 400,000. For some supporters of the AES the City was highly dispensable and its liquidation was expected to 'reduce dramatically the hold of international capitalism over the British economy'.[23] Members of the Cambridge Political Economy Group took this view, as did the Conference of Socialist Economists, and the logic of Stuart Holland's analysis pointed in this direction. But it was never embraced by the Labour Party

The more radical proposals for programmatic renewal of the Labour Party were not however confined to the margins of the organisation. Tony Benn came to be seen as the leading figure in this project by the end of the 1970s and a contender for the leadership of the party. In 1970 he announced his conversion to the 'New Politics' which he identified with alienation from existing power relationships and the call for participatory democracy throughout industry and society.[24] Benn subsequently championed industrial democracy, constitutional reform of the Labour Party, democratisation of the media and greater transparency and decentralisation of power in government – just the sort of 'expressive values' which Inglehart associated with the post-materialist left. Benn encouraged the extra-parliamentary movements and saw the growth of pressure groups and special interests as both a source of rank-and-file creativity and an indispensable force for change.[25] This undoubtedly attracted those who saw the AES as part of a wider programme that would mobilise people for radical change and create a momentum that would propel Labour towards even more fundamental reforms. The apparent tension between the Bennite stress on pluralism, popular participation and decentralisation, on the one hand, and a greater role for the state on the other, attracted criticism, as we have seen, but was answered for others by the promise of industrial democracy and broader popular participation in the planning process. But there was also the sense, in the mid- to late 1970s, that the AES consisted of emergency measures that addressed the crisis caused by international factors such as the collapse of the Bretton Woods system and Britain's adjustment to the EEC, both of which were overlaid on the 'deep-rooted structural problems' of the UK economy.[26] Dramatic evidence was provided for this thesis by the rising unemployment and rapidly rising inflation which the Labour government of 1974–79 inherited from the Heath government, coupled with the regime of deflationary cuts and financial crises which preceded the IMF loan of 1976, which in turn led to the abandonment of Keynesianism, the turn to monetarist policies and further deflationary measures. There was a perception on the left that the crisis could be resolved by a revivification of market forces on the basis of deregulated labour markets and there was a real urgency to prevent this outcome. Moreover, as economic problems mounted the left agenda for state action grew, while the prospects for a vibrant extra-parliamentary campaign in support of 'Bennism' diminished.

The election of the Conservatives under Mrs Thatcher in May 1979 and the end of the Labour government brought about an intensification of the factional warfare which had been a feature of the Labour Party throughout the decade. The demand for internal constitutional change climaxed in the convening of a special conference which adopted mandatory reselection of MPs and election of the leader by the mass party. In a pre-emptive move, Callaghan resigned as party leader so that his successor could be elected by the old method; the parliamentary party voted for Michael Foot, a veteran left-winger but a moderate by Bennite standards. The party nevertheless split when leading MPs on its revisionist wing resigned to form the Council for Social Democracy, forerunner of a Social Democratic Party. For these people, Labour had fallen irretrievably to the extremists. Yet when Benn challenged the right-wing candidate for the deputy leadership in 1981, the divisions on the left – personal and political – quickly came to the surface. Benn's challenge failed by less than 1 per cent because members of the parliamentary left either abstained or voted for Denis Healy, the right-wing candidate. Later that year the Bennite majority on the NEC was lost. Foot's shadow chancellor, Peter Shore, followed his Keynesian instincts and was inclined to ignore the AES. The NEC nevertheless continued to elaborate upon the decade-old policy and arguably the fullest statements of the AES were published in 1982. The following year Labour contested the general election with a programme recognisably inspired by the thinking that had originated in the mid-1960s.

France

The recent history of the French left must begin with the explosion of discontent which began in May 1968. Although small vanguard organisations in the Marxist-Leninist mould were conspicuous in these events, there is no doubt that May 1968 is also strongly associated with the emergence of a left radicalism which was critical of both the communist and the social democratic traditions. The socialist left began regrouping in 1969 when the *Section Française de l'Internationale Ouvrière* (SFIO) became the *Parti Socialiste* (PS) and merged with the Convention of Republican Institutions, two years later, at the Congress of Epinay in 1971. Since the war the French left had been dominated by the ideologically inflexible Communist Party (PCF), but even the PCF could see that the constitution introduced by General de Gaulle in 1958 entailed institutional pressures which effectively forced the parties of the left to seek electoral collaboration. Essentially, the left had to come to terms with the sheer strength of Gaullism in the context of the new arrangements. Not only did the electoral system encourage the PCF and SFIO to support each other in second ballots, with whichever was the weaker after the first ballot stepping down;

presidential elections also encouraged a logic of polarity with the leading candidate of the left taking on his counterpart of the right.

The Communists initially gained the most advantage from this alliance and could contemplate the eventual absorption of the Socialists' electoral support. By 1967, however, it became clear that the short-lived federation of socialist groups (FGDS) put together by François Mitterrand had made the non-Communist left a formidable electoral force. Presidential campaigns, moreover, showed that the Communists could get nowhere near the 45 per cent second ballot vote which Mitterrand achieved against de Gaulle in 1965. The showing of the FGDS in 1966–68 and its emerging dialogue with the PCF made left unity a practical proposition. For the PCF, which regarded the 1968 events as an infantile ultra-left disturbance and showed not the slightest interest in insurrection, the only way to remove the right from power was by means of elections. In practice this meant an electoral pact with the Socialists and slowly it became clear that such a strategy also entailed a Socialist presidential candidate, rather than a Communist.

Within the non-Communist left ideological change visibly accelerated in 1968. Distrust of the state and statist forms of socialism informed the renewed interest in workers control which was one of the strongest themes to survive the student and workers' protests. *Autogestion* was sufficiently radical-sounding (suggesting self-government, popular or workers' control) – and vague – to command the support of all those socialists looking for a libertarian alternative to the bureaucratic and authoritarian socialism of Eastern Europe and the paternalistic, welfare state socialism of the West. At one level, of course, France had experienced neither, but the history of state planning since the war had been as determinedly preoccupied by economic growth as it was uncritical of the existing power structure of industry and society. The invasion of American multinationals, which proceeded apace after 1965, was 'exposed' in a bestseller by the journalist Jean-Jacques Servan-Schreiber in 1967, who called for a European counter-attack via 'the creation of large industrial units capable of competing with the American giants, both by their size and their management'.[27] Servan-Schreiber was as fulsome in his praise of the perceived superiority of technocratic management in the US conglomerates as he was insistent on the need for French and European responses in kind. Around the same time as *The American Challenge* was surpassing all post-war book sales records in the republic, French employers 'launched a vigorous offensive against state intervention in industrial investment'. Such trends may help in our understanding of socialist trade union policy, for example within the CFDT. Economic growth had increased the purchasing power of workers but had 'not given rise to any increased participation in economic decision-making on their part. Quite the contrary: the major part of post-war social legislation dealing with worker representation in organs of decision-making, both within the firm and at national level ... [had] been emptied of all meaning ... At the same time, since the mid-1960s [firms] ha[d] turned to the international market' with uncertain, but anxiety-making, consequences for employees.[28]

Though wage demands predominated overwhelmingly in industrial disputes, the May events 'encouraged reflection within the labour movement ... on themes of self-management'.[29] May 1968 inspired confidence in both the feasibility and the popularity of a 'third way'. In part this was because of what actually happened in the course of the strike wave of that summer. The striking workers, for example, spontaneously formed occupation committees in some factories and raised demands that challenged managerial prerogatives. The student revolt raised demands for, and expectations of, direct democracy. Both confounded fashionable theories of affluent, post-ideological societies drifting towards consumerist contentment. The feeling survived that there was something new in the air. In part the 'third way' was made necessary because something new had come into existence – the New Left, which none of the variants of the old left properly catered for, whether the new emphases were on the environment, gender issues, alternative lifestyles or other critiques of conventional politics. *Autogestion* came to stand for the overcoming of alienated labour, and the rejection of the atomised, consumerist lifestyle required by modern capitalism, and the desire for social solidarity which united the otherwise disparate groups of the left.

Edmond Maire, secretary-general of the CFDT, and Michel Rocard, then secretary-general of the *Parti Socialiste Unifie*, a left-wing secession from the SFIO, identified themselves with *autogestion* in the midst of the May revolt. Both talked about the need to de-bureaucratise society and denounced traditional social democracy for its naive faith in progress via state-guided economic growth and technological change. Maire envisaged workers collectively determining all facets of production – what will be produced, how, when and where. Rocard was similarly concerned to secure workers' control and by means of *autogestion* saw prospects for the realisation of the ideals of individual self-development and creativity.[30] Evidence from strike analyses in the early 1970s suggested that a majority of disputes for increased pay were 'linked to frustrations over hierarchical relationships and alienation due to working conditions'.[31] The CFDT explicitly regarded the wage hierarchy as 'an expression of the hierarchical form taken by established authority' and adopted the strategy of putting demands that were both incompatible with capitalism and which prefigured the self-managed future in which the capitalist oligarchy was absent.[32] Thus by 1970 this erstwhile Christian alternative to the Communist-controlled trade union federation, the CGT, had embraced class struggle and the objectives of *autogestion*, social ownership and planning, when it deconfessionalised after 1964.

The growth of the left within the PS was signified by the growing influence of Jean-Pierre Chevènement's *Centre d'Etudes, de Recherches et d'Education*

Socialistes (CERES). This group saw itself as sensitive to the New Left concerns which surfaced in 1968 while also favouring an expansion of the state and pressing the argument that for Marxists there were no enemies on the left. A common front with the PCF was the logical outcome of such a mentality – a position François Mitterrand had personally arrived at for purely electoral purposes. As the recipient of the highest percentage of the vote ever given to the left candidate in a presidential election,[33] Mitterrand was able to exercise a leadership role in favour of close alliance with the Communists. Two-thirds of the large towns already possessed PCF-PS alliances by 1971 and the total left vote in the municipalities had averaged 47 per cent.[34] That year Mitterrand was elected first secretary of the PS with the support of CERES, committing the organisation to close collaboration with the PCF. Twelve months later he negotiated the Common Programme of the left with George Marchais of the PCF. During the next four years the PS membership grew from 80,300 to 149,623[35] and the proportion belonging to CERES of this swollen total advanced from one-twelfth to one-quarter. Meanwhile, the PS at last caught up with the PCF in electoral support and swept ahead of it in the years following Mitterrand's marginally unsuccessful bid for the presidency in 1974.[36]

From the beginning the PS encouraged fractionalism by adopting a form of leadership election based on principles of strict proportionality. Mitterrand, Rocard and Mauroy each had their factions within the party. CERES, which originated in the old SFIO, was the one which developed an analysis of modern capitalism along lines similar to those of the Bennite left in Britain. As in Britain, the left saw MNCs exercising power to restrict the scope for national politics whilst they exacerbated problems of regional inequality, inflation, currency volatility, and balance of payments.[37] A new international division of labour was emerging in which the labour intensive industries were relocated to newly industrialising countries. Though CERES did not advocate a strongly protectionist policy, a marked nationalist sentiment informed its analyses. These depicted the US as the guardian of the MNCs and chief beneficiary of the emerging capitalist world order. France needed an industrial policy if it was to exercise control over its economic development and achieve sustained economic growth in this US-dominated world in which internationalising trends were growing stronger. Government intervention would have to affect investment decisions, research and development, the development of new technology, the level of import penetration, and the maintenance of strategically important industries. The state would have to take over large chunks of industry and finance. An incomes policy would be required to help narrow differentials.

The enlarged public sector would also be the laboratory for experiments in *autogestion* and this would be one of the main antidotes to the bureaucratising and centralising dangers inherent in the statist measures which the fraction regarded as essential for a rupture from capitalism. CERES also advocated citizen's referenda and greater autonomy for communes. But it also situated *autogestion* within the imperatives of the national plan, without being able to explain how this would work. It made clear that the public companies would have to make a profit. It fought hard to strengthen the alliance with the PCF – an organisation not known for its democratic proclivities – and it conducted its own fractional activities without bothering to elect its leaders. Contradictions were not confined to its democratic credentials. CERES feared US foreign policy more than that of the USSR. In the early 1980s, like most of the European left, it could see the possibility of a US-initiated nuclear war fought in Europe. But unlike the leftists of most other West European countries it unequivocally favoured the national nuclear deterrent. Though it focused on the need for a national industrial policy, however, CERES did not advocate withdrawal from the EEC. It envisaged collaboration with left governments in Southern Europe, imagining that they would be soon governed by the socialists, and held out the prospect of detaching Germany from the American embrace as a basis for an alternative European policy. In this way CERES wanted to end the cold war polarisation in Europe.

It also loudly denounced the Rocardians, who joined the PS in 1974, as mere liberals, at best libertarians, representing the class interests of the salaried white-collar workers. This Leninist style of polemic was another of the things at odds with CERES claim to champion more democracy. Rocard placed it in the Jacobin tradition. He and his supporters' emphasised the passing away of the old class forces and the emergence of a richer civil society. They saw the New Left and its agenda arising from the autonomous actions of new social movements and claimed, on this sort of reasoning, to be closer to the real spirit of *autogestion* than CERES. In fact, for all the talk of 'two cultures' within the PS both fractions were led by career-minded leaders whose ideological posturings must be read as in part displays for personal advancement.

Socialism in one country

In rejecting state planning as a mere device for the maintenance of the existing regime of inequality, sections of the French, Italian[38] and British left converged in their determination to challenge multinational capital through an extension of public ownership. This derived from similar analyses of contemporary capitalism rather than conscious cross-fertilisation. In France awareness of the American multinational challenge and wariness of American foreign policy objectives transcended the parties. So did the rhetoric of planning of course. The French Socialist and Communist Parties actually named the companies that they intended to appropriate in their Common Programme of the left, whereas the Green Paper on the National Enterprise Board which the British Labour Party published in opposition was content to mention merely the number of such companies. The French left argued that extended public ownership would help to break down the dominance of big capital. Public ownership would embrace the entire banking and financial sector and strategic industrial groups and firms. This would include armaments, aeronautical, nuclear and pharmaceutical industries and the country's mineral resources. Parts of the electronics and chemical industries, steel, petrol and transport would also enter the public sector.

While the Labour Party talked about the need to renegotiate the terms of Britain's membership of the EEC and held a referendum on entry in 1975, the French and Italian left parties had either accepted the Community or were positively in favour of it. The Common Programme observed that an extension of the public sector was not precluded by the Treaty of Rome. The programme stressed the need for democratic planning and a democratised public sector. Parliamentary control would be supplemented by a decentralised process of plan formulation beginning with plants in the public sector, but also in consumers' organisations and regional bodies. A battery of controls would seek to determine industrial location, price controls and the structure of foreign trade. In Italy the state holding companies, IRI and ENI, had apparently demonstrated that real control over industrial conglomerates was feasible on a minority shareholding and this persuaded the PCI to drop its hitherto exclusive reliance on full nationalisation. Instead it began to stress the democratisation of the public sector and better planning agreements.

Stuart Holland argued in 1975 that any left government 'would be ill-advised to try to "go it alone" in attempting a programme of socialist transformation' without the support of the other two.[39] In his view, however, the Socialist International had handicapped itself by abandoning an offensive strategy decades before as a result of the cold war, and by its acceptance of the permanence of liberal capitalism and the consequential loss of initiative as against multinational capital that these policies entailed. As an alternative he recommended the creation of a permanent international committee of the executives of all the parties concerned – socialist and communist – but also international trade union coordination, though this would depend on the prior coordination of the leading left parties of Italy, France and Britain. However, Holland was forced to acknowledge that the West European reformist parties differed in both their conceptions of socialism and their national situations. The German SPD, the Italian left and the Dutch Labour Party favoured a federal Europe but with quite different motivations, according to Holland, for whom it was obvious that the PCI and the SPD were poles apart in their understanding of the meaning of socialism. In reality, despite some dialogue between the SPD and the PS in preparation for the first elections to the European Parliament in 1977, each party operated independently of the others.

It could also be added that much more democratic accountability was needed in the EEC and that its intergovernmental bodies were unacceptably opaque and unaccountable. But it was already clear, on the basis of Holland's own analysis of international capital, that effective action to rescue social democracy was required on a transnational basis, as well as at the level of the nation-state, and that impediments to such action would have to be overcome sooner or later. In the 1980s these truths became blindingly obvious.

Sweden

While other parties merely dreamed of radical change, in Sweden the reform initiatives of 1968–76 sponsored by the unions and the social democrats 'challenged the power and prerogatives of corporate managers and owners of capital. Hence they departed from the essentially welfarist orientation of Swedish social democracy between 1948 and 1968'.[40] The Swedish economy was much stronger than those of Britain, France and Italy but, far from rejoicing in this, it is clear that

> The reform offensive challenged the power and prerogatives of managers and capitalists at different levels. Some initiatives addressed specific aspects of the relationship between wage earners and employers. For instance, the labour movement pushed through legislative measures that restricted employers' right to fire people (the Employment Security Act of 1974) and that allowed shop-floor safety stewards to shut down production if they determined conditions were hazardous or unhealthful (the Work Environment Act of 1977). Other reforms addressed systemic features of the labour-capital relationship. The wage-earner funds proposal endorsed in 1976 by LO, the confederation of blue-collar unions, usually called the Meidner Plan ... went furthest, by calling into question the very principle of private ownership.[41]

The new concern for power and equality in industry and society in Sweden can be traced to the second half of the 1960s. The SAP programme of 1968 included a critique of the concentrated economic power represented by Swedish banks and industrial conglomerates. It saw the need for measures to democratise decision making in industry and, with an eye on regional policy, proposed that the state should become directly involved in economic restructuring. Such rhetoric translated into a number of institutional changes designed to promote state enterprise in pursuit of regional policy and cherry-picking, but there was no attempt to introduce planning and the nationalisation of industry was not resorted to on a large-scale at governmental level until the social democrats were defeated in the general election of 1976 and a coalition of bourgeois parties took over. The reform offensive after 1968 was in any case mainly driven by the unions affiliated to LO, rather then the SAP itself.

Resolutions on the theme of industrial democracy were supported at the Metalworkers' Union conference in 1968 and taken up by the TCO

(Confederation of Professional Employees) congress of 1970. But the leadership of the blue-collar unions received a rude shock when a wave of wildcat strikes surprised Sweden in 1969–70, especially at the LKAB mines. These disputes revealed rank-and-file discontent with the trade union bureaucracy, as well as with the structure of power at work. As Pontusson says, the strikes were 'widely interpreted as expressing growing worker discontent with the working conditions and managerial practices characteristic of Fordist-style mass production'.[42] But the evidence of alienation and discontent with union leaders among workers in the state-owned iron mines of Kiruna above the Arctic Circle prompted the idea that a degree of union decentralisation was required, as well as worker participation in the boardroom, if worker alienation was to be overcome. 'State-owned! What does it matter? We never feel that it's ours. And the company board – you don't feel as if you had something to do there. It's the company board that decides every issue.' Such were the views expressed by the striking miners of Kiruna.[43] The LO responded quickly by creating a committee on industrial democracy in June 1969. As the white-collar confederation of unions TCO also supported the demand for co-determination at work, and the Liberals and Centre Party had been advocating some form of participation at work since the second half of the 1960s, the demand to democratise work emerged as a cross-society concern by the time it stood as the main theme of the 1971 LO congress.

Some influential social democrats believed that the time was ripe for a move towards 'economic democracy'. The party, it was argued, had achieved both political democracy after the First World War and social democracy by the welfare measures of the post-1945 period. So even before the unofficial strikes of 1969–70 the SAP was talking about economic democracy as its third great project. In 1968 it set up a study group chaired by Alva Myrdal which produced *Towards Equality* the following year. This document saw inequality as a breeding ground of social and industrial dissatisfaction, stagnation and disloyalty. Equality of opportunity, according to Myrdal, required a significant shift of power and resources to employees and involved greater participation in decision making. Only then could society find the social solidarity it needed for stable development. In policy terms the report stressed the necessity for a progressive taxation system, future legislation to promote the economic independence of married women, a flattened hierarchy in firms and schools and steps towards industrial democracy. Thus the LO congress of 1971 reflected this thinking within the SAP, as well as the demands for greater employee influence at work that had been raised by the miners of Kiruna.

The LO adopted the policy statement *Industrial Democracy* in 1971, by which it approved worker representation in the boardroom, and the congress of that year addressed other radical themes that were to become law during the following few years. The SAP's 1975 programme also emphasised the importance of industrial democracy and underlined the need to transform capitalism because of its inability to prevent unemployment and inflation.[44] Democratic control of the economy was central to this vision. As the party programme declared:

> The Social Democratic Party therefore wishes to replace the present concentration of power in private hands by an order of things in which each individual is entitled as a *citizen*, *wage earner*, and *consumer* to determine the direction and distribution of production, the shaping of the productive apparatus and the condition of working life. This will be done by engaging the *citizens* in the national planning of resource management in order to make the best use of the country's potentialities. It will be done by guaranteeing the *wage-earners* influence on their work places and firms and by expanding their participation in the formation of capital and the administration of collective savings.[45]

The SAP governments of 1970–76 achieved improvements in health and safety (Working Environment Act 1977); a level of worker representation in the boardroom (Joint Regulation of Working Life Act 1976); recognition of shop stewards (Position of Trade Union Representatives at the Workplace Act 1974); provision against unfair dismissal (Security of Employment Act 1974); and restrictions on the ability of managers to reduce manpower (Promotion of Employment Act 1974) by requiring employers to notify the public labour-market authorities of planned cutbacks in manpower and to enter discussions about such proposals. Legislation on paid educational leave, giving the unions substantial rights in the interpretation over what constitutes appropriate education and training, was also passed in 1975. The result of this legislative onslaught, according to Kesselman, was 'extraordinary changes on the shop floor' in health and safety, the quality and organisation of work and employee protection.[46]

Employers resented much of the legislation which established new employee rights, seeing it as an infringement on the Basic Agreement reached at Saltsjobaden in 1938 – one of the cornerstones of the post-war consensus – which had left management to the managers. Some of the big firms such as Volvo, however, also expressed an interest in the 'participation' idea in order to emulate Japanese standards of flexibility, concern for 'quality', and lower levels of employee turnover and absenteeism. Their conciliatory approach undoubtedly assisted the corporate lobbying which was designed to remove the less palatable proposals for rights of worker self-determination. Their intention was to confine 'participation' to plant-level issues. By the time the Joint Regulation of Working Life Act was passed in 1976, the more radical ideas – such as the workers' veto – had been dropped and, despite Olof Palme's conviction that the new law was the greatest reform since universal suffrage, the new measure left managerial prerogatives unscathed. Furthermore, an unforeseen consequence of the 1976 co-determination law when it finally became operational in 1982 was that it localised industrial relations and undermined centralised bargaining; gradually local agreements on profit sharing, share ownership and locally determined, results-based pay awards accounted for a growing proportion of the total wage.[47]

The Meidner Plan

From the late 1960s the Swedish left had begun to regard investment as one of those prerogatives of management that created problems for labour. More investment was going abroad. That which remained in Sweden created fewer jobs in successful advanced sectors than were being lost in old basic industries, such as mining and timber, faced with declining competitiveness. The evidence also accumulated that one of the unforeseen consequences of the solidaristic wage policy – the policy of concentrating bargaining priorities on the low paid – was that wealth and capital in Sweden became ever more concentrated in the giant companies of the most dynamic sectors, as 'excess profits' were accumulated in these most efficient industries where workers were subject to pay restraint. Excess profits threatened to undermine the solidarity which the LO depended on because workers in the affected sectors could hardly be expected to show wage restraint in the interests of egalitarianism, if their employers made a laughing stock of them by appropriating bigger and bigger profits. Pay restraint in successful enterprises did not necessarily benefit low-paid employees in other firms. The biggest firms, furthermore, were increasingly financing investment out of retained profits to avoid climbing interest rates on loans and to meet the growing cost of research and development. Such firms could do what they liked.

It was in this context that the LO chief economist, Rudolf Meidner, was asked at the 1971 LO congress to form a committee of enquiry to develop employee investment funds. This idea had more than one objective. The LO wanted to promote industrial democracy so that workers would exercise real influence in economic matters and challenge what it called the industrial 'oligarchy [which] has no counterpart anywhere in our democratic society'. Meidner talked of 'democratic control over the process of capital formation itself'[48] and drew attention to the falsity of the 'managerial revolution' thesis of dispersed corporate ownership, and the reality of increasing concentration of voting power at company meetings. The LO wanted to do something about unequal distribution of wealth – 'the inevitable concomitant of industrial self-financing' – in a context in which 89 per cent of the population owned no shares at all and small stockholders exercised zero influence. The LO was also trying to do something about wage drift, or the tendency for the most profitable sectors to pay further wage rises after the central wage negotiations had fixed a general increase. This practice had the effect of fuelling inflation and endangering the survival of less profitable firms compelled to increase their own wage rates. It also undermined the solidaristic wage policy. The employee investment trusts, by contrast, would shore-up the wage policy by allowing workers in the more profitable sectors who exercised wage restraint to see that their sacrifice did not benefit the employers in the form of above-normal profits. Instead the wage funds would grow and the workers as a collective would reap the benefit. For all these reasons the wage funds idea recommended itself, but only if – as Meidner was at pains to point out – it was not allowed to prejudice the maintenance of full employment and its essential condition, a high level of capital formation.

The basic idea put forward by Meidner was that a portion of profits would be transferred annually to collectively owned employee funds from which they would be used to buy company stocks, eventually giving the unions a major say in the running of private industry. Meidner proposed that 20 per cent of the profit should be set aside for the employees. Meidner's first version of the scheme was presented in August 1975. It was then subject to a consultative process in the winter of 1975–76, during which thousands of union members responded to the report. In June 1976, just three months before a general election, the LO quinquennial congress adopted Meidner's plan as a basis for further work on the subject.What was impressive was the unanimity with which the unions adopted it. Something like 18,000 union members had participated in LO study circles during 1975 to consider and modify Meidner's proposals before the 1976 congress unanimously adopted them. The social democratic leadership, by contrast, was ill prepared and unenthusiastic and the scheme was subject to a ferocious campaign of opposition from the bourgeois parties and the SAF.

The SAP's declared interest in greater economic democracy had none the less been evolving since the 1968 *Programme for an Active Industrial Policy* acclaimed by the party congress. It envisaged various forms of planning and even a greater role for state enterprises. The following year the party approved *Towards Equality*, with its emphasis on measures to promote gender equality in fiscal policy, family law, and the labour market. In 1975 the SAP party programme even talked of economic democracy as the successor to political and social democracy in the party's historic campaign to extend rights.[49] This was also the context for optimistic academic analyses of the SAP which ascribed its success to its ability to mobilise popular forces so that the balance of class power was shifted to its advantage.[50] Reformism and the transformation of capitalism were deemed to be compatible as long as the party skilfully pursued a strategy of encroachment on capitalist prerogatives, rendering the capitalists functionless and bringing their power into the collective management of employees. Co-determination and employee participation in collective ownership could be seen as stages in this process. In the event the election of 1976 deviated from the customary left–right cleavage, which had consistently benefited the SAP since 1932, as the issue of nuclear power dominated discussion and the social democrats stuck doggedly to their growth ideology. The Social Democratic Party was removed from power for the first time in forty-four years. Meanwhile the original Meidner Plan came to be perceived as an electoral liability rather than a mobilising focus for the next stage of advance against private capital.

The SAP accepted the LO's proposal for employee investment funds only on a revised basis. The excess profits of just the largest firms would be taxed, employees would also make a contribution, and the funds would be regional to prevent concentrated power falling into the hands of the unions. The 1978 party congress made much of the new international volatility of exchange rates and inflation which were believed to be responsible for the decline of savings and investment. It was argued that the investment fund idea would have to be reworked to take this into account. Fears about the future of Sweden's pension scheme were also in evidence, consequent upon the growth in the number of pensioners expected by the end of the century and the strain upon solidarity which an increase in contributions would entail. The SAP and the LO concluded that additional collective savings were required and by the 1982 general election the employee investment funds 'came to be seen as a cornerstone for guaranteeing the pension system'.[51]

The 1982 election was dominated by debate about the funds with the bourgeois parties predicting that they would soon allow the unions to control the economy, while the Left Party Communists (VKP) claimed that Meidner's original proposal had been diluted to the point of irrelevance. The public was largely indifferent, though 20 per cent was strongly opposed to the funds and a proportion of these agreed with the communists. Five wage funds were eventually introduced within the general pension system, each with its own government-appointed board, largely composed of employees. They became fully operational in 1984 and by the end of the year were worth 1.54 billion crowns. They were financed by profit sharing on the basis of 6 per cent of the wage bill or 500,000 Swedish crowns – whichever the company preferred. Only large companies were affected and their real contributions, after tax allowances, were half the stipulated amount. Contributions, moreover, were scheduled to stop in 1990, by which time 14 billion crowns was expected to have been amassed, or 6–7 per cent of the collective value of Sweden's largest companies. The money bought shares in Swedish (industrial) companies and was required to earn a real return of 3 per cent. But each fund was only allowed to hold a maximum of eight per cent of the voting shares of any given company and collectively no more than 40 per cent of the voting rights. The bulk was invested in Volvo, ASEA, Ericsson and other large engineering companies.

Divisions within the SAP on the direction of economic policy were papered over in the 1982 election in the idea of a 'third way' between neo-liberalism and the public ownership radicalism of the French socialists. The party regained power and remained in office for the rest of the decade, seeming to perform wonders in the maintenance of full employment. Commentators had already discerned, however, both a 'pervasive mood militating against egalitarianism in most strata of Swedish society' and the breakdown of the Swedish model of welfare capitalism.[52] Arguably, welfare state egalitarianism had reached its upper limit in Sweden and the scope for further provision was accordingly limited. Strains had begun to show in the social consensus and the employers' organisations began to withdraw their support from the institutions that had once served them so well.

West Germany

By the mid-1980s green parties – which had secured representation at various levels of government in Belgium, Italy, Luxemburg, the Netherlands and West Germany – were the most successful expression of the post-materialist challenge to social democracy. West Germany provides the best example of all because it produced both the strongest of these new parties – *Die Grünen* – and currents which brought New Left politics inside the SPD. The change is traceable to the thaw in the country's peculiar acceptance of the cold war *status quo* in the 1960s. The SPD – always anti-communist under Schumacher – became a supporter of the Western Alliance after his death. Some on the left were reconciled to a state of affairs – which featured a permanently divided country – that could be seen as proof of the acceptance of war guilt. Only a tiny and marginalised body of socialist opinion had rejected NATO and Atlanticism and objected to West Germany's front-line status in the confrontation of the cold war enemies. The Socialist Student Union (SDS) – expelled from the SPD in 1961 for refusing to endorse the Bad Godesberg Programme – was one such but exercised little influence at the time of its expulsion. The situation began to change, however, when Western foreign policy fell into profound disrepute with the young at the very time when domestic developments raised alarms of a return to the old authoritarian state.

The stultifying anti-communism of the 1950s depended on factors that could hardly be sustained. It had almost become official state ideology and was turned against anyone or anything that questioned the wisdom of the state's main commitments – even the SPD. A ruling of the Constitutional Court in August 1956 had declared aspects of socialist analysis unconstitutional, such as the idea that wage labour is a form of exploitation.[53] Such cultural conformity was born out of the fascist defeat. The generation which came of age at the time of the American war in Vietnam suffered from this complex much less and were provided with compelling evidence that the Manicheanism of the cold war was false. Closer scrutiny of cold war history actually led many of them to conclude that the US initiated most, if not all, of the technological developments leading to the contemporaneous threat of nuclear Armageddon. Added to this was a new awareness that the 'Free West' included numerous notorious dictatorships supported by the US; and that the Third

World was in fact largely under Western control, and subject to the exploitation of its governments and companies. The student population of West Germany expanded rapidly in the 1960s just as these questions were being openly discussed to an unprecedented extent.

The West German state itself had illegitimate origins in the minds of many of this generation who were trying to come to terms with the sins of their fathers. The Nazi past was seen to linger on in the personnel who had run the state since its creation in 1949 and former fascists held high positions throughout the institutions of West German society. The obsessive anti-communism of the state looked sinister to those who perceived it running in a straight line all the way back to Hitler. The Allies had set this state up, or so it was argued, as a counter to Soviet communism. They had turned a blind eye to its former Nazi functionaries, who were regarded as rather useful for ensuring stability. The Allies had in any case restricted West Germany's sovereignty, reserving the right to encamp troops and station missiles on its soil. After the Cuban missile crisis it dawned on more Germans than ever before that their country was a future battlefield for nuclear weapons. The campaign for disarmament, launched at Easter in 1960 with only 1,000 members, had grown to 50,000-strong by 1963 and 150,000 members in 1967. Opposition to nuclear weapons had stirred the population before but had faded, as in the mid-1950s when Adenauer made light of 'tactical' nuclear weapons in accordance with fashionable NATO thinking. This time, however, other developments helped to swell the ranks of the peace protestors and the socialists who had been ignored in 1960.

The SDS, which had been expelled from the SPD in 1961 and had participated in the peace demonstrations, evolved as a centre for New Left analysis developing positions on modern society drawn from Herbert Marcuse and the Frankfurt School and learning about the Third World from Franz Fanon and Che Guevara. The growth of dissent over Vietnam, NATO and nuclear weapons broadened its milieu. When the SPD entered the so-called Grand Coalition in 1966 – leaving the country without a parliamentary opposition – many liberals expressed concern, but the emerging New Left sounded the alarm. Fear that West Germany had not learned the lessons of its past – because no clean break with that past had ever occurred – was fuelled even more by the pending emergency legislation, initiated by the Erhard government, for which the Grand Coalition assumed responsibility. This allowed for the suspension of elections in the event of some future crisis. The legislation was presented as unfinished business – something that every democracy allowed itself but was anomalously denied the Bonn state in 1949. In the West German context, however, the student left took this measure as a sign of creeping authoritarianism.

From the student milieu a self-styled 'extra-parliamentary opposition' (APO) emerged by 1966 attacking the cold war order and the cultural conformity of West German society. This was a highly heterogeneous movement which contained advocates of participatory democracy such as the SDS but also various Leninist groups which had persuaded themselves not only that the West German state was inherently authoritarian, but that the DDR, with its nationalised property and 'clean break' with fascism, was to be given the benefit of the doubt if not actually supported. The wider context was one of a sea-change on the left with regard to East Germany. Kurt Schumacher's policy on national reunification was long gone and many on the left took the view expressed by the philosopher Karl Jaspers that a united Germany meant an authoritarian Germany. For some, the argument that the DDR was a permanent fact of life was little more than a pragmatic acceptance of the *status quo*. Others hoped to 'normalise' relations with the former pariah in the name of what Egon Bahr called '*Wandel durch Annaeherung*' (change through rapprochement). Willy Brandt's *Ostpolitik* was of this order, attempting to promote reform in the DDR by regularising interaction with it. One author has argued that many on the left came to regard the DDR as a permanent legitimate independent state within the context of Soviet hegemony leading to 'the shameful situation' in which they 'became perhaps the most solid supporter of the status quo in eastern Europe and the Soviet Union throughout the 1970s and 1980s, publicly forsaking the plight of opposition movements'.[54] But for most of the left acceptance of the DDR's right to exist was bound up with fear of nationalism – which had become something to keep at arms length – and the conviction that anti-communism was an instrument of the cold war which played into the hands of the right.

To some extent sympathy for the DDR on the far left derived from the argument that nationalised property provided the sure progressive basis for some future evolution towards democracy. The stronger sentiment in the 'extra-parliamentary' milieu was the conviction that the West German state was a tool of American imperialism and big business. The formation of the Grand Coalition, the emergency legislation, the fatal shooting of a student demonstrating against the visit of the Shah of Iran in June 1967, and the success of the neo-Nazi National Democratic Party in the *Lander* elections of 1967–69, when it obtained between 7.4 and 9.8 per cent of the vote – this was the sort of empirical evidence which counted among those convinced that the Federal Republic was going fascist. When SDS leader Rudi Dutschke was shot by a right-wing assassin, while preparing demonstrations against the emergency laws in April 1968, large-scale protests were held throughout West Germany. Out of these events – and later measures of *Berufsverbot* – competing Leninist sects emerged that might have added up to some 40,000 members by the early 1970s. Better known than these was the Baader-Meinhof terrorist gang, or Red Army Faction, which gave rise to the anti-terrorist laws of the 1970s, which in turn excited more talk of the state's propensity to repression.

More important than the sects and terrorists were those elements of the

New Left, which in advancing a new social and political agenda – on the environment, gender, and peace in particular – had a lasting impact on the SPD, whether they entered the party and strengthened the hand of the radicals, or challenged the Bad Godesberg Programme from outside party ranks. Some joined the party to begin that 'long march through the institutions' which Dutschke indicated as the only way to bring about the democratic revolution. Others joined the SPD after 1969 when the inspirational Brandt became chancellor. Some were attracted by the evident radicalisation of the SPD's youth wing, the Jusos, an erstwhile supporter of the Bad Godesberg Programme but one that was demanding dialogue with the APO by 1968. In 1971 the SPD severed its ties with the Social Democratic University League (SHB) – so radical had the latter become – but the Jusos groups that were formed in the universities to replace it were just as bad from the party leadership's viewpoint. SPD membership grew from 710,448 in 1965 to 998,847 in 1975 and the Jusos groups continued to increase in number during the same period. The influx in 1968–72 in particular increased the proportion of well-educated, middle-class members among the SPD membership. Braunthal makes the point that this new, youthful membership, though its vocabulary was often Marxist, was distinguished by post-materialist rather than traditional views in the emphasis it gave to quality-of-life issues such as participatory democracy and environmental protection.[55]

The SPD also began attracting more female members and voters around this time and the New Left forced it to challenge the 'proletarian antifeminism' that had previously relegated the 'woman question' to the status of a secondary issue.[56] In 1972 the SPD vote was greater among women than men for the first time in its history. The new social movements – the feminists, peace campaigners, citizen's initiatives and environmentalists – were beginning to change the party in ways 'which amounted to a redefinition of its very political identity', according to one observer.[57] At their peak 'those movements had more members than all the political parties put together' but they also displayed 'a remarkable overlap with the SPD'.[58] The advance of New Left and feminist ideas within social democracy was not confined to the SPD of course – it was visible throughout Scandinavia in particular. In the Netherlands the process of New Left infiltration of the Labour Party (PvdA) had proceeded much faster than in Germany when a loosely structured, post-materialist group drawn from the student and single-issue campaigns of the late 1960s actually took over the party in the 1970s.[59] The PvdA became more radical, more factionalised and more inclined to polarise party competition as a result, refusing to countenance certain coalitions – such as with the Catholic Party – and inclined to announce in advance of elections exactly what sort of cabinet it wanted. When the party revised its statement of principles in 1977 the document was much more militant about gender issues, the environment and the need to transform capitalism. It talked of the need for a new world order, especially in North–South relations, and was critical of NATO, US foreign policy and the arms race.

The idea that a real transformation of capitalist societies was on the immediate agenda in the 1970s gained force from the revolution in Portugal in 1974 and the unrelated collapse of dictatorship in Spain and Greece soon afterwards.[60] In Greece the end of the military regime in 1975 also seemed to herald radical change in view of the growth of the socialist movement led by PASOK, which had declared that the country had been the victim of imperialist subjugation, principally at the hands of the US, to serve 'the military and economic interests of the great monopolies'.[61] The 'movement' aimed to restore Greek sovereignty by withdrawing from NATO and effecting a social transformation based on the socialisation of the entire financial system, much of basic production, the strategic monopoly industries and the largest trading concerns. PASOK also promised constitutional guarantees for the right to work, self-management in the larger firms, universal health care and social insurance and an attack on inequality. Judged by its rhetoric PASOK was far too militant to work with the Socialist International which its leader Papendreou described as instrument of 'US-oriented German social democracy'.[62] Closer inspection of PASOK's Marxist-sounding polemics, however, revealed that 'national liberation' was designed to appeal to all social strata; the enemy was either foreign or one of the privileged few who benefited from the tutelage of foreigners. PASOK – completely dominated by Andreas Papendreou – soon showed its true colours after forming a government in 1981.

Similarly, the Spanish Socialists quickly retreated from the militant rhetoric of the 1970s when they entered office. Spanish labour had been the most militant in Europe in the mid-1970s, when measured by the number of strikes.[63] Legislative gains were won in areas of labour law and the right to form political parties was achieved. As late as the election of 1977 the PSOE and PCE[64] defined their ideologies as Marxist,[65] revolutionary and democratic, though it was already clear that the major left parties had dropped their radical policies in the interests of democratic consolidation and fear of provoking military intervention.[66] By the end of the decade Felipe González emerged strengthened by this process within the PSOE, assisted by such factors as the rise of unemployment (reaching over 13 per cent by 1981), which weakened the militants in the unions; the explosion of membership after 1977 which diluted the influence of party veterans and opened the way for careerism and patronage; and, it must be acknowledged, popular support for a moderate electoral strategy which the party's successes reinforced within the organisation. Though this led to government in 1982, it also led away from the PSOE's socialist identity while consolidating the cult of personality around Felipe González and an authoritarian party regime which brooked no dissent. Upon taking office, party leaders had already concluded that there was to be no socialist experiment as in France (where the Mitterrand government was in retreat) and that it would not be handicapped by too close an association with the unions and the working class (which was presumed to be the British Labour Party's problem).

We shall see that the 1980s marked a retreat for all the parties of the Socialist International (which PASOK joined in 1986). This chapter has tried to give some indication of the way the increasingly adverse economic conditions of the 1970s, combined with the appearance of the New Politics, produced an initially radical response from the reformist socialist parties. Of particular interest is the growing awareness of the power of international capital on the left of social democracy. Though the strategies for addressing this problem proved inadequate, the problem itself was real enough and it may be noted here that a large agenda was potentially opened up. Would the social democrats now devise answers to the problems of corporate tax avoidance, threats of corporate exit, the Dutch auction of subsidies to induce inward investment, the 'race to the bottom' in welfare and collective provision? We will return to these questions shortly. But first we turn to an examination of how the social democrats have adapted to the challenge of the most successful of the new political forces in the electoral field – the greens.

Notes

1 F. Fox Piven and R. A. Cloward, *The New Class War: Reagan's Attack on the Welfare State and Its Consequences* (New York, Praeger, 1980), pp. 116–18.

2 D. Vogel, 'Why businessmen distrust their state: the political consciousness of American business executives', *British Journal of Political Science*, 8:1 (1978) 24.

3 G. Myrdal, *Beyond The Welfare State* (New York, Bantam, [1960] 1967).

4 In the 'hot autumn' of 1969 rank and file initiatives were militant, numerous and generally ahead of trade union officialdom. See J. Barkan, *Visions of Emancipation: The Italian Workers' Movement Since 1945* (New York, Praeger, 1984), p. 68.

5 By July 1976 the PCI held power in six of Italy's twenty regions and most of the big cities. The Chamber of Deputies elected a Communist president and the the Party held the chair on six parliamentary committees. In the years 1966 to 1977 PCI membership rose from 1.5 to 1.8 million with an average annual intake of new members of the order of 100,000 – thus evincing an extremely high turnover.

6 R. Pryke, *Though Cowards Flinch: An Alternative Economic Strategy* (London, MacGibbon and Kee,1967), pp. 124–25

7 *Ibid.*, p. 127.

8 L. Panitch and C. Leys, *The End of Parliamentary Socialism: From New Left to New Labour* (London, Verso, 1997), pp. 25, 52.

9 Early analysis of multinational capital include P. Baran and P. Sweezy, *Monopoly Capitalism* (New York, Monthly Review Press, 1967); R. Veron, 'Multinational enterprise and national sovereignty', *Harvard Business Review*, March–April (1967); P. Baran and P. Sweezy, 'Notes on the multinational corporation', *Monthly*

Review, 21:5 (1969) 1–13; J.-J. Servan-Schreiber, *The American Challenge* (Harmondsworth, Penguin, 1969); P. Uri (ed.), *Les Investissements etrangers en Europe* (Paris, Editions Dunod, 1967); E. Mandel, *Europe versus America* (London, New Left Books, 1970).

10 See L. Minkin, *The Labour Party Conference* (London, Allen Lane, 1978).

11 M. Hatfield, *The House the Left Built* (London, Gollancz, 1978).

12 *Labour's Programme 1973* (London, Labour Party, 1973), p. 1.

13 C. A. R. Crosland, *Socialism Now and Other Essays* (London, Cape, 1974), p. 32.

14 S. Holland, *The Socialist Challenge* (London, Quartet, 1975) pp. 33–5.

15 *Ibid.*, p.91

16 The radical view was put, for example, by the Conference of Socialist Economists in *An Alternative Economic Strategy* (London, CSE Books, 1980).

17 See for example CPSA/SCPS, *Cuts That Puzzle:The Case Against the Cuts* (London, CPSA/SCPS, 1975).

18 See J. Bearman, 'Anatomy of the Bennite left', *International Socialism*, 6 (1979).

19 See A. Coote, 'The AES: A New Starting Point', *New Socialist*, November–December (1981) 4–7.

20 S. Aaronovitch, *The Road From Thatcherism: The Alternative Economic Stratgey* (London, Lawrence and Wishart, 1981), pp. 58–9.

21 B. Rowthorn, 'Britain in the world economy', in his *Capitalism, Conflict, and Inflation* (London, Lawrence and Wishart, 1980), p. 81

22 S. Holland (ed.), *Out of the Crisis: A Project for European Recovery* (Nottingham, Spokesman, 1983), p. 153.

23 Cambridge Political Economy Group, *Britain's Economic Crisis* (Nottingham, Spokesman, 1975), p. 17.

24 A. Wedgwood Benn, *The New Politics: A Socialist Reconnaissance* (London, Fabian Society, 1970).

25 T. Benn, *Arguments For Socialism* (London, Cape, 1979) and *Arguments for Democracy* (London, Cape, 1980).

26 M. Barratt Brown, K. Coates and J. Eaton, *An Alternative* (Nottingham, Spokesman, 1975).p. 1.

27 Servan-Schreiber, *The American Challenge*, pp. 125, 69–71.

28 P. Dubois, C. Durand and S. Erbes-Seguin, 'The contradictions of French trade unionism', in C. Crouch and A. Pizzorno (eds), *The Resurgence of Class Conflict in Western Europe Since 1968, Volume One: National Studies* (London, Macmillan, 1978), pp. 57–8.

29 *Ibid.*, p. 63.

30 B. E. Brown, *Socialism of a Different Kind: Reshaping the Left in France* (Westport, CT, Greenwood Press, 1982), pp. 46–52.

31 Dubois *et al.*, 'Contradictions', p. 65.

32 Quoted in *ibid.*, p. 66.

33 Mitterrand received 45 per cent in the second ballot against de Gaulle in 1965.

34 R. W. Johnson, *The Long March of the French Left* (London, Macmillan, 1981), pp. 65–6.

35 G. Voerman, 'Le paradis perdu. Les adherents des partis sociaux-democrates d'Europe occidentale, 1945–1995', in M. Lazar (ed.), *Le Gauche en Europe Depuis 1945: Invariants et Mutations du Socialime Européen* (Paris, Presses Universitaires de France, 1996).

36 Mitterrand received 49 per cent of the vote in 1974 against Giscard d'Estaing.

37 See D. Hanley, *Keeping Left? CERES and the French Socialist Party* (Manchester, Manchester University Press, 1986), ch. 3.

38 The PCI developed its own alternative economic strategy in the mid-1970s to address the economic crisis as it affected Italy, but with both eyes on its international dimensions. Interestingly the Communists made the struggle against inflation a priority, opposed protectionism and – in the context of an already swollen public sector – made no demands for further public ownership. See D. Sassoon (ed.), *The Italian Communists Speak for Themselves* (Nottingham, Spokesman, 1978).

39 Holland, *Socialist Challenge*, p. 344.

40 J. Pontusson, *The Limits of Social Democracy* (Ithaca, NY, Cornell University Press, 1992), p. 2.

41 *Ibid.*, pp. 3–4.

42 *Ibid.*, p. 165.

43 Quoted in H. Heclo and H. Madsen, *Policy and Politics in Sweden* (Philadelphia, PA, Temple University Press, 1987), p. 145.

44 M. B. Hamilton, *Democratic Socialism in Britain and Sweden* (London, Macmillan, 1989), p. 207.

45 Translated by R. G. Tanner and quoted in Hamilton, *Democratic Socialism in Britain and Sweden*, p. 207.

46 M. Kesselman, 'Prospects for democratic socialism in advanced capitalism: class struggle and compromise in Sweden and France', *Politics and Society*, 11:4 (1982) 414.

47 K. Ahlen, 'Swedish collective bargaining under pressure: inter-union rivalry and incomes policies', *British Journal of Collective Bargaining*, 27:3 (1989) 333, 336.

48 R. Meidner, *Employee Investment Funds* (London, Allen and Unwin, 1978), pp. 39–40, 14.

49 Political citizenship preceded social citizenship in Swedish history; by the late 1960s the time was said to be ripe for economic citizenship via industrial democracy.

50 See W. Korpi, *The Working Class in Welfare Capitalism* (London, Routledge, 1978).

51 K. Ahlen, 'Sweden introduces employee ownership', *Political Quarterly*, 56:2 (1985) 190.

52 S. Lash, 'The end of neo-corporatism? The breakdown of centralised bargaining in Sweden', *British Journal of Industrial Relations*, 23:2 (1985) 234.

53 W. Hulsberg, *The German Greens: A Social and Political Profile* (London, Verso, 1988), pp. 19–20.

54 A. S. Markovits, 'The West German Left in a Changing Europe', in C. Lemke and G. Marks (eds.), The Crisis of Socialism in Europe (London, Duke University Press, 1992), p. 178.

55 G. Braunthal, *The West German Social Democrats, 1969–1982: Profile of a Party in Power* (Boulder, CO, Westview Press, 1983), p. 70.

56 See E. Kolinsky, 'Political culture change and party organisation: the SPD and the second "Fauleinwunder"', in J. Gaffney and E. Kolinsky (eds), *Political Culture in France and Germany* (London, Macmillan, 1991), pp. 210–25. See also H. Schissler, 'Social democratic gender politics', in D. E. Barclay and E. D. Weitz (eds.), *Between Reform and Revolution: German Socialism and Communism From 1840 to 1990* (Oxford, Berghahn, 1998), pp. 507–31.

57 T. Meyer, 'The transformation of German social democracy', in D. Sassoon (ed.), *The Rise and Success of Green Parties and Alternative Lists* (London, I. B. Tauris, 1997), p. 125.

58 *Ibid.*, p. 126.

59 R. Inglehart and R. B. Andeweg, 'Change in Dutch political culture', *West European Politics*, 3 (1993) 359 and B. Tromp, 'Party strategies and system change in the Netherlands', *West European Politics*, 4 (1989) 92.

60 See R. M. Fishman, 'Rethinking state and regime: Southern Europe's transition to democracy', *World Politics*, 42:3 (1990) 422–40.

61 From PASOK's Declaration of September 1974, quoted in R. Clogg, *Parties and Elections in Greece* (London, Hurst, 1977), pp. 217–18.

62 A. Elephantis, 'PASOK and the elections of 1977', in H. Penniman (ed.), *Greece at the Polls* (London, Hurst, 1981), p. 135.

63 V. Navarro, 'The decline of Spanish social democracy, 1982–1996', in L. Panitch and J. Saville (eds), *The Socialist Register 1997* (London, Merlin, 1997), p. 199.

64 The Communist Party, initially handicapped by its association with the Stalinist regimes of Eastern Europe, memories of the Civil War and its own history of authroitarianism, rapidly shifted to the Right under Santiago Carillo's leadership in the late 1970s but failed to dent the PSOE's vote. By the 1982 election it was factionalised beyond repair and could only secure 4.1 per cent of the vote against the socialists' 48.4 per cent.

65 D. Share, *The Making of Spanish Democracy* (New York, Praeger, 1986), p. 139. Up to 1977 most members of the PSOE even thought of Felipe Gonzàlez and the 'Sevillians' as Marxist.

66 See, J. F. Coverdale, *The Political Transformation of Spain After Franco* (New York, Praeger, 1979), p. 64; Share, *Making of Spanish Democracy*, p. 113; R. Gillespie, *The Spanish Socialist Party: A History of Factionalism* (Oxford, Clarendon Press, 1989), pp. 379–80. Plans for a coup, incriminating 200 officers, and scheduled to prevent elections, were exposed as late as October 1982. See P. Preston, *The Politics of Revenge: Fascism and the Military on Twentieth Century Spain* (London, Routledge, 1995), pp. 165–202.

4

Challenge from the left: the greens and social democracy

New social movements

The challenge to social democracy of the new social movements went beyond a new issue agenda to encompass the meaning of politics itself.[1] Social democrats in the golden age had stood for growing prosperity, greater equality and social security through the instrument of the state. Politics was largely confined to the arena of party competition, corporatist bargaining and parliamentary government. The New Politics of the late 1960s, by contrast, sought to politicise civil society as well as to advance a new issue agenda. The new social movements stressed wider political participation, decentralisation, direct action and self-transformation. They rejected the traditional hierarchical forms of political organisation and sought to mobilise support around particular issues, though the range of issues salient for them was vast since they embraced questions of power and domination, gender relations, the environment, North–South issues, problems of peace and war and so on. The demands associated with the new social movements ranged all the way from the particular to the universalistic, but tended to depart from the class-specific. Analyses of their social base consistently revealed the prominence of the new middle class and those outside the labour market such as students.[2] Though social democratic parties themselves were becoming more middle class in composition at their activist base, they still depended on the blue-collar working class for much of their electoral support and were confronted by a wide-ranging problem of adjustment. When green parties began to make an electoral impact in the 1980s the process of adjustment quickened. All the new social movements were internally divided, of course, and the social democratic left could reckon on attracting their more ambitious elements on the grounds that no system change was conceivable unless organised labour was part of the equation.

Economic growth versus the environment

But the conflict of interests between growth-oriented policies and environmental concerns had already become increasingly obvious in the 1970s and was by no means confined to the West German left, where the new social movements were arguably at their strongest. In Austria, for example, where young, leftish people had been drawn into the SPÖ during the decade (locally attributed to Kreisky's dynamic leadership), the decision to build the country's first nuclear reactor at Zwentendorf, which was ready to go on-stream by 1978, produced acute tensions within the party and vociferous opposition to the leadership. The trade union federation, the ÖGB, was just as keen to support the nuclear programme as its critics opposed it, but when Kreisky forced a referendum on the Zwentendorf plant, the vote was narrowly lost. The unexpected victory for the environmentalists gave a boost to the Austrian green movement and caused the SPÖ to begin taking the 'Alternatives' seriously.[3] Green ideas also advanced within the party – notably through the Socialist Youth, as well as through attempts by a new party department to adapt to the new agenda – but the rift between trade unionists and environmentalists surfaced again when the SPÖ-led government endorsed the construction of a hydroelectric power station on the Danube and in 1984 began clearing central Europe's last surviving wetland forest to prepare the ground. The fact that the leader of the protesters was himself a leading trade unionist – Gunther Nenning of the Union of Journalists – is a caution against simplification, but there is no doubt that the unions were suspicious of the environmentalists when the latter denounced economic growth and job creation.

Polling evidence in Austria showed that the growth of environmental awareness was particularly strong among the young and the educated voters. If, as the evidence suggested, the old working class was in decline, and the post-materialist, green electorate was potentially one-fifth of all voters, the party had to take note of the trends, particularly in view of the way polls conducted between 1980 and 1984 suggested that job security was less important to voters than environmental protection.[4] The SPÖ also had reason to worry, however, that it would lose working-class voters to its major rivals the ÖVP if it changed too quickly. After the 1978 referendum the independent green organisations became a force of attraction for socialists disillusioned with the SPÖ and one commentator has even described the green alternatives as 'a crucial factor in the demise of the so-called "Kreisky era" ...'.[5] But the idea that the social democratic left in affluent societies is inevitably placed on the defensive by environmentalism is not borne out by the evidence.

In Denmark, where three left-wing alternatives to the Social Democratic Party (SD) already existed, no green party has managed to establish itself in what would otherwise be considered fertile post-materialist ground.[6] In Norway, the green agenda found its way into the Labour Party (DNA) and environmentalism was certainly an electoral issue by 1989, but the Socialist Left Party accrued extra seats in the *Storting* rather than the Norwegian Green Party. In Sweden, the former Communist Party (since 1990 the Left Party) and the Centre Party were quicker to adapt to environmentalism than the SAP and the social democrats were made to suffer. Again nuclear energy was the issue that brought the conflict between economic growth and environmental protection to a head. Nevertheless, Lewin observes that ordinary party members 'seemed to understand the need to do something about the uninterrupted rise in energy consumption, even if this meant a lower rate of growth in private consumption'.[7] But having announced their support for the building of eleven nuclear reactors in 1970–71, the party leadership subsequently added two more to the list and the issue became the main concern of the 1976 general election. The SAP entered the contest as the only party definitely committed to the nuclear energy programme and narrowly lost the election. An unbroken period of social democratic government lasting forty-four years thus came to an end.

The environment remained a salient issue thereafter but it was not until the 1988 election that the Greens surmounted the 4 per cent electoral barrier to enter the *Riksdag*. The SAP meanwhile adjusted its image and programme, trying to find the balance between the ecological agenda and its traditional stress on growth, welfare and redistribution.[8] It was also helped by the fact that the Greens regarded the Conservatives as their principal opponents and could be relied upon to join with the Left Party in sustaining the SAP governments of the late 1980s and 1990s.[9] Nevertheless, the SAP found that while its female members, youth organisation and middle-class members were especially likely to make environmental issues their first priority, the LO and the metalworkers in particular were more concerned about jobs. Issues such as the future of nuclear power or the plan for a rail bridge to link Sweden and Denmark brought these divisions into the open. But it was only after the Greens emerged from the general election of 1988 as one of the strongest parties of this type in Europe that the SAP moved closer towards a decision on the abolition of nuclear power. In 1990 the party conference agreed to enter negotiations with the other parties on the decommissioning of nuclear power stations. By then the 'greening' of Swedish politics had affected all the left parties and the Centre Party too. But the left majority in the *Riksdag* had survived the process.

Greens versus Social Democrats

In West Germany the emergence of the Greens, the self-proclaimed 'anti-party party', was more troublesome to the Social Democrats because the electoral arithmetic favoured their opponents, the CDU/CSU, which had been in governmental alliance with the liberal Free Democrats since 1982. Any adjustment of the SDP to court the green vote threatened to drive working-class voters to the CDU/CSU; while neglect of the environmental agenda might allow the Greens – with their undoubted appeal to leftists – to advance at the SDP's expense. Well before *Die Grünen* was formed, however, the new social movements, as we saw in the last chapter, had established a milieu which crossed into the SPD and drew upon the energies of its left activists in the movements for peace, feminism and environmental protection which emerged at the end of the 1960s.

The SPD left demanded arms reductions at the party conferences of 1971 and 1973 and argued for greater distance from NATO and the end of compulsory military service. Half the delegates at the 1973 convention supported a freeze on defence spending. The Jusos also called for these measures, but additionally for the withdrawal of foreign troops and the end of the cold war military blocs. The party leadership managed to hold off this challenge on defence.[10] Environmental issues surfaced in relation to energy because of the 1973 oil crisis and the oil embargo on West Germany imposed by the Arab states. By 1977 the SPD was divided over nuclear power.[11] The SPD chancellor, Helmut Schmidt, and the unions were pro-nuclear, but an anti-nuclear movement was growing at the base of the party. The unions stressed full employment and economic growth, the left opposition – with former cabinet member Erhard Eppler its unofficial spokesman – called for a pause in future constructions to allow a full evaluation of the alternatives. Large demonstrations were organised to oppose the nuclear construction programme and in 1977 the party convened an energy conference. Schmidt announced a huge investment programme in atomic technology research the day before the conference met. The unions and *Bundestag Fraktion* (the SPD parliamentary wing) right supported Schmidt.[12]

The trade union federation, the DGB, however, later in the year came to the view that a moratorium on new plant construction was required so that the problem of waste could be resolved. Some SPD deputies also threatened to vote against the government on the issue of the country's plutonium fast-breeder reactor programme. Before the party convention in 1977, the party executive came out in support of a moratorium on nuclear power. Schmidt announced that he would ignore the executive and the DGB switched to support Schmidt. An ambiguous compromise was adopted giving both sides the illusion of victory. The problem rumbled on and surfaced again during the second oil crisis in 1979 when perhaps as many as 40 per cent of party delegates opposed Schmidt's policy. The Baden-Württemberg SPD voted for a ban on plants in their area. But Schmidt dominated the party convention again when it considered defence and energy, even though the stationing of neutron bombs in West Germany had aroused oppositional passions on the left at this time. Two years later the issue of NATO's deployment of cruise missiles divided the party and Schmidt threatened to resign unless he got his way in supporting the Western alliance. In October 1981 the largest demonstration in the Federal Republic's history took place against cruise missiles with about one-quarter of the parliamentary *Fraktion* supporting the protestors.

When the party lost power in 1982 there was no great swing to the left but on the issues of environment and peace the party had apparently changed. At the 1983 Cologne congress the delegates overwhelmingly rejected the stationing of medium-range NATO missiles in West Germany and Schmidt was isolated. The party also became more anti-nuclear and the argument that economy had to be reconciled with ecology gained force. By this time young people were turning to *Die Grünen*[13] and the SPD had to pay attention to its left critics for electoral reasons. There was also the realisation that the internal divisions generated by the new social movements were damaging the party and had to be addressed. The party congress at Essen in 1984 voted to begin the process leading to a new Basic Programme. The programme commission, overseen by Willy Brandt, naturally sought a policy synthesis that would appeal to the party's traditional supporters and those with a New Politics orientation. The central idea was that of qualitative economic growth which brought considerations of the quality of life and the democratic control of technology to the forefront. The programme also stressed the need to end the arms race, address world inequalities and promote gender equality at home. It also referred to new forms of democracy involving workers and citizens. In short, the programme was proof that the party was adapting itself to an agenda that had arisen beyond the control of party managers. Those who had resisted it, such as Helmut Schmidt, were increasingly marginalised.

Some commentators argued that the party was transformed 'in the course of the 1980s into something fundamentally different than it was before'.[14] In 1983, for example, the SPD withdrew its support for NATO's double-track decision on the siting of cruise missiles. The 1986 conference agreed to phase out all nuclear plants within ten years. Nuclear deterrence was also repudiated. Markovits and Gorski see these decisions as rejections of the Atlanticist and growth-oriented positions of the previous quarter-century and more.[15] Similarly, the decision in 1988 to embark on a campaign to raise the female membership to at least 40 per cent of all party positions by 1994 is also attributed the impact of the New Politics. More precisely, the SPD left's pressure for a change of direction had finally borne fruit with the help of the Greens. The emergence of the new party was arguably the result 'of a division of the SPD from below' which the leadership was belatedly trying to heal.[16] From 1983 – the year in which *Die Grünen* broke through the 5 per cent threshold in elections to the *Bundestag* – this certainly meant making concessions to the post-materialist agenda and the SPD's parliamentary *Fraktion* now harried the Kohl government to change its course on the salient issues.

Länder SPD governments in Schleswig-Holstein and Hamburg in 1988 also began to move in the new policy direction. Merkle suggests that the post-materialist activists were now in charge of the lower- and middle-level leadership ranks in the big cities and university towns and had begun to determine the course of the party.[17] These university-educated, middle-class activists seized the initiative away from the old working-class supporters whose power bases in industry were shrinking. The cost, according to Merkle, was the SPD's declining ability to integrate the working class in the big city branches. A sectarian preoccupation with ideology and disregard for vote maximisation was supposed to characterise elements of this New Left,[18] though this judgement is clearly not true of those New Leftists who conspicuously moved to the right as they climbed the party hierarchy or who left the party in exasperation to join the Greens, or the peace movement or the politically inactive.[19] In fact the process of adjustment to the New Politics was far from straightforward. For example, it was not clear if the SPD had done enough to steal the Greens' clothes. Even if it had done so there was nothing to stop the other parties following suit in specific areas of policy. Unless the Greens were simply to disappear as an electoral force, and thus conveniently solve the problem, the SPD would still have to decide whether it could afford to ally with the new party or try to isolate it.

Another possibility was that the SPD, having adopted aspects of the Greens' programme and rejuvenated itself in the process, would strengthen the hand of the 'realists' within *Die Grünen* and enable them to steer the new organisation towards compromise with the Social Democrats. For their part the Green 'realists' might be expected to want to strengthen the SPD left by cementing an alliance of the two parties. The SPD right had every reason to fear such a move and produced arguments to the effect that any association with the new social movements could only be achieved at the expense of alienating the SPD's working-class base. Most of the prominent Green politicians were former SPD activists, many of them wary of being stifled in the Social Democratic embrace.[20] Alliances nevertheless emerged at local level in the town councils and in state legislatures such as Baden-Württemberg and Lower Saxony. The first, at Hamburg in June 1982 with the Green Alternative List, provoked divisions within the city SPD and led to impasse over nuclear energy policy. A more significant experiment was conducted in the state of Hessen when the Greens under Joschka Fischer's 'realist' leadership sought policy concessions from the SPD in return for their support in the state parliament. Hessen's SPD leader, Holger Börner, previously noted for his enmity towards the Greens, entered into protracted negotiations with them which resulted in a deal. Though this was denounced by the Green '*fundis*' (or fundamentalists),[21] the 'realist' wing of the Greens was strengthened, as was Willy Brandt's argument that the Greens were the 'lost children' of the SDP with whom a new centre-left majority could be forged. Börner himself stressed that the Hessen red-green alliance represented a new historical initiative rather than an exercise in pragmatism.

Despite such rhetoric the alliance, which in 1985 became the first formal red-green coalition at regional level, faced formidable ideological problems. Divisions within both parties threatened to undermine it from the beginning and it was clear that the Green realists and SPD left had the greatest stake in its survival. The Greens extracted agreements on nuclear energy and road construction, but most of what they wanted was deferred in one way or another.[22] The SPD nationally let it be known that the Hessen experiment was 'a purely instrumental' affair and not a model for the future, while Börner behaved as if this entailed integrating the Greens into the SPD. In February 1987 the coalition fell apart when the SPD economics minister granted an operating permit to plutonium reprocessing plants that had been functioning on a quasi-legal basis for the previous decade. Yet there were signs in other parts of the country that a *modus operandi* between the two parties could be found, as at Kassel where a red-green alliance survived the electoral cycle of 1981–85, probably because the local left-dominated SPD could not countenance a grand alliance with the CDU/CSU.[23] Rising figures within the SPD such as Gerhard Schröder and Oskar Lafontaine talked of the Greens as 'long-term companions' and Lafontaine even attracted their supporters to the SPD in the Saarland, where the party was notably more radical than in the nation as a whole. Within *Die Grünen* too a majority could be found in 1986 which wanted negotiations with the SPD if the forthcoming national elections produced the possibility of a federal red-green majority.

In the 1987 federal elections, however, the SDP chancellor candidate Johannes Rau distanced the party from the Greens. In part this was inspired by the example of North Rhine-Westphalia, where the Greens had seemingly been forced below the 5 per cent threshold by SDP determination to go it alone. Rau's case was also informed by the damaging divisions within *Die Grünen* as the conflict between '*realos*' and '*fundis*' reached new heights. The SDP federal strategy in 1987 nevertheless returned the party's worst vote since 1961 and revealed that though Rau had gained some voters from the right he had also lost leftist SDP voters to the Greens.[24] The two parties were evidently in competition for a floating leftist vote 'largely composed of the young and upwardly mobile, the "new" middle class and women'.[25] Many observers stressed the dilemma the SDP faced; shun the Greens and lose votes on the left, court the Greens and lose votes in the centre.[26] According to Meyer, 'many social and political indicators pointed to a scenario where the SPD and the Greens would have to compete for an almost constant and finite proportion of the votes; a zero-sum game which would never resolve itself in losses for parties to their right'.[27] This reckoned without the actual dynamism that characterises politics. For example there was the question of the extent to which Green ideas would continue to spread through the electorate; the extent to which the SDP, as a new generation of ecology-minded leaders came to the fore, would successfully adapt its ideology; whether the ideological strife within *Die Grünen* would be resolved in favour of the '*fundis*' or '*realos*'; and so on.

In fact the decade-old strife within the Green party reached a climax in the wake of German reunification, which the Greens had opposed. Sections of the ecosocialist left opted for a broad alliance with the former East German communists of the PDS, leaving the Greens and enabling the realists to take over the party. The organisation was then subject to reforms which ended some of its 'anti-party' characteristics – such as the rotation of official positions. During the Gulf War of 1990–91 leaders of the party such as Petra Kelly and Joschka Fischer criticised the party's instinctive pacifism and anti-Americanism, though they were well aware that the Greens had emerged in part from the peace movement of the early 1980s. In January 1993 the Greens formally coalesced with East German dissident groups styling themselves *Bundnis 90* and though they only amounted to around one-tenth of the membership, the East Germans strengthened that wing of the party which placed human rights before suspicion of NATO and the US, as became clear during the war in Bosnia in 1993 when some sections of the party actually called for military intervention by the United Nations. The party nevertheless remained deeply divided over the issue and in 1994 adopted a manifesto which among other things demanded German withdrawal from NATO and dissolution of the *Bundeswehr* (armed forces).[28] But at the time of writing the Greens were thrown into another crisis as the NATO bombing of Kosovo and Serbia unfolded. The German government, formed in 1998 on the basis of a red-green coalition at federal level, came out in support of NATO's campaign against the Serbian government of Slobodan Milosevic, begun in April 1999, and it was the Green '*realo*' Joschka Fischer as foreign minister in that government who necessarily played a major role in justifying the decision, which involved the German air force. Not only does talk of the 'transformation' of the SPD's Atlanticism look a little premature in the light of this, it is surely the Green Party's ideological journey that seems the more striking.[29]

We do not have the space to develop the point here, but it seems reasonable to assume that it is not only the social democratic parties that are forced to change to remain politically relevant. What we can also say is that it has too readily been assumed that the social democratic parties would prove unable to survive the growth of the New Politics. In purely electoral terms the extent of the challenge is apt to be exaggerated.[30] In Britain, Denmark, Spain, Greece and Norway the greens had no parliamentary representation by 1999 – fully twenty years after an identifiable green politics had first arisen.[31] The most successful of these parties in Western Europe, *Die Grünen*, first broke through the 5 per cent electoral barrier in 1983, achieving 5.6 per cent of the vote in elections to the *Bundestag*. In 1998 the party – known as *Bundnis 90/Die Grünen* since 1990 – secured 6.7 per cent of the vote. Though the German Greens obtained just over 10 per cent of the vote in the European election of

1994, the most spectacular aspect of the party's life so far is its survival as an electoral force capable of keeping above the 5 per cent threshold – rather than its electoral growth or the extent of its membership base (51,000 in 1999). Significant green parties, in electoral terms, also exist in Sweden, the Netherlands and Austria, but with less electoral support than in Germany. The Swedish party broke through the 4 per cent threshold in elections for the *Riksdag* in 1988 and was still able to do the same thing in 1998 (falling from 5.5 per cent to 4.45 per cent of the vote). The Austrian Green Party achieved similar results in federal elections and the Dutch Green Left Party was just behind, with less than 4 per cent of the vote in elections to the first chamber (though over 7 per cent in the 1998 elections to the second chamber of parliament). In France and Italy the green parties respectively held 7 of 577 seats in the Assembly (1997) and 14 of 630 seats in the House of Representatives (1996).

Programmatic change

It would be wrong to minimise the political significance of the green parties on the basis of these figures, after all they sometimes hold the balance of power in parliament. But since they are the biggest electoral challenge to social democracy emanating from the new social movements, the figures at least help to put that challenge into perspective. What they do not reveal is the extent of the influence of the new social movements. One measure of this relevant for environmentalism might be a rough correlation of the extent of the green electoral challenge and the effect that has on focusing legislative efforts to improve environmental standards; it is argued, for example, that 'as a direct consequence of the Greens' engagement, the Federal Republic developed the strictest environmental protection laws anywhere in the world'.[32] The measure that concerns us, however, is evidence of ideological change in social democracy itself. Though scepticism about the value of party programmes, in terms of their relationship to what actually gets done, is often justified, we will refer to them here as a rough guide to ideological change in social democracy in respect of ecological issues.

It is of no surprise to find that the Basic Programme adopted by the SPD at Bad Godesberg in 1959 had nothing to say on environmental issues since a modern ecological awareness did not exist then. It is instructive to note, however, that when the SPÖ – to turn to another, more recent example – adopted its new programme nearly twenty years later, the Austrian social democrats only made perfunctory mention of such problems. The issues raised were those of pollution, traffic congestion and the 'waste of the world's resources of raw material and energy'. These issues apparently called for no major rethink of the party's ideology and could be subsumed under traditional categories such as regional planning, though there was brief mention of the need for new forms of international cooperation, mostly in recognition of the ways in which the 'internationalisation of capital' impaired the powers of national governments.[33] However, ten years later the Basic Policy Programme of the SPD, adopted in December 1989, asserted that 'the ecological restructuring of our industrial society has become a matter of survival' and 'the preservation of nature must become a mission for all areas of politics'.[34] Here the SPD acknowledged that the industrial nations, which had done most to destroy 'the natural bases of existence ... must bear the main responsibility ... for [their] restoration'. Ecology 'is no addendum to economics', the programme argued, 'It is becoming the basis of responsible economic activity'. Hence it saw the immediate need for 'an ecological assessment of all forms of energy production and energy conversion'. The 'plutonium-based economy' was described as 'a mistake' and transport, agriculture and chemicals were identified as the industries most in need of an ecological reassessment.[35]

A similar shift is evident in other social democratic parties. In Denmark, for example, the Social Democratic Party talks of the need for 'environmentally sustainable growth' and the phasing out of agricultural subsidies 'in favour of supporting the development of ecological farming' and 'animal welfare'.[36] Its 1996 programme, *Common Future, Common Goals*, criticises economic markets for their blindness to the environmental costs of growth. Neither the party nor its programme are very radical, but it is clear that concepts have invaded them that were utterly alien to most socialists in the recent past. In Norway, where the greens are as weak as in Denmark, the DNA's 'mission statement' also reveals the influence of their ideas. This speaks of 'a vision of a just world without poverty, in peace and ecological balance, where the people are free and equal and have influence on the conditions affecting their lives'.[37] Of its four major challenges, the first is identified as finding 'a development that the earth can sustain' and one that will also fight poverty. According to the DNA

> At present those who already have the most ... are the ones who continue to take a disproportionately large share of the earth's resources. The unfair distribution of resources and environmental destruction are not only a challenge to our ideals of freedom and equality here and now, but also a threat to future generations. This lack of equality and ecological balance challenges our social democratic values more than anything else.[38]

The DNA argues that

> sustainable development entails that production and consumption must be reorganised in the rich parts of the world so that the conditions of those who have least may be improved. Here at home the reorganisation will especially have to include the energy and transport sectors. Increased welfare in the Norway of the future cannot be based on a steadily increasing consumption of energy and

> generation of waste. Instead we must implement measures to limit the consumption of energy and increase recycling and re-use.[39]

The idea of 'sustainable development' derives from the recognition – present in green literature since the 1970s – that economic development since the industrial revolution was achieved, as the Swedish SAP put it in 1990, 'at the cost of plundering the environment and shortsightedly exploiting nature'. The consequences, it adds 'threaten to undermine the very foundations of human existence'.[40] Like the greens, the SAP recognises that

> environmental problems pose the question of the lifestyle of the small affluent community in a world where several billion people ... are also rightly demanding a growth of development, consumption and production ... If large sectors of the world's population are kept in poverty and under-development there will be a growth of worldwide unrest. The same will happen if the countries of the Third World are forced to take over the hazardous waste and extravagant technology of the industrialised world.[41]

As in the other programmes we have briefly considered there is the realisation that while 'internationalisation has already taken place – on market terms – with regard to capital', there is an unsatisfied 'need for cooperation' at governmental level and an 'imperative necessity of subordinating the ambitions of the nation state to a wider interest' that is greater than ever before. The programme is unambiguous in identifying the unregulated private profit motive and market forces as the principal causes of growing inequalities and environmental destruction.

The SAP programme of 1990 thus acknowledged that the internationalisation of the economy posed problems for labour movements as worldwide corporations determined global movements of capital and limited the ability of trade unions and governments to achieve democratically defined national objectives.[42] Yet the party argued that 'environmental stipulations must permeate every sector of society' and law-breakers must pay the cost of environmental hazards. Global action, through agencies such as the United Nations Environmental Programme, would only be able to address the problem, according to the SAP, if the UN was transformed into 'an efficient instrument of mandatory international cooperation' able to 'create an international legal order and responsible management, so that the Earth's resources can be fairly distributed and the gaps between the peoples of the world made narrower. The conversion of military to civilian production is part of this process'.[43] The DNA programme adopted in 1996 argued for the same objectives saying that 'in important matters concerning peace, the environment and the distribution of wealth, the UN must be given the authority to pass binding resolutions that will apply to all nations'. This would entail strengthening the UN economically – perhaps by taxing currency transactions

– but also through the creation of a 'global democratic legal system'. The DNA envisaged an 'economic security council' to coordinate the work of transnational organisations such as the World Bank, World Trade Organisation and IMF and ensure that political control and leadership were established in global economic matters.[44]

It might be objected at this point that strong social democratic parties based in small, politically insignificant countries can indulge in such wishful thinking at no cost to themselves. But the DNA is insistent that Norway, 'as one of the world's richest nations ... has a special responsibility to help equalise the disparities of the world' and will provide increased development aid, debt relief and protection for refugees.[45] It is not, then, simply a case of waiting until the appropriate changes are made at the international level. Furthermore, the example of the SPD shows that social democrats in Western Europe's leading nation are just as concerned as their Scandinavian neighbours about uncontrolled economic power transcending national borders. The party programme argued that 'in order to avoid competition among economic regions on questions of industrial location resulting in worldwide pressure on wages, a deterioration of working conditions, social services and environmental standards, we need binding international rules for the social and ecological conditions of production'.[46] The internationalisation of capital and financial investment, having reduced national opportunities for controlling capitalism, demands a global political response, according to the SPD:

> Wherever the loss of national competence is not compensated for by international regulations, the law of the jungle prevails. National economies everywhere become more susceptible to crises. Therefore, we want to regain, broaden and extend the possibilities of controlling the economies through international cooperation and frameworks, without absolving national economic policy of its responsibility.[47]

Again, it is recognised that the poor and developing countries have the biggest need of a new world economic order. These are the countries forced into a 'humiliating dependency on the banks' and agencies dominated by the West such as the IMF and World Bank. The SPD wanted the debts of the poorest nations remitted and the removal of punitive conditions tied to debt relief, since these were said to increase the deprivations of the poor in the poorest countries. While warning that 'those who only wait for European or global regulations will not get them in the end', the SPD clearly favoured 'national and international control mechanisms [to] ensure that international capital does not withdraw from its social and ecological responsibilities and tax obligations'. It wants a stronger and restructured UN (and affiliated organisations) through which to realise some of these goals. But it is clear that the SPD sees that the European Community in particular 'opens the way for the freedom to act ... a chance of self-assertion and influence in the world market'. In this arena the SPD stands for harmonisation of economic policies, an active employment policy, parity of social policy and economic policy, co-determination and economic democracy, active promotion of gender equality, and ecological renewal.[48]

Many greens would not be at all persuaded by the attempts of social democrats to merge environmentalism into their old growth ideology through such verbal formulae as 'managed growth', 'sustainable growth' and so on. They would say that this is at best an attempt to reconcile the irreconcilable. It is also true that left reformist parties have not all 'greened-up' to the extent of the SPD, SAP, PvdA[49] and DNA. But I am only concerned to establish that a renewal of the social democratic programme has taken place in the countries we have considered, at least partly in response to the ideas associated with the new social movements. The influence of the new social movements in these countries is visible in what the social democrats now have to say about North–South issues, global capital, gender equality, sexuality, solidarity between different cultures, peace and industrial democracy. What is also striking about the programmes of the SPD, DNA and SAP is that the new ideas inject vitality into the old social democratic critique of untrammelled markets, the dominion of capital and private profit, the claims of equality, social justice and responsibility.[50]

In Northern Europe Britain provides the outstanding example of a country in which the greens have made the least impact electorally. The Green Party has no MPs and only a handful of councillors in local government. In the 1997 general election its vote was well below 1 per cent and had to be lumped in with 'Others' to register on the scale.[51] Environmental issues have never been significant electoral issues in any of the general elections fought in Britain since the greens first appeared in the 1970s. Of the established parliamentary parties the Liberal Democrats were the first to show much interest in green issues, but this could be attributed to their remoteness from power. Throughout the 1980s neither the Thatcher government nor the Labour opposition showed any interest in environmentalism until the Green Party shocked the political establishment by securing almost 15 per cent of the vote in the European elections of 1989.[52] Though this was the largest percentage of the poll for any green party within the EU, it translated into zero MEPs for the Green Party in Britain – which was thwarted by the first-past-the-post electoral system. This gave the party cartel enough time to adjust, and a flurry of speeches and documents was produced in the immediate aftermath of the European election to show that both Labour and the Conservatives were concerned about environmental issues. The Green vote subsequently faded away and the dominant parties returned to the pattern of ignoring environmental issues during election campaigns. The difference after 1989 was that the parties were now careful to include statements about environmental improvement in their manifestos. Labour Party policy makers now began to think how this could be done and by 1992 the party even claimed that it had made 'environmental modernisation an integral part of [its] industrial strategy'.[53]

British Labour

The evidence suggests that it was the electoral challenge of the Green Party, facilitated by various forms of proportional representation, which initially forced some social democratic parties to take the new issues and ideology seriously. Because this challenge was sustained in some countries, organisations such as the SPD progressed from making *ad hoc* programmatic responses to develop a more thorough overhaul of party ideology. They encountered resistance along the way, principally from sections of their traditional blue-collar support. But they also had to accommodate their own middle-class activists – a growing phenomenon in all social democratic parties since the 1970s. More important, there was a growing middle-class vote to capture and in the countries where a vote for the greens was not a wasted vote, the social democrats had to reckon with the possibility that a growing proportion of it would support environmentalism. It is too simplistic to see this process as a matter of simply diluting the social democratic programme. Yet in explaining British Labour's relative lack of interest in green issues in the 1970s and 1980s some analyses stress 'The party's roots in the organised labour movement and its reliance on support from the urban working class [which] provided powerful constraints against the adoption of a comprehensive environmental programme. Among Labour's traditional supporters and financiers the environment has been regarded, at best, as an irrelevance and, at worst, as inimical to economic growth and employment'.[54]

Unfortunately for this argument, the Labour Party is not alone among social democratic parties in having intimate ties with organised labour, dependency on its financial support and a history of urban, working-class electoral support. It does, however, lead to another error which is to suppose that New Labour gave greater attention to environmental issues after 1994 and that this was 'a symbol' of a shift that has involved the party in shedding 'its image as a representative of the working-class producer and its social democratic or socialist ideological character'. In this view the greening of New Labour is related to its move away from class-based issues, since the environment 'is not easily located on a left/right ideological spectrum – perfect credentials for inclusion as part of a so-called "third way" agenda'.[55] Though this faithfully records the 'modernising' propaganda of New Labour, the reality is rather different. By comparison with the DNA, PvdA, SPD and SAP, the Labour Party is both less concerned with traditional social democratic values and policies, and less affected by environmentalism. No 'comprehensive environmental programme' has emerged in New Labour. This is just what we might expect. The Labour Party faces no electoral challenge from its left and does not have to compete with an electorally viable Green Party; therefore it is not that interested in environmental issues and cannot be punished for retreating from social democratic values. It does, however, face a mighty challenge from its right and was kept out of power for eighteen years by a Conservative Party that was more committed to the rhetoric of 'the market knows best' than any governing conservative party in Western Europe; therefore Labour moved its programme to the right, as we shall see in the next three chapters.

These two considerations help to explain why the British Labour Party is relatively mute on North–South issues, and the need for a stronger UN and EU, and the problems posed by multinational capital – issues which green and New Left activists helped to bring to the fore in Germany and Sweden. It also explains why New Labour accepts many of the previous Conservative government's reforms which stand in the way of just the sort of environmental progress that might be expected to appeal to organised labour. In the latter category one thinks of better health and safety standards at work, an integrated transport policy, greater regulation of markets, stricter controls and punishments for polluters, higher taxes to deter environmental destruction and the like. The transition to 'New' Labour, far from seeing a deeper greening of the party, actually involved it dropping many of the policies that figured in the 1992 manifesto as proof of its environmental concerns, such as the restoration of public control of the National Grid and public ownership of water; reining back open-cast mining; opposing the privatisation of railways; ending the deregulation of buses and so on. Here we will simply observe that this was related to the Labour Party's ongoing conversion to markets (such as 'flexible labour markets') and the way that it came to champion the logic of 'globalisation'; and its retreat from state intervention, planning, state ownership, equality and the redistribution of income; and its seeming inability to publicly champion beneficial EU-wide regulations on the environment – all this stands in the way of its emergence as a real spearhead of environmental progress. Although its 1997 manifesto asserted that environmental policy 'is not an add-on extra, but informs the whole of government, from housing and energy policy through to global warming and international agreements', this was precisely the opposite of the truth.[56]

Notes

1 See C. Offe, 'New social movements: challenging the boundaries of institutional politics', *Social Research*, 52:4 (1985) 817–68.

2 See for example, F. Parkin, *Middle Class Radicalism* (Manchester, Manchester University Press, 1968).

3 M. A. Sully, 'Austrian social democracy', in W. E. Paterson and A. H. Thomas (eds), *The Future of Social Democracy: Problems and Prospects of Social Democratic Parties in Western Europe* (Oxford, Clarendon Press, 1986), p. 164.

4 J. Fitzmaurice, *Austrian Politics and Society Today* (Basingstoke, Macmillan, 1991), pp. 111, 117–18, 153–4.

5 C. Haerpfer, 'Austria: the "United Greens" and the "Alternative List/Green Alternative"', in F. Muller-Rommel (ed.), *New Politics in Western Europe: The Rise and Success of Green Parties and Alternative Lists* (Boulder, CO, Westview Press, 1989), p. 24.

6 N. F. Christiansen, 'Denmark: end of an idyll?', in P. Anderson and P. Camiller (eds), *Mapping the West European Left* (London, Verso, 1994), p. 93

7 L. Lewin, *Ideology and Strategy: A Century of Swedish Politics* (Cambridge, Cambridge University Press, 1988), p. 241.

8 See D. Sainsbury, 'Swedish social democracy in transition: the party's record in the 1980s and the challenge of the 1990's', *West European Politics*, 14:3 (1991).

9 H. Bergstrom, 'Sweden's politics and party system at the crossroads',*West European Politics*, 14:3 (1991) 12.

10 G. Braunthal, *The German Social Democrats Since 1969: A Party in Power and Opposition* (Boulder, CO, Westview Press, 994), p. 278.

11 M. T. Hatch, 'Corporatism, pluralism and post-industrial politics: nuclear energy in West Germany', *West European Politics*, 14:1 (1991) 73–87, 80.

12 See Braunthal, *German Social Democrats Since 1969*, p. 256 and J. Delwaide, 'Postmaterialism and politics: the "Schmidt SPD" and the greening of Germany', *German Politics*, 2:2 (1993) 247

13 Originating as the Alternative Political Alliance-The Greens (SPV) in March 1979, the organisation became know as *Bundnis 90/Die Grünen* after German reunfication when it fused with smaller groups based in Eastern Germany.

14 A. S. Markovits and P. S. Gorski, *The German Left: Red, Green and Beyond* (Cambridge, Polity Press, 1993), p. 268.

15 *Ibid.*, p. 268.

16 Delwaide, 'Postmaterialism and politics', p. 249–51.

17 P. Merkle, 'The SPD after Brandt: problems of integration in a changing urban society', *West European Politics*, 11:1 (1988) 47.

18 *Ibid.*, p. 48.

19 Braunthal, *German Social Democrats Since 1969*, pp. 109–110.

20 W. E. Paterson, 'The German Social Democratic Party', in W. E. Paterson and A. H. Thomas (eds), *The Future of Social Democracy* (Oxford, Clarendon Press, 1986), p. 149.

21 See W. Hulsberg, *The German Greens: A Social and Political Profile* (London, Verso, 1988), pp. 152–9.

22 See C. Spretnak and F. Capra, *Green Politics* (London, Paladin, 1985), pp. 131–2 and E. G. Frankland, 'Federal Republic of Germany: Die Grünen', in Muller-Rommel (ed.), *New Politics in Western Europe*, p. 73.

23 T. Scharf, 'Red-green coalitions at local level in Hesse', in E. Kolinsky (ed.), *The Greens in West Germany: Organisation and Policy-Making* (Oxford, Berg, 1989), p. 166.

24 G. Braunthal, *Parties and Politics in Modern Germany* (Boulder, CO, Westview Press, 1996), pp. 76–6. See also W. P. Burklin, 'The split between the established and non-established left in Germany', *European Journal of Political Research*, 13 (1985) 283–93.

25 Markovits and Gorski, *German Left*, p. 221.
26 *Ibid.*, p. 224 and Meyer, 'The transformation of German social democracy', p. 127
27 Meyer, *ibid.*, p. 128.
28 G. Braunthal, 'The perspective from the left', *German Politics and Society*, 34:1 (1995) 41
29 By May 1999 the Greens were plunged into 'an existential crisis' by the German government's participation in the Kosovo war and its congress at Bielefeld, which was marred by violence, only narrowly voted to support Fischer by 444 votes to 318.
30 Though left alternatives to the social democrats exist in Austria (United Greens), Belgium (Agalev, Ecolo), Denmark (Socialist People's Party, Left Socialists), France (Ecolo, PCF), Italy (Refounded Communists, Ecologists), Netherlands (Green Progressive Accord), Spain (United Left), Sweden (Left Party, Greens) and Germany (Greens). Britain is notably absent from this list.
31 In fact the first green party, the Values Party in New Zealand, was founded in the late 1960s and captured close to 5 per cent of the vote as early as 1975. Green ideology had taken form through such publications as *Blueprint For Survival*, the seminal work of Edward Goldsmith published in *The Ecologist* magazine in 1973. See C. Spretnak and F. Capra, *Green Politics*, pp. 157–81.
32 C. Joppke and A. S. Markovits,'Green politics in the new Germany', *Dissent*, Spring (1994) 235.
33 SPÖ, *The New Programme of the Austrian Socialist Party (SPÖ)* (Vienna, SPÖ, 1978).
34 SPD, *The Basic Policy Programme of the Social Democratic Party of Germany*, adopted 20 December 1989 (Bonn, SPD, 1990), p. 35.
35 *Ibid.*, pp. 35–7.
36 Social Democratic Party, *Common Future, Common Goals* (Copenhagen, Social Democratic Party, 1996), p. 9.
37 Labour Party [Norway], *Statement of Principles and Action Programme* (Oslo, DNA, 1996), p. 7.
38 *Ibid.*, p. 15.
39 *Ibid.*, p. 30.
40 SAP, *The Swedish Social Democratic Party Programme*, adopted by the 31st party congress, 1990, translated by Roger Tanner (Stockholm, Tryckeri AB, 1992), p. 7. The SAP gave some attention to environmental issues from as early as 1968 but from the mid-1970s lost ground over the issue of nuclear energy. Economic issues subsequently dominated its agenda until 1987.
41 *Ibid.*, pp. 8–9.
42 *Ibid.*, p. 17.
43 *Ibid.*, pp. 42–3.
44 Labour Party [Norway], *Statement of Principles*, pp. 30–4.
45 *Ibid.*, p. 30. Norway's response to the Kosovo crisis in April 1999 was to immediately take thousands of refugees.
46 SPD, *Basic Policy Programme*, p. 33.
47 *Ibid.*, p. 33.
48 *Ibid.*, pp. 34–5.

49 Partij van de Arbeid, *Platform of Principles*, trans. J. Rudge (Amsterdam, PvdA, n.d.).

50 For a detailed analysis of the SAP's recent programmatic renewal see D. Sainsbury, 'Swedish social democracy in transition: the party's record in the 1980s and the challenge of the 1990s', *West European Politics*, 14:3 (1991) 42–4 and especially the same author's 'The Swedish Social Democrats and the legacy of continuous reform: asset or dilemma?', *West European Politics*, 16:1 (1993) 39–61.

51 With the adoption of a form of proportional representation for the European elections in 1999, the Green Party managed to return two MEPs.

52 See M. Robinson, *The Greening of British Party Politics* (Manchester, Manchester University Press, 1992).

53 Labour Party, *It's Time To Get Britain Working Again* (London, Labour Party, 1992), p. 21.

54 R. Garner, 'How green is Labour?', *Politics Review*, 8:4 (1999) 26.

55 *Ibid.*, p. 26; A. Giddens, *The Third Way: The Renewal of Social Democracy* (Cambridge, Polity Press, 1998).

56 Labour Party, *New Labour: Because Britain Deserves Better* (London, Labour Party, 1997), p. 4.

5

Ideological retreat of the left in the 1980s

During the 1980s the evidence of left governments – in Spain, Portugal, Greece, Australia and elsewhere – generally demonstrated the dominance of neo-liberal economic orthodoxy.[1] Parties confined to opposition were also inclined to adapt to the reigning hegemony of neo-liberalism in one way or another – though the SPD began programmatic renewal in 1984 by giving more emphasis to gender equality and was significantly less complacent than it had been about the prospect of economic growth dissolving distributional conflicts. The first draft of the new Basic Programme even talked of the need for 'a new social and economic order' that would break the 'the power of capital over working people'.[2] By the final draft in 1989, however, the stronger anti-capitalist passages had been deleted. The PvdA in the Netherlands, confined to opposition from 1977 to 1989, apart from a short-lived experience of coalition in 1981, made a more spectacular transformation when one recalls that a New Left faction had taken it over in the early 1970s. By the end of the period of opposition it had been returned to a policy of making markets work rather than abolishing them altogether. The post-materialist agenda of the 1970s had not always translated well into policy in any case, but it was the economic crisis of the early 1980s which led to the collapse of the 1981 coalition and brought about a period of sustained revisionism. After its defeat in the 1986 election the PvdA invoked the internationalisation of the economy as the rationale for its rejection of Keynesianism, state intervention and socialisation. By the time Ruud Lubbers' government came to an end in 1989, the PvdA leadership around Wim Kok was able to decide what went into the manifesto, *Vote of Quality*, and the party distanced itself from too close an association with society's 'losers'. It entered government prepared to dismantle regional policy, cut back the welfare state and thereby create 'incentives' for the unemployed to find work.[3] Unemployment had averaged 14 per cent throughout the 1980s. In the poorer countries of Southern Europe socialist governments managed capitalism in a similar way, but here it was arguable that the consolidation of democracy and the process of integration into the European Community were the real achievements of the 1980s. It was France, however, that presented the most dramatic example of socialist retreat and the most powerful case against 'socialism in one country'.

The French economy was one of those suffering from declining rates of productivity and profit after 1973. Corporate debt rose and investment rates fell, while industrial policy focused on infrastructure and prestige exports such as weapons and aircraft. The traditional labour-intensive industries such as steel, shipbuilding, textiles and coal experienced sharp decline. Stagflationary conditions in the 1970s produced the usual symptoms of fiscal crisis as claims on public money outpaced the growth of tax revenues. By the end of the decade inflation was around 13 per cent, unemployment approached 2 million and a persistent balance of payments deficit gave testimony to the weakness of the consumer goods sector of the economy. This is the situation the Socialist Party stepped into in May 1981 when it secured a majority in the Assembly for the first time, shortly after François Mitterand had assumed the presidency.

The Socialists introduced a substantial programme of reform from the moment they formed the government. Its purpose was to sponsor structural reforms in the French economy, which would both foster growth and champion social justice. The government's social reforms greatly increased family allowances and increased access to health insurance benefits for the (1.8 million) unemployed and part-time workers. Pensions were increased in absolute terms and as a percentage of the minimum wage. Allowances to the handicapped rose by 20 per cent and some prescription charges were abolished. Housing subsidies were increased, as was aid to poor farmers. The minimum wage – which affected 1.7 million workers – was increased by 15 per cent in real terms between May 1981 and December 1982. In all, these social measures amounted to 200 million francs of expenditure in the second half of 1981 and 800 million in 1982.[4] The purchasing power of social transfers increased by 4.5 per cent in 1981 and 7.6 per cent in 1982.[5] The cost of these measures was to a significant extent met through progressive taxation. The top rate of taxation was raised to 65 per cent, death duties on large estates rose, a wealth tax affecting 200,000 households was introduced in 1982, a crackdown on tax evasion was instituted and the anonymity of gold transactions was ended. Nevertheless, indirect taxes also rose on such items as petrol, tobacco and alcohol.

Mitterrand's 'dash for growth' involved more than these welfare and redistributory measures. The Socialists also attempted to increase effective demand in the economy by directly increasing employment. The government itself took on an extra 200,000 employees in 1981–82, particularly in the postal service, the civil service, education and health. Indirect measures were also utilised. The working week was cut by one hour, annual leave was increased by one week, early retirement was encouraged by generous pension schemes and older workers were able to go part time on 80 per cent of their former income. Various inducements were introduced to foster 'contracts of solidarity' between employer and employee. For example, employers who cut the working week and created more jobs were exempt from making social security contributions for the extra employees. These measures also helped to absorb some of the young unemployed but fell short of the major reform that had been promised – the thirty-five-hour week.

The government's much-vaunted break with capitalism centred on an extensive programme of public ownership. In the judgement of some commentators this went 'far beyond the established boundaries set for European mixed economies'.[6] It was intended not only to stimulate growth and investment but also, in the words of the *Programme commun de government*, to 'break the domination of big capital'[7] – the prerequisite in the Socialists' view of a successful social and economic policy. Public firms were conceived, much as they were in British Labour's AES, as an irreplaceable instrument for the stimulation and direction of the entire economy. In France the largest banks were already state owned, but that did not prevent the Socialists from nationalising thirty-six smaller ones, plus two investment banks. The government also acquired the remaining minority of private shares in the *Credit Lyonnais*, *Banque Nationale de Paris*, and the *Societe Generale*. These measures were accompanied by the purchase of all the shares in six industrial conglomerates involved in electronics, telecommunications, textiles, chemicals, aluminium, glass, paper, metals and electricity generation. The government also took a majority shareholding in two major steel firms and nationalised three groups that were partly or entirely owned by foreign multinationals. The nationalisation programme affected over 800,000 employees and increased state employment in industry from 11 to 22 per cent of the total workforce. It gave the government apparent control of up to 60 per cent of industrial investment.

The rationale for this industrial policy followed a similar logic to that of the left in Britain. Manufacturing industry was to be given priority, deindustrialisation and the loss of the domestic market to foreign competitors had to be stopped. Employment, growth and investment were to be increased. National control of the economy was to be restored and planning given a new lease of life. But industry was to be rejuvenated in a way that would harness the competitive dynamic of the market. The Socialists intended to channel funds into industry through measures designed to reduce the cost of borrowing and increase the rate of saving. New agencies were created to help small and medium-sized business, particularly in the hi-tech sector. Much of the government's intervention in the economy, however, was necessarily concerned to rescue industries in decline (given its full employment aspirations). Banks were instructed, for example, to direct half their 1981–82 profits into the loss-making steel industry. At the same time the Socialists engaged in cherry-picking, in such industries as machine-tools and electronics, with the latter receiving 140 billion francs of investment in the five years after 1981. Investment in research was increased from 1.8 to 2.3 per cent of GNP in the same period.

In chapter three we saw that in the 1970s the Socialists made much of their commitment to greater democracy. Planning itself was to be democratised by increasing the role of the Assembly and involving the relevant sectors of the economy in the planning process through the *contrats de plan* elaborated both regionally and sectorally. At plant level industrial relations were to be transformed by legislation. The Aurox laws required employers to engage in annual negotiations over wages and working conditions with unions that actually represented the workforce. The laws made more time and information available to works committees. A charter of rights and rules was adopted for the workplace and stiffer health and safety rules were introduced. Measures were taken to involve previously excluded groups of workers in the works committees such as homeworkers, part timers and those on fixed-term contracts. Companies employing less than fifty staff were obliged to make arrangements for the representation of employees. In the public sector, the Aurox laws established workshop councils which would meet at least every two months. One-third of the seats on the board of public-sector firms was to be reserved for employees. It was all a long way short of *autogestion* – Mitterrand's '110 propositions' had promised that factory committees would be able to veto decisions on employment, redundancy, work organisation and the like – but it also stood in sharp contrast to what was happening in Britain at the same time.

Similarly, while power was increasingly centralised by the British Conservative government, the French Socialists undertook a programme of decentralisation between 1982 and 1986 which curbed the power of the prefects (officials of the central state), strengthened the *departements conseil generale* and eventually transferred significant decision-making capacities to twenty-three elected regional assemblies. The prime minister, Michel Rocard, explained that the main aim here was to encourage private investment. Regions acquired responsibilities for adult education and training, school construction, industrial development, tourism and infrastructure, utilising a budget composed in equal measure of a centrally provided lump sum and their own independent fiscal resources. The *departement* became responsible for running welfare and social services, while the *communes* (most of them villages) took responsibility for local town planning and environmental issues. In all cases the authorities were given latitude for raising their own finances as well as spending central government grants in ways they saw fit. Devolution of power was nevertheless qualified by the fact that the prefecture remained in charge of the police and law and order while the central state retained control of the health service, education and the administration of justice – matters that are largely devolved in a country like Germany.

The Socialist reforms fell a long way short of the 1970s rhetoric promising a rupture with capitalism, but they went completely against the grain of policy in other capitalist states. French employers predictably complained that the private sector would be ruined by the extra costs imposed upon it – a 34 billion franc increase in wages and social security contributions and an estimated 65 billion franc bill for the extra week of holidays in 1982 alone. These extra 'burdens' would only cause bankruptcies, a further fall in investment and international competitiveness, and more unemployment.[8] The *patronat* (the employers' organisation CNPF) foresaw doom if the socialist rhetoric – particularly the *autogestion* rhetoric – was taken seriously. Employers' organisations such as the CGPME and CNPF stridently opposed the Aurox laws which, they claimed, could only undermine the work ethic and managerial prerogatives, leading to industrial paralysis. The nationalisation programme was likewise depicted as an attack on free enterprise which could only strengthen the Communist-dominated CGT. While organised labour was weak and divided, without strong links either to the state or to the Socialist Party, the employers enjoyed close relations with the central bureaucracy.

Less than six months after taking office, finance minister Jacques Delors called for a 'pause' in the reform programme from within the government. Doubts had accumulated because unemployment and inflation had refused to respond to the government's medicine. Public expenditure increased by over 11 per cent in 1981–82, the budget deficit expanded to 3 per cent of GDP and at around $16.7 billion in 1982 it stood as a post-war record. The economy grew because of the stimulus it had received, but not as fast as real disposable income. Imports were sucked in to such an extent that the trade deficit doubled in twelve months and by 1982 it was already necessary, according to Lionel Jospin, for the left to relinquish its 'lyrical illusions'.[9] The French Socialists had had the misfortune to enter office when deliberately deflationary policies promoted by President Reagan helped to bring about a global recession in 1981–82. Nor was there any solidarity forthcoming from the social democratic government in West Germany, where Chancellor Schmidt stuck to his emphasis on export-led growth, based upon productivity increases and support for the tight financial regime favoured by the *Bundesbank*. The 'Keynesianism on a world scale' which Claude Cheysson, minister of foreign affairs, hoped for had no chance, as Mitterrand discovered on his trip to Ottawa in July 1981 and Delors realised at the Franco-German summit in the same month when Schmidt described his idea of a concerted reduction in interest rates as a 'utopia'. A retreat was all the more likely in the absence of a radical popular movement behind the reforms.[10]

In June 1982, a year after electoral victory, the *plan de rigeur* (stringent austerity), was adopted. The franc was devalued, prices and wages were frozen for four months. Wages were then de-indexed from the cost of living and severe anti-inflationary policies pursued across the board – leading to cuts in social security and redundancies among public-sector workers. Nor was the change of heart confined to economic policy. Initially, the Socialists had displayed a certain libertarianism in respect, for example, of immigrant workers by ending the policy of expulsion and simplifying the renewal of work permits; a similar impression was made by measures such as the abolition of the executive-dominated *Cour de Surete de L'Etat*, the generous amnesty law, and of course the enlargement of union rights. By August 1981, however, Gaston Defferre, minister of home affairs, was already talking of tightening immigration policy. Mitterrand's promise to give France's 3.5 million immigrants the right to vote in local elections was never redeemed. Instead, public discourse on immigration returned to familiar preoccupations with controls and offers of repatriation. Similarly, promises to suspend twelve nuclear sites – which Mitterrand repeated in the second round of the presidential elections – proved to be misleading, with the government actually taking measures to complete the nuclear programme begun by Pompidou.

Mitterrand is easily dismissed as an opportunist who reinvented himself at intervals over five decades adopting positions across almost the entire political spectrum.[11] His fellow leaders also made use of policy statements and ideological rhetoric to advance their careers within the factionalised PS. Their collective manoeuvrings also made pragmatic sense in terms of unifying the PS and in making and keeping the alliance with the PCF – with a view to displacing it as the left's dominant electoral force.[12] It could be said that the appointment of Delors – a long-standing opponent of the more radical Socialist policies – to the Ministry of Economy and Finance also indicated the government's real intentions. In a similar vein, the immediate downgrading of *autogestion* can be read as a signal that the new regime was not a serious threat to the established forces.[13] All this is intended to cast doubt on the Socialist government's commitment to the programme of 1981. Yet Mitterrand continued to proclaim his intention of implementing the programme after the election and contrary to expectations set about doing so. It also has to be remembered that the huge Socialist majority was obtained by a party that employed a Marxist rhetoric and promised radical policies. It thus had sought a mandate for change on this basis. It also had pragmatic reasons to go ahead with its policies. The Socialists wanted to keep the Communists inside the government – confined to four minor ministries – instead of opposing the government from outside and possibly reversing their declining electoral fortunes.

Does this mean that the Socialists' retreat was simply forced upon them by global constraints over which they exercised no influence? There is some truth in this, but it overlooks policy mistakes that might have been avoided, such as the misprojection which predicted worldwide reflation in 1981–82, instead of the deflation that actually occurred. The Socialists might have rallied their supporters by telling them what the stark choices were and that industrial strategy needed time to work before demand could be allowed to rise to the desired levels. It is arguable that the government's investment drive and economic restructuring should have preceded the stimulation of demand.[14] The franc had been overvalued since 1979. The changing terms of trade between France and West Germany justified a large and immediate devaluation of the currency to stimulate exports when the Socialists entered office.[15] One obvious option for the government was a massive devaluation of the franc and withdrawal from the European Monetary System (EMS), another was devaluation within the EMS. The U-turn was chosen only after a prolonged battle within the government which the left lost.[16] Even before the election, Chevènement and Bérégovoy had argued for devaluation and exit from the EMS. After the election these ministers were joined by Laurent Fabius in additionally proposing measures of protectionism.[17] An early warning had been supplied by the loss of 15 billion francs of 'hot' money that flowed out of the country in anticipation of a Mitterrand victory; a third of the country's reserves were lost in the run up to his inauguration. The flight of capital could not have come as a shock because it had been foreseen, but no measures had been designed to deal with it.[18] In chapter three we saw that this concerned Marxist advocates of the AES in Britain, though the Labour NEC, like the PS, neglected the issue.

Real policy proceeded in the opposite direction by making life easier for the speculators. In October 1979 the Conservative government in Britain abolished Britain's forty-year-old exchange controls which were scrapped as an obsolete feature of an obsolete Keynesian order. The lobby in favour of this measure included the insurance companies, pension funds and many other City agencies who wanted to diversify and expand their international activities. As Hellheiner puts it, the Bank of England

> saw the abolition of exchange controls as a way of attracting more financial business to London. Because London's emergence as an offshore Euromarket center in the 1960s had depended in part on the US capital controls program, the US decision to abolish these controls in 1974 had threatened London's competitiveness as an international financial centre. Unless it abolished its exchange controls, London stood to lose its reputation as the most liberal and deregulated of such centres, which was key to maintaining and attracting footloose global financial business.[19]

Mitterrand introduced financial reform in 1984 and the West German government liberalised and deregulated around the same time. Denmark (1984) and the Netherlands (1986) jumped on the bandwagon. The European Commission promoted this process of liberalising capital movements as part of the movement towards a single European market.[20] The opening up of the London Stock Exchange to foreign securities firms in October 1986 was another step to protect the City's position at a time when much of the international business in finance was transferring from banking to securities. In the same year all controls on capital movements directly related to trade and investments in the EU were lifted. In 1987 plans were made to lift restrictions on all EU capital movements. These were approved by the Council of Ministers in June 1988, committing all members to implementation by mid-1990, though Spain, Portugal and Ireland were given until December 1992.

Though the process still had some way to go in 1981, the experience of the French Socialists has been invoked by those claiming that qualitative changes in the degree of world economic integration had effectively undermined the economic management capacities of nation-states.[21] Clearly, the deregulation of financial markets represented a growing problem, but it was not a new one. In fact the Blum government had been faced with similar problems to those of 1981 in 1936 – international deflation, capital flight, chronic trade deficits, domestic inflation, currency speculation and the hostility of business.[22] Halimi notes that Blum was presented with the choice: 'either enact exchange controls, strict government supervision of the economy, autarky and authoritarianism, or open borders, [and] the free trading of currencies ...'[23] It was not much of a choice. But Blum also refused to devalue on the required scale, early in the life of his government. Like the left government of 1945–47, moreover, Blum and Mitterrand both entered government at a time of economic stress, financial disorder and capital flight. If anything, as Ambler argues, Mitterrand was in a stronger position than his predecessors.[24] It is hard to think of worse international circumstances than those of 1936 and one could argue that by 1981 the French economy was much stronger and the state exercised considerable control over it.

Of course, the reflation of 1981 could not be sustained in the circumstances France found itself in, but at least some elements of the unfolding situation were related to design faults of the Socialist project as well as the manner of its implementation. To those that we have already mentioned we can add the nationalisation programme. An expensive and contradictory catch-all, it was simultaneously supposed to be a means of rescuing failing industries, increasing investment and productivity, promoting research and technological change, promoting self-management and equality, assisting central planning and securing national sovereignty. The state-owned banks were likewise supposed to bail out industries in decline and provide venture capital to dynamic sectors and firms, while making their own profits and improving their capital base. The public sector – already a complex array of agencies, quangos and bureaux of various degrees of operational independence – became so vast that it outstripped any feasible expertise and plan that the government may have had. Any benefit that the state sector may have produced for either the economy or the structure of power in French society could only be long term. But confidence in the efficacy of the swollen state sector by 1982 was not great. The contradiction was not lost on those New Left supporters of *autogestion* who had backed the Socialists in the name of participatory democracy rather than statism. And more generally the French left, having belatedly discovered the gulag, was in the process of turning its back on both planning and social transformation as discredited ideas just as the Socialists were getting into a mess.

Before we pursue the Mitterrand U-turn any further it is worth observing that some of the more radical supporters of the AES in Britain began to reappraise the programme in the light of 1979–81 conjuncture. In other words, at least some long-standing advocates of a very similar programme to that pursued by the PS realised before the Mitterrand U-turn that new problems had arisen. The international scope of the recession and the consolidation of neo-liberal policy were among these problems. In Britain the recession of 1979–81 eliminated around 20 per cent of manufacturing, destroying a large part of the very constituency for which the AES was intended. The Thatcher government also followed the US, as we have mentioned, in deregulating financial markets, thus helping to set off a competitive scramble by other European governments seeking similar short-lived advantages. Britain's advancing economic integration into the EEC also underlined, as many of these other issues did, that the AES offered 'no coherent analysis of the world economy'. Yet any attempt to implement the programme, it was now seen, would simply isolate the country and bring home its interdependencies with the outside world. Since the more radical versions of the AES represented a real threat to capital, moreover, enormous opposition would be mobilised against it both at home and abroad. To meet this challenge the programme would require a coherence and degree of popular support which it simply did not possess.[25]

The Labour Party continued to adhere to the AES in one form or another up to and including the general election of June 1983 when it was decisively beaten. But even before this trauma, individuals on the left of the party were beginning to see that a new European framework was the only future for the sort of policies they favoured. Withdrawal from the EEC was in this view 'absurd'[26] when economic interdependence was growing so quickly and the common economic problems of stagnation and unemployment demanded a common response. The only beneficiaries of the lack of a transnational policy response were the MNCs, with US multinationals in particular occupying the commanding position within the EEC with regard to subsidies, tax evasion and the general flouting of national regulations. The Brandt Report, *North-South: A Programme for Survival*, had highlighted these issues in 1980 – the whole thrust of the report was on the need for a 'globalisation of policies' to meet the challenge of global forces. In Bob Rowthorn's view, it was 'Europe or bust' for the left and this message, publicly expressed in May 1982, soon acquired additional force in the wake of the about-turn in Socialist France. By July the example of Mitterrand's government had already been invoked as evidence of the defects of a purely national reflationary strategy in the discussions of the Labour left. France was also said to demonstrate what would happen if the financial system in the broadest sense was not brought under strict regulation.[27] But the developing thrust of these 'French lessons', at least for some people on the Labour left, was on 'the search for an AES for Europe'.[28]

After the general election of June 1983 the Labour Party leadership under Neil Kinnock set about 'modernising' the party and its programme. By the autumn of 1983 the emphasis on Britain's relations with the EEC had moved from 'withdrawal' to 'working with European socialists to promote a European policy on employment and social justice'.[29] In fact little progress was made in this direction. The main preoccupation of the leadership was making Labour electable in Britain and we shall see that this was conceived as a question of jettisoning the AES rather than transferring it, or something like it, on to a European stage. In practice it was from among the more radical proponents of the AES that work in this direction was undertaken, with Stuart Holland, Ken Coates, Bob Rowthorn, Francis Cripps and Ken Livingstone among those recognising the need for such a change.[30] In *Out of the Crisis* (1983), Holland, Rowthorn and Cripps diagnosed deflation as the dominant factor in bringing about the 15 million unemployed in Western Europe, rather than falling competitiveness or loss of market share, though they recognised the slowdown of the growth of markets and competition from the Far East as contributory factors. Any reflation had to be accompanied by restructuring and redistribution across Europe, they reasoned, because the crisis was structural as well as cyclical – reflecting major changes in the structure of production and employment – and demand was saturated at prevailing levels of income distribution. The supply side had been transformed by a mesoeconomic sector impervious to Keynesian measures.

The situation had been made worse, in this view, by the refusal to see this. Governments had undermined their tax base because subsidies to private enterprise had offset nominal corporation tax and deflationary policies exacerbated the fiscal crisis. Benefits payments increased as tax revenues fell due to rising unemployment and higher levels of poverty. Since more than 80 per cent of public spending provided demand for the private sector, policies of retrenchment simply made things worse, as did cuts in transfer payments and the public-sector wage bill. Unless governments took measures to bring the leading sectors of the economy under public control there would be little likelihood of promoting investment, productivity and growth or of harnessing economic dynamism to finance public services in the social interest. Similarly, the authors argued that 'a wider international control over financial institutions is both necessary and feasible to make reflation more secure', as were national controls to prevent exit by savings and pension funds built up within the countries concerned.[31]

No one would expect the ideas of a handful of socialist intellectuals to change much in the short term. But the motive for a transnational left strategy within the EEC was broadly based to judge from the speed with which the experience of the French Socialists gave rise to a conventional wisdom against unilateral national reflationary policies. It is true that the European Commission under Jacques Delors' leadership eventually encouraged investigations along the lines advocated by Stuart Holland.[32] But there was no echo of this in the Labour Party during the 1980s even though, as the leader of the Labour group in the European Parliament asserted in 1988, 'important democratic socialist objectives can no longer be accomplished within the boundaries of a single country'.[33] Within eighteen months of Labour's 1983 defeat the new leader, Neil Kinnock, had accepted the view that a shift in popular values had underpinned the Conservative's victories since May 1979 and that Labour was too closely associated with regions and socioeconomic forces subject to secular decline.[34] The leadership's project was to catch up with these modernising trends which Thatcher's government had harvested and encouraged. If the Labour leadership thought that the future of any form of social democracy was uncertain in Britain, there not much chance of the party championing the idea of transferring the old programme, or a modernised version of it into the European Community. Until Delors became the champion of the Social Charter at the end of the decade, the European Community in any case seemed to be dominated by the right. In West Germany the Christian Democrats formed a government under Helmut Kohl in 1982, Thatcher was returned to power in Britain a year later and the French Socialists had moved to austerity policies which gave priority to the suppression of inflation, rather than the elimination of unemployment.

Mitterrand committed the country to a strong franc, tied to the German mark within the EMS. The Socialists now began to praise private enterprise and 'modernisation'. There was much talk of excessive taxes and red tape and some measures to reduce the 'burden' on business and shift it to employees via a greater reliance on regressive indirect taxes. In October 1985 at Toulouse, the Socialist Party congress formally acknowledged the change, when the delegates accepted that there would be no future break with capitalism, just social democratic reform. The French 'Bad Godesberg' was summed up in the final resolution put before the congress which said that 'The crisis has put this brutal truth in sharp light: the only revenue that can be distributed is the counterpart of that which can be produced and sold. The Socialists have taken better account of the necessity to remain competitive, to make profits in order to invest, to contain the costs of production'.[35] The new realism meant mass unemployment and greater inequality. Massive job losses were inflicted on the steel and shipbuilding industries, car manufacture and mining. While state-subsidised loans were cut back in the public sector, in accordance with European Community competition policy, grants to the private sector soared.

By 1986, 70 per cent of nationalised subsidiaries had been sold off and private capital had been brought into the public sector via the sale of stock. After 1986 the Chirac government began a large privatisation programme of its own which the Socialists largely accepted.

Indeed, the Socialists remained fastened to the policy of competitive disinflation until 1993, even though unemployment rose to 3.3 million and growth rates remained low. Massive electoral defeat in 1993 occasioned a reappraisal and future presidential candidate Lionel Jospin began to stress the 'margin of manoeuvre' available to the state in the creation of jobs. The idea of defective demand was rediscovered and policies such as the shorter working week were adopted with the intention of finding work for 700,000 people (half in the public sector). But it took the rebellion of French public-sector unions in December 1995 – when millions demonstrated against the Juppé Plan for major welfare cuts and measures of privatisation and deregulation – to concentrate minds. Until then the Socialists had been indistinguishable from the centre-right in domestic economic policy. It was within the EC that a measure of progress was made.

By aligning the *franc fort* with the deutschmark Mitterrand had made possible a policy offensive within the EC which prepared the ground for the single market and European monetary union. Greater integration within the European Community would appeal to business – as it had done before – but also offered improved prospects for the reformist left. As Ross says, it

> could preserve, perhaps even enhance, what Delors came to call the 'European model of society', a mixed economy in which market harshness was mitigated by welfare states and civilised industrial relations systems, with an important regulatory role reserved for the state ... The new vision was meant to be one of social democracy on a European scale led by the French.[36]

Business would obtain as broad a base as those enjoyed by its North American and Japanese competitors. The lifting of exchange and capital controls was sold as part of the logic of economic integration. But Mitterrand also pressed, after 1988, for a 'social dimension' to the Single European Market, warning that it must not 'abandon workers on the other side of the road'.[37] It is true that the French labour market was subject to measures of 'flexibilisation' in respect of working schedules, the hiring of temporary employees, the inspection of factories, the procedure for layoffs and programmes to reduce employment costs to firms. But a strong *dirigiste* tradition survived and during the 1980s there was nothing like the 'There-is-no-alternative' conviction which prevailed in Britain. It was here, under the Thatcher governments, more than anywhere else in Western Europe that the neo-liberal offensive against organised labour was most systematic and a model of capitalism came to prevail that was said to go with the grain of increasing economic internationalisation.

The British model

Though average unemployment rates rose everywhere in the years 1974–82, there was significant variation between OECD countries. The UK, in common with the US, Italy and Ireland, averaged just over 7 per cent unemployed at the highest end of the scale, whereas Austria, Norway, Sweden and Japan averaged around 2 per cent at the other extreme. By 1983 Britain had become a net importer of manufactured goods for the first time since the industrial revolution. Unemployment rose to above 13 per cent of the workforce in 1981, or well over 3 million, peaking at 14 per cent in mid-1986 (at 3.25 million) even though economic growth had been improving since 1982. The phenomenon of persistent mass unemployment, combined with annual economic growth averaging more than 3 per cent per annum during 1982–89, inspired speculation about a new era of 'jobless growth'. But the prosaic reality was that unemployment was much larger than official figures disclosed – the government having repeatedly changed the method of calculation and removed as many people as possible from the register.

The destruction of so many jobs in car manufacture, textiles, engineering, steel, mines, shipbuilding and ancillary industries ensured that the worst affected areas were the Labour and trade union strongholds. The depressed regions of the UK had higher unemployment rates in 1983 than anywhere in Europe except Sardinia, Campania, Corsica and Denmark. Even Greater London lost over one-third of its manufacturing jobs in the decade 1973–83 and the West Midlands was added to the familiar list of depressed regions of Britain for the first time. Trade union membership was bound to suffer, especially in view of the fact that 'only 55 per cent of the adult male population were in full-time jobs' by 1983 and only 24 per cent of women. Part-time work represented over 20 per cent of all jobs by the end of the first Thatcher government and it was in this area that employment was growing. Thus, while full-time male employment fell by a further 60,000 in 1984, total employment grew by 343,000 with 54 per cent of these additional jobs being part-time positions taken by women.[38] Part-time employment constituted a rising proportion of all female employment in the UK, reaching over 40 per cent of the total in the early 1980s; but the earnings of women workers relative to men were lower than in any other European Union country.[39]

By the mid-1980s the labour market in the UK was characterised by high levels of long-term unemployment among young and middle-aged men and a rising proportion of part-time jobs increasingly taken by women. It was also characterised by growing inequalities of income. The Institute of Fiscal Studies calculated that by 1984 the average unemployed man had lost about 15 per cent of weekly income as a direct result of tax changes introduced by the Conservative government in the years 1979–84; meanwhile the income of company directors and senior managers had risen by 43 and 19 per cent respectively. Excluding taxes and benefits, the relative income of the poorest

20 per cent of households fell by about 60 per cent between 1975 and 1983. As Standing pointed out in the mid-1980s; 'If the poor are increasingly on state benefits it implies a chronic failure of the labour market to help them retain some semblance of socio-economic status'.[40] The Conservative government drew different conclusions from the persistence of mass unemployment and the rise in the numbers of people claiming welfare benefits; it concluded that the labour market was beset by rigidities which prevented people from taking jobs.

The new emphasis on 'labour-market flexibility' coincided with the abandonment of monetarism. The new conventional wisdom preached by the right from the spring of 1985[41] was that the only inflation-proof way to boost employment was to attend to those 'supply-side measures' which would remove obstructions to the working of the labour market. These obstructions included employment protection legislation, health and safety regulations, wages councils for the low paid, trade unions, income taxes, the employer's contribution to national insurance, regulations governing the hiring and firing of labour and welfare benefits. The inspiration for this line of attack was the US under Ronald Reagan's presidency – an economy which absorbed well over 8 million legal immigrants in the 1980s and produced millions of new, largely poorly paid, jobs. At the opposite extreme stood the major economies of Western Europe, which suffered, according to the Conservative view, from 'Eurosclerosis' – or the presence of all those evils which stood in the way of flexibility.

The clearest expression of the fact that all of this was driven by ideology was that total labour costs in the UK were already lower, according to the National Institute for Economic and Social Research in 1984, than in any other of the sixteen industrialised countries in its study.[42] Furthermore, the UK's total labour costs had been relatively low for at least the previous ten years. The leading instances of 'Eurosclerosis', on the other hand, were countries such as Sweden and Germany which had always enjoyed higher levels of employment, growth, productivity and real incomes than the UK since the world economic crisis had begun in the 1970s. Though the government-induced recession of 1979–81 had effectively eliminated jobs in precisely the industries that possessed the strongest trade unions – the ones that had supplied the relatively well-paid, full-time jobs; though hourly rates of pay for full-time manual workers had subsequently grown at less than the overall rate of growth of productivity, while the share of profits in net domestic product 'rose considerably';[43] though membership of trade unions had fallen in every year since 1979; the government's strategy for job-creation in 1985 centred on measures to further weaken the unions and drive down the incomes of wage earners and the unemployed.

As we have noted in a previous chapter, the Conservative government had always explicitly believed that the major incentive for effective participation in the economy for those who were already poor was less income, while for those who were already rich the best incentive was even more money. Successive budgets accordingly redistributed income to the rich, beginning with the first in June 1979 which cut the top rate of income tax from 83 to 60 per cent and the standard rate from 33 to 30 per cent, whilst increasing regressive indirect taxes such as VAT which rose to 15 per cent. Between 1979 and 1982 the gross pay of the highest paid decile of non-manual workers raced ahead of that of the lowest paid decile of manual workers. The Low Pay Unit calculated that the proportion of the workforce on less than two-thirds average pay had increased from one in ten male manual workers in 1979 to one in six in 1982, while among women the proportion had increased from two-thirds to three-quarters.[44] Nevertheless, in 1984 the chancellor of the exchequer, Nigel Lawson, indicated that there was more to be done in widening the gap which separated the worst paid from the rest of the population when, in his Mais Lecture, he praised wage cuts as a cause of the recovery of the American economy.

As part of this offensive the government also embarked on the erosion of the welfare state. It began to alter the criteria of eligibility and the basis of entitlement within a year of taking office. Long-term benefits were de-indexed from movements in real wages in 1980, the same year in which taxation of unemployment benefit was introduced and the first of a series of measures took benefits away from unemployed school leavers. The families of those involved in industrial disputes lost social security entitlements under the provisions of the Social Security (No 2) Act 1980. The value of child benefit was allowed to fall annually; changes in the method of calculation and the timing of payments made further economies; while to these often niggardly changes in the rules were added other measures to demoralise and stigmatise claimants, such as cuts in social security staff and constant minatory rhetoric about social security fraudsters. While the numbers of factory inspectors and employees of the Health and Safety Executive were cut, the number of social security investigators and prosecutions brought for social security fraud increased. Yet at the end of 1983 the social security minister announced that only two in three of those eligible to claim supplementary benefits actually bothered to do so.[44]

Similar economies were made in housing benefit and health care during the first Thatcher government. Soon after its re-election in 1983, the government announced a wholesale review of social security spending. Further measures to provide bespoke incentives to rich and poor were soon introduced. By the end of its first ten years of office the Conservative government had whittled away at the right to unemployment benefit on no less than seventeen occasions and produced over twenty other changes to welfare adversely affecting the income of the unemployed. According to Frank Field, one of the British Labour Party's experts on social policy, savings on the welfare budget in

1989–90 alone amounted to around £5 billion, an amount which covered the £4.2 billion in tax cuts received by the richest 1 per cent of taxpayers in the same year.[46] Government policy was to drive down the real incomes of the unemployed and all those dependent on state benefits. The total number of people dependent upon supplementary benefit grew by more in the first ten years of the Conservative governments than it had done in the whole of the post-war period prior to 1979, rising from 4.4 million as the Conservative Party entered office to 8.2 million by May 1988. The unemployed were by far the largest group affected, followed by pensioners living on the state pension – an amount that was allowed to fall far behind the rise in average incomes during the 1980s.

Whereas the share in net income of the top 5 per cent had fallen slightly during the 1970s, it rose sharply after 1979. The range of inequality widened – not only between the top and bottom deciles, but also between the poorest worker's wages and those on average wages. The government found numerous ways to assist the wealthy. The tax on unearned income was abolished in 1984 and successive budgets found ways to extend tax relief to inherited wealth and capital gains. By 1989 the richest 1 per cent received tax cuts which gave each one of them more income than the total annual income of any individual in the bottom 95 per cent of the population.[47] Meanwhile, the government did what it could to reduce the relative pay of the low paid by dismantling the regulatory and protective measures which previous governments had erected. Thus the provision that employers tendering for public contracts should pay the generally accepted wages for the trades in question – known as the Fair Wages Resolution – was scrapped in 1983. Similarly the wages councils, which predominantly affected low-paid workers, had their powers to determine holiday entitlements, weekend rates of pay, shift premiums and other related issues so diminished that they were no longer able to guarantee an income above the poverty line. The thrust of this policy, of course, was to force people to accept any work available and thus reinforce the flexible labour market. Abolition of the wages councils and other forms of regulation ensured that the proportion of very low-paid work rose.[48]

As recently as January 1997, official figures showed that 13.7 million people (4.2 million children) in the UK were living below the poverty line, compared with 5 million in 1979. A European Commission survey of 1997 showed that 22 per cent of the UK population lived in poverty – defined as an income of half the average or less – and 32 per cent of its children, compared with EU averages of 17 and 20 per cent respectively.[49] Until the end of its tenure in May 1997, the Conservative government continued to pursue policies that hurt these people in particular, such as the continuing shift to indirect taxation and income tax cuts funded from cuts in state expenditure on public goods and transfer payments. Thus the entitlement to non-means-tested benefit was cut from twelve to six months, while the qualifying period of

National Insurance payments was extended from one to two years. The minimum qualifying period during which employees could claim unfair dismissal was raised from six months to two years. The Unemployment Unit calculated that the numbers struck off benefit nearly trebled from 113,000 to 317,000 between 1993–94 and 1995–96, on the grounds that those involved were failing to actively seek work or were refusing to take up training. Yet officially acknowledged levels of unemployment in the period 1978–97 averaged 8.9 per cent of the workforce, or 2 million people. Furthermore, the 3.2 million extra jobs in the service sector created in the same period paid about 25 per cent less than the 3.5 million manufacturing jobs that were lost in these years. The new workforce was feminised and casualised and an increasing number of manual workers of both sexes were caught in jobs with no prospect of rising real incomes. Certainly real wages stagnated for twenty years for both full-time manual workers in manufacturing and female part-time workers in services.[50]

This is the context in which the Workplace Industrial Relations Survey showed that union recognition had declined since 1979. Sixty-six per cent of all establishments recognised trade unions in 1984, but only 53 per cent did so by 1990. Labour Force Survey data in 1994 showed that 48 per cent of employees belonged to workplaces where unions were recognised, varying from 34 per cent in the private sector to 86 per cent in the public sector (compared with 60 per cent and over 90 per cent respectively in the early 1980s).[51] The measures that were introduced by the Labour government of 1974–79 to encourage trade union recognition were naturally repealed. Six acts concerned with trade unions were passed between 1980 and 1993. Their combined effect was to eliminate the closed shop, which covered only 3–500,000 workers in 1990, compared with anything between 3.5 and 3.7 million in 1984; enforce postal ballots before strike action could be called; render unions liable for damages arising from 'secondary industrial action' and unofficial strikes not formally repudiated by the union; and make strikers – official and unofficial – vulnerable to dismissal. Trade union membership dropped from over 12 million in 1979 to 7,780,000 in 1992 and union density fell from nearly 55 per cent to just over 35 per cent. Other measures also helped to swing the balance of power decisively in the employer's favour, such as the change of the law governing unfair dismissal in 1985, mentioned above. British employers notably made less use of fixed-duration contracts than their counterparts in the EU, despite the higher proportion of part-time workers in Britain – possibly because it was so much easier to fire workers on permanent contracts in Britain. How much of the collapse in union membership is due to unemployment, changes in trade union law, changing employer attitudes, changes in the size and occupational mix of workplaces, more general economic restructuring or other factors such as poverty and fear is difficult to say.[52]

The combined effect of these factors certainly accounts for the dramatic decline in the numbers of days lost through strikes, which stood at only 528,000 in 1992 compared with an annual average of 7–10 million in the 1970s. They also facilitated the 'steady decline in industry level bargaining towards either single-employer bargaining ... or ... unilateral decision by the employer' observed by Wolfgang Lecher. By 1990, according to his figures, 'multi-employer bargaining was the main basis for pay increases for only 19 per cent of manual employees in private manufacturing and for only 6 per cent of non-manual employees'.[53] The British experience 'has offered a striking demonstration of the vulnerability created by the absence of legally enforceable rights, in particular rights of employee representation', according to Lecher who notes that the National Association of Citizen's Advice Bureaux has been obliged to deal with a growing number of employment-related problems in the absence of effective representation at work. Citizen's Advice dealt with 850,000 separate cases in 1991–92.[54]

Labour's modernisation

The Labour Party, confined to opposition for eighteen years, adapted itself to many of these changes. When Kinnock became leader of the party after the 1983 general election there was already a majority in the parliamentary party in favour of a policy rethink and the isolation of the 'hard left'. This process was assisted by the defeat of the miner's strike of 1984–85 and the failure of militant Labour councils to resist the government's rate-capping policy – a failure which led to the isolation of the Liverpool City Council and ultimately facilitated a purge of the 'Trotskyists' who were said to have infiltrated it. These events were used to highlight the bankruptcy of the Bennite left and the electorally damaging consequences of its confrontationist rhetoric. But the Kinnock leadership had not only decided that change was needed to make the party electable again, it was also driven by the idea – derived from public opinion research and election studies – that this entailed shifting to the right in order to catch up with a similar shift in public opinion. The right of the party had accepted this analysis since 1979, while the Campaigns and Communications Directorate (CCD) created in October 1985 under Peter Mandelson's tutelage embraced the same logic from its inception.[55] Over the period of readjustment 1983–94, taken as a whole, Labour began to see that the performance of its traditional role in government – speaking for the nation, not the interests of the working class – involved acceptance of most of the Thatcherite economic and social legacy. This realisation came gradually as Labour persuaded itself that a new hegemony existed reflecting a new social and economic reality.

By the 1987 general election the Labour Party had divested itself of such policies as withdrawal from the EEC, the adoption of exchange controls and import controls. Labour was less convinced by the idea that public ownership, planning and state intervention could inject new vigour into the UK economy. It had also departed from measures that rested on corporatist arrangements such as incomes policy. The party's relationship with the trade unions was thought to be something that had to be downplayed for electoral reasons. Industrial democracy was accordingly resculpted in the report *People At Work: New Rights, New Responsibilities* (1986). An idea that had been concerned with changing the power structure at work in favour of workers throughout much of the 1970s and early 1980s was in due course transformed into a consensual proposal for 'legislation to foster good industrial relations and democratic participation' in the 1987 manifesto, *Britain Will Win*. For all these changes Labour was still broadly interventionist. It was only when the result of the election increased the Conservative majority in parliament to 144 seats – Labour having gained just twenty seats over the 1983 result – that the leadership reacted by instituting a full-scale 'policy review' which lasted until 1989 and produced a further wave of revisions to its economic analysis.

Before examining this new stage in Labour's policy shift it is worth recalling some of the interventionist measures outlined in the 1987 manifesto, *Britain Will Win*. In the light of subsequent developments it is instructive to note that the manifesto referred to a whole panoply of measures designed to regulate the labour market, including the replacement of Tory legislation that enabled 'employers and non-unionists the means to frustrate legitimate trade union activity'; protection against unfair dismissal, applicable from the time of employment, with reinstatement the normal outcome of a successful appeal; 'extended employment protection to all workers, including part-timers'; improved statutory protection in respect of health and safety at work; restoration of provision for fair pay in the form of the wages councils, the Fair Wages Resolution and Schedule 11 of the 1975 Employment Protection Act; the strengthening of the Advisory, Conciliation and Arbitration Service (ACAS); steps to 'promote trade union membership and organisation' including those that would 'encourage union recognition by employers'; restoration of the right to belong to a trade union; and, finally, legal protection for 'workers and their unions to organise effective industrial action'.[56]

Official unemployment had peaked at 3.35 million the year before the manifesto was published, but the real figure continued to be much higher and the drive for greater labour-market flexibility was at its peak.[57] At this point Labour was still publicly persuaded that the economic changes wrought over the previous eight years, far from amounting to a new settlement in tune with the needs of the age, involved a good deal that was destructive of economic efficiency as well as social justice. Its stated priority was 'to concentrate resources on the essential tasks of combating unemployment and poverty' and this involved a pledge to reduce unemployment by one million in two years, partly by spending on housing, schools, hospitals and infrastructural investment. The state pension was to be linked once again to average earnings or living costs – whichever was the most favourable to pensioners – and the State Earnings Related Pension Scheme was to be restored. Similarly, the party promised to restore the death grant and maternity grant and to increase these and other payments such as child benefit. A new disability income scheme would be introduced and extra resources found for young people with disabilities. Long-term supplementary benefit was to be extended to the long-term unemployed and a statutory national minimum wage was to be introduced as part of 'a comprehensive strategy for ending low pay'.[58]

Far from accepting the idea that the economy had been modernised by the Conservative reforms, Labour saw evidence of 'drift and decline' and took as proof of government neglect 'the huge capital outflow of £110 billion since 1979'. Though much diluted since 1983, Labour still had a commitment 'to rebuilding [the British] industrial base' and the party saw a role both for state-provided, long-term industrial investment and regional policy. There was still talk of extending social ownership via a new body called British Enterprise which would 'take a socially-owned stake in high-tech industries' in particular. A new British Industrial Investment Bank with its own regional bases would supply finance for investment. While the Department of Trade and Industry would be strengthened to spearhead the 'new industrial strategy', Labour proposed measures to regulate the City and create a 'capital repatriation scheme'. In short, the thrust of the manifesto was redolent of Labour rhetoric of old; it was a case of science, industry and technology aided by the state against the forces of finance, short-termism and capital export.[59] Electoral defeat, however, reinforced the hand of the modernisers.

The Labour leadership saw the purpose of the policy review begun in the autumn of 1987 as an exercise in programmatic renewal informed by evidence that the party was electorally handicapped by being out of step with social, economic and cultural change.[60] In practice this entailed another step in the party's growing affirmation of the role of markets in promoting economic welfare, but we will see that the Wilsonian idea of Labour as the champion of British industry was not yet dead. The first report of the policy review, *Social Justice and Economic Efficiency*, drew attention to the increasingly open nature of the British economy and the way in which 'the freedom of action of national governments is seriously constrained by international trading arrangements, competitive pressures, the huge flows of capital across frontiers, and the decisions of multinational firms'.[61] For our purposes it will suffice to note that the report argued that 'this does not mean that national governments or a Labour government in particular have no power'. Indeed, it talked of the need for intergovernmental cooperation in 'reconstructing international economic relations to overcome the deficiencies of the post-Bretton Woods era' because 'the deregulation of international trade and finance and the climate of "international monetarism" has resulted in persistent slow growth and high unemployment'.[62] But there was no evidence that Labour saw European unity as part of the solution. The EC featured as an obstacle to British economic regeneration in so far as the Single Market Act paved the way for 'an uncontrolled "free" market on a European-wide scale' capable of reinforcing 'the current imbalances in the European economy, concentrating industry in those parts of Europe where it is already strongest, and enhancing the potential for rapid and destabilising capital movements'.[63] After Jacques Delors had stressed the social benefits of membership of the EC at the 1988 TUC conference, the mood in the party nevertheless became significantly more pro-European as closer ties with the EC came to be seen as a way of circumventing Thatcherism.

In 1989 the second phase of the policy review was completed with the publication of *Meet the Challenge, Make the Change*. Neil Kinnock's introduction to the document stressed that the state's economic role was largely to facilitate the workings of the market, but this still meant that the government had a role in providing the framework which enabled markets to work 'fairly and efficiently'. In this view 'the Conservatives are the party for the City. We [the Labour Party] are the party for industry and, like the governments of our competitors, we will form a government that helps industry succeed.'[64] Ideological blindness in the form of a dogmatic conviction that the markets always know best was said to be a reason why the Conservatives refused to intervene at either national or European level in order to secure efficiency and social justice. But as the party of the City, the Conservatives, in Labour's view, represented a constituency whose self-interests militated against industrial regeneration. According to Labour, the UK's lack of competitiveness derived from a 'fixation with the short-term', a 'disease' which the policy review traced to the habits of the City. This was said to be the main cause of the UK's lamentable record in respect of training, research and investment in new technologies.

Labour had now discovered a 'supply-side socialism' which consisted of recognising that private enterprise, in Neil Kinnock's words, 'can be the most efficient way of producing and distributing many goods and services' as long as 'government regulates commercial behaviour in the interests of the consumer, and restricts monopoly practices in the interests of competition'.[65] Helping the market to work properly, in Labour's view, involved acting on the insight that education was the key to future competitiveness.[66] The policy review had also concluded that 'new working patterns should be used to increase efficiency' and achieve ' social and economic flexibility'.[67] Two years later, *Looking to the Future* hit upon the formulae 'Business where appropriate; government where necessary' and left little doubt that the party now endorsed 'the efficiency and realism which markets can provide'.[68] Education and training had now been elevated to 'the commanding heights' of a modern economy. But it was clear that Labour's priority was stable prices. There would be no 'irresponsible dash for growth'. Government borrowing would only be for long-term investment. The over-riding goal of price stability was seen as the precondition for inducing higher rates of investment and securing long-term competitiveness.[69] The same themes were reiterated in a spate of policy statements published in 1991.[70] Kinnock talked of the 'old ideologies' of 'crude laissez-faire' and the 'command economy'. Labour would chart a 'third way' between them involving cooperation between government and industry.[71] A Labour government would get interest rates and inflation 'down to German and French levels' and keep them down.[72] Industrial policy became increasingly submerged as the language and thrust of the policy statements gave more and more ground to economic liberalism. Yet as late as 1994 Labour described its policies as being 'designed specifically to build the long-term industrial strength' of the British economy which was perceived as 'the only secure foundation of national prosperity'.[73] By now this was largely empty rhetoric. The thought had gained ground that a vigorous, long-term industrial policy modelled on the experience of a country like Germany simply could not be adapted to British conditions where a sort of institutional degradation had arguably taken place under the Conservatives, undermining the most basic conditions for such an experiment.[74] Not that this was the way Labour politicians argued the case. Gordon Brown and Tony Blair in particular saw only virtue in the British economic condition by 1994 and actually enjoined the other states of the EU to emulate the model, as we shall see in the next chapter.

Sweden's 'third way'

The Swedish Social Democrats returned to power in 1982 armed with a 'third way' strategy of their own. They promised to avoid the extremes of French socialism and British conservatism and they retained their grip on government in 1985 and 1988. The first act of the newly installed SAP was to devalue the krona by 16 per cent. Unemployment stood at a record post-war high of 3.5 per cent (peaking at 4 per cent in 1983), with another 3 per cent in government-financed programmes. In return for implementation of the investment funds, the LO agreed to wage restraint and in this context the effects of the devaluation were sustained. By 1984 an economic recovery was in motion. In the period that followed the party defied political trends in Western Europe by returning Sweden to economic health. The huge government deficit was eliminated without endangering full employment and the welfare state and the promised 'third way' seemed vindicated. From 1983 to 1988 the economy grew at an average rate of 2.7 per cent, the rate of unemployment fell from 3.5 per cent to less than 2 per cent and the balance of trade deficit was turned into a surplus. The evidence provided by three consecutive election victories showed that the SAP managed to retain the loyalty of its traditional supporters, by obtaining 70 per cent of the working-class vote, despite some evidence of issue voting and the decay of partisan identification.[75] At this stage the party could still boast strong mass organisations, an extensive state-subsidised social democratic press, and numerous social and recreational organisations.[76] Trade union membership rose to new heights in the early 1980s.

The cost of this recovery was paid for in inflation, which accelerated even as it slowed down in the rest of the OECD during 1989–90. By that time Swedish inflation was 6.6 per cent compared with 4.5 per cent for the OECD, and at the end of 1989 the balance of payments returned to deficit at a higher level than in 1982 as Swedish competitiveness suffered. The economy was now deflated and the austerity measures introduced in February 1990 involved a two-year ban on strikes and a freeze on wages. These crisis policies confirmed trends that had been in operation since 1989, the year of the collapse of the communist regimes, when the much-vaunted 'third road' (which could also be conceptualised as lying between the command economies and the New Right) was suddenly no longer in the moderate 'middle'. Relations with the LO predictably deteriorated, the party leadership was no longer so sure of itself and the social democratic 'image of society' lost much of its sheen.

In the years 1982–89 Swedish wage costs rose by 76.5 per cent compared with a rise of 64.9 per cent in Britain and 36.6 per cent in West Germany.[77] By 1990, 18 per cent of Sweden's population was aged sixty-five or more and the proportion was expected to grow over the next thirty years. Demographic changes at the other extreme showed a 25 per cent increase in the number of babies born each year in the early 1990s. Single-parent families and one-person households also grew.[78] The pressure for reform of Swedish public services derived from more than just demographic change and technological progress; it was also driven by slower growth rates and the ideology of post-Fordism.[79] Though the Social Democrats managed to maintain full employment for most of the 1980s – largely by increasing the public-sector workforce – unemployment began to rise after 1989 and reached 11 per cent in 1994, under the four-party centre-right government which was elected in 1991 (dominated by the conservative Moderate Party). A further 4 per cent of the workforce were kept out of the unemployment figures only by virtue of various labour-market schemes. People in receipt of social assistance grew from 4 per cent in 1980 to 8 per cent in 1993, with a continued rise expected because of long-term unemployment. The new regime elected in 1991 was committed to a Thatcherite 'system shift' involving privatisation and marketisation, but lacked the *Riksdag* majority required to see it through. Nevertheless, employers and the political right generally sought to mould public opinion with complaints about the growth in the numbers of those claiming sickness benefit and disability pensions, and the fact that the combined proportion of those working for the state or claiming social benefits from it had risen from 30.6 per cent of the population in 1972 to 53.6 per cent in 1992.[80] The great size of the public sector, the high levels of taxation, the legacy of corporatist institutions and expectations, the abuse of the benefit system, the damage to the work ethic and investment which the welfare system allegedly entailed – all these familiar complaints entered public debate from 1989.

The centre cannot hold

In reality the marriage of Swedish capitalism and social democracy had been under severe strain since the attack on managerial prerogatives in the 1970s. Sweden had operated as the closest approximation to the ideal-type of corporatism since the end of the war. Features of this system included the LO's near-monopoly representation of organised manual labour in a country of exceptionally high levels of union density, and its special influence within the social democratic state, which allowed it to trade wage restraint for economic growth, full employment and social reforms. The LO's authority over the industrial unions federated within it ensured that deals negotiated with the employers were generally made to stick, evidence for which can be seen in the low incidence of strikes – both official and unofficial. For their part the employers were also concentrated and centrally organised to an exceptional degree. The Swedish economy has long been dominated by export-oriented giants such as Volvo and all the largest firms (and 40,000 others) were represented in the SAF. It was in the interests of wage restraint that the Swedish employers favoured central bargaining and it was when this mechanism was no longer useful that they turned against it from the late 1970s. It was the LO's masterstroke to turn this need to its own advantage by using centralised bargaining to pursue wider economic and social issues than simply higher pay. This was another reason for the employers' dissatisfaction, since wage compression was said to undermine all sorts of incentives (to acquire skills, etc.). The model worked for as long as unions and employers outside the two confederations – particularly white-collar and professional workers – followed the lead of the LO-SAF and for as long as blue-collar workers dominated the labour market.

The service sector expanded throughout the 1950s and 1960s so that by 1970 it employed over half of all Swedish workers; twenty years later this proportion had risen to two-thirds, while the proportion of workers in the industrial export industry had shrunk to under one-fifth.[81] The growth of the service sector produced a corresponding growth of white-collar and public-sector unions in all three union confederations; the LO, the TCO and the Central Organisation of Professional Employees (SACO). The balance of power within each one of these confederations changed in consequence. For example, by 1978 the traditional dominance of the metalworkers inside the

LO was displaced by the largely female Municipal Workers' Union SKAF. The simple model of LO-SAF bargaining was called into question in the 1970s when three bargaining cartels were formed within the TCO and two of them encompassed public-sector workers also organised by LO and SACO. At the same time that collective bargaining became more complex, it was taking place in circumstances of more conspicuous scarcity. As elsewhere, the slow-down of economic growth in the 1970s brought into question the compatibility of rising personal incomes and the expansion of public service provision. Swedish firms complained that they had the highest paid workers in the world and the most lavish welfare facilities, requiring the highest personal taxes.

Four bourgeois governments grappled with the problems of structural crisis in Swedish industry and the growing inflationary problems exacerbated by high wage settlements in the mid-1970s and the two oil shocks. In spite of the severe economic crisis the bourgeois coalition did everything it could to maintain welfare entitlements and full employment, while avoiding tax increases and welfare cuts, with the result that the government deficit amounted to 13 per cent of GDP by 1982. The krona was devalued in 1976, 1977, 1981 and 1982, but any benefit to the economy was cancelled by wage increases. A wage freeze introduced by the Falldin government in 1980 provoked lockouts and strikes and the policy of confrontation probably assisted the SAP's electoral recovery two years later. The government also resorted to nationalisation – more than the Social Democrats had done in the previous forty-four years – and state ownership of overmanned, declining industrial sectors was bequeathed to the incoming SAP government to sort out. But the deadlocked collective bargaining of 1980 which had produced 'the most widespread strikes and lockouts in Swedish history' was also evidence of a new mood among Sweden's employers.[81] The SAF made clear its desire to quash the 1938 Basic Agreement and impose an incomes policy on the LO, while the SAP itself moved to the right by openly supporting cuts in social expenditure and increased taxes.

By the time the Social Democrats were returned to power, after the interregnum of 1976–82, the decay of the decades-old, peak-level collective bargaining was well advanced. Three white-collar industrial unions departed from their bargaining cartel in 1983 to do a separate deal with the employers in the engineering industry. In the 1987–88 bargaining round all the unions from this cartel conducted separate negotiations. The engineering employers, the most powerful group within the SAF, representing an industry responsible for one-half of total Swedish exports, was especially keen to bargain apart from the central LO-SAF agreement.[83] It was dissatisfied with the solidaristic wage policy in particular and resented the *de facto* incomes policy which the government introduced in the mid-1970s by making the public sector first in any bargaining round. It argued that there was little incentive for workers to train, so far had differentials between skilled and unskilled narrowed. Yet the number of skilled jobs in engineering tended to increase. Meanwhile, the leaders of this group of employers – such as Volvo, Electrolux, Ericsson and SKF – became conscious of new conditions of international competitiveness as their dependence on exports increased. The fact that Sweden's dependence on these particular exports also increased could only heighten the employers' power within the country. The engineering employers thus became zealous advocates of decentralised bargaining, productivity deals and the free market from the late 1970s. They were faced with severe labour shortages, but had the means to overcome them with higher wages. They were also faced with new international conditions and the need to restructure to remain competitive. Separate bargaining was presented as a solution to these problems.

But their employees – organised in *Metallarbetareforbundet* (the metalworkers' union) – had their own reasons for breaking ranks with the LO in 1983 to conclude a separate deal. Fear of losing members to the white-collar union active in engineering, SIF, was a motivating factor because members of SIF received better pay than workers in *Metall* who were classified as blue collar. This gave rise to jurisdictional disputes between the unions. The desire for big pay rises in a sector that could afford them also motivated *Metall* to pull out of LO. Higher than average wage rises followed for metalworkers. Such was the dominance of the big engineering companies within SAF that they were able effectively to veto suggestions by those employers outside of the tradeable goods sector to return to central coordination. A year later the rest of the LO's private-sector unions conducted separate bargaining and came out with deals of varying durations, but all calculated to make a return to centralised bargaining very difficult to achieve. It was the first year since 1956 that there had been no central LO-SAF talks. By the end of the decade centrifugal forces were evident within SACO, where groups such as the doctors and civil engineers were demanding the right to break away from central bargaining at will. And within LO the problem reproduced itself in the form of tension between the SKAF and the metalworkers, with the former having much more interest in the preservation of central bargaining and labour movement solidarity.

The Social Democrats resorted to a *de facto* incomes policy in 1984–85 and 1986 when Olof Palme conducted a series of meetings with the union confederations and the employers. It was an attempt to control the wage-price spiral, but in 1985 Sweden's biggest ever public-sector strike brought a virtual stop to the country's foreign trade. To finance the settlement, the government introduced a compensatory credit squeeze and raised interest rates. In 1986 nearly two-thirds of the public-sector unions struck for wage rises and compensation for wage drift in the private sector. Inflation averaged 6.5 per cent in 1988 and public-sector pay settlements broke the government's cash limits to cancel it out. The highest marginal rate of taxation was reduced in the same year (72 to 60 per cent) as an incentive for people to work harder and evade payment less.

Scott Lash suggested a number of reasons for this fragmentation in the mid-1980s. One was the new salience of the highly paid, skilled workers in the export-oriented sector. Another was the growing proportion of public-sector employees and a third was the growth in size of the white-collar workforce. The last two changes led to a parallel growth of separate white-collar trade union federations, some of which were content at first to follow the lead provided by LO. By the mid-1980s, however, the white-collar confederation TCO had a membership 75 per cent the size of the LO private-sector unions, and three 'cartels' had emerged among its constituent unions as bargaining forces in their own right. A new balance of forces came into existence as early as 1973 when the first of these white-collar bargaining bodies was set up. According to Lash it was evidence of labour-market fragmentation,[84] as was the decision of the white-collar cartels to distance themselves from the Social Democrats in the early 1980s. As labour markets fragmented, so did organised interests come to favour decentralised bargaining.

The changing gender balance of the workforce added to this fragmentation within the LO, where two of the four largest unions were dominated by women to the extent of over 70 per cent of the membership. One of these, the 600,000-strong SKAF was both 80 per cent female and 50 per cent part-time, and 68 per cent of its members were involved in care for others. SKAF grew larger than the traditionally dominant metalworkers' union. Disruptive conflicts, such as the one involving SKAF in 1980, became more common as the decade progressed. Sectional conflicts developed between LO and the non-manual federations, but also along the public/private-sector axis so that four rival union blocs obstructed central bargaining

In circumstances of chronic labour shortages, as Sweden returned to full employment, wage drift came to compose as much as two-thirds of the pay rises for certain workers in the 1980s and 45 per cent for the whole labour market in 1988. Rising rates of inflation, wage drift and decentralised pay bargaining produced, according to Ahlen, 'a civil war in which rank order and relative pay levels [were] more important than actual purchasing power. The resulting leap-frog bargaining ha[d] created a wage-wage spiral that undermine[d] the country's economy'.[85] It is clear that the employers encouraged wage drift and that this undermined collective bargaining. Schemes of profit sharing and bonuses undermined the solidaristic wage. The very largest exporters, such as Volvo, Electrolux and Ericsson, were inclined to blackmail government with threats of relocation – Datatronic's move to the US was invoked as a warning example. The decision to apply for membership of the EU was itself influenced by the outflow of capital preparing for the single market in 1992. These firms, already independent of the domestic capital market, had benefited from the bourgeois governments' easing of foreign exchange policy. In 1989 the SAP abolished all currency controls.

Notes

1 Although these governments added to the general gloom concerning the condition of the Left in the 1980s they clearly had special conditions attached to them. Each was faced with transition from dictatorship in the context of relative economic backwardness compared with the most of the countries with whom they wanted to integrate within the European Union. The legacy of excessive statism, the need for modernisation and democratic consolidation – these were the preoccupations which predominated. The workers who bore the brunt of this modernisation – in the form of mass unemployment, labour-market deregulation and the rest – responded with general strikes.

2 Quoted in S. Padgett, 'The German Social Democrats: a redefintion of social democracy or Bad Godesberg Mark 2', *West European Politics*, 1 (1993) 27.

3 G. Falkner and E. Talos, 'The role of the state within social policy', *West European Politics*, 3 (1994) 65.

4 P. Hall, 'Socialism in one country: Mitterrand and the struggle to define a new economic policy in France', in P. Cerny and M. Schain (eds), *Socialism, the State and Public Policy in France* (London, Frances Pinter, 1985), p. 85.

5 W. Northcutt, *Mitterrand* (London, Holmes and Meier, 1992), p. 88; D. S. Bell and B. Criddle, *The French Socialist Party: The Emergence of a Party of Government* (Oxford, Clarendon Press, second edition, 1988), p. 156.

6 G. Ross and J. Jenson, 'Political pluralism and economic policy', in J. S. Ambler (ed.), *The French Socialist Experiment* (Philadelphia, PA, Institute for the Study of Human Issues, 1985), p. 39.

7 Quoted by J. McCormick, 'Apprenticeship for governing: an assessment of French socialism in power', in H. Machin and V. Wright (eds), *Economic Policy Under the Mitterrand Presidency, 1991–1984* (London, Frances Pinter, 1985), p. 46

8 V. Lauber, *The Political Economy of France: From Pompidou to Mitterrand* (London, Praeger, 1983), pp. 219–20.

9 Quoted by M. Kesselman, 'Lyrical illusions or a socialism of governance: whither French socialism?', in R. Miliband and J. Saville (eds), *The Socialist Register 1985* (London, Merlin, 1986), p. 234.

10 Only 39 per cent of those polled a year after the election favoured a radicalisation of policy. See B. H. Moss, 'Economic and monetary union and the social divide in France', *Contemporary European History*, 7:2 (1998) 233–4.

11 M. Maclean, 'Introduction', in her *The Mitterrand Years: Legacy and Evaluation* (Basingstoke, Macmillan 1998), p. 3; J. Laughland, *The Death of Politics: France Under Mitterrand* (London, Michael Joseph, 1994), p. xiii.

12 C. Nay, *The Black and the Red: Francois Mitterrand, The Story of an Ambition* (London, Sheridan, 1984), p. 347.

13 D. Singer, *Is Socialism Doomed?* (Oxford, Oxford University Press, 1988), p. 126.

14 Ross and Jenson, 'Political pluralism', pp. 43–4; see also A. Cole, 'A house divided: socialism a la francaise', in G. Raymond (ed.), *France During the Socialist Years* (Aldershot, Dartmouth, 1994), pp. 68–9.

15 An econometric study by Blanchard and Muet demonstrated the efficacy of this approach. See Moss, 'Economic and monetary union', p. 233.

16 D. R. Cameron, 'Exchange rate politics in France, 1981–83: the regime-defining choices of the Mitterrand presidency', in A. Daley (ed.), *The Mitterrand Era: Policy*

Alternatives and Political Mobilization in France (Basingstoke, Macmillan, 1996), p. 58.

17 Chevènement was minister for research and technology until 1984, and then minister for education; Bérégovoy was minister of finance from 1984; Fabius was prime minister from 1984.

18 D. S. Bell and B. Criddle, *The French Socialist Party: The Emergence of a Party of Government* (Oxford, Clarendon Press, second edition, 1988), p. 154; D. S. Bell, 'The socialists in government', in D. S. Bell and E. Shaw (eds), *The Left in France* (Nottingham, Spokesman, 1983), p. 80.

19 E. Helleiner, *States and the Reemergence of Global Finance* (Ithaca, NY, Cornell University, 1994), p. 151.

20 *Ibid.*, p. 157.

21 J. S. Ambler, 'French socialism in comparative perspective', in Ambler (ed.), *The French Socialist Experiment*, pp. 208–10.

22 *Ibid.*, M. Liebman, 'Reformism yesterday and social democracy today', in Miliband and Saville (eds), *The Socialist Register 1985*, p. 14.

23 S. Halimi, 'Less exceptionalism than meets the eye', in Daley (ed.), *The Mitterrand Era*, p. 86.

24 J. S. Ambler, 'Is the French left doomed to fail?', in Ambler (ed.), *The French Socialist Experiment*, pp. 19–20.

25 B. Rowthorn, 'The politics of the Alternative Economic Strategy', *Marxism Today*, January (1981) 5–10.

26 B. Rowthorn, 'Europe ... or bust', *New Socialist*, May–June (1982) 23.

27 F. Cripps and T. Ward, 'Road to recovery', *New Socialist*, July–August (1982) 23.

28 F. Cripps and T. Ward, 'Government policies, European recession and problems of recovery', *Cambridge Journal of Economics*, 1: March (1983).

29 L. Minkin, The Contentious Alliance: Trade Unions and the Labour Party (Edinburgh, Edinburgh University Press, 1991), p. 455.

30 S. Holland (ed.), *Out of the Crisis: A Project for European Recovery* (Nottingham, Spokesman, 1983); P. Teague, 'The Alternative Economic Strategy: a time to go European', *Capital and Class*, 26 (1985); K. Livingstone, 'Reassembling the left', *Chartist*, 115, May–June (1987); K. Coates, 'Europe without frontiers', *New Socialist*, 59, February–March (1989).

31 Holland (ed.), *Out of the Crisis*, pp. 66–7.

32 See S. Holland (ed.), *The European Imperative: Economic and Social Cohension in the 1990s* (Nottingham, Spokesman, 1993).

33 D. Martin, *Bringing Common Sense to the Common Market* (London, Fabian Society, tract 512, 1988), p. 3.

34 'The face of Labour's future', Neil Kinnock interviewed by Eric Hobsbawm, *Marxism Today*, October (1984), pp. 8–15. This analysis was promoted by I. Crewe in, 'The Labour Party and the electorate', in D. Kavanagh (ed.), *The Politics of the Labour Party* (London, Allen and Unwin, 1982); 'The disturbing truth about Labour's rout', *Guardian*, 13 June 1983, and 'The electorate: partisan dealignment ten years on', *West European Politics*, 7 (1984).

35 Quoted by J. W. Friend, *Seven Years in France* (Boulder, CO, Westview Press, 1989), p. 134.

36 G. Ross, 'The limits of political economy: Mitterrand and the crisis of the French left', in Daley (ed.), *The Mitterrand Era*, p. 40
37 Quoted in Northcutt, *Mitterrand*, p. 288.
38 G. Standing, *Unemployment and Labour Market Flexibility: the UK* (Geneva, ILO, 1986), pp. 7–8.
39 *Ibid.*, p. 34.
40 *Ibid.*, p. 21.
41 As in the White Paper, *Employment: The Challenge for the Nation*, March 1985.
42 See Standing, *Unemployment and Labour Market Flexibility*, p. 50
43 *Ibid.*, p. 47.
44 Cited in M. Loney, *The Politics of Greed* (London, Pluto Press, 1986), p. 64.
45 *Ibid.*, p. 73; see also pp. 78–80.
46 F. Field, *Losing Out: The Emergence of Britain's Underclass* (Oxford, Blackwell, 1989), pp. 14–15.
47 *Ibid.*, pp. 54–6, 73–4.
48 S. Beavis, 'It's boom-time for the cynical tendency', *Guardian*, 31 January 1997, p. 21
49 R. Exell, 'Arousing suspicions', *New Times*, 28 February 1998.
50 J. Froud *et al.*, 'Stakeholder economy? From utility privatisation to New Labour', *Capital and Class*, 60 (1996) 131
51 D. Farnham, 'New Labour, the new unions and the new labour market', *Parliamentary Affairs*, 49:4 (1996) 591
52 For an empirical review of the evidence see D. Gallie, R. Penn, and M. Rose (eds.), *Trade Unions in Recession* (Oxford, Oxford University Press, 1996). Gallie and Rose find no evidence of a general hardening of employer attitudes to trade unions. See pp. 33–64.
53 W. Lecher, 'The current state of the trade unions in the EU member states: Britain', in W. Lecher (ed.), *Trade Unions in the European Union: A Handbook* (London, Lawrence and Wishart, 1994), p. 37.
54 *Ibid.*, p. 39.
55 See E. Shaw, *The Labour Party Since 1979: Crisis and Transformation* (London, Routledge, 1994), pp. 23, 54–7.
56 Labour Party, *Britain Will Win* (London, Labour Party, 1987), p. 13.
57 As in the White Paper, *Employment: The Challenge for the Nation*, March 1985.
58 Labour Party, *Britain Will Win*, p 4.
59 *Ibid.*, p. 6.
60 See A. Thorpe, *A History of the Labour Party* (London, Macmillan, 1997), p. 222.
61 Labour Party, *Social Justice and Economic Efficiency* (London, Labour Party, 1988), p. 6.
62 *Ibid.*, p. 6.
63 *Ibid.*, p. 6.
64 Labour Party, *Meet The Challenge, Make the Change* (London, Labour Party, 1989), p. 6.
65 *Ibid.*, introduction, p. 6.
66 *Ibid.*, pp. 6–7 , 17–20.
67 *Ibid.*, p. 22.

68 Labour Party, *Looking to the Future* (London, Labour Party, 1991), p. 6. The slogan quoted was an obvious paraphrase of the German Social Democrats' formula, adopted in 1959, 'As much competition as possible, as much planning as necessary'.

69 *Ibid.*, pp. 8-10.

70 Labour Party, *Labour's Better Way for the 1990s* (London, Labour Party, 1991); *Modern Manufacturing Strength* (London, Labour Party, 1991); *Made in Britain* (London, Labour Party, 1991).

71 Labour Party, *Labour's Better Way for the 1990s*, p. 4.

72 *Ibid.*, p. ii.

73 Labour Party, *Made in Britain*, p. 3.

74 David Soskice argued this plausible point and came to see the US experience as more relevant to Britain. See D. Goodhart, *The Reshaping of the German Social Market Economy* (London, IPPR, 1994), pp. 73–4.

75 Sainsbury, 'Swedish social democracy in transition', pp. 45–9.

76 M. Linton, *The Swedish Road to Socialism* (London, Fabian Society, tract 503, 1985), p. 20.

77 J. Fulcher, 'The social democratic model in Sweden: termination or restoration?', *Political Quarterly*, 65:2 (1994) 205.

78 J. Clasen and A. Gould, 'Stability and change in welfare states: Germany and Sweden in the 1990s', *Politics and Policy*, 23:3 (1995) 195.

79 B. Burkitt and P. Whyman, 'Public sector reform in Sweden: competition or participation?', *Political Quarterly*, 65: 3 (1994) 276–7.

80 Clasen and Gould 'Stability and change in welfare states', p. 195.

81 K. Ahlen, 'Swedish collective bargaining under pressure: inter-union rivalry and incomes policies', *British Journal of Industrial Relations*, 27:3 (1989) 331.

82 M. Kesselman, 'Lyrical illusions', p. 416

83 S. Lash, 'The end of neo-corporatism: the breakdown of centralised bargaining in Sweden', *British Journal of Industrial Relations*, 23:2 (1985) 218.

84 *Ibid.*, p. 225.

85 K. Ahlen, 'Swedish collective bargaining', p. 338.

6

Warfare on welfare?

The advance of conservative and neo-liberal theories, which began in the English-speaking world in the 1970s, grew stronger in the 1980s. During these decades, as chapter two revealed, the institutions of the corporatist welfare state were variously identified as a source of governmental 'overload' and 'ungovernability'; fiscal crisis; inflation; poor growth rates; sclerotic over-regulation; cultures of dependency; and so on.[1] The conservative right believed that the state could regain its lost authority and capacity to act in countries such as Britain by reducing the claims and responsibilities placed upon it; the neo-liberal right favoured a disengagement of the state from the economy in order to 'set free' markets. For both camps the welfare state had gravely exceeded its utility and become evidence of the swollen power of trade unions, the anti-'enterprise' left and a range of vested interests. In reality, the various institutional arrangements which different European countries had adopted to buttress the welfare state in the 1960s and 1970s – active labour-market policy, 'indicative planning', social partnership, co-determination, social contract and the like – were also adopted to make free enterprise work better. It might be expected that corporatist arrangements were despised by the right to the extent that they had failed to do so, and this was a matter of wide variation between states.

It is also true that in countries such as Britain, Italy, Sweden, France and the Netherlands, rank-and-file trade unionists had become impatient with corporatism themselves since the late 1960s.[2] The push to decentralise wage bargaining was not just evidence of employers' dissatisfaction, though it was often a feature of the broader programme promoted by big business at this time. For example in the Netherlands in the 1970s the Dutch employers' associations complained of a profits squeeze caused by excessive wage demands. As in Britain the growth of unemployment and inflation strengthened the hand of those who wanted a break with the old consensus. In the later 1970s the Wagner Commission, set up by the centre-right government and consisting disproportionately of representatives of the multinationals under the chairmanship of a director of Royal Dutch Shell, demanded a programme of reforms which dominated subsequent policy. It wanted cuts in public spending, decentralised wage bargaining – with a separate policy for the public sector – greater private-sector wage differentiation, more flexible labour markets and changes to the social security system to provide greater incentives to work and greater work discipline. Subsidies to declining industries and regions needed to be phased out, while more money was needed for research and development, education and training.[3] By the end of the 1980s there was a familiar ring about this programme in most countries of Western Europe.

Van der Pijl argues that in effect big capital revolted against the sort of proposals for greater regulation of markets that emanated from social democracy in the 1970s and culminated in the Brandt Report.[4] Faced with a profits squeeze, growing economic uncertainty and demands for incursions against managerial prerogatives, the big employers turned to policies that would restore the sovereignty of capital. It has been argued often enough that the internationalisation of capital ultimately lay behind this programme. By the mid-1980s it was becoming fashionable to talk about 'globalisation', one alleged aspect of which was the growing ability of MNCs to hold government and trade unions to ransom with threats of relocation unless social costs (welfare), wages, taxes and labour markets were to their liking. If the managing director of Aga was right when he said that 'Sweden needs Swedish companies but Swedish companies do not need Sweden',[5] it could be argued that the whole post-war model had been called into question – by the globalisation of production and financial markets, and the spread of information technology and Japanese management techniques.[6] In this view it was no longer necessary for the big employers to recognise trade unions or engage in centralised bargaining where they already existed, or feel any obligation to support the institutions of the post-war social consensus. They now had the big stick and could wield it.

But higher levels of unemployment in the quarter century since the collapse of Bretton Woods would have weakened trade unions anyway, just as slower growth rates and higher inflation would be expected to cause strains in the welfare state, with or without 'globalisation'. If globalisation was at the root of growing inequality, the erosion of welfare states and the development of increasingly exploitative labour markets, small, open economies might be expected to show greater evidence of its ravages over the last quarter century than that of the US – the biggest economy of all and one in which the degree of openness, as measured in the trade to GDP ratio, hardly changed in the years 1980–95 (at 21 per cent). In fact inequality of incomes and wealth, labour-market deregulation and the erosion of welfare have all advanced further in the US than in small, open economies such as Sweden. A possible explanation for this apparent paradox is that these signs of increasingly ruthless exploitation are all the effects of 'a business political mobilisation'[7] – rather than just the impersonal forces of global economic integration – a mobilisation which began in the US as early as the 1970s in response to its flagging performance. This succeeded in returning the state to the ideology of *laissez-faire* in the avowed interest of restoring business competitiveness. US-dominated institutions such as the IMF and World Bank were similarly galvanised to promote nineteenth-century economics during the 1980s. Throughout the 1980s, though free-market 'America' was in many respects as outperformed by 'sclerotic' West Germany and Sweden[8] as Thatcherite Britain, the US decision-making elite pressed on with its project until it created some of the dog-eat-dog conditions attributed to globalisation. The growing internationalisation of capital was real enough but as yet insufficient to merit the idea that growing inequality, poverty and unemployment was simply one of its effects. The global market in which locational and institutional constraints to the free movement of investment capital and firms no longer existed was (and still is) a myth, though some governments found it an increasingly useful rationale for the policies they pursued.

Britain

We have noted that on almost all counts the economic circumstances of the 1970s were worse in Britain than anywhere else in Western Europe and the polarisation of the political parties reflected it. The main employers' organisation, the Confederation of British Industry (CBI), vehemently opposed the proposals for industrial democracy emanating from the Labour Party, was alarmed by the power of the unions and the ambitions of the left, and ascribed the country's economic woes to the corrosive values that they were said to represent. It also complained when the first Thatcher government allowed much of British manufacturing to disappear in the slump of 1979–81. The CBI's influence in government declined somewhat thereafter compared with more passionate advocates of neo-liberal doctrine such as the Institute of Directors. All business organisations in Britain nevertheless 'gave fulsome backing to the Conservatives in the 1983 and 1987 elections',[9] though the City of London was particularly satisfied because it benefited directly from financial deregulation and had always placed economic liberalism and sound money at the centre of its world view. The attack on the post-war consensus was nevertheless spearheaded by the Conservative Party, acting through the state and championing all things to do with 'markets' and 'enterprise' against anything remotely connected to 'socialism', the unions and the welfare state. This revealed the extent to which class conflict does not solely concern the struggle between employers and workers but embraces the budget, the incidence and character of taxation, conflicts over social welfare expenditures and trade union rights, labour-market regulation and much else besides.[10] In this context dramatic confrontations with particular unions were staged in particular industries by 'macho' managers – some of them appointed, all of them encouraged, by the government – and by the end of the 1980s the proportion of the British workforce covered by collective bargaining agreements was whittled down to 47 per cent, and falling.[11] British employers, again following the government's lead, aggressively opposed social legislation emanating from the EU as they sought to protect these gains.

The Thatcher governments did not approve of the 'social dialogue' which Jacques Delors, president of the European Commission, opened in 1985 with the intention of bringing the unions 'on-side' for the project of creating a single European market in 1992.[12] Delors was also concerned to address the issue of 'social dumping' which was of concern to the wealthier member states, and was interested in correcting at least some of the imbalance which the single market project entailed by strengthening capital as against labour. Both factors help to explain why the British government refused to sign up for the Charter of Fundamental Social Rights of Workers which the other eleven member states put their names to in December 1989. This was accompanied by a Social Action Programme containing legally binding measures and an attempt to bring the European Trade Union Confederation (ETUC) and Union of Industrial and Employers' Confederations of Europe (UNICE) into regular bargaining – a situation unfamiliar to both organisations. Progress was made with agreement in October 1991 that the Treaty on European Union should include a procedure for consultation with each of the 'social partners' on the content and direction of EU legislation in the social field. In the absence of Britain agreements were reached on part-time work and parental leave. The adoption of the European Works Directive in September 1994, which required European-wide firms to establish works councils or procedures for employee consultation, also seemed to pave the way for European collective bargaining. But the future purposes of the works councils remain in doubt, given the reluctance of both the unions and the employers to operate at this level. Even if the unions proved able to overcome their national preoccupations they would find coordination extremely difficult given the complexity and opacity of the multinational companies they would have to work within. But this aspect of the Delors project remains significant as evidence of the commitment to consensus-style policies in much of continental Europe and of the extent that Britain had taken a singular divergent path.

Sweden

While the British experienced an 'institutional collapse' in collective bargaining as employers chose 'to opt out of branch level agreements', the move to decentralise bargaining in Scandinavia, by contrast, has been described as 'a controlled and deliberate decision' by certain engineering employers and trade unions to disengage from the peak-level organisations.[13] We saw this was the case in Sweden in chapter five, but also that there was a sharp reaction to social democracy's ambitions of the 1970s.[14] Centralised wage bargaining, in so far as it promoted a narrowing of differentials, was viewed as an aspect of the wider incursions on managerial prerogatives promoted by the LO and the SAP. Esping-Andersen observed that the unions had begun to 'question the continued relevance of indisputable managerial rights to control the labour process'[15] and Olsen explained that the push for legislation in respect of rights at the workplace was a reaction to the SAF's 'persistent resistance to labour's attempts to impinge on its right to manage the workplace via negotiation and collective bargaining'.[16] The SAF was dominated by the major exporters and it was from this quarter that the stiffest resistance to the LO came in the 1970s. The 1977 wage round lasted a record seven months and was accompanied by employer demands for lower taxes and a war against absenteeism.The employers then used the investment funds initiative to mobilise the entire business sector against the labour movement's turn to the left. In the run up to the 1979 election the Meidner Plan was thus subject to an 'ideological barrage from the employers and the bourgeois parties' which some observers judged to be more feverish and sharp than anything witnessed since the 1920s.[17] In 1980 the employers refused to negotiate with the LO and replied with a lockout of almost all manufacturing employees when strike action was threatened. Though the SAF backed down after one week, its president declared that it had just made an 'investment in the future'.[18] The employers saw the investment funds as 'a semi-revolutionary attack on the market economy, a plan to confiscate their profits and to use the money to buy away their ownership and give it over to the trade unions'.[19]

By 1980 they had taken over responsibility from the bourgeois parties to prevent the return of an SAP government. During the 1982 election Swedish business spent almost as much on propaganda against the wage-earner funds as the five largest parties spent altogether.[20] In 1983 the employers organised a demonstration in Stockholm in which 75-100,000 people made known their opposition to the funds. Subsequent demonstrations and rallies broadened the opposition to include attacks on centralised wage bargaining, the solidaristic wage policy and the generosity and scope of the welfare state. Throughout the 1980s the SAF kept up its campaign for decentralised pay bargaining. The Swedish Metal Trades Employers' Association led the way and the cry of 'flexibility' was in the air. The slogan 'Wages – A Tool For Management' expresses something of their motivation.[21]

Germany

The SAP and LO were left to do what they could with the remnants of the centralised system of wage bargaining after the exit of the big employers and some of the biggest trade unions. In Spain, Ireland, Finland and to some extent Greece and Portugal, corporatist strategies survived the 1980s. In Germany and Italy, employers' organisations actually enhanced their importance in bargaining with the trade unions. The West German employers organised in the BDA (80 per cent of firms) were of course one of the pillars of the social market economy. Membership of the DGB unions was also slightly higher at the end of the 1980s than at the beginning and the initial effect of reunification increased the total further. Nevertheless, within the right-wing coalition formed in 1982 the Free Democratic Party persisted in calling for greater deregulation of the economy even as the share of employee incomes in total national income fell from 70 per cent in 1981 to 62 per cent in 1990, reflecting a surge in profits.[22] The BDA had already flexed its muscles by describing the SPD's 1980 election manifesto as 'a threat to the market economy' and targeted the proposals to extend co-determination as 'anti-democratic and unconstitutional'. Relations deteriorated thereafter, even though the proposals were duly watered down. Some observers reported that the BDA looked on enviously at the Reagan administration's policies as it demanded reform of welfare at home to reduce indirect labour costs.[23] Van der Wurff notes that business supported the neo-liberal elements in the Kohl coalition, but the dominance by those sections of industry which were successful in the 1980s, such as capital goods manufacturers, perhaps explains why gradual adaptations of the *status quo* sufficed and there was no stampede for the dismantling of the post-war order.[24] In this context the old, relatively consensual, institutionalised relations between labour and capital largely survived the decade intact. Collective bargaining covering whole industries in specific regions remained the norm, though as Thelen points out the discourse of 'flexibility' was a constant on the employers' side from the mid-1980s and entered into discussions over reduced working time.[25]

The Kohl government established an official commission on deregulation which reported in 1991 and proposed that the legal status of collective agreements should be weakened. Though this came to nothing, the costs of reunification, including higher taxes and mass unemployment, fuelled the debate about social benefits, indirect labour costs, labour law and the even the role of the works council system. Lecher and Naumann note that deregulatory proposals emanating from the Kohl government 'were immediately incorporated into the employers' bargaining agenda'.[26] As the reunified economy slowed down in the late 1990s, amid high unemployment, the Germans heard more and more about 'globalisation' and the necessity of change (that is, more inequality, more deregulation and less welfare) from the employers' organisation. When the metalworkers' union IG Metall negotiated a wage rise above the rate of inflation in 1994 and a cut in hours from thirty-six to thirty-five several employers quit the *Gesamtmetall* employers' federation claiming that the price of industrial peace was too high and had become 'untenable'. The bargaining system was blamed for everything from short hours and high wages to high absenteeism. Some of the bigger firms such as Daimler-Benz and Pirelli-Spa and including the three largest chemical companies – Hoechst, Bayer and BASF – made threats of relocation and disinvestment, shortly after announcing record profits.[27] While a prominent British supporter of the 'Rhineland model' could accurately report at the end of 1998 that Germany's export performance was at record levels, that it had reduced unit labour costs more than any other industrialised country in the 1990s and that it had no shortage of inward investment, it was also observed that the German trade unions, so long the shining model of 'restraint', had become 'the bete-noire of the international financial press', along with its allegedly sclerotic Handwerk system, ludicrously generous welfare entitlements and the rest.[28]

France

Pressures for the decentralisation of wage bargaining, falling trade union membership and various arrangements to bypass collective bargaining were also visible in France in the 1980s. The objectives of neo-liberalism were championed by the right-wing monthly *Les Quartes Verites* from 1973, whose main themes stressed the vital role of the company in generating economic dynamism and the menace it faced from union power and the Common Programme of the left.[29] One of its founders, Yvon Gattaz, became president of the dominant employers' organisation, CNPF, at the end of 1981. Patriarchal employers who regarded unions as the enemy were already well represented in French business, of course, but an aggressive neo-liberalism came to characterise the outpourings of the CNPF from the moment the Socialist government first entered office.[30] The CNPF argued for the greatest decentralisation of pay bargaining that was possible and was assisted in some ways by the Socialist Aurox laws of 1982 which made collective negotiation over terms of employment obligatory in firms. The reforms also boosted the number of company agreements and further reduced industry-wide bargaining. Meanwhile, the unions had lost members since the economic crisis of the mid-1970s and only represented about 10 per cent of the workforce by 1999 – these being divided between six national confederations. Unlike the British case, however, the state had actually increased its protection of workers as in the 1989 national employment plan of the Rocard administration, the initiative on working time cuts introduced in 1993, and the Jospin legislation for the thirty-five-hour week in 1997. French employers had also given broad support to the European Social Charter, unlike their British counterparts.

Welfare under attack

The broader context for much of the period since 1973 has been one of budgetary constraint – for all the reasons that we have already discussed – and welfare states have been subjected to a certain amount of erosion by means of cuts in benefits, stricter principles of eligibility, means testing, marketisation of services, and so on. The welfare states in question are of various types[31] and degrees of generosity and have responded differently to economic and social change. But the social democratic ideal can be applied to all of them and was probably best expressed by T. H. Marshall in 1950. He conceptualised the modern welfare state as the culmination of a centuries-old struggle for citizenship rights, which had passed from the beginnings of legal and civil rights in the eighteenth century, to the nineteenth-century struggle for political rights and on to the acquisition of rights of social citizenship in the twentieth century.[32] The return of persistent mass unemployment is one of the principal reasons why this ideal was put under strain, but it is not the only problem and it should be remembered that the countries of Western Europe were 50 per cent richer in real terms by 1999 than they were when the talk of welfare state crisis first began in the early 1970s. Welfare states are certainly in need of modernisation to keep up with changes in family structure and the new demands placed upon them. The combination of lower fertility rates and longer life expectancy in particular can increase the fiscal burden on the working population and increase the pension bill. No doubt there are complex political problems attached to the required modernisation.

But none of this adds up to crisis. The OECD calculated that the extra pension costs implied by an ageing population could be met by modest growth rates of 0.5 to 1.2 per cent and some states – such as Sweden and Germany – have already pushed back the retirement age and taken other steps to increase the proportion of economically active people of working age – principally by encouraging female employment.[33] The atmosphere of crisis owes more to the efforts of the right to identify the welfare state as one of the blockages on economic dynamism in Western Europe, as compared with areas of the world economy such as the US, which created more jobs in the period 1992–99. Typically, the *Economist* solemnly warned in June 1999 that in the light of this divergent performance – and overlooking the contradictory evidence of the twenty years before 1992 – 'it is still more vital that Germany, along with most of Europe, attacks the high taxes, over-generous welfare benefits, onerous labour-market restrictions and red tape that are choking growth in output and jobs'.[34] Once again the conservative ideological preferences of the hour acquired authority from the fashionable 'globalisation' thesis, variants of which supposed that capital would flow to economies with free-market characteristics of the sort preferred by the *Economist* and that the higher growth rates associated for a time with some of the small nations of South and South East Asia had something to do with their lower social policy 'costs'. While academic analysts disputed every aspect of the globalisation thesis,[35] there is no doubt that by the mid-1990s many of the opinion formers in Western Europe – employers' organisations, finance 'experts', leading journalists and the like – believed that the American 'model' of capitalism was the one that was best prepared for the future. Economic problems were thus increasingly attributed to the alleged defects of other 'models' – Swedish, German, Japanese, French and so on.

It is interesting to note that the internationalisation of capital had not led to the convergence of welfare states in the period with which we are concerned, let alone their dismantling, which is no doubt why the *Economist* believed there was still so much to be done in 1999, nearly thirty years after the crisis of the welfare state was first announced. The EU average for spending on social protection grew from 24 to 26 per cent of GDP between 1980 and 1991 as rising unemployment and ageing populations forced expenditure to rise despite cutbacks in provision.[36] The erosion of pensions, unemployment and care payments across the EU states ensured that cash payments were 'getting meaner and their conditions harder to fulfil'.[37] But, as Esping-Andersen reported in 1996, with the exceptions of Britain and New Zealand, 'the degree of welfare state roll-back ... has so far been modest'; other experts concurred with this view, believing that the fundamentals of most welfare systems remained unchanged by the late 1990s.[38] According to Daly, 'Only in the United Kingdom and the Netherlands could far-reaching structural changes be said to have taken place, with the virtual "privatization" of pensions in the former and the alteration of the principle of entitlement (largely to give women an equal right) in the latter'.[39] Indeed, the UK was alone in Western Europe in experiencing 'a radical regime shift' in welfare as the government adopted a deliberate policy of deregulation and 'marketisation' which, as Esping-Andersen astutely pointed out, was intended to 'manage economic decline' by reducing the social wage, weakening the unions and obtaining greater labour and wage flexibility with the assistance of mass unemployment.[40]

This had been achieved by numerous measures such as the elimination of the earnings-related element in national insurance, the abolition of grants to the poorest for necessities, the abolition of income support to sixteen to eighteen-year-olds, the rolling together of social assistance and social insurance for the unemployed into a new Job Seeker's Allowance, under which claimants had to prove that they were genuinely seeking work and so on. Accompanying these measures and others like them was the constant refrain that welfare payments *created* the 'underclass' that survived on them. Alongside this rhetoric a 'communitarian' lament became fashionable which argued that the decay of the social fabric derived from poor parenting, inadequate education systems and the weakening of 'community' – this latter translating into the policy that parents and teachers must pick up the pieces. Labour-inclined 'think tanks' soon adopted the language of 'dependency' and the 'problem family', while Labour social policy experts wanted 'zero tolerance' of beggars and the undeserving poor.[41]

It was noted in chapter five that the success of this policy was reflected in growing inequality such that the lowest-decile earners lost ground, relative to the median, by 14 per cent in the course of the 1980s. In 1995 the social policy expert Peter Townsend, using government-compiled statistics, showed that

> between 1979 and the early 1990s the richest 20 per cent improved their share of disposable income from 36 per cent to 43 per cent. The poorest 20 per cent experienced a fall in their share from 10 per cent to 6 per cent. Had the percentages stayed the same the richest 20 per cent would be £35 billion or £6,000 per household worse off than they now are. The poorest 20 per cent would be £17 billion or £3,000 per household better off than they now are.[42]

Yet the occasion for these observations was the publication of the Labour Party's Commission on Social Justice report in November 1994 which, in Townsend's words, 'appeared to have been governed by the belief that to win the next election the Labour party must bow to the pressures of the international market, reduce long-standing aspirations to social equality and withdraw from the most costly commitments to the welfare state'.[43] Social democratic values and principles were brushed aside in this document in the interests of a 'realism' which worried about 'tax-and-spend' policies that would drive the rich abroad and inflate the social security budget, while ignoring completely the structures of inequality that had deepened during the previous fifteen years. While the report dismissed Beveridgean principles of universality and pointed to more means testing in the future, it paid no attention to evidence from the Annual Survey of Social Attitudes that the British public favoured improved benefits and would support the higher taxes required to finance them.[44]

New Labour

Under Tony Blair's leadership, after 1994, Labour's 'realism' retained these dual characteristics of looking for further economies in welfare expenditures while attaching no significance to evidence of popular support for improved universal benefits. Yet by 1994 one of the most distinctive aspects of the British welfare system was its punitive meanness. Britain was near to the bottom of the EU league in the percentage of its national income spent on social protection, and social security spending was growing only very slowly when New Labour formed a government in May 1997. By this time the party had renounced income redistribution via the tax system and accepted the former government's spending limits. It was nevertheless one of New Labour's main objectives to modernise the welfare state. In January 1997 Blair identified the 'underclass' as 'the single biggest threat to social stability in western democracies', but his government announced from its inception that Britain 'had reached the limits of the public's willingness simply to fund an unreformed welfare system'.[45] Not surprisingly modernisation and cost-cutting were conflated from the outset, even though the government actuary himself denied that there was a major problem with rising welfare costs.[46] Tony Blair launched the crusade by declaring at the 1997 Labour conference – in language reminiscent of the Victorian Charity Organisation Society – that 'the new welfare state must encourage work, not dependency'. He then proceeded to highlight the spiralling cost of the social security bill which was variously denominated as taking £80 per household per week, or three times the education budget or twice the cost of the NHS. All this implied the urgent need for cuts rather than a modernisation of the system to take account of changing patterns of living.

Two groups almost immediately identified as problems were single parents and the disabled. The former – 1.4 million of them – were said to be under greater obligation to retrain and look for work in return for the benefits they received. Indeed, a form of 'workfare' borrowed from American precedent was said to be needed to break the 'dependency culture' allegedly fostered by the benefits system. In July 1997 the Labour government announced that it would end the One Parent Allowance, worth £6.30 per week, and abolish the higher child benefit for new claimants. By October the minister responsible, Harriet Harman, announced that 400 lone parents had found jobs in 'welfare-to-work' pilot schemes, an estimated 1 per cent of the women covered by the scheme.[47] In December the same minister refused to rule out means testing of disabled people in an attempt to distinguish between the deserving and undeserving among them. This was subsequently revealed as involving a new test of employability, compulsory job interviews, new tests for the disability living allowance and attendance allowance and means testing for incapacity benefit. The plan was to cut the number of claimants, which was running at 1.5 million by 1998.

The number of claimants on incapacity benefit had undoubtedly increased in the 1980s and 1990s as the Conservative governments removed people from the unemployment register by reclassifying them as disabled. But the number also rose because compared with unemployment benefit, incapacity benefit was relatively generous. It thus became the object of New Labour's cost-cutting attention and in the spring of 1999 legislation was introduced to means test unemployed claimants and all those in receipt of more than £50 per week from an occupational pension. This was expected to 'save' £750 million and make more money available for the 'genuinely disabled'. Most of the money would in fact be lost to the social security budget and to the poorer households of the country. Also notable was the government's lack of interest in fighting for the social insurance principle, according to which benefits are claimed as a right by citizens who pay into a national insurance fund. Instead of tightening the rules of eligibility to deter the abuse of the existing system, the measures introduced cleared the way for a new layer of claimants to be branded as dependants on the state who must be rigorously means tested and weeded of the feckless. All this was in accordance with a diagnosis – 'welfare dependency' – which British socialists first took issue with in the 1880s.

The Labour government's welfare reforms during its first two years also included modest amounts of extra cash for child benefit, health and education; a Working Families Tax Credit for the low paid; privatisation of the Benefits Agency medical service and plans to sell off the entire property estate of the Department of Social Security; and part-privatisation of hospitals through the operation of the Private Finance Initiative, which would finance their construction. In line with European-wide developments to encourage female employment, Labour also made money available to cover a proportion of the costs of childcare for low-income families. When a minimum wage was introduced Labour fixed it at £3.60 an hour but insisted that twenty-one-year-olds and younger would only receive £3. The law was also notably weak in the measures adopted for the enforcement of the minimum wage in the 2 million workplaces affected by it. Employers were not required to inform employees of their minimum wage rights on their pay slips. Only 115 inspectors were appointed to patrol the system and companies found to be in breach of the law could only be fined a maximum of £5,000. All this was in sharp contrast to the ruthless package of measures contained in the Asylum Bill in 1999 designed to deter refugees. Here severity and policing were reminiscent of the workhouse. Yet when the Labour government brought Britain into alignment with the rest of the EU over paternity leave it did so in a way that maximised the red tape and minimised the chances of take-up, by determining that the leave would be unpaid if it could be obtained at all. Critics complained, unsurprisingly, of the reform programme's lack of coherence; for the centre-left *Observer* it appeared that

> The Government does not know whether it is cutting spending because the social security budget is too high, because it wants to end the 'dependency culture', because it wants to reframe the great compromise between capital and labour that the welfare state represents, or because the system of social insurance needs modernising in order to protect it.[48]

But if there was any pattern in Labour's policies it was surely about increasing the supply of low-paid workers – a policy eminently compatible with means testing, cuts in benefits, subsidised childcare, and the rest of the package introduced in the government's first two years.

Western European experience

The discourse of welfare reform has invoked the need for competitiveness and flexibility throughout Western Europe, though no social democratic party has embraced individualism to the extent of New Labour. In Denmark there had been a slight shift to 'workfare' in the 1990s in the form of new requirements that claimants maintain job seeking activities and receive training in return for benefits. In 1996 it was decided that benefits could be withdrawn if job offers were refused. Measures were already in place to provide counselling on work, subsidised job training, employment projects and further education.[49] So far, so Blairite. But benefit levels were much higher than in Britain and the period of eligibility for unemployment benefit was all of five years. New rights had been added in the 1990s, such as paid childcare leave and allowances for carers. The much-trumpeted tax revolt of 1973 was short lived and did not continue into the 1980s.[50] The same is true in Norway where the period of eligibility for unemployment benefit was increased from forty to eighty weeks in the mid-1980s and the qualifying conditions were liberalised in 1990.[51] Child allowances have also been made more generous and maternity leave lengthened to twelve months with full pay for the first forty-two weeks and 80 per cent replacement for the whole period. While Norway weathered the 1980s with the aid of its oil and gas resources, Germany did so on the basis of its status as Europe's strongest economy. Changes to its welfare system were thus not very extensive and by comparative standards it remained a big spender enjoying strong popular support for state provision.[52]

In the late 1980s the Kohl government introduced new parental leave allowances and improved pension entitlements for women, while the *Länder* improved social assistance benefits. Commitments after reunfication raised social expenditures to record levels by 1994 as the social security system was extended to the former East Germany where unemployment affected two-fifths of the workforce (4 million people). As the recession of the early 1990s also affected the rest of the country, extensive cuts in social benefits were introduced in 1994 across the board, but especially affecting the poorest, including the swollen ranks of the refugees and asylum seekers. The Germans remained strongly committed to their relatively generous public social insurance schemes, however, and these were even extended in 1994 to cover the care of the elderly and disabled. Pension rights for women were also improved and extended to carers in 1992. At the same time the tough monetary policy of the *Bundesbank*, which also enjoys popular support, combined with the enormous costs of reunification has ensured that economies in social spending have remained on the political agenda throughout the 1990s, just as they did for the Schmidt and Kohl governments when faced with economic difficulties in the late 1970s and early 1980s. Mass unemployment in the 1990s also gave credence, as we have noted, to the argument that the German economy suffered from various disabilities in the face of 'globalisation', especially insufficient job creation which neo-liberals attribute to high taxes, high wages and generous welfare entitlements. There was also pressure to adapt the welfare policy menu to address the low fertility rate – which is a bigger problem in

Germany than ageing – and the growth of poverty in lone-parent households. Reform remains a subject of debate but has not yet altered the system.

Sweden had been held up as evidence of the irreversible nature of the welfare state as recently as the mid-1980s, a polity in which social democracy had become 'the highest form of capitalism'.[53] By the end of the decade its public sector employed more than one-third of the workforce and disposed of 60 per cent of GDP. In former times the SAP had increased its natural constituency, it was argued, by promoting universal welfare rights, extending employee rights and increasing the number of state employees, from among whom a large proportion of its white-collar supporters were drawn. In Sweden, moreover, transfer payments constituted a smaller proportion of public expenditure than in neighbouring states, such as Denmark, where the public believed that the state expended too much of taxpayers' money as early as 1970. The Swedish social democrats, by contrast, required the employers to pay some of these costs – 38 per cent of old-age pension contributions for example – while being much more actively engaged themselves in the promotion of investment, work retraining programmes and the dynamic sectors of the economy generally.[54] The social democrats were thus long associated with economic health and modernisation. Expansion of the state sector in the 1980s seemed to show this once again as the SAP kept unemployment around 2 per cent while the economy grew at an average of 2.7 per cent between 1983 and 1988 and the balance of trade deficit bequeathed by the bourgeois coalition of 1976–82 was turned into a surplus. Important new steps were taken to facilitate rising female employment, not least in the welfare sector itself. The SAP also won three consecutive election victories after 1982 and managed to retain 70 per cent of the working-class vote as trade union membership rose to new heights.[55]

Swedish inflation rates however became a major problem, Swedish wage costs had risen by 76.5 per cent in the years 1982–89 compared with a rise of 64.9 per cent in Britain and 36.6 per cent in Germany, and the balance of payments returned to deficit despite repeated devaluations.[56] The social democrats now consciously deflated the economy and relations with the LO deteriorated in the context of austerity measures, wage freeze and strike bans. Unemployment climbed steeply to 12.5 per cent under the four-party bourgeois government returned in 1991 as the deflationary turn of public policy was maintained. By 1994, 11 per cent of the workforce was still unemployed, with a further 4 per cent on various labour-market schemes and a rising proportion of people in receipt of social assistance. Public debate continued to focus on the high levels of taxation, the size of the public sector, the legacy of corporatist institutions and the unrealistic expectations allegedly derived from them, the abuse of the benefit system, and the damage to the work ethic and productive investment entailed by the welfare system. The bourgeois government demanded a system shift based on privatisation and marketisation of welfare, but lacked the *Riksdag* majority to see through such a transformation. Pressure for radical change was nevertheless sustained by the big employers and the right generally with complaints about the numbers on sickness and disability benefits, the parasitical nature of the state sector, the growth of single-parent households and the proportion of the population on retirement pensions.[57]

The centre-right government's public expenditure cuts on welfare in the years 1991–94 were not as radical as its rhetoric. The social insurance system no longer averaged a 90 per cent replacement income for sickness benefit, parental benefit, unemployment benefit and disability pension; it was reduced to 80 per cent, with talk of further reducing it to 70 per cent. Eligibility rules became more stringent; the system of voluntary unemployment insurance administered by the unions to their members was replaced by an obligatory system in which employees, as well as employers, made contributions; state pensions have been reduced in value and made more actuarially sound; schools, nurseries and home help services have lost staff; private agencies have been encouraged. The effect of all this on the scale of public expenditure was negligible in 1991–94, partly because entrenched interests fought their corner in the *Riksdag* and partly because the coalition was divided – notably in the person of the minister for health, Bengt Westerberg, leader of the Liberal Party, who refused to embrace the culture of cutbacks and actually introduced a disability law giving the disabled the right to a personal assistant. But most important was the obstruction of Swedish political culture which, with no tradition of hostility to the state, showed little evidence of turning against state expenditure in repeated opinion polls conducted between 1986 to 1992, despite the crisis talk of the right.[58] The Social Democrats actually regained the support of the working class in 1994 and together with the other left parties the SAP enjoyed its best result for over two decades, while the bourgeois parties suffered their worst.

Nevertheless the terms of debate undoubtedly changed. The Social Democrats accepted the need for further public expenditure cuts to deal with the budget deficit (12 per cent of GDP in 1993) and the national debt (80 per cent of GDP). A significant section of the electorate (5 per cent in 1994) supported the Green Party and the country was divided by the referendum on membership of the EU in November 1994 (52 per cent for, 47 per cent against). The turn of the big engineering employers and the *Metall* workers' union against centralised wage negotiations, combined with the rise in unemployment, effectively destroyed the Rehn-Meidner strategy for wage egalitarianism, full employment and stable prices. Fundamentally, the alliance between blue-collar and white-collar employees over welfare issues was also jeopardised by divisions according to gender, life chances and the public/private cleavage. 'Whereas support for the welfare state has diminished among the private-sector employees in general, the public-sector working class and specifically public white-collar groups have come increasingly to favor state welfare programs.'[59] Private-sector workers worry about their jobs, it may be argued, precisely because right-wing propaganda links the future of these jobs to levels of taxation and social costs. Public-sector workers, especially the lower white-collar workers in the welfare state system, and women of all occupational strata, support the public sector more strongly than men.[60]

Kitschelt's explanation of the Swedish social democrat's predicament is worth examining because of its general applicability and the fact that it echoes a number of conventional wisdoms. It invokes three factors. First, he asserts that 'increasing internationalization of capital flows has undermined ... domestic policy autonomy and thus reduced the beneficial effects of corporatist social democratic policy strategies'. Second, he perceives a

> transformation of the social and occupational structure, resulting in a large tertiary sector of personal and financial services, a highly educated labor force, and an increased proportion of public sector employees [which] has given rise to quality of life, postmaterialist, or libertarian demands for individual autonomy and collective participatory governance beyond the institutions of market and state.[61]

The third element in his argument proposes that it is how social democratic parties react to these environmental changes that determines their fate – this reaction being dependent on the behaviour of competitors in the party system and the internal organisation of the Social Democratic Party itself. Kitschelt judged that the SAP – faced with left competitors such as the greens, feminists, and former Communists – was sluggish in adapting to the new political agenda which they represented in the 1980s, just as it was slow to appreciate that the old Keynesian-corporatist prescriptions were obsolete. He nevertheless found plenty of Social Democrats who showed 'a keen sense that close party-union linkages [were] no longer strategic assets, but liabilities'.[62] Collective affiliation of the unions to the SAP was in any case ended in 1990 by mutual agreement, but Kitschelt's argument clearly implied that the SAP's survival as a major force depended on acquiring freedom of manoeuvre to jettison all those elements of the old ideology and organisation which stood in the way of the necessary mix of post-materialist and liberal market policies.

Kitschelt assumed, rather than demonstrated, that globalisation must lead to loss of policy autonomy together with an unspecified degree of convergence around liberal economic policies. There is no recognition in his argument of the dysfunctions of globalisation in those areas where it really exists – notably in the speculative financial sector – and the scope for new forms of state intervention which these problems may provoke. Kitschelt also overlooks the fact that Sweden has always been an open economy since the Second World War and that recent years have not witnessed a marked increase in the extent of its trade dependence. The SAP did, however, contribute to its own difficulties by phasing in financial deregulation in the 1980s and aggravating the estrangement of the unions with such 'third way' policies as the squeeze on wages to the benefit of profits and tax concessions for the corporate rich. This does not mean, however, that the social democrats have lost their distinctive policy bias in the countries where they have traditionally been strong such as in Scandinavia and Northern Europe, or that they are losing electoral support in such countries.[63]

Kitschelt also assumes that the old social democratic values cannot be reconciled with those of the new social movements. Yet in Sweden no political party has done more for the cause of women's equality than the SAP. In the 1980s women's employment grew rapidly, some of the largest public-sector unions acquired more female members than men, and the SAP facilitated these changes not only through expansion of the public sector, but by virtue of policies such as parental leave and expansion of public childcare centres which the party had supported since the late 1960s. The SAP and LO did not change as fast as feminists within their own ranks demanded, but the feminisation of the SAP could be seen in the growing proportion of its female MPs as well as in the changing composition of the party's voters, a majority of whom were women by 1985. It could also be seen in the SAP's declared determination to improve the quality of work in the feminised social services sector – a policy commitment taken up in the late 1990s. In chapter four we showed that the SAP renewed its programme in 1990 – as it has done at intervals throughout its history – and that it involved reassertion of traditional social democratic values and a stronger commitment to environmentalist and feminist policies. The achievement of a classless society remained the SAP's principal aim and the public sector figured in the programme as its main instrument. Sainsbury notes that when the party drafted the new manifesto it considered arguments stressing non-class cleavages in society and the emergence of post-materialist values, but concluded that new divisions, such as those based on knowledge and education, ran alongside and actually reinforced the materialist divisions of old.[64] Nevertheless, the SAP also placed environmental progress on a par with the achievement of full employment and, introducing the idea of a 'green GDP', insisted that ecological requirements would inform all areas of policy.

It is not fanciful to imagine that a mix of social democratic, feminist and green policies will appear both realistic and necessary to wide sections of society in the future, including sections of the employers, but it is not going to happen automatically. It will be a matter of political contestation as to how policy is renewed and shaped, but there is no reason to believe that the odds are weighed in favour of the right, especially in countries with a strong social democratic tradition. If there is any position which affords a clear view of the future it is not that of fractional, competitive and speculative capital. This is a factor making for uncertainty, generalised risk and insecurity. It is more likely to be public authorities at local, national and transnational levels that will be expected to respond to problems of social and economic insecurity with appropriate policies – which was why people turned to social democracy in the first place, of course. In Britain, however, where the liberal-capitalist ideology is now embraced by all three major parties, it will be necessary to first of all find a social democratic alternative.

Delors

Before concluding this chapter we should briefly consider the Delors strategy for the creation of jobs and social security in the whole of Western Europe – a strategy which one writer described as 'the most elaborate proposal for a new left-of-centre vision we have yet seen'.[65] According to Ross 'its fundamental mark' was its Europeanism, advocated 'in response to the dramatic devaluation of national policy tools by globalisation'. Delors conceded many of the arguments made about the need for greater flexibility and competitiveness but combined them with a desire to defend what he called 'the European model of society' – a model that valued solidarity and cohesion. These qualities might be defended on many ground, including the economic, against those who stressed the advantages of low wages and low social costs.[66] Although the basic prerequisite for the Delors strategy was conceived as an open integrated European market – the policy for which the British Conservatives signed up – Delors saw that such an economy would need organisation, regulation, and unified policies, including common social policies. Economic integration would also make certain socially desirable policies possible – monetary union, for example, would help in the fight against speculative financial markets and enable governments to retrieve lost powers to spend and invest without the constant fear of reprisal from the markets. A vigorous regional policy – which the poorer EU states insisted upon – would be needed to make integration work and to facilitate the process with infrastructural and environmental projects, vocational training and the like. From 1991 the Delors team expanded the original project to encompass a so-called 'Keynes-Plus' European recovery programme aimed at generating 15 million jobs by reflation, the restructuring of firms, industries and regions and a variety of schemes for reducing working hours and closing inequalities. Among those enthusiastically behind this project were individuals such as Ken Coates MEP and Stuart Holland, architects of the Labour Party's old Alternative Economic Strategy.[67]

Working against this scheme from the outset were all those governments committed to the anti-growth bias of monetary policy in the late 1980s and early 1990s which was compounded, of course, by the strict convergence criteria for monetary union adopted at Maastricht. Those who argued that items of social expenditure should be exempt from these constraints were ignored. Their hopes that the European Investment Fund, adopted at the

Edinburgh summit in December 1992, would prove to be an instrument of Keynesian expenditure policies were likewise dashed. The European Council nevertheless approved various infrastructural schemes in October 1993, but the plans for work sharing got no further than the Brussels summit which met that December. The Council of Ministers proceeded to block the plan to create 15 million jobs – too many of the governments concerned were worried about budget deficits or just ideologically opposed to such thinking. Large majorities in favour of the Delors Plan in the European Parliament, recorded in 1994 and 1995, counted for nothing. Finally, at Florence in June 1996 the Council even failed to agree on the financing of trans-European transport and communications networks. With the election of the Socialist government in France headed by Lionel Jospin in 1997 there was hope that the Delors agenda might be reopened. There was certainly talk to this effect and the balance of forces inside the EU was changing in favour of centre-left governments. By the beginning of 1999 thirteen of the fifteen EU governments contained social democrats[68] and the issue of job creation was the subject of much rhetoric.

Whether it would result in concerted action of the sort Delors envisaged was another matter. Job creation by this time was increasingly identified as the work of markets and supply-side policies such as training schemes. The shift was most conspicuous in the case of the British Labour Party. In the 1980s its leading members had called for a common manifesto of European socialist parties in recognition of the fact that the only viable reflation was one that was European-wide.[69] Admittedly, none of the party's Front Bench campaigned for such a reflation and the party's European policy evolved by the end of the decade into a demand for British membership of the Exchange Rate Mechanism, partly on the grounds of securing Labour's credibility 'as a party of fiscal and monetary rectitude' – something that would have been hard to square with support for the Delors Plan.[70] The discovery of 'globalisation' around 1992–93 also led leading party figures such as Gordon Brown to discard Keynesianism, though this did not stop the party from giving support to the Delors initiative in such documents as *Labour's Budget for Jobs* and *Labour's Economic Approach*, as well as in its submission to the Delors commission in November 1993.[71] The party's private opinion polling, however, seem to have frightened it off and no mention of the Delors Plan was made in its 1994 European election campaign. This did not prevent Tony Blair calling for active support of the Delors initiative in a speech in Brussels in January 1995, and the idea of a counter-cyclical spending programme on a European-wide basis surfaced in *A New Economic Future for Britain*, which Labour produced in the summer of that year.[72] One of Labour's most active supporters of the Delors Plan, however, was already aware that the advent of Tony Blair had signalled a change of attitude on this as on so much else and complained about the new frigidity of New Labour towards a European Keynesianism.[73] Certainly the draft manifesto of 1996, *New Labour; New Life*, contained no reference of this sort and by the time Jospin was elected the New Labour government wanted nothing to do with his talk of a 'Delors-Plus' programme. After all of its vacillations New Labour had apparently decided to go with the grain of the post-Thatcher UK economy. Its focus groups taught, furthermore, that a Eurosceptic electorate would punish promotion of big schemes emanating from Brussels.

Notes

1 See C. Offe, *Contradictions of the Welfare State* (London, Hutchinson, 1984), pp. 65–87.

2 C. Crouch, 'The fate of articulated industrial relations systems', in M. Regini (ed.), *The Future of Labour Movements* (London, Sage, 1992), p. 172.

3 S. B. Wolinetz, 'Socio-economic bargaining in the Netherlands: redefining the post-war policy coalition', *West European Politics*, 1 (1989) 90–8.

4 He gives examples such as the 1975 ECOSOC Eminent Persons' Report and the ICTUs proposal for the regulation of multinationals. K. Van der Pijl, 'The sovereignty of capital impaired: social forces and codes of conduct for multinational corporations', in H. Overbeek (ed.), *Restructuring Hegemony in the Global Political Economy: The Rise of Transnational Neo-Liberalism in the 1980s* (London, Routledge, 1993), pp. 28–49.

5 Quoted in M. Rhodes, 'Globalisation and West European welfare states: a critical review of recent debates', *Journal of European Social Policy*, 6:4 (1996) 312.

6 J. Visser, 'Traditions and transitions in industrial relations: a European view', in J. V. Ruysseveldt (ed.), *Industrial Relations in Europe: Traditions and Transitions* (London, Sage, 1996), p. 31.

7 F. Fox Piven, 'Is it global economics or neo-laissez-faire?', *New Left Review*, 213 (1995) 111.

8 The *Economist*, no friend of the left, opined in 1987 (7 March) that 'Sweden is an economic paradox. It has the biggest public sector of any industrial economy, the highest taxes, the most generous welfare state, the narrowest wage differentials, and powerful trade unions. According to prevailing economic wisdom, it ought to be suffering from an acute bout of "Eurosclerosis", with rigid labour markets and arthritic industry. Instead, Sweden has many large and vigorous companies and one of the lowest unemployment rates in Europe'.

9 A. Gamble, *Free Economy and Strong State* (London, Macmillan, 1988), p. 190.

10 This does not mean that the 'leader' had all this worked out in advance. See H. Young, *The Iron Lady: A Biography of Margaret Thatcher* (New York, Noonday Press, 1989), pp. 96–7.

11 By 1999 the figure stood at around 36 per cent nationally, but only 22 per cent in the south east outside London.

12 See C. Grant, *Delors: The House that Jacques Built* (London, Nicholas Brealey, 1994) and P. Teague, *The European Community: The Social Dimension* (London, Kogan Page, 1989).

13 C. Crouch, 'The fate of articulated industrial relations systems', pp. 180–1.

14 R. Scase, *Social Democracy in a Capitalist Society* (London, Croom Helm, 1977), p. 166.

15 G. Esping-Andersen, *Politics Against Markets* (Princeton, NJ, Princeton University Press, 1985), p. 295

16 G. M. Olsen, *The Struggle for Economic Democracy in Sweden* (London, Avebury, 1992), p. 26.

17 Esping-Andersen, *Politics Against Markets*, pp. 114, 299. This is also Swenson's view in *Fair Shares: Union Pay and Politics in Sweden and West Germany* (Ithaca, NY, Cornell University Press, 1989), p. 139.

18 G. Rehn and B. Viklund, 'Changes in the Swedish model', in G. Baglioni and C. Crouch (eds), *European Industrial Relations: The Challenge of Flexibility* (London, Sage, 1991), pp. 300–1.

19 G. Rehn and B. Viklund, 'Changes in the Swedish model', p. 308.

20 G. M. Olsen, *The Struggle For Economic Democracy in Sweden*, p. 82.

21 K. Amark, 'Afterword: Swedish social democracy on a historical threshold', in K. Misgeld, K. Molin and K. Amark (eds), *Creating Social Democracy – A Century of the Social Democratic Party in Sweden* (Philadelphia, PA, Penn State University Press, 1993), p. 90. See also G. Baglioni, 'Industrial relations in Europe in the 1980s', in Baglioni and Crouch (eds), *European Industrial Relations*, pp. 22–4.

22 W. Lecher (ed.), *Trade Unions in the European Union* (London, Lawrence and Wishart, 1994), p. 21.

23 J. A. Helm, 'Codetermination in West Germany', *West European Politics*, 1 (1986) 34; D. Webber, 'Combatting and acquiescing in unemployment? Crisis management in Sweden and West Germany', *West European Politics*, 1 (1983) 70, 75.

24 R. van der Wurff, 'Neo-Liberalism in Germany?', in Overbeek (ed.), *Restructuring Hegemony*, pp. 182–3.

25 K. A. Thelen, *Union of Parts: Labor Politics in Post-war Germany* (Ithaca, NY, Cornell University Press, 1991), pp. 11, 2, 157. See also M. Upham, *Trade Unions and Employers' Organisations of the World* (Harlow, Longman, second edition, 1993), p. G-37.

26 Lecher (ed.), *Trade Unions in the European Union*, ch. 1, p. 29.

27 'German firms turn sour on system that kept peace with workers', *Wall Street Journal*, 17 October 1995, and 'Germany's chemical giants post gains', *Wall Street Journal*, 10–11 November 1995.

28 W. Hutton in the *Observer*, 4 October 1998. For the the equally accurate bad news see L. Panitch and R. Miliband, 'The new world order and the socialist agenda', in Panitch and Miliband (eds), *The Socialist Register 1992* (London, Merlin, 1992), p. 9. See also M. Glassman, 'The siege of the German social market', *New Left Review*, 225 (1997). Glassman points out that some 12 million persons are involved in the Handwerk system of standards and skill in which there were 500,000 apprenticeships in 1993. He concludes that in the face of globalisation 'the virtues of German economic governance have been declared vices and the cause of its problems' (p. 138).

29 S. Berger, 'Liberalism reborn: the new synthesis in France', in J. Howorth and G. Ross (eds), *Contemporary France: A Review of Interdisciplinary Studies* (London, Frances Pinter, 1987), p. 87.

30 M. Upham, *Trade Union and Employers' Organisations of the World*, p. G-19.

31 One influential typolgy comprises the socialist, as in Denmark, the Netherlands and Sweden; the conservative-corporatist, as in France and Germany; and the liberal as in the US and, increasingly, the UK. See G. Esping-Andersen, *Three Worlds of Welfare Capitalism* (Cambridge, Cambridge University Press, 1990).

32 T. H. Marshall, *Citizenship and Social Class* (Oxford, Oxford University Press, 1950).

33 OECD, *Ageing Populations* (Paris, OECD, 1988), cited by G. Esping-Andersen, 'After the golden age?', in G. Esping-Andersen (ed.), *Welfare States in Transition* (London, Sage, 1996), p. 7.

34 *Economist*, 5 June 1999, p. 15.

35 This vast literature might be entered via the following and their bibliographies: D. Gordon, 'The global economy', *New Left Review*, 168 (1988); M. Albert, *Capitalism Against Capitalism* (London, Whurr, 1993); M. Mann, ' As the twentieth century ages', *New Left Review*, 214 (1995); W. Ruigrok and R. van Tulder, *The Logic of International Restructuring* (London, Routledge, 1995); P. Hirst and G. Thompson, *Globalisation in Question* (Cambridge, Polity Press, 1996); L. Weiss, *The Myth of the Powerless State* (Cambridge, Polity Press, 1998).

36 S. Kuhnle, 'Political reconstruction of the European welfare states: a critical review of recent debates', in H. Cavanna (ed.), *Challenges to the Welfare State: Internal and External Dynamics for Change* (Cheltenham, Edward Elgar, 1998), p. 52.

37 M. Daly, 'Welfare states under pressure: cash benefits in European welfare states over the last ten years', *Journal of European Social Policy*, 7:2 (1997) 143.

38 G. Esping-Andersen, 'After the golden age?', p. 10, and *ibid.*, p. 144; see also M. Rhodes, 'Globalisation and West European welfare states', p. 318.

39 Daly, 'Welfare states under pressure', pp. 135–6.

40 Esping-Andersen, 'After the golden age?', p. 15.

41 See J. Smith, 'The ideology of "family and community": New Labour abandons the welfare state', in L. Panitch and C. Leys (eds), *The Socialist Register 1997* (London, Merlin, 1997), pp. 184–8.

42 P. Townsend, 'Persuasion and conformity: an assessment of the Borrie Report on social justice', *New Left Review*, 213 (1995) 145. His figures came from the Central Statistical Office publication *Social Trends*, 1995, p. 94.

43 *Ibid.*, p. 137.

44 For example, D. Lipsey, 'Do we really want more spending?', in R. Jowell (ed.), *British Social Attitudes*, 11th Report (Aldershot, Dartmouth, 1994); P. Taylor-Gooby, 'Comfortable, marginal and excluded', in R. Jowell (ed.), *British Social Attitudes*, 12th Report, 1995; and L. Brook, 'Public spending and taxation' in R. Jowell (ed.), *British Social Attitudes*, 13th Report, 1996.

45 Quoted in Anderson and Mann, *Safety First: The Making of New Labour* (London, Granta, 1997), pp. 224, 225.

46 'Halting welfare errors', *Guardian* editorial comment, 17 May 1999.

47 P. Kellner, 'It just doesn't add up, Harriet', *Guardian*, 25 October 1997.

48 Leading article, 'Do we want to privatise hope?', *Observer*, 28 December 1997.

49 J. Torfing, 'Workfare with welfare: recent reforms of the Danish welfare state', *Journal of European Social Policy*, 9:1 (1999) 5–28.

50 The literature on this also suggests that the progress parties which led the way in Denmark and Norway were harvesting a support that was less concerned with

the costs of welfare and more concerned to prevent immigrants availing themselves of the system's benefits. See P. Kosonen, 'From collectivism to individualism in the welfare state?', *Acta Sociologica*, 30: 3–4 (1990) 204, 206; F. Castles, 'Scandinavian social democracy: achievements and problems', *West European Politics* (1978) 26; J. G. Andersen and T. Borklund, 'Structural changes and new cleavages: the progress parties in Denmark and Norway', *Acta Sociologica*, 33:3 (1990) 204, 206.

51 S. Kuhnle, ' Political reconstruction of the European welfare states', p. 69.

52 R. Lawson, 'Germany: maintaining the middle way', in V. George and P. Taylor-Gooby (eds), *European Welfare Policy: Squaring the Circle* (London, Macmillan, 1996), pp. 36–8.

53 See, G. Therborn and J. Roebroek, 'The irreversible welfare state: its recent maturation, its encounter with the economic crisis, and its future prospects', *International Journal of Health Services*, 16:3 (1986) 177–93; and M. Kesselman, 'Prospects for democratic socialism in advanced capitalism: class struggle and compromise in Sweden and France', *Politics and Society*, 11:4 (1982) 402.

54 G. Esping-Andersen, 'Social class, social democracy, and the state', *Comparative Politics*, 11 October 1978, p. 47.

55 D. Sainsbury, 'Swedish social democracy in transition: the party's record in the 1980s and the challenge of the 1990s', *West European Politics*, 14:3 (1991) 45–9; see also M. Linton, The Swedish road to socialism, (London, Fabian Society, tract 503, 1985), p. 20.

56 J. Fulcher, 'The social democratic model in Sweden: termination or restoration?', *Political Quarterly*, 65:2 (1994) 205.

57 See, J. Clasen and A Gould, 'Stability and change in welfare states: Germany and Sweden in the 1990s', *Politics and Policy*, 23:3 (1995) 195; B. Burkitt and P. Whyman, 'Public sector reform in Sweden: competition or participation?', *Political Quarterly*, 65:3 (1994) 276–7.

58 *Ibid.*, p. 197.

59 S. Marklund, 'Welfare state: policies in the tripolar class model of Scandinavia', *Politics and Society*, 16:4 (1988) 478.

60 *Ibid.*, p. 481.

61 H. Kitschelt, 'Austrian and Swedish social democrats in crisis: party strategy and organisation in corporatist regimes', *Comparative Political Studies*, 27:1 (1994) 3–4. This was the thesis of his *The Transformation of Social Democracy* (Cambridge, Cambridge University Press, 1994).

62 *Ibid.*, p. 60.

63 See on this G. Garrett, *Partisan Politics in the Global Economy* (Cambridge, Cambridge University Press, 1998). The countries in question include Sweden, Norway and Austria.

64 D. Sainsbury, 'Swedish Social Democracy and the Legacy of Continuous Reform', p. 50.

65 G. Ross, *Jacques Delors and European Integration* (Cambridge, Polity Press, 1995), p. 243.

66 See the European Commission White Paper, *Growth, Competitiveness, Employment: The Challenges and the Way Forward in the Twenty-First Century* (Luxembourg, EC, 1994), p. 112.

67 See, for example, K. Coates, 'The dimensions of recovery', in K. Coates and M. Barratt Brown (eds), *A European Recovery Programme: Restoring Full Employment* (Nottingham, Spokesman, 1993), pp. 11–18, and S. Holland, *The European Imperative: Economic and Social Cohesion in the 1990s* (Nottingham, Spokesman, 1993).

68 The percentage of parliamentary seats occupied by social democrats by 1998 was as follows:

Portugal	48.7
France	42.6
UK	63.4
Belgium	29.3
Netherlands	30
Germany	37.5
Austria	38.8
Czech Republic	37
Denmark	36
Norway	37.6
Sweden	46.1
Finland	31.5

69 Robin Cook made such a call. See P. Anderson and N. Mann, *Safety First*, p. 120.

70 *Ibid.*, p. 71.

71 *Ibid.*, pp. 71, 89, 93, 95.

72 *Ibid.*, pp. 403, 87.

73 K. Coates, 'Tide may be turning toward the left', *Tribune*, 6 November 1998. According to Coates, Tony Blair helped to block attempts to address the unemployment problem in the Council of Ministers. See his 'Unemployed Europe and the struggle for alternatives', *New Left Review*, 227 (1998) 131.

7

Social democratic responses to globalisation

In his insider's account of the Labour Party's transformation, Philip Gould is quite explicit in showing how the party sought to catch up with the modernising changes which were presumed to have taken place under the Thatcher governments.[1] Though the policy review instituted by Neil Kinnock had achieved much in this view, it still left a great deal to do and as the 1992 general election approached the party's focus groups revealed that the targeted voters of 'middle England' perceived its policies as insufficiently 'aspirational' and too much concerned with issues such as unemployment, the rights of minorities and people who 'haven't made it'.[2] The shadow chancellor's tax-and-spending plans made matters worse in the view of the team around Kinnock. Two years later, after John Smith's brief time as party leader, Gould's advice to his successor Tony Blair was that he should start by recognising the 'Conservative hegemony' and continue to revise Labour's policies accordingly.

The party's commitment to an industrial policy survived the programmatic renewal which led to the erasure of the AES after 1983. The German or Rhineland model of capitalism in particular intermittently exercised an attractive force for party leaders that was never entirely suppressed in Neil Kinnock's or John Smith's time as party leader. The demotion of Bryan Gould from the shadow trade and industry job in November 1989 nevertheless marked a significant stage in Labour's retreat from this policy and his defeat in the leadership contest in 1992 cleared the way for those who saw the defeat of inflation as the necessary focus of macroeconomic policy.[3] The main thrust of policy change had undoubtedly been towards a celebration of the efficacy of markets, rather than greater emphasis on the institutional changes required to make them work more efficiently and fairly in the British context. The 1992 manifesto asserted that 'Britain needs a Labour government which will back British industry in the way our competitors back theirs' and this was conceived in the document as putting industrial policy 'at the heart of economic policy'.[4] But government policy was to be chiefly concerned with creating conditions in which markets worked properly and consisted of measures such as tax incentives for small business investment. Rhetorical emphasis was also placed on stable interest rates and low inflation. The fight against inflation was to entail emphasis on education, science and skills as part of a strategy to increase productivity in the medium term. The manifesto also evinced a conversion to labour-market flexibility in the sense that there was now to be no return to the *status quo ante* in regard to trade union legislation, beyond promising 'a fair framework of law for both employers and unions'. Nevertheless, Labour's emphasis was on education, training and skills rather than further labour-market deregulation. In *Labour's Campaign for Recovery* (1992) the party insisted that there was no dispute about the importance of the market between itself and the Conservatives. It also reasoned that 'the response to the emerging global economy – and the inevitably more limited scope for national governments acting on their own – is not to espouse policies for more deregulation but to improve the mechanisms for international economic co-operation'.[5]

In reality Labour increasingly emphasised improved education and training of the workforce as the effective response to the internationalisation of capital. It is true that Labour returned repeatedly to the need for 'partnership' between government and industry, stressing government's role in providing the framework for economic success and social justice. 'More than ever before', according to *Opportunity Britain* (1992), 'British industry now needs a long-term commitment from government, not in the form of indiscriminate subsidies or second guessing industry, but in the form of cooperation to meet clearly-defined goals – improving skills, crossing new technological frontiers ...'[6] But central to this perspective was Labour's call for a 'training revolution'. After the 1992 general election, but especially after Tony Blair and Gordon Brown took over the party leadership in 1994, this emphasis on skills and education was increasingly linked to the theme of globalisation. In *Rebuilding the Economy* (1994) the 'new global economy' was said to be one in which 'inventions, technology, raw materials and capital are tradeable worldwide'. For this reason the difference between success and failure in a company was determined by the 'level of skill' that the company could draw upon. Thus 'a policy for national economic renewal must mean enhancing individual economic potential as the route to rebuilding the industrial base'.[7] The development of global markets was seen as being connected to the 'knowledge revolution' in the sense that in a 'world of modern value-added products, of technologically-driven innovations, precision working and persistent change, there is now a premium on the skills of the workforce with the new knowledge-intensive industries demanding new highly-skilled labour forces'.[8] Further deregulation of the labour market was no answer, according to Labour, because it had already led the UK to 'the worst [combination] of high European unemployment and US-style low wage employment and rising in-work poverty'.[9]

In 1994 Gordon Brown, the shadow chancellor, invoked the 'Asian Tigers' and the newly industrialising economies of Latin America as evidence of the intensified competition that was 'bringing three billion more people into the economic mainstream' and threatening the prospect of Europe's economic eclipse by 2010. Those who attempted to 'go-it-alone', he warned, could now be punished at 'a flick of the switch' as billions of dollars flowed back and forth at the command of punitive financial markets. This new world of global communications, of digitalisation and fibre optics, and 'the global sourcing of companies' was 'more truly trans-continental than multinational' in the words of the future Labour chancellor.[10]

Labour's policy conclusions owed something to the fashionable hyperbole of Robert Reich, President Clinton's secretary of state for labor, who had dramatically embraced the globalisation thesis in *The Work of Nations*, where he announced that there would soon be no such thing as the economy of the USA – or of any other nation – such was the degree of global economic integration taking place.[11] Labour followed Reich in stressing investment in the skills of the workforce, the primary national asset in a world of mobile, transnational capital. Reich's advocacy of steeply progressive taxation on the rich, tough action against tax evasion, elimination of corporate subsidies – all on the grounds that globalisation made these measures *feasible* – was ignored altogether. New Labour was content, as President Bush had been, to talk up education. 'The competitiveness of nations', according to *Rebuilding the Economy*, 'is now determined by the skills and talents of their citizens. In the modern economy where capital, raw materials and technology are internationally mobile and tradable worldwide it is people – their education and skills – that are increasingly the most important determinant of economic growth'.[12] All of this would have been a surprise to the highly educated and highly skilled people of Russia and Eastern Europe, still starved of inward investment ten years after the collapse of the communist regimes.

The Reich-Brown argument exaggerated both the mobility of capital and the economic significance of education, but its prime local function was to support Labour's increasing emphasis on 'supply-side' deficiencies – in investment, education, training, capital and infrastructure – in explaining 'Britain's chronic economic weakness'. Brown rejected what he called 'the old-style corporatist economics [which] saw its task as curbing the market economy, and pursuing "quick-fix" tax and borrow politics in one country ... Labour's new economic approach means equipping people, industry, and communities to make the investments which are essential in a dynamic market economy for opportunity and prosperity'.[13] It was in Labour's view 'no longer sufficient to rely on the old national levers of demand management ... It is in failures of supply' that a future Labour government would act by encouraging 'public-private partnerships' in rail and infrastructure but also in less obvious areas such as childcare, the health service and training.[14] By this time Brown and

Blair were at pains to distance themselves from the ideas expressed in Will Hutton's bestseller, *The State We're In*, which advocated the German social market model, or something like it, for Britain. It was seen to involve corporatism, labour-market regulation and legal obligations for firms that had just been 'set free' by the Thatcher governments. Blair toured the chambers of commerce assuring business leaders that nothing would be done to undermine flexible labour markets. In any case, the Labour leadership did not want the burden of advocating policies that went against the grain of British society and that involved a risky institutional upheaval with no guarantee that the model would succeed on British soil. They were markedly less cautious in their admiration for the economy of the US and less sceptical about Britain's capacity to emulate it.[15]

The by-now familiar themes were reiterated in 1995 in *A New Economic Future For Britain*. Britain's economic potential had to be realised, according to the document, in the context of 'a rapidly changing, competitive and tough global economy' characterised by 'fast-moving markets, rapidly growing world trade and footloose companies'. While technology, raw materials and capital 'can be bought from anywhere by just about anyone', the success of companies depends, or so the document tells us, on 'the level of skill' available to them.[16] Here the party pledged to deliver the highest sustainable level of growth consistent with low and stable inflation and underlined its fiscal rectitude by stressing the 'Golden Rule' that a future Labour government would only borrow in order to invest – not to finance consumption.[17] Investment would be induced primarily by securing stable and low inflation, rather than by pump-priming, though once again the idea of rebuilding infrastructure through public-private partnerships was raised. The document also mentioned the issue of direct intervention in the form of 'more effective regulation and supervision of currency and financial markets to ensure that the growth of derivatives and other financial instruments does not destabilise world capital markets'. It also wanted a restructuring of the IMF and World Bank 'to increase their public accountability, to promote growth and sustainable development' and to enable the IMF to support currencies 'under unjustifiable short-term attack'. Labour at this stage thought that the IMF could help to pre-empt crises by engaging in independent auditing to check the sustainability of national economic management.[18] Such ideas were the common currency of social democracy in the mid-1990s.

By this time, however, the party's City spokesman, Alistair Darling, had already publicly ruled out 'draconian measures' against the City on the grounds that, as journalistic observers put it, it 'would simply lead to a mass exodus of investment to financial centres with a lighter regulatory framework'.[19] Voluntary self-regulation would therefore continue except in financial services and in respect of takeovers where Darling proposed that companies would have to prove a public interest. In general, Labour was anxious to convince business that it was opposed to 'unnecessary outdated regulation' and in favour of 'cutting red tape' – especially for small and medium-sized enterprises, a sector which it identified with job creation and promised to stimulate with new tax advantages.[20] The same could be said of the labour market. The party had championed the Social Charter of the Maastricht Treaty since the Conservative government had secured a British opt-out from its provisions after leading a campaign of furious opposition. But by 1996 Labour's rationale for supporting the Social Charter was as much concerned with securing Britain a seat in future negotiations than with the intrinsic value of strengthening workers' rights, a cause for which the party leadership was singularly unenthusiastic.[21] Likewise, Labour's minimum-wage commitment promised to take the prevailing economic circumstances into account and the advice of both sides of industry. Labour increasingly presented itself as the proponent of a 'third way' between Conservative *laissez-faire* and European over-regulation. Certain abuses and unfair practices were seen to prevail in Britain because 'among major developed countries Britain has amongst the fewest basic legal standards to protect the working conditions of employees'. But the party also embraced 'proper flexibility' and distanced itself from an equally vague 'over-regulation' which had entered public debate under the name of 'Eurosclerosis'.[22]

There would be no return to the employment laws of the late 1970s under a future Labour government and no repeal of the Conservative laws on trade unions enacted in the 1980s. Precision in party policy statements after 1992 was increasingly confined to what a Labour government would not do. This was to a large extent the product of repeatedly falling foul of Conservative estimates of the 'tax-and-spend' implications of Labour's promises at the general elections of 1987 and 1992. But there was also an apparent acceptance of the greatly reduced role of government which the Labour leadership linked to the process of 'globalisation'. The 'pre-manifesto' of 1996, *New Labour: New Life For Britain*, for example, rehearsed the themes now associated with the 'New Times' thesis of the 1980s:[23] Britain was subject to incessant, rapid change in economic markets, in workplace technology and organisation, in culture, in social structure, attitudes and lifestyle. But it also stressed 'change in the political balance of power. A trillion dollars is now traded every day on the international markets.'[24] This 'trillion dollars' was also invoked in Tony Blair's speeches;[25] the implication seemed to be 'what can a government do in the face of this?'. The answer appeared to be to go with the grain of irreversible change which placed more and more power in the workings of markets. Blair's introduction to the 1997 manifesto, for example, suggested that in accepting 'the global economy as a reality' New Labour would strive to facilitate even faster economic change by working for government and business collaboration with the objective of 'enhancing the dynamism of the market'.[26] Gordon Brown sounded a similar note in *Labour's Business Manifesto*, where the 'old national economic policies' were found wanting in the face of 'continuous innovation and the need to adapt old certainties such as a job for life or a skill for life' – neither of which could any longer be taken for granted. Indeed, the future chancellor confessed that 'Embracing change and equipping people for change is the only way we can provide opportunity for all'.[27]

The *Economist* noted that Labour's fondness for 'globalisation' 'may be partly because it provides a politically acceptable way to ditch old ideas – "it is not that we were wrong you see, it's just that times have changed."'[28] But this was to overlook the fact that most of the old ideas had already been ditched before the globalisation mantra was adopted. The journal was on firmer ground in pointing out that Blair's emphasis on flexibility – allegedly both a key effect of globalisation and a necessary response to it – was 'an acceptance of the economic legacy of Thatcherism'.[29] The Labour leadership had been won by degrees to the view that a new 'settlement' had come into being based on the 'achievements' of four successive Conservative governments. More and more aspects of its own identity were jettisoned or downgraded as the party sought to catch up with the spirit of the times. Globalisation entered the frame both as a reinforcement for the arguments that had already been mobilised against 'tax-and-spend' socialism and as a symbol of modernity and proof of Labour's forward-looking realism. There was no public debate in the Labour Party about the meaning and policy implications of 'globalisation'. What had happened was that the party had gradually adapted to Thatcherism in the late 1980s and had then discovered by the mid-1990s that the 'modernising' that had taken place might be in the swim with a bigger world movement. Globalisation was simply invoked as a *deus ex machina*: 'it is as if', Tony Blair told Japanese businessmen, 'someone has pressed the fast-forward button on the video, and there is no sign of it stopping'.[30] This might help to explain why Labour's conversion to a pro-European position in the late 1980s, when it discovered the social benefits of 'Europe', later had a critique of 'Eurosclerosis' grafted on to it.

Blair's 'globalisation' was as irresistible and benign in its impact as it was mysterious in origin. Protectionism, by contrast, was condemned as self-evidently 'wrong and impractical'. Successfully competing in the new environment, Blair asserted in Japan, demands that two things be done. 'A country has to dismantle barriers to competition and accept the disciplines of the international economy'.[31] But this was a logic which had been brought about by the decisions and 'non-decisions'[32] of governments in the 1970s and 1980s, through which international finance acquired its current power. Blair's reasoning in Tokyo suggested that there had to be more of the same thing.[33] It also invoked the merciless punishment meted out by the financial markets on governments with less than an absolute commitment to an anti-inflationary policy. He expressed the belief that the same globalising market forces demanded that 'our tax rates need to be internationally as well as nationally competitive' – and his reasoning accepted this conclusion.[34] The central economic changes made by the Conservatives in the 1980s were now pronounced 'inevitable and here to stay'. Blair prophesied something that his Japanese audience had practised for fifty years: 'The next era ... will be dominated by those countries that save, invest, innovate, and above all develop the potential of the one resource which will be exclusively theirs: their people.'[35] This platitude was later given the characteristic New Labour 'spin': 'knowledge' had become the key to wealth, and lifelong learning was the route to knowledge.

The 'old way' of social democracy, Blair told Singaporean businessmen later the same month, 'was through redistribution in the tax and benefit regime. But in a global economy the old ways won't do'.[36] Instead, according to the Labour leader, the direction which 'a new economics of the centre and left-of-centre must go' is 'towards an open economy working with the grain of global change: disciplined in macro-economic and fiscal policy'. The economics of the right, by contrast, was misrepresented in this speech as consisting of a 'laissez-faire passive' approach – an analysis which overlooked the fact that the 'grain' of global change was in large measure the result of deregulatory measures taken by the right. Labour's active alternative to the alleged passivity of the right consisted of 'a willingness to act to prepare the country for this change'.[37] Blair used the occasion to pay obeisance to the model of the 'Asian Tigers' which he identified as the 'broad notion of a unified society with a strong sense of purpose and direction'. This would have different applications in different societies. At the time of the Singapore speech Blair used the notion of 'a stakeholder society' to express his belief in the possibility of combining social cohesion with market economics. A better balance between savings, investment and security than that afforded by the welfare state was the goal he apparently had in mind. There was not, he said, sufficient movement in the welfare system from benefits to work and this had to be changed. The more ambitious idea of stakeholding associated with Will Hutton's *The State We're In* – with its call for action against unrestricted, unaccountable finance capital – was already far from his mind.

When he addressed Rupert Murdoch's Newscorp Leadership Conference in July 1996 Blair was content to define the economic role of government 'in this world of change' as involving the creation of 'a competitive base of physical infrastructure and human skills to attract the capital that will produce the wages for workers and the profits for investors' while situating it in the context of forces that are 'reducing the power and capacity of government to control its domestic economy'.[38] An expansionary fiscal or monetary policy which went against the grain of global conditions had been specifically ruled out years before.[39] Budget deficits and tax regimes out of line with other major industrial countries were also ruled out, though the significance of Blair's emphasis on the need for a 'tax structure ... to attract enterprise into the UK' was not obvious, given the facts about taxation in the UK. These revealed that the UK was thirteenth out of twenty countries ranked in order of taxes and social security contributions as a percentage of national income, with only Switzerland, Spain and Portugal below the UK among the major European economies. Taxes on corporate profits in the UK stood around the European average, but social security contributions paid by employers as a proportion of national income were (and still are) the lowest in Europe and less than those paid in the US and Japan. While UK workers worked longer hours than anywhere else in the EU, UK employers had the lowest proportion of indirect labour costs in total industry labour costs – that is the 'burden' of vocational training, statutory and non-statutory social security contributions and other services paid for by the employer was lighter in the UK than anywhere else in the EU. The UK, at the time when Blair was stressing the need for flexibility, was also distinguished by the fact that its poorest 20 per cent shared a smaller proportion of the national income than its counterpart in any other major industrial economy, while its richest 20 per cent took more than anywhere else except Switzerland.[40]

Blair lectured the German employers' federation (BDI) in the summer of 1996 on the virtues of labour-market flexibility and the evils of 'over-regulation' as a crusader for conditions that had actually been created by the Thatcher governments. The BDI president, Hans-Olaf Henkel, noted for his hard-line approach, praised the speech, as did most of those present, many of whom contrasted the 'modernising instincts' of the Labour leader with the 'mildewed ideology of his counterparts in the German opposition led by Oskar Lafontaine'.[41] Lafontaine, the SPD party chairman, was so out of touch with reality, in the view of his critics, that he was wont to argue for international cooperation against speculation and to oppose wage dumping, tax dumping and welfare dumping as self-defeating responses to globalisation. Unlike Blair, Lafontaine stressed the instability caused by increasing levels of income inequality, continued erosion of the welfare state, tax evasion by the rich and the emphasis on a supply-side economics that caused all of this and unemployment too.[42] While Lafontaine questioned both the extent and the results of globalisation, the Labour Party leader, according to sympathetic observers, saw it as both inevitable and desirable.[43] His acceptance of 'broad swathes of the Thatcherite agenda including her labour reforms and privatisation' was perceived in some quarters as part of an attempt to turn Labour into a party more like the Democrats in America.[44] But it was also designed 'to make Britain "a better bet" for the allegedly footloose multinational investment every government is trying to attract'.[45]

This became apparent in Blair's economic arguments within the EU soon after Labour formed a government in May 1997.[46] To the evident dismay of social democratic 'modernisers' like David Marquand and Martin Jacques, his emphasis on labour-market flexibility and globalisation and the obvious lack of sympathy with the European left showed that Blair had accepted the basic assumptions of Thatcherite political economy including the notion that Britain's international competitiveness was enhanced by relatively low wages, long hours, casualisation, strict labour laws and low levels of social protection.[47] Seen in these terms the Labour victory of May 1997 was another 1951 rather than a 1945; in other words, an adjustment to someone else's agenda and an acceptance of the new *status quo*.[48] The idea that neo-liberal economics was an answer to the crisis in the UK had been contested within the Conservative Party in the 1970s; by the mid-1990s Labour was seen to accept its main precepts and behaved as if Thatcher had accomplished a necessary modernisation of the country. More than that, Labour now wanted to carry the message into the EU. The election of a Socialist government in France within one month of the formation of the Labour government set this ambition back. Lionel Jospin's administration was perceived with a 'disdain' that was 'instinctive' and 'profound' – and which New Labour normally only reserved for Old Labour.[49] For as *The Times* immediately noted, Jospin's government would 'strengthen the forces opposed to Mr. Blair's attempt to create a new European social policy based on flexible labour markets'.[50] The exaggerated perception of France as a bastion of the left could also be found in other sections of the 'quality' press and was especially visible in the reports of the *New York Times*' Paris correspondent, Roger Cohen, who persuaded himself that the French clung to a closed socialist system dominated by labour unions and technocrats. This hyperbole reached a peak in October 1997 when Cohen warned that 'France has set itself up as perhaps the nearest thing the US has to a serious ideological rival in the last decade of the twentieth century'.[51] It was a place of 'internal paralysis', 'threatened by innovation', where fossilised unions paraded 'the rags of an exhausted socialist dream'.[52]

New Labour, by contrast, had apparently accepted the argument that governments had to respond to globalisation by attracting 'footloose' multinational capital by means of tax incentives, subsidies, skilled labour and flexible labour markets, while avoiding policies that might be punished by global financial markets. Yet the election of the Labour government in Britain in May 1997 coincided with a turn against the policies that had dominated since the beginning of the previous decade – mass unemployment, rising poverty levels, and general austerity policies. Within months of Labour's election victory a world financial crisis was in full spate reminding everybody of the dangers of untrammelled markets. The Socialists in France apparently also wanted radical policies to deal with unemployment and promised to introduce a thirty-five-hour week – something that was anathema to New Labour.[53] But the Amsterdam summit of June 1997 had already showed that nobody was prepared to support Jospin over the issue of jobs except through face-saving formulae.[54] The Kohl government in Germany wanted debt reduction to take priority in the disposal of any budget surpluses, while the Jospin government wanted priority for job creation. The French Socialists had already pledged themselves to introduce the thirty-five-hour week by the year 2000 – to the horror of the employers – but only obtained public support, among left governments, from Romano Prodi's 'Olive Tree' coalition in Italy. But 'The remedies for unemployment adopted almost everywhere and recommended by the European Commission are altogether different', one commentator observed. 'They can be summed up in one word; flexibility.'[55] This is what emerged from the Luxembourg Job Summit in November 1997, when all agreed to reform welfare in a way that integrated the unemployed into the labour market and broke with 'dependency'.

Social democrats in Britain lamented New Labour's inability to see that

> the only worthwhile rationale for the European Union in a post-Cold War world is to defend the European social model from destruction at the hands of renascent global capitalism. In the struggle between globalisation and the European model, the central theme of European politics today, their instincts are with the globalisers, as their visible embarrassment at Lionel Jospin's victory in France demonstrate[d].[56]

Certainly it had been Blair who took the lead at the Amsterdam summit in sinking France's employment plan. The British prime minister predictably argued that the 'priority objective' on employment was deregulation to create an adaptable workforce. European unity simply did not figure in New Labour discourse as a challenge to neo-liberalism. Every member of the Labour government had become a crusader for 'flexibility'. Thus it was the unlikely figure of the British foreign secretary, Robin Cook, who told the Institute for European Affairs in Dublin that the challenge of globalisation could only be met by 'skills and competitiveness' and the avoidance of regulations that 'over-burden business'. In particular, Cook saw the need to reduce 'the non-wage costs of taking on new people' – a reference, presumably, to the employer's social contributions and costs of training – and to 'tear down the remaining barriers to borderless trade'.[57] By February 1998 Blair was ready to take this message to the world when he announced his intention to bring 'centre-left parties' together in a standing conference, beginning in late 1998 or early 1999. Explaining himself, he said that he wanted 'to start with the ideology which links Labour and the [US] Democrats' in order 'to put ourselves at the forefront of those who are trying to manage social change in a global economy'.[58]

Reports that the French Socialist government would represent a radical challenge to New Labour were soon shown to be overstated. Immediately after his election Jospin was converted to support for the economic constraints necessary for the launch of the Euro – the long-standing convergence criteria. Yet France had 6 million people living on the bare minimum, 3 million unemployed and another 3 million on less than 5,000 francs per month. If reduction of the budget deficit and a strong franc were to be Jospin's economic priorities there could be no sustained campaign for a European-wide public-works programme, reduced hours, and increased welfare entitlements. Jospin's minister for economy, Strauss-Kahn, actually boasted of the savings on state and social security expenditures that had helped to bring the deficit down.[59] He also told both the G7 and the IMF that the Asian crisis occurred because the liberalisation of these economies had not proceeded far enough.[60] France had addressed structural changes in the labour market, he reminded the Franco-American Chamber of Commerce in November 1997 on a visit to the US, where, as we have seen, the Jospin government was widely misunderstood. Strauss-Kahn denied that all the EU's 'rigidities' needed removing, but accepted that most of the EU's unemployment was structural and that France had made progress by increasing the proportion of temporary workers in the economy and by taking such measures as privatisation and providing tax incentives to encourage firms to spend more on research and development.

If these observations put Jospin's challenge to the 'third way' into perspective, the formation of the SPD-Green coalition in Germany in October 1998 nevertheless strengthened the prospects for greater interventionism in the EU, if only because there were now thirteen governments within it with a social democratic presence. The SPD had also stressed the need to put job creation at the top of its priorities. And yet the European Central Bank created for the launch of the Euro in January 1999 had already been designed to be independent of the politicians and solely concerned with price stability (unlike the Federal Reserve of the US, which has a wider brief). It was given in effect a power to veto the economic policies of the national governments within European monetary union and prevent the emergence of an alternative economic strategy. When judged in terms of the debates they generated within their own parties, however, as we saw in chapter four, various social democratic parties within the EU did not at all take the Blairite line on globalisation and remained committed to a strong state and social democratic values. But there is no consistent line on this within the EU, the Party of European Socialists or the Socialist International, as we shall see below after considering the contrasting cases of the SPD and PvdA.

At its conference of December 1997 the SPD, in preparation for the 1998 elections, recognised the limits on national governments in a globalised economy. But the party argued that to protect the welfare state and the environment, to limit the extent of inequality, a social and environmentally friendly economy had to be constructed on a global scale.[61] Power would have to be transferred to transnational organisations such as the EU and UN so that binding regulations might produce the degree of cooperation required in respect of human rights, world trade, international payments, financial controls and the elimination of the poorest countries' debts. Social and ecological minimum standards had to be integrated into WTO thinking. A social democratic EU would give priority to democratic policy and common minimal standards before the needs of blind markets. Indeed the 'decisive project' for social democracy had to be a social democratic Europe or it would not survive 'since otherwise it will lose its power of policy-shaping and therewith the confidence of the people'.[62] The reduction of mass unemployment would be the test of this approach and some comfort could be taken from the inclusion of an employment chapter in the Treaty of Amsterdam which permitted the EU to take initiatives in this field.

The SPD also wanted EU measures to prevent downward competition on company taxes, welfare and working conditions. The existing tax havens would have to be eliminated. EU-wide regulations on labour markets would have to be designed to ensure the maintenance of standards and workers' rights and the prevention of unprotected casualised labour often disguised as 'self-employment'. A social stability pact could prevent welfare dumping. It was understood as a case of transferring the social market economy and improving environmental standards on to a European-wide basis. This would enhance Europe's competitiveness, not undermine it. Economic and Monetary Union (EMU) could be the start of an answer to globalised financial markets in that it provided the possibility of regaining control from them. While taking a much more confident position on the capacities and potential of the EU than New Labour, the party also adopted a good deal of Blairite rhetoric.

At Leipzig in April 1998 the SPD asserted that Germany could not win in a race for the bottom, but must stick to quality products at competitive prices based on 'the best education system worldwide, the most effective research, the newest technologies and the most modern infrastructure'.[63] Only the interlinkage of social stability and economic efficiency would create the conditions for general prosperity. Thus the party wanted improved education, technological innovation, reduced indirect wage costs, support for small to medium-sized firms, and reduced corporation taxes to get more investment and make them 'internationally comparable'. The employers' social welfare contributions would be reduced. The national debt would also be reduced. Excessive regulation would be cut. Flexible solutions were to be found in wage policy and the organisation of work. It also proposed to reduce initial tax rates on income, introduce 'lifelong learning' and reduce benefits for those who refuse work, while insisting that society imposes obligations as well as providing rights. All these banalities were recognisably New Labour.

On the other hand, the SPD also talked of developing co-determination at home and in the EU, strengthening workers' rights regarding wrongful dismissal, and regulating the labour market against social dumping, wage dumping, illegal employment and the black economy. 'We want joint and compulsory regulations on tax evasion and social dumping' at EU level, asserted the 1998 manifesto. 'We urgently need European agreement on effective minimum taxation for trade and industry and the elimination of tax havens'. The reduction of unemployment was seen as the priority – it had to be given the unprecedented post-war levels it had reached in the aftermath of national reunification. It was to be achieved through tripartite cooperation and also action at the EU level. The manifesto adopted at Leipzig also contrasted the rising tax burden for individuals with the falling tax burden for company profits and the wealthy – something that New Labour in Britain was unable to bring itself to mention.

The Dutch coalition government led by the PvdA was much closer to New Labour's mentality on these issues than the SPD. It argued (through its Ministry of Economic Affairs)[64] that companies 'have a growing choice of locations for each of their activities' and face fiercer international competition, especially in open economies like the Netherlands, forced to attract business by a variety of devices because 'as competition between companies increases, so does competition between countries'. The 'business climate' had thus to be improved through fiscal measures, improvement of the operation of markets – including the labour market – measures to 'optimise our investment climate' and an emphasis on knowledge-based activities. Price competition alone would not be enough, in this view, because of the emergence of the Tiger economies and Eastern Europe, where labour costs were much lower than in the Netherlands. Even among the knowledge-intensive, specialist areas of the OECD, countries had lost their monopoly, according to the Dutch government, as could be seen, or so it argued, from the doubling of research and development expenditure as a percentage of GDP in South Korea and Taiwan in the ten years after 1985. The Southeast Asian economies appear in this perception as combining a formidable blend of low costs and high investment and knowledge. The Dutch response thus had to stress a mutually reinforcing industrial, technological, educational and scientific policy funded by government in partnership with business.

Vidal observes that the PvdA-led government cut the budget deficit to 2.8 per cent of GDP in 1996 and brought public spending down from 60 per cent to 54 per cent of GDP by the same year. Privatisation programmes and tax cuts accompanied these measures. The social security system – based on a monthly minimum wage – was cut by 20 per cent in real terms by freezing it for almost a decade. Since benefits were indexed to the minimum wage these fell too. Principles of eligibility and periods of eligibility had already been changed to save money and the law had been tightened to force claimants to take work. Taxes, meanwhile, continued to fall and labour-market reforms made it easier for business to employ workers on temporary contracts. Paul Kalma, the Labour Party's head of research, thought that Wim Kok's accession to the prime minister's office in 1994 was 'a miracle' in view of such measures and of the PvdA's loss of voters and members – the price, he thought, of wage restraint and labour flexibility. Dutch firms, on the other hand, celebrated their increased profits in a leaked document of the employers' association, VNO-NCW, which observed that profitability now lagged behind only the UK within the EU. It nevertheless bemoaned the fact that 2.5 million people under sixty-five received some sort of social assistance 'for lack of incentives to work'.[66] Different incentives were required for business. In 1997 the government was still looking at further reductions in company taxation on the grounds that it is 'a significant factor for international concerns in the choice of locations'.[67] Similarly, the regulatory 'burden' on business had to be reduced, especially in the small company sector.[68]

While member parties of the Socialist International argued that 'deregulation of international financial markets ... has permitted rampant currency speculation to destabilize the global economy by undermining real, productive economic activity and killing jobs', even these critics put their hope in a future international multilateral framework of regulation and taxation developed through the existing transnational organisations such as the IMF, ILO, World Bank, WTO and G7.[69] These were the very organisations which had proselytised and enforced neo-liberalism up to the Asian financial and economic crisis of 1997–98. For firefighting purposes even President Clinton was prepared to see changes to the functions and role of the IMF and World Bank and said so at the Naples G7 meeting in 1994. The financial crises which swept the world in 1997 and 1998 brought this type of reform on to the immediate agenda.

At the IMF's annual meeting in Hong Kong in April 1998, Gordon Brown called for greater transparency and disclosure by nations in respect of financial information and analysis, budgetary practices and fiscal integrity. He also wanted a code of conduct on social policy so that financial crises did not lead – as they had on every previous occasion – to punitive measures in respect of welfare, public services and labour standards. At the end of September 1998 Blair joined those who wanted the IMF strengthened so that it could effectively monitor standards for national fiscal and monetary polices, central bank reserves and corporate transparency. The latter would cover accounting standards, insolvency regimes and securities markets to prevent speculative activities such as those which led to the demise of the misnamed Long-Term Capital Management in the US. Dominic Strauss-Kahn, Finance Minister in Lionel Jospin's French Socialist government, outlined a similar blueprint which stressed the need for accurate information and effective monitoring, adding that offshore financial centres stood in the way of both.[70] Both Strauss-Kahn and Jospin called for enhancing the power of the IMF's Interim Committee, but Jospin talked specifically of extending its control over capital flows to deter speculation. He foresaw the Interim Committee becoming 'a sort of political government ... providing control over the world financial system'.[71]

Other measures to address the globalisation problem have been advocated by the parties of the Socialist International. The Belgian Socialist Party (SP) is one of several member parties of the International that favoured the Tobin tax[72] – originally proposed as a 1 per cent levy on currency transactions with the intent of deterring at least some speculation. But noting that something in the region of 70,000 billion Belgian francs was speculated daily, the SP argued that a 0.5 per cent levy on all foreign currency transactions would raise an enormous sum that might finance a global 'social fund', even if it had no effect in reducing speculation. The Swedish SAP saw a similar opportunity, proposing that a capital trading tax of this sort might be a new way of financing the UN.[73] When the Socialist International Council (SIC) met in Oslo in May 1998, Torbjorn Jagland, former prime minister of Norway, supported the Tobin tax, pointing out that those who argued that controls were impossible were advocating an unacceptable alternative to socialists. The DNA recognised that since such a tax would have to be genuinely international and binding, it would be necessary to empower the UN to pass binding resolutions – a point observed by several parties as we saw in chapter four. Similarly, the elimination of tax evasion required international cooperation in this view to compel banks and other financial institutions to investigate and report wherever there was suspicion of criminality.[74]

Lionel Jospin supported the idea of the Tobin tax during the French presidential campaign of 1995, noting that it would have to be universally applied and confined to speculative activities. The Swedish social democrats also recognised the utility of such a tax as a new way of financing the UN and the new global public sector which they saw as necessary to regulate the global economy. In the interim the SAP was as keen as any other party in power to counteract currency speculation by keeping public finances in order at the national level. Jagland referred to a choice between the principles of 1789 and those of 1933, and argued that the first meant a strengthening of the role of the state in national economies and a global welfare society based on a stronger UN. Pierre Mauroy, as president of the Socialist International in 1998, was keen to insist that there was – contrary to New Labour's logic – an alternative to neo-liberalism. Social democracy operating within the EU could be that alternative, according to this argument, if the undoubted economic and commercial power of the EU, supported by a single currency, was used to promote social justice and democracy. Specific proposals did not feature in Mauroy's speech to the SIC, but socialism – a word expelled from British Labour's lexicon – was invoked as a source of hope in a world of increasing inequality.[75]

When the Party of European Socialists (PES) met at Malmo a month later, it agreed to investigate policy themes redolent of the 'third way' including 'Reduction of non-wage labour costs' and 'the employment-friendly character of taxation systems', but also asserted that

> there is a strong need to elaborate a social agenda for the European Union in parallel with Economic and Monetary Union by identifying the objectives and instruments of a coordinated policy for the promotion of employment and the setting of social standards ... The Malmo Congress ... marks the start of a PES

> employment policy network which is based on an interlinkage of Social Democratic and Socialist ministers and spokespersons responsible for EU labour market policy, fiscal policy, education and environment. Its aim will be to maximise EU support to fight unemployment.[76]

Oskar Lafontaine of the German SPD had observed that the emergence of the EU as a regional trade bloc was itself evidence of growing economic interdependence – there was no argument about that.[77] Indeed, regional economic integration was the most impressive evidence of globalisation and as such provided the basis for an EU-wide system of regulation and macroeconomic policy. Lafontaine stressed that government within the EU could ensure that it maintained the best education system, the most innovative research environment and the best public infrastructure. The nations of the EU could collectively avoid a race to the bottom which would see the reduction of company taxes, real wages and social standards if each member state competed for inward investment as if the only thing that mattered was lower business costs. This process would only engender xenophobia, public squalor, growing inequality and the corrosion of social cohesion. It would finally lead to political extremism. But if that happened, according to Lafontaine, it would be the logical result of incorrect political choices rather than ineluctable processes of globalisation. The correct response to the latter, in Lafontaine's view, would be international cooperation and the creation of a new political framework through the existing transnational organisations – the EU, OECD, International Currency Fund and WTO. The EU could create a 'social and ecological market economy'. It could begin by working for a stabilisation of exchange rates and lower interest rates – both conducive to higher rates of investment and employment. Though EMU was perceived as a step in this direction, Lafontaine also saw the need for reductions in structural government deficits and harmonisation of tax policies.

Lafontaine argued that corporate tax evasion reduced effective demand in the economy by shifting the tax burden 'to the labour sector', a view shared by the PES-ECOFIN (European Council of Finance Ministers) Group.[78] But he also observed that successful tax evasion is evasion of a responsibility to share in the funding of public services. It thus weakened social cohesion. It also led to the erosion of national tax bases. The elimination of tax havens was something that the New Labour government was supposed to be examining and other EU governments were certainly pressing for.[79] Britain needed to do something about this as a report in the *Economist* showed when it revealed that Rupert Murdoch's Newscorp International had paid no tax on the £1.387 billion profits which it had made in Britain over an eleven-year period. The same report demonstrated that its most profitable British operation, incorporated in the tax haven of Bermuda, had no employees and produced nothing.[80] Lafontaine, supported by Schröder, the Austrian social democratic chancellor Viktor Klima and Dominique Strauss-Kahn, also demanded qualified majority voting on tax harmonisation at the end of 1998 when the issue briefly became public news in Britain.[81] Prior to this date there had been no public debate sponsored by the British Labour Party on the issue of corporate tax evasion and the danger of competitive tax dumping within the EU. However, the European Commission had pronounced itself in favour of tax union and advocated effective minimum taxes on companies, capital and the environment. The British chancellor of the exchequer seemed also to favour 'coordinating savings and corporate taxation' in a paper originally drafted by his economic adviser when the public debate first began.[82]

It became clear, however, that the member states of the EU were far from united over tax harmonisation. New Labour quickly asserted its tax cutting propensities and preparedness to use the veto to get its way – which was precisely to prevent majority voting on tax harmonisation. While the popular newspapers in Britain denounced Lafontaine as 'the most dangerous man in Europe' for speaking out in favour of corporate tax harmony, there was more relevance in the observation that 'the strength of the City of London ... depends on investors' intent on tax evasion'. This, it was claimed, accounted for Gordon Brown's rapid *volte-face* on the issue and his 'Thatcherite insistence that he would veto any effort by Brussels to influence British tax rates'. It was also described as another example of a British political discourse on the EU that was 'dishonest and self-defeating'.[83] It was left to the Italian and Swedish governments to find a compromise position on the issue which saw the need for international cooperation to combat tax evasion and tax competition, while affirming national democratic sovereignty over tax policy.[84]

In December 1998, Blair and Schröder agreed a joint statement which said that they opposed a unified European system of corporate taxation and eschewed any measures 'leading to a higher tax burden and jeopardising competitiveness'.[85] The German government nevertheless reiterated its goal of 'tax coordination' – the term now preferred to tax harmonisation – precisely to avoid 'tax dumping and unfair competition', and these positions were prominent in its 'objectives and priorities' for the German presidency of the Council of Ministers in 1999, which referred to the need for 'a regulatory framework including ecological and social aspects for the world economy and lasting development'. This position was backed by Jospin, who expressed the hope that Britain would 'digest this reality'.[86] Lafontaine and Strauss-Kahn also emphasised macroeconomic coordination to create jobs, though both accepted that the Maastricht agreement to limit budget deficits made fiscal policy virtually redundant in this regard. Lafontaine stressed the need for lower interest rates (though these were set by an independent European Central Bank with a brief to control inflation), regulation of financial markets, exchange rate stabilisation, and an international social charter protecting both workers and the environment.[87]

EMU, as the PES-ECOFIN report *The New European Way* pointed out in October 1998, would enhance the potential for tax evasion unless the EU coordinated tax policy.[88] This report also argued that improved governance of international financial institutions combined with greater transparency in both the public and private sectors would increase the resilience of the international financial system and improve the multilateral surveillance of national policies. By the end of the month the G7 backed these ideas and the IMF was given extra credit facilities to assist countries in trouble. The SIC talked about the need for 'the regulation of globalisation and the globalisation of regulation' the following November. Among the measures it advocated for these purposes was the enforcement of a code of conduct, with appropriate sanctions, to be applied to market operators. It called for a worldwide system for monitoring financial and economic risks and improved political accountability of the IMF, World Bank, WTO and ILO. In particular it repeated the earlier demand for transformation of the IMF's Interim Committee into a Political Council with decision-making powers and favoured closer cooperation between the multilateral institutions mentioned. The stronger institutional framework which it promoted for purposes of collective responsibility and effective coordination of international economic policy would include an enlarged G7. This Economic Security Council, operating within the UN framework, would address global issues such as the stability of exchange rates, international capital flows, the avoidance of fiscal competition and global programmes for growth and employment. Indeed a global recovery programme promoting investment, trade, income and employment would be top of its agenda.[89] The statement argued that

> If we want to maximise gains and minimise losses from globalisation, we need to restructure the global imbalance between public and private financial power. If we want financial markets to serve people rather than master governments, we need to ensure that they can maximise employment and welfare and minimise risks to the environment. They need rules of the game which can promote positive outcomes for themselves and the world economy, rather than their recent record of zero or negative sum outcomes. This implies a governance framework for the global economy and to safeguard the global environment.[90]

The SIC also admitted that

> it is evident that structural adjustment policies, reinforced by cross conditionality, imposed by the IMF since the mid-80s, have in large part been paid for by the poor, and that trickle-down rarely occurs while upward income shifts have been marked. To break this circle means taking a Gordian knot approach to cutting poverty by a global programme for direct expenditures on nutrition, housing, sanitation, health and education for the poorest people in both the less and least developed countries.[91]

Developing countries, in this view, should not be penalised for trade deficits if they are pursuing investment in the social sector. The SIC argued that all projects undertaken by the World Bank should be subject to 'environmental conditionality' and that both the World Bank and the IMF should be given more resources and clearer roles based on the original distinction that the IMF should act as an agency for short-term balance of payments support while the World Bank acts as a long-term development agency. The SIC countenanced capital controls too, but as a short-term crisis measure designed to avoid costly bail-outs of the sort that repeatedly saw governments rushing to the financial aid of private firms that had damaged themselves in speculative financial activities.

The larger problem of global financial crisis also moved the PES to observe that it had exposed 'the limits and risks of world-wide uncontrolled capital liberalisation'. The usual call for transparency, prudence and upgraded governance and coordination of the IMF and World Bank was made. Its report on 'the creation of an orderly world economy' recognised at least some of the damage which IMF structural reform programmes did to development in the countries subjected to them. It also called for financial regulation to discourage short-term capital flows and currency stability between the major trading blocks. It pointed out that if the private sector had to bear some of the cost of bail-outs, it might be deterred from speculation in the first place. Much of the speculation might also be reduced by the creation of regional monetary unions designed to narrow the range of currency fluctuations. But it rejected capital controls and talked only in terms of new codes of conduct.[92]

Concluding remarks

The world's currency markets daily trade an amount that dwarfs the total currency reserves of the world's central banks. Such banks have been eclipsed by market operators in terms of their control over capital markets. Power in the world economy has shifted to finance and away from the producers of goods and services. Politicians took some of the decisions that led to this situation and made other decisions – such as the rules governing the European Central Bank – in deference to the power of finance. Institutions such as the IMF hastened the process by insisting on the deregulation of foreign exchange and stock markets whether or not local economies could cope with the consequences. Emerging market economies in particular experienced huge capital inflows which turned to abrupt withdrawal at the first loss of confidence, triggering exchange crises, dramatic depreciations, draconian credit squeezes, precipitous public debt and the collapse of production and employment. Speculative activity on this scale, operating at great speed and perforce with only imperfect information, proved conducive to herd behaviour of the sort that generated crises in Latin America in the 1980s and Southeast Asia in the late 1990s. The European economy was necessarily affected by these and other speculative frenzies such as the one that brought Britain out of the Exchange Rate Mechanism in 1992. The risks of global deflation became obvious in the biggest of these crises, as did the recourse to social dumping and the sacrifice of the living standards of the poorest. In the wake of the Asian crisis in 1997–98 even the supporters of unbridled globalisation started to talk about reining it in.

Control of speculative finance requires the concerted action of the most powerful governments – at a minimum – for this is the most truly global economic activity of all. Unless the government of the US accepts the need for this, the EU is probably powerless to do anything about it. Other aspects of economic behaviour do not inevitably undermine social democratic governance. MNC's are not 'footloose', for example. They operate overwhelmingly within the three regional blocs that dominate the world economy – the EU, North America and the Japanese-dominated Pacific. They need the resources of these blocs such as skilled workers, sophisticated infrastructure, political stability and strong markets for their products. The European bloc is especially integrated economically. Multinationals from this region largely operate within it, whether we are measuring their employment, investment or sales strategies. If the EU insists upon the maintenance and improvement of standards affecting the environment, health and safety at work, employee representation and the like, there is no reason to believe that MNCs would simply pull out and find more 'flexible' alternatives. Concerted action by EU governments could probably also lead to effective action against corporate tax evasion and eliminate the 'Dutch auction' which currently leads to expenditure on unnecessary bribes and subsidies in an effort to induce inward investment to particular countries. To talk of the need for internationally 'competitive tax rates' and flexible labour markets and the obsolescence of 'tax-and-spend' socialism – a socialism that stood for the redistribution of income and the narrowing of inequalities – is to suggest that mobile capital will simply punish with impunity countries which deny these truths. But there is no evidence to support this conclusion.[93] Even if there had been one might expect social democratic parties to look to processes of transnational political integration as the appropriate response, and it is significant that the party which appears to be most convinced of the need to 'go with the grain of globalisation' is one of the least enthusiastic about political union within the EU – New Labour. But then British capital is about equally divided between Europe and the US in terms of investment and attracts foreign investment about equally from the US and the EU. Likewise, while domestic investment by domestic capital easily dominates both direct investment overseas and foreign investment at home in most European countries, this is not true of Britain.[94] It would be too simple, however, to reduce Labour policies to these factors.

In the absence of a European-wide coordination the spectre of further deregulatory bias will continue to haunt anxious, employer-pecked governments who will be told that the high wage/ high value-added economy with strong social institutions will be swept aside by the 'Anglo-American' model. The pessimists already doubt that world markets will be big enough to sustain the strategy that made Germany and Sweden admired 'models' in the 1970s and 1980s. They question their ability to innovate, point to the pool of cheap East European labour that will destroy their internal labour markets, with or without immigration, and observe that financial internationalisation already corrodes the erstwhile long-termism of local banks and breaks their intimacy with local firms.[95] But, as in much of the globalisation literature, this is at least for now crystal-ball gazing and a counsel of despair.

Notes

1 P. Gould, *The Unfinished Revolution* (London, Little Brown, 1998), p. 24.
2 *Ibid.*, pp. 49–54, 258.
3 R. Ramsay, *Prawn Cocktail Party: The Hidden Power Behind New Labour* (London, Vision, 1998); S. Driver and L. Martell, *New Labour: Politics After Thatcherism* (Cambridge, Polity Press, 1998), pp. 17–18.
4 Labour Party, *It's Time to get Britain Working Again* (London, Labour Party, 1992), p. 11.
5 Labour Party, *Labour's Campaign For Recovery* (London, Labour Party, 1992).
6 Labour Party, *Opportunity Britain* (London, Labour Party, 1992), p. 5.
7 Labour Party, *Rebuilding the Economy* (London, Labour Party, 1994), p. 13.
8 *Ibid.*, p. 14.
9 *Ibid.*, p. 14.
10 *Ibid.*, p. 13.
11 'There will be no national products or technologies, no national corporations, no national industries. There will no longer be national economies, at least as we have come to understand that concept. All that will remain rooted within national borders are the people who comprise a nation. Each nation's primary assets will be its citizen's skills and insights'. R. B. Reich, *The Work of Nations* (New York, Vintage, 1992), p. 3.
12 Labour Party, *Rebuilding the Economy*, p. 4.
13 *Ibid.*, p. 2.
14 *Ibid.*, p. 4.
15 P. Anderson and N. Mann, *Safety First: The Making of New Labour* (London, Granta, 1997), pp. 38–9, and Driver and Martell, *New Labour*, p. 50.
16 Labour Party, *A New Economic Future For Britain* (London, Labour Party, 1995), p. 6.
17 *Ibid.*, p. 14.
18 *Ibid.*, pp. 17–18.
19 L. Elliott and R. Kelly, 'Labour admits city is needed', *Guardian*, 4 October 1994.
20 Labour Party, *Vision For Growth* (London, Labour Party, 1996), pp. 12, 47, 50.
21 *Ibid.*, pp. 57–9.

22 Labour Party, *Building Prosperity – Flexibility, Efficiency and Fairness at Work* (London, Labour Party, 1996), p. 3.
23 In Britain a thesis connecting sweeping changes in social structure, employment, gender relations, ideology, state-society relations and much else was promoted by the journal *Marxism Today*. In effect the journal stressed every development that could be interpreted to mean that all forms of socialism and social democracy were redundant. This work was continued by the new journal *Soundings* whose first editorial announced the impotence of national governments in the face of globalisation and the unravelling of the even the social democratic strongholds by virtue of competition from low wage/low social benefit economies. S. Hall, D. Massey, and M. Rustin, 'Uncomfortable times', *Soundings*, 1 (1995) 5–6.
24 Labour Party, *New Labour: New Life for Britain* (London, Labour Party, 1996), p. 5.
25 For example in Blair's speech to the Keidanren in Tokyo, January 1996.
26 Labour Party, *New Labour: Because Britain Deserves Better* (London, Labour Party, 1997), p. 3.
27 Labour Party, *Labour's Business Manifesto: Equipping Britain For the Future* (London, Labour Party, 1997), p. 1.
28 'All mod cons: Tony Blair's economic inheritance', *Economist*, 27 September 1997.
29 'The vision thing: Tony Blair says his mission is to modernise Britain', *Ibid.*
30 T. Blair, speech to the Keidanren, Tokyo, January 1996, in his *New Britain: My Vision of a Young Country* (London, Fourth Estate, 1996), p. 118.
31 *Ibid.*, p. 118.
32 See S. Strange, *Casino Capitalism* (Manchester, Manchester University Press, 1997).
33 Which might explain why it was not the British government that brought the two-year-old Multinational Agreement on Investment negotiations to an end in 1998.
34 Blair, *New Britain*, pp. 121–3.
35 *Ibid.*, p. 118.
36 Blair, 'From a speech to the Singapore Business Community', 8 January 1996, in *New Britain*, p. 293.
37 *Ibid.*, p. 296.
38 T. Blair, speech to Newscorp Leadership Conference, Hayman Island, Australia, 17 July 1996, in *New Britain*, p. 204
39 T. Blair, Mais Lecture, City University, London, 22 May 1995, in *New Britain*, p. 86.
40 See, M. Barratt Brown, *Defending The Welfare State* (Nottingham, Spokesman, 1998), pp. 869.
41 B. Johnson, 'Herr Blair takes a bow, but cannot take the credit', *Daily Telegraph*, 19 June 1996.
42 See O. Lafontaine, 'The future of German social democracy', *New Left Review*, 227 (1998) 72–87.
43 P. Riddell, 'Blair plays new economy card to trump Tory appeal', *The Times*, 5 January 1996.
44 'Blair does the business', *Guardian* leader, 22 January 1997.
45 W. Keegan, 'Deep depression and severe weather warning for the Tories', *Observer*, 7 January 1996.

46 Speeches by Blair at the launch of Britain's Presidency of the EU, Gordon Brown at the British-American Chamber of Commerce (both on 5 December 1997) and Blair again at The Hague on 20 January 1998 talked about the need to 'reform the European social model not play around with it' and advocated 'flexible labour markets' against 'the old European model which stifled job creation with over-regulation and inflexibility'.
47 M. Jacques, 'New Europeans', *Guardian*, 7 July 1997; D. Marquand, 'After euphoria: the silemmas of New Labour', *Political Quarterly*, 4 (1997) 335.
48 C. Crouch, 'The terms of the neo-liberal consensus', *Political Quarterly*, 4 (1997) 352.
49 M. Kettle, 'Labour's bright new dawn ends at Dover', *Guardian*, 21 June 1997.
50 P. Riddell, 'Opening a doorway to the past', *The Times*, 2 June 1997.
51 R. Cohen, *New York Times*, 20 October 1997, quoted by T. C. Frank, 'France: an unforgivable exception', *Le Monde Diplomatique*, April 1998.
52 R. Cohen, *New York Times*, 31 October 1997, quoted by Frank, 'France'.
53 T. Jagland, Speech to the Socialist International Council, 18 May 1998, DNA website, accessed January 1999.
54 I. Ramonet, 'Europe under the Bundesbank', *Le Monde Diplomatique*, July 1997.
55 C. Gobin, 'Taming the unions', *Le Monde Diplomatique*, November 1997.
56 D. Marquand, 'After euphoria', p. 336.
57 R. Cook, speech to the Institute for European Affairs, Dublin, 3 November 1997.
58 M. Kettle, 'The next step: a blueprint for New Labour's world role', *Guardian*, 7 February 1998.
59 D. Strauss-Kahn, Speech at the Forum Paris Europlace, New York, 17 April 1998.
60 French Embassy and Information Service, *News From France*, April 1998.
61 SPD, 'Globalisation and sustainable development', adopted by SPD Hanover conference, 2–4 December 1997, SPD website, accessed January 1999.
62 SPD, 'Europe: a united continent of peace, welfare and social security', adopted by SPD Hanover conference, 2–4 December 1997, SPD website, accessed January 1999.
63 SPD, 'Work, innovation, and justice, SPD Manifesto 1988', adopted at Leipzig, 17 April 1998, SPD website, accessed January 1999.
64 Dutch Ministry of Economic Affairs, 'Knowledge in action', Ministry of Economic Affairs website, accessed January 1999.
65 D. Vidal, 'Uncertainty over the welfare state: miracle or mirage in the Netherlands?', *Le Monde Diplomatique*, July 1997.
66 *Ibid.*
67 Dutch Ministry of Finance, 'The Dutch tax authorities and foreign businesses', Dutch Ministry of Finance website, accessed January 1999. See also Dutch Government Press Release, 'White Paper: taxes in the twenty-first century: an investigation', 11 December 1997.
68 Dutch Ministry of Economic Affairs, 'Knowledge in action'.
69 New Democratic Party, Resolution from the 18th Federal Convention at Regina, Saskatchewan, 11–13 April 1997.
70 D. Strauss-Kahn, 'Six of the best', *Financial Times*, 16 April 1998.
71 See D. Buchan, 'Jospin plea over capital flows', *Financial Times*, 12 September 1998.

72 First proposed by the Nobel prize winner James Tobin.

73 SAP, 'Stepping into the year 2000: the congress of the future, Sundsvall 1997: policy guidelines adopted by the Party Congress' (SAP, n.d.), p. 86.

74 Labour Party [Norway], *Statement of Principles and Action Programme* (Oslo, DNA, 1996).

75 P. Mauroy, 'Draft of speech to SI Council', 18 May 1998, DNA website, accessed January 1999.

76 PES, PES press release, June 1997, PES website, accessed January 1999.

77 See O. Lafontaine, 'Globalisation and international cooperation' (Bonn, SPD, 1996); see also his 'The future of German Social Democracy' and 'Globalisation and international cooperation – social democratic policy in an age of globalisation', in D. Dettke (ed.), *The Challenge of Globalisation for Germany's Social Democracy: A Policy Agenda for the 21st Century* (Oxford, Berghahn, 1998), pp. 1–11.

78 PES-ECOFIN-Group, 'The new European way – economic reform in the framework of EMU', 12 October 1998, PES website, accessed January 1999.

79 R. Atkins, 'Lafontaine links tax to EU budget', *Financial Times*, 17 December 1998. 'Stockholm: Swedes press EU to move against tax havens', *Financial Times*, 28 November 1997.

80 *Economist*, 20–6 March 1999.

81 R. Atkins, P. Norman and R. Peston, 'Schröder backs Lafontaine', *Financial Times*, 3 December 1998.

82 Ed Balls apparently authored the paper 'Economic reform in the framework of EMU' which Brown presented for an Anglo-German Economic Working Party. Reported by R. Peston in 'Brown plans Anglo-German working party', *Financial Times*, 19 November 1998.

83 Editorial, *Observer*, 29 November 1998, p. 28.

84 J. Blitz, 'Italy seeks to defuse dispute over policy', Financial Times (3 December 1998); SAP, 'Stepping Into the Year 2000: The Congress of the Future, Sundsvall, 1997: Policy Guidelines Adopted By the Party Congress', p. 18.

85 R. Peston and F. Studemann, 'UK plays down chance of veto over European Tax on savings', *Financial Times*, 10 December 1998.

86 G. Graham, A. Parker and D. Wighton, 'Chirac seeks to soothe UK', *Financial Times*, 4 December 1998.

87 I. Traynor and D. Walker, 'Analysis: social democracy: pretty in pink', *Guardian*, 15 September 1998.

88 PES-ECOFIN-Group, 'The new European way'.

89 Socialist International Council, 'To regulate globalisation and to globalise regulation', agreed in Geneva, 23–24 November 1998, Socialist International website, accessed January 1999.

90 *Ibid.*

91 *Ibid.*

92 PES, 'Creating an orderly framework for the world economy: towards a more efficient, stable, and fair global financial and monetary system', PES website, accessed January 1999.

93 See F. Vandenbroucke, *Globalisation, Inequality, and Social Democracy* (London, IPPR, 1998). Vandenbroucke qualifies the globalisation phenomenon in ways

similar to Hirst and Thompson in *Globalisation in Question*, but argues explicitly that the most fundamental long-term constraints on the social democratic Keynesian programme for full employment are internal to the nation-state and concern distributional conflicts (p. 41).

94 See A. Glyn and R. Sutcliffe, 'Global but leaderless? The new capitalist order', in L. Panitch and R. Miliband, *The Socialist Register 1992* (London, Merlin, 1992), p. 84.

95 See for example, W. Streeck, 'German capitalism', in C. Crouch and W. Streeck (eds), *Political Economy of Modern Capitalism* (London, Sage, 1997), pp. 50–2.

8

Changes in party organistion

The social democratic parties were formed for a variety of purposes which affected their structures and organisation. Germany's SPD was created with the intention of transforming capitalist society; the Labour Party in Britain was chiefly concerned to acquire parliamentary representation for the organised working class with a view to pursuing its interests by achieving particular reforms. As early as the publication of Eduard Bernstein's *Evolutionary Socialism* in 1899 it was realised in some quarters that these parties had to reach beyond their 'natural' constituency to obtain the support of other social classes. Labour was in any case keen to demonstrate its national credentials from the first time it formed a government in 1924. In Britain the logic of the two-party system after 1945 reinforced the party leadership's conviction that only moderate policies would secure the crucial middle-class and 'floating' voters. The doctrinal left of the Labour Party was perceived as a problem precisely to the extent that it was able to criticise the leadership ('generate internecine controversy') and insist on principle ('indulge in superfluous ideological rhetoric'). In chapter one we saw that all the parties of the reformist left were subject to pressures which forced them towards the centre ground and consensus.

The revisionists were in charge of the direction of policy. Here we will only consider the organisational bases of this dominance. Some of them were as old as those uncovered in Robert Michels' classic study[1] of the German Social Democratic Party – notably the culture of deference among the ranks, the belief in loyalty and unity, the personal and organisational powers enjoyed by the leadership. But the sources of revisionist dominance of the Labour Party in Britain were also derived from its unique federal structure which gave the affiliated trade unions a massive representation at its annual conference and on its National Executive Committee, as well as the dominant role in party finance. The 'social democratic centralism' that operated in the party in the 1940s and 1950s – a centralism which one leading MP compared to Lenin's[2] – was securely rooted because it rested on an alliance between the parliamentary leadership and the biggest of the affiliated trade unions. Labour's organisational structures ensured that between them the union officials and the professional politicians dominated the policy-making bodies of the party, with the unions generally following the lead given by the politicians. Trade union finance also made the political leadership less dependent on the subscriptions of individual members and lessened the need for a mass individual membership. And since influential voting studies from the 1950s emphasised the declining significance of activists in getting out the vote, as mass media became more important and attention focused on floating voters in the minority of (marginal) constituencies, the activists could be seen as little more than a noisy nuisance.

Many of the parties of the continent also enjoyed intimate relationships with trade unions which acted as a moderating influence, but they were also shaped by different points of departure. Most were conceived as weapons in the struggle to transform the social system and accordingly set out to become counter-cultural parties of social integration, almost states within the state. The mobilisation of the working class that was thought to be required in order to effect this transformation, involved the parties in building a mass membership serviced by their own cultural, sports, educational and news organisations, reaching out via ancillary organisations to bring women, youth, and other sections of the population into its embrace. In the 1920s Egon Wertheimer observed that British Labour had none of these protective skins and stood exposed to the full blast of the dominant value system. Labour never set out to rupture the political and socioeconomic order like the pre-1914 SPD in Germany, where the party of social integration model reached its peak. Parties that had set out to achieve a revolution still bore organisational evidence of this original ambition long after they had officially or practically renounced it. Commentators like Sigmund Neumann saw continued relevance for the party of social integration in the 1950s, and the remnants of this form of organisation certainly survived well beyond the Second World War in countries such as Austria, Sweden and Italy as well as in West Germany.[3] Kircheimer argued in the mid-1960s however that the project of 'intellectual and moral *encadrement* of the masses' had actually been abandoned, as competitive pressure forced such parties to become 'catch-alls' seeking vote maximisation.[4] A process was underway, according to Kircheimer, that would see the elimination of ideological baggage that stood in the way of this objective, and the downgrading of the role of the activists and the party's core constituency as an increasingly powerful leadership reached out to other social strata in search of votes. Leadership control in the parties of social integration had always relied on a degree of bureaucracy and patronage that had been unnecessary in the British Labour Party because of the collaboration of the trade union and parliamentary elites – a collaboration that had been the norm for most of Labour's existence. But except in the Scandinavian countries where hegemonic social democratic parties did not face competitive pressures to transform themselves into catch-all parties, in the 1960s a degree of convergence in party organisation was already taking place.

Social democratic parties have generally enjoyed close links with the trade unions, as we have observed, though the unions' 'symbiotic attachment' to British Labour is exceptional.[5] Nevertheless, many of them have enjoyed cooperative relationships which have undoubtedly assisted party managers and parliamentary elites. This is particularly true of the Scandinavian parties in the 1950s and 1960s, but also of West Germany and Austria[6] where moderate, centralised and disciplined unions have enjoyed access to decision-making bodies in the social democratic parties on the basis of overlapping membership.[7] It is noteworthy that in the Netherlands, where the trade union federation, NVV, decided against a formal link with the PvdA in 1945 and further loosened its links with the party at the end of the 1960s, the New Left was able to exert a major influence in the party – because the traditional forces were not there to block its way. The NVV, having decided that too close a relationship with the party would restrict its appeal – in a context where tripartite corporatist structures ensured that it exerted influence on government via more effective channels – remained detached for fear that the New Left activist virus would spread into its own ranks.[8] Unions have more generally been constrained by the fact that elected social democratic parties are of more use to them than unelected social democratic parties. If evidence accumulates suggesting that programmatic 'modernisation' is required to render a party electable, it is difficult for union leaders to block its path. From the beginnings of social democracy unions have recognised the primacy of the electoral struggle and the dominant role of party leaders in shaping the social democratic image and tactics. Except in the Scandinavian countries, unions do not generally represent a majority of the workforce and can be credibly depicted by social democracy's opponents as a mere sectional interest. Neither union leaders nor party managers have an interest in the perception of a union-dominated social democracy under these circumstances, and so another reason is added to the case for trade union restraint. Union leaders are also aware that not all of their members are social democratic voters and that too intimate a relationship might jeopardise effective pursuit of their primary functions.[9]

When social democratic parties themselves threaten these functions unions can be expected to resist. The British TUC was notably more committed to the defence of working-class living standards than the self-avowed socialists who led the Labour government during the financial crisis that almost split the party in 1931.[10] Relations between the TUC and the Parliamentary Labour Party (PLP) were notably strained after the latter floated the idea of legislating in industrial relations in 1969. The unions effectively blocked this idea and went on to play a leading role in the construction of the Social Contract, the centrepiece of Labour's programme for government in 1974. The stronger Scandinavian unions have also been a source of social democratic policy. As we have seen the active labour-market policy of the SAP in Sweden originated with LO economists, as did the Meidner Plan for employee investment funds which the SAP was conspicuously less enthusiastic about and successfully watered down. In Denmark the LO acts as a significant faction of the Social Democratic Party and when a union official, Anker Jorgensen, became leader of the party in 1972 he was said to have consulted former trade union colleagues before his own cabinet members. Between February 1975 and August 1978 'the economic policy of the minority [social democratic] government was effectively co-determined by the LO and the government' in Denmark.[11] When the Social Democrats entered a coalition with the Liberals, LO criticism was vociferous and helped to bring the coalition to a speedy end. Thereafter (October 1979–82) the unions returned to a prominent role in devising social democratic economic policy and continued to exert real influence in this area into the 1990s.

In Norway the trade unions (LO) are collectively affiliated to the DNA at local level and there is LO representation throughout the organisation, including the party executive and Cooperating Committee on which Labour ministers meet with the union leadership. The party has always depended on trade union finance and from the 1920s it became 'unthinkable' that the two sides of the movement would divide on a major political issue.[12] What was true for Norway applied also in Sweden where there was collective affiliation of union branches at district level of the party until 1990 and the general secretary of the LO was always a member of the senior party leadership. Major decisions were rarely taken without LO agreement.[13] As recently as the early 1980s LO members accounted for 60 per cent of SAP local councillors, 46 per cent of county councillors and 40 per cent of MPs; the LO president was accustomed to being one of these members of the *Riksdag*.[14] One aspect of the 'Swedish model' which attracted Labour politicians in Britain in the 1950s and 1960s was the wage restraint exercised by the LO in return for progressive policies from SAP governments. Such restraint was also secured in West Germany, even though the SPD was rarely in power and no organic relationship tied it to the unions.

Former trade union officials nevertheless formed a significant proportion of SPD parliamentarians, and office holders at local level are often acting union functionaries. Though the union confederation, the DGB, plays no formal role in protecting the dominance of the party elite, the trade union members of the party exercise influence through such media as the *Arbeitsgeneinschaft fur Arbeitnehmerfragen* (AfA), a working circle founded in 1972 to consider questions relating to employees. In the 1970s and 1980s trade union influence was invariably exercised against the left of the party.[15]

We will shortly see that the ability of the unions to protect party elites has waned, a fact that has been obscured perhaps, rather than highlighted, by the growing conflict between trade unions and social democratic parties since the 1970s. But first it is necessary to register the point that the strength and authority of the Scandinavian unions is exceptional and even the levels of trade union support enjoyed by the social democratic parties in Britain, West Germany and Austria were unknown in France, Greece, Portugal and Italy.

In France, where the Communists took control of the CGT in 1947, a weak and divided trade union movement has not been able to supply significant support to the socialists. This 'seriously affected' the credibility and strength of the Socialist Party.[16] The union link might have brought the financial support, organisational stability and the mass membership that the PS lacked. Overshadowed by the PCF until the 1970s, the PS's overwhelmingly white-collar membership disqualified it as a workers' party at a time when that was what it aspired to be. Though it wooed the CFDT following the 1974 presidential elections, it was ultimately unsuccessful[17] and party membership became increasingly composed of white-collar, tertiary employees. The violent fluctuations in membership recorded in the 1980s seem to lend weight to Criddle's claim that the party is more vulnerable to the fickleness of the 'new middle class' than its counterparts in other countries, even though one must acknowledge the trend against blue-collar participation in social democratic parties everywhere.[18] A trade union presence could be found among the rank and file of the PS, but it was small, drawn from different confederations and sprinkled across the different factions of the party, all of which goes some way to explain 'its relative silence and paralysis' on industrial issues.[19]

There is no doubt that some social democratic parties now look on the French Socialists with envy when it comes to the question of its detachment from the unions. As social democratic governments turned to neo-liberal policies, conflict with the unions became inevitable. In Spain the PSOE was historically linked to the trade union federation, the UGT, which acted as its trade union wing while remaining formally independent of it. Under the Franco dictatorship the stronghold of Socialist activity was based in the north of the country where it was organised on a UGT basis.[20] But neither the UGT nor the PSOE were as well organised as their Communist rivals when the transition to democracy began. Reorganisation of the PSOE was largely the work of aspiring professional politicians with little or no experience of union affairs. This group quickly transformed the party into a model of elite domination based on professional politicians largely drawn from middle-class backgrounds. While this cohort took the view that the future of the party depended on its ability to break free from the constraints of working-class identity and embrace the economic 'modernisation' that would swell the ranks of the new middle class, the UGT experienced rapid membership decline – from more than 5 million members in 1978 to a quarter of a million by the mid-1980s.[21] Though the Socialist government pursued an orthodox monetarist policy after 1982 – denounced by the Communist-led workers' commissions – the UGT tried to defend its policy until austerity and unemployment bred discontent and industrial unrest in the late 1980s culminating in UGT support for a general strike in 1988.

The adverse economic conditions which prevailed after 1973 were made worse by government policies – often social democratic government policies – to give priority to price stability, balanced budgets and the Maastricht convergence criteria. In Greece, as well as Spain, this strained relations between the unions and socialist governments. The Norwegian Labour Government of Gro Harlem Brundtland justified its own deflationary policies between 1981 and 1986, against those who demanded Keynesian measures, by the now familiar argument that such measures would no longer work in the conditions of 'the new liberated, international economy'.[22] But the stresses evident in the relationship between organised labour and social democracy are not merely the consequences of recession, unemployment and welfare cuts. There is a strong perception that changes in the social structure and occupational mix are also relevant – not just because they signal the relative, often absolute, decline of the blue-collar workers' organisations and the rise of newer white-collar unions, but also because these changes promote membership changes in the parties themselves and help to explain the rise of new issues.

Even in Sweden the harmonious relationship between the LO and SAP had begun to break down as early as the 1970s during the period of the Meidner Plan for employee investment funds. The growth of rival trade union federations representing white-collar workers undermined the LO's authority, as did the employers' increasing dissatisfaction with centralised bargaining in the same decade. By the 1980s the tensions between the SAP and the unions was indicated by the mutual agreement to phase out collective affiliation and the increasing number of disagreements which the media dubbed 'the war of the roses'. Public-sector cuts, tax concessions for the rich, deregulation of the economy, wage freezes and strike bans aggravated the LO membership. The Swedish case also illustrates some of the problems which have emerged as the old social democratic agenda is challenged by the New Left. In the 1980 referendum on phasing out nuclear power stations the unions found themselves on the same side as the employers in raising fears of lost competitiveness and jobs, and commentators were already warning of a burgeoning division in the SAP between 'competing factions, one industrially based and committed to growth, the other based on the service sector and sceptical of growth'.[23] The issue of reconciling traditional social democratic concerns with green issues is certainly ongoing and was also visible in the drafting of the 1981 environmental programme and the construction of the 1990 party programme.

The rise of the agendas associated with the new social movements within social democracy is paralleled by the relative growth of a white-collar, university-educated, middle-class membership in these parties and the relative decline of the blue-collar, working-class membership. In West Germany, the SPD's disappointing election results of 1976 – revealing losses that were highest among women and blue-collar workers – prompted an internal reassessment of the party which concluded, among other things, that the membership was dangerously passive. Two empirical surveys of the membership followed, but official complaints about the closed and inactive ethos of the branches continued to be voiced into the 1980s.[24] Working-class membership of the SPD has declined from the 60 per cent recorded in 1930 to 22 per cent in 1978. Though the SPD vote was more working class than the population as a whole, its membership was substantially less so and working-class interests had become only one of many battling for influence within the party. Furthermore, the party's working class members derived chiefly from the skilled workers.[25] Increasingly, the better educated, together with workers from the public-sector professions, are represented disproportionately in the membership. The influx of new members from the beginning of the 1970s accelerated this process creating, according to one 1995 study, 'a serious problem of communication between the labour movement and its erstwhile most important clientele – the working class'.[26] The low representation of working class members in official positions within the party is mirrored in the branches where working-class members are reportedly 'alienated by the academic and expert nature of much of the discussion'[27] and much less inclined to assert themselves than the middle-class members – much as Michels argued in 1911.

There is be a price to be paid for declining working-class involvement. According to Kolinsky, writing in 1984, an increasing proportion of the party membership stipulated personal influence within the organisation, as well as wider political issues, as reasons for membership rather than mere loyalty to the organisation. Such members were more likely to be drawn from the ranks of the white-collar workers and an internal discussion paper produced in 1982 reported membership losses of 10–20 per cent and low rates of activism in urban areas. Yet middle-class loyalty to the organisation is more conditional on the realisation of personal objectives and more than one in twenty of this section of the membership, in a survey cited by Kolinsky, expressed either a readiness to resign because of frustration or a conviction that their aspirations had been blocked by the way the party functioned. Kolinsky concluded that a way of accommodating these aspirations had yet to be found, but it is relevant in this context to note that the old working-class deference which party elites used to take for granted is also in decay.[28] More recently, Berger has suggested that the removal of party functionaries from everyday working-class realities can be seen in the 'vague and badly thought through' line adopted by the SDP on problems of social integration associated with foreign workers and asylum seekers in a period of high and rising unemployment, a position apparently 'rejected by substantial numbers of manual workers who have increasingly looked to right-wing parties'.[29]

These frustrations were expected to be compounded by the perception that 'old left' issues belong to the right of the political spectrum as New Left green issues come to occupy the opposite pole. Certainly in the 1980s 'the defection of blue-collar voters to the CDU was blamed by many in the unions on the SPD abandoning its traditional constituency'.[30] Taylor adds that the party's flirtation with the Greens – with Oskar Lafontaine leading the charge of those who wanted a closer alignment with the allegedly 'post-materialist middle class' – angered the DGB unions who saw it ' as symptomatic of the baleful influence of white-collar, middle-class activists out of touch with core SPD blue-collar supporters'.[31] The chemical and miners' unions were among those opposed to the SPD's ecological concerns in the 1980s and once the costs of national reunfication became an issue many unions argued that Germany could not afford the environmental agenda of the party's New Left. 'Lafontaine-ism' met with concerted opposition at the 1989 party congress, but the evidence since then is that the unions are having to live with the party's growing concern for environmental issues. After Engholm resigned as party chair in 1993, Schröder put himself forward as representative of the strategy of Green coalition against those, such as Scharping, ready to do business with the centre-right. Though personal rivalries within the leadership elite contributed to its very public divisions in the 1990s, the party contained 'competing social and cultural milieux', some of which are institutionalised in organisations such as the AfA, as we observed earlier, while others derive from recruitment in the east of the country.[32]

The influx of educated, middle-class recruits experienced by the SPD after 1969 was even more dramatic in the case of the Dutch Labour Party with the result that the New Left dominated the party until the mid-1980s, changing its political as well as its class culture. Issues such as participatory democracy, peace and environmental progress were of more concern to the new members than the old preoccupations of jobs and welfare.[33] In 1970 right-wing members left the party to form the Democratic Socialists. Increased factionalism nevertheless characterised this period of the PvdA's recent history as it did in that of the DNA, which recorded the same rise of New Left issues – especially green issues and those of the peace movement – but also divided internally over the issue of membership of the European Community. The SAP in Sweden has experienced less factionalism – perhaps because there are (former Communist and Green) parties to its left capable of securing representation in the *Riksdag* – but the same divergence between 'concrete socialists' and 'eco-socialists', to use Arter's terms, has been evident in the recent past.[34]

As shown in Table 8.1 (pp. 190–1), the general trend of social democratic party membership in the years 1974–94 has been down, though there are exceptions. Social democratic parties compete with their rivals for the greater share of the votes of national electorates in a context in which it has been extremely unusual for them to win half of the votes cast. The membership of these parties is generally to the left of the party's electoral support and this has been a source of persistent friction between the activists and the parliamentary leadership. Oppositional forces within the membership have taken a wide variety of forms, ranging from quasi-clandestine organisations such as Militant within the British Labour Party, with its own membership and programme, to the groupings around individual leaders characteristic of the French Socialists. Clearly this is also a spectrum that ranges from fundamental ideological opposition to the party's chosen strategy and tactics, to pragmatic conflict based on rival egos and career paths. It has been suggested that the rapid ideological shifts in the French and Spanish parties in the 1980s shows that 'ideas were as much counters to be played in the power game as signifiers of political conviction'.[36] We might add that the journey taken by many socialist politicians in the British Labour Party in the 1980s and 1990s is illustrative of the same point. Indeed, this may constitute the special contribution of social democracy to the apparent popular disenchantment with politics across Western Europe, as the public has been treated to a veritable 'permanent revolution' of jettisoned principles in such countries, as well as a plague of corruption scandals.

Certainly the upheavals associated with the issues raised above – the influx of new middle-class members, factionalism and the conflicts caused by recession – seem to have demoralised the membership in some of the social democratic parties. Though there was doctrinal debate in the SPÖ in the 1970s and discontent with the party's performance in office,[37] a left opposition in the party was virtually non-existent by the 1990s. Similarly, there was no organised alternative within PASOK by the 1990s. When the PvdA began to move closer to the centre after its failure to get back into government in 1986, it nevertheless encouraged expectations of a different socioeconomic approach than that of the CDA/VVD (Christian Democratic Appeal/People's Party for Freedom and Democracy) coalition. When this failed to materialise in the early 1990s there was an exodus of members (17 per cent) leaving behind a splintered and reduced left-wing seemingly incapable of real opposition. A pattern of declining rates of activism and grassroots demoralisation also emerges in the case of the Norwegian DNA, which was without 'institutionalised expression of opposition' by 1993.[38] In Spain, opposition to the policies of González within the PSOE was difficult because of the party's authoritarian internal regime until 1988, but also because of what Gillespie calls 'ideological self-policing' arising from the conviction that there was no alternative.[39] When factionalism re-emerged in 1988 it was largely based on personalities, but an attempt to raise an ideological challenge by internal party groups was also made as the Socialists lost working-class support in the 1993 election. No left

Table 8.1 *Membership of socialist and social democratic parties, 1945–94*

	BSP/PSB Belgium	*DNA Norway*	*Labour UK*	*SPÖ Austria*	*PASOK Greece*	*PS France*	*PS Portugal*	*PSI Italy*	*PSDI Italy*	*PSOE Spain*	*PvdA N'lands*	*SAP Sweden*	*SD Denmark*	*SDP Finland*	*SPD Germany*
1945		191,045	487,047	357,818		335,703		700,000			56,000	563,981	260,566	63,745	
1946	95,260	197,638	645,345	500,181		354,878		860,000			116,551	558,584	285,634	65,611	711,400
1947	105,134	202,043	608,487	570,768		296,814		822,000			111,722	588,044	305,606	75,379	875,479
1948	113,201	203,094	629,025	616,232		223,495		531,031			119,509	635,658	316,027	75,951	844,653
1949	123,764	204,055	729,624	614,366		157,897		430,258			112,504	668,817	294,969	69,309	736,218
1950	127,158	293,094	908,161	607,283		140,190		700,000			105,609	722,073	283,907	67,268	683,896
1951	134,558		876,275	621,074		126,898		720,000			111,885	739,474	275,994	71,230	649,529
1952	143,977		1,014,524	627,435		116,327		750,000			111,351	746,004	277,658	65,730	627,817
1953		178,004	1,004,685	657,042		113,455		780,000			112,823	753,785	283,525	62,442	607,456
1954	153,014	174,575	933,657	666,373		105,244		754,000			119,561	757,426	283,221	62,669	585,479
1955	167,531	174,080	843,356	691,150		107,653		770,000			124,641	770,140	278,299	58,962	589,051
1956	172,530		845,129	687,972		120,000		710,000			142,139	777,860	275,363	60,547	612,219
1957	182,496		912,987	683,249		117,331		477,000			142,849	774,866	265,174	57,774	626,189
1958	187,000		888,955	716,208		115,000		486,652			137,778	780,686	256,759	51,144	623,816
1959			847,526	710,378		102,000		484,652			147,074	796,106	257,219	46,263	634,254
1960	199,000	165,096	790,192	727,265		100,000		489,337	119,167		142,583	730,305	259,459	42,926	649,578
1961	196,700	164,799	750,565			98,000		465,259	129,125		138,829	740,608	252,667	39,035	644,780
1962		162,842	767,459	698,705		91,000		491,216	153,717		139,375	758,073	237,671	44,828	646,584
1963		164,562	830,346			88,000		491,676	150,717		138,567	788,559	228,137	42,124	648,415
1964	204,500	163,712	830,116	717,624		88,000		446,250	165,980		142,426	803,964	229,275	49,308	678,484
1965	202,223	150,262	816,765	707,972		85,000		437,458	185,269		140,389	798,662	223,977	51,656	710,448
1966	203,078	152,305	775,693	707,972		84,000		697,588			134,476	824,616	188,859	51,681	727,890
1967	196,619	164,250	733,932	702,296		82,000		633,573			130,960	831,712	177,997	51,417	733,004
1968	207,145	163,163	701,299	705,634		81,000					116,736	818,416	176,729	60,079	732,446

1969	215,686	157,536	680,656	716,196		72,000					107,005	851,382	179,609	56,542	778,945
1970	224,950	155,254	680,191	719,389		70,392		537,000		2,000	98,671	835,741	177,507	60,707	820,202
1971	235,069	158,295	699,522	702,083		80,300	40,000	592,586	250,181		96,337	857,151	165,645	73,511	847,456
1972	241,317	153,186	703,030	696,438		92,230		575,000	284,772		94,229	889,582	152,174	76,869	954,394
1973	250,337	145,724	665,379	687,375		107,757		465,189	303,026		97,787	877,936	130,476	82,795	973,601
1974	254,462	130,489	691,889	687,650	8,000	137,000	40,000	511,741	279,396		103,140	935,379	122,722	92,372	957,253
1975	253,993	137,954	674,905	693,156	8,000	149,623		539,339	308,211		100,524	978,662	123,140	99,463	998,471
1976	254,830	143,934	659,058	700,146		159,548	91,000	498,542		9,141	95,548	1,028,574	111,139	101,725	1,022,191
1977	252,481	152,935	659,737	703,624	17,426	160,000		482,916	149,610		109,659	1,073,926	106,204	101,236	1,006,316
1978	259,213	153,032	675,946	706,039	30,834	180,000		472,277	148,131		121,274	1,106,506	109,389	99,644	997,444
1979	257,735	158,724	666,091	721,262	55,000	159,000		484,044	217,212	101,082	118,522	1,141,847	109,000	99,722	981,805
1980	268,720	153,507	348,156	719,881	75,000	189,580		514,918	108,470		112,929	1,159,655	104,842	100,161	986,972
1981	283,817	153,335	276,692	713,104	100,000	196,501		530,083	199,588	99,999	109,557	1,159,970	105,000	98,247	954,119
1982	272,469	165,479	273,803	702,414		213,584		552,587	126,015	119,101	105,486	1,184,321	105,000	97,365	926,070
1983	261,627	171,796	295,344	694,598	200,000	203,535	119,000	557,619	215,000	144,865	101,724	1,188,574	101,000	95,461	925,630
1984	259,171	172,108	323,292	690,533	250,000	189,282		571,821	165,733	157,260	99,347	1,170,482	103,000	93,872	916,485
1985	248,685	174,143	313,099	685,588		176,878		583,292	165,733	165,053	100,818	1,160,707	102,000	92,032	919,457
1986	244,597	164,222	297,364	674,821		177,284		589,697	133,428	185,663	103,217	1,166,410	100,000	90,109	912,854
1987	249,697	153,447	288,829	654,397	100,000	183,210		614,815	133,428	216,138	101,141	1,124,164	100,000	87,872	910,063
1988	241,631	140,042	265,927	637,469		202,083		656,126	110,000	232,665	98,001	1,077,876	98,000	86,944	911,916
1989	231,009	127,099	293,723	617,163		204,172			110,000	242,661	96,472	978,265		85,242	921,430
1990	228,623	128,106	311,152	597,426	160,000	165,186				273,535	93,673	838,822		81,896	919,129
1991	224,717	130,092	261,233	585,063		155,000				309,401	91,784	260,346		79,417	919,900
1992		114,863	279,530	561,338	150,000	137,000				327,456	79,000	261,605		77,159	902,193
1993		103,475	266,270	535,345	159,327	112,405				350,416	74,000	259,888		74,758	861,480
1994		97,922	305,000	512,838		103,000	206,518			361,609	70,000		90,000	74,174	849,374

Source: G Voerman, 'Le paradis perdu. Les adhérents des partis sociaux-démocrates d'Europe occidentale, 1945–1995', in M. Lazar (ed.) *La Gauche en Europe Depuis 1945: Invariants et Mutations du Socialime Européen* (Paris, Presses Universitaires de France, 1995).

alternative to González's economic policies came forward however, even after the party fell from office mired in corruption scandals. It would seem that the Socialists have disgusted the veterans of the 1930s or coopted them, while losing support among youth.

We saw in the first three chapters that the elite consensus in the Labour Party in Britain broke down in the late 1960s and 1970s. The parliamentary and industrial wings of the party clashed over wage controls and trade union reform at a time when the big unions were no longer led from the right. Croslandite revisionism was in ideological retreat, the party moved to the left and the authoritarian party regime was undermined when its main policing agent, the NEC, abandoned a number of candidate selection controls, allowed the constituency organisations greater autonomy and discarded the list of proscribed organisations. These organisational changes followed from the party's shift to the left – a process which came to an end after the electoral trauma of 1983. By this time, however, the culture of the party had changed to such an extent that it was not a simple matter to reassert managerial control. Shaw identifies a breakdown in deference associated with the younger, middle-class radicals who had entered the party in the 1970s and early 1980s as one element of the changed environment. Another was the left's resistance to a reintroduction of social democratic centralism even when it was directed at the small groups of Trotskyist infiltrators, such as Militant, which the media seized upon as evidence of Labour's extremism. Finally, the parliamentary leadership found that the courts were brought in to set limits on the exercise of the NECs disciplinary powers – limits which it had been accustomed to exceed in the 1920s and 1950s.[40]

The 'iron law of oligarchy' was challenged in the 1970s by activist organisations such as the Campaign for Labour Party Democracy (CLPD), established in 1973. This challenge culminated in the constitutional reforms adopted by the party's special conference at Wembley in 1980, when mandatory reselection of candidates was adopted and an electoral college was set up to elect future leaders of the party. Within a year, however, the party's movement to the left had reached its climax and the serious electoral defeat of 1983 began a new process of centralisation, originally set in train by Neil Kinnock, which included the loss of trade union influence as well as that of the constituency activists, as power was concentrated in the leader's office. State finance to assist research by opposition parties, introduced for the first time by the Labour government in 1974, helped to finance this centralism by providing the Labour front bench with an additional income of £440,000 in 1983, rising to £1, 445,000 by 1992. Alongside the growth of the leader's personal advisory staff, which this money made possible, measures were taken to marginalise the NEC, the PLP-TUC Liaison Committee and the annual conference in the policy-making process. Kinnock created joint policy committees, composed of equal numbers of MPs and members of the NEC, to bypass the

NEC itself and provide the leadership with control of both the agenda and any policy recommendations actually made.

In 1985 the Campaigns and Communications Directorate (CCD) was established, with Peter Mandelson as director, responsible only to the leadership. From this a Shadow Communications Agency was born liasing directly with the leader's office. The first report of the CCD, written by the advertising executive Philip Gould in 1987, stressed the outmoded image of the party in the perceptions of voters, many of whom associated it, not only with the 'cloth-cap' working class, but also with unappealing 'minorities'. It argued that the party indulged in a redundant campaigning style geared more to the needs of unrepresentative activists than winning general elections, and it stressed the need for more advertising specialists and better use of, and greater reliance on, the media. Voters were perceived increasingly as consumers with fixed views; the job of the party was to make its programme attractive to as many of these people as possible, but especially to the decisive minority of floating voters in the marginal constituencies. The various elements of the new media professionalism advocated by Mandelson were conspicuously present during the 1987 general election but failed to prevent Labour from losing with just 31.7 per cent of the vote compared with the Conservatives' 43.4 per cent.

At this point the 'policy review' was launched by Kinnock, taking the form of a two-year reappraisal of all existing policies by seven policy review groups under the control of the leadership. A thinly disguised public relations exercise called 'Labour Listens' was conducted during 1988–89, purportedly to allow members of the public to influence this policy review process, but the events held under its auspices created little interest and it was never clear how the public's opinions would be measured and made to count. In reality policy was made from the leader's office, as political journalists were only too well aware.[41] In 1989 the results of the prolonged policy deliberation were adopted by the annual conference after it was made clear that the policy review reports under consideration could only be adopted or rejected without amendment. In accepting these reports the leadership obtained the results it desired and the party thereby dropped its former commitments to three measures now deemed to be electoral liabilities – the repeal of the Conservative's labour laws, unilateral disarmament and the reversal of Thatcher's privatisation programme.

Steps were also taken to eliminate the activist nuisance at source. If the entire membership was allowed one postal ballot per person – in the election of the leader, the selection of candidates and reselection of MPs, and, finally, the selection of delegates to annual conference – it could be expected that the unrepresentative activist minority would lose its power in the party; all the more so if the individual membership could be greatly increased at the same time. One member one vote (OMOV), as it became known, was also in principle at odds with the trade union block vote at annual conference and it was pressure from Kinnock which eventually persuaded the unions to reduce that power from 90 to 70 per cent in 1993, falling to 50 per cent when individual membership passed the 300,000 mark. However, Kinnock only succeeded in getting the 1987 annual conference to accept a compromise between OMOV and trade union power at constituency level, in the selection of parliamentary candidates (with the unions having up to 40 per cent of the vote); but that was as far as he could go. Nevertheless, after John Smith succeeded Kinnock in the wake of the 1992 general election defeat, the OMOV issue was taken up again. In 1993 the annual conference adopted OMOV for candidate selection. The unions also agreed at the same time that in elections for the leader, union members affiliated to the party would vote as individuals and collectively carry 30 per cent of the total vote – the rest of the vote would belong to MPs and MEPs or constituency members.

The evidence collected from a major academic survey of the Labour membership in 1989–90, however, revealed an ageing and increasingly passive membership. Seyd and Whitelely argued in 1995 that the membership was 'typically male, middle class, ... and middle aged', with a mean age of 48.[42] They also found that Labour was 'dominated by the middle class salariat', with teachers the largest single grouping. Seyd and Whiteley's first survey was conducted during a period of considerable change in Labour Party membership and on the cusp of dramatic changes brought about after the emergence of Tony Blair as party leader in July 1994. In 1980 the membership had stood at 348,156, but it was never that high again for the rest of the 1980s, and between 1984 and 1988, 60,000 members left the party. In 1989–90, when the Seyd and Whiteley survey was conducted, membership fluctuated around 300,000, but in 1991 it fell to 261,233. A period of membership growth only began in 1994 – the year Tony Blair replaced John Smith – and by 1997 it had risen to 405,328, a 40 per cent increase. This was achieved on the basis of a well-resourced national campaign which largely bypassed the party branches. It was motivated by a desire to transform the ethos of the party and facilitate doctrinal and organisational changes as old Labour members were either replaced or diluted by New Labour recruits.

We know, for example, that in 1995, when 113,000 new members joined the party, 38,000 members resigned from it. In many ways the new members were encouraged to adopt a more passive role. Face-to-face contact between members was reduced as the national membership drives brought people into the organisation simply by payment of subscriptions transferred by standing order. No contact between the new recruit and the existing membership was necessary. Obviously the function of the new enlarged membership is partly to supply finance to an organisation determined to distance itself from the trade unions that it had always relied on for this purpose. But diluting the strength of activist minorities had been an objective of the party leadership since 1983. We have already seen that Mandelson's CCD regarded the sort of canvassing activities favoured by the activists as self-serving, and it is also apparent that the membership now plays a very subordinate role in policy making. The Seyd and Whiteley survey unsurprisingly found that manual workers were only 26 per cent of the Labour membership. Contrary to media perceptions, however, this membership appears to be not markedly to the left of Labour voters – even the activist minority within the membership was not distinctively radical on particular issues by the end of the 1980s.

In June 1987, when he was a little-known MP, Tony Blair proposed that a new Labour Party was required, distinguished by the conviction that efficiency and social justice were inextricably linked.[43] Unlike his predecessor John Smith, Blair took over the leadership in 1994 convinced that the 1992 general election defeat indicated that a great deal more was left to be done before the transformation of the Labour Party was complete. The perceived need in the 1980s was to transform Labour's 'ideology, policies, membership, and organisation' to create an effective election-winning and governing party. 'Effective' meant going with the grain of the economy and being correspondingly modest in commitments that cost money. The party itself had to be transformed to block or eliminate the overload of demands that would otherwise be funnelled through it. However, the 1992 defeat – despite the changes in organisation and policy already made by Kinnock – could be laid at the door of spending plans revealed in the party's 'shadow budget', as prepared by John Smith; the Conservatives costed these plans as involving an extra £1,000 on the average family's tax bill. Lingering doubts about Labour's 'fitness to govern' thus had to be eliminated according to the Blairite analysis by taking steps to centralise decision making further in the party, protect policy making from the organisation's special interests and modernise the party's image.

Blair expanded the team of party functionaries loyal to the leadership office and strengthened the managerialist and media-oriented ethos that had developed under Kinnock but which had stalled when John Smith took over the leadership. The growth of party membership after the advent of Blair did not obstruct the continuing process of centralisation. A majority of members approved the general direction of Blair's leadership, according to an internal survey of membership in May 1995. This survey also revealed that the blue-collar membership stood at only 10 per cent of the total and that the retired (25 per cent) and white-collar workers (47 per cent) were the best-represented sections of the population.[44] Blair addressed up to 30,000 party members in 1995 as part of his campaign to excise Clause IV of the party constitution – an objective declared the previous year. At the special conference convened for this purpose in April 1995, 90 per cent of the constituency delegates voted for the change. The annual conference of 1995, which followed in the autumn, was an even greater success for the leadership in that it won every vote that was taken. The same hitherto unlikely event recurred in 1996 and 1997. In March 1996, Blair bypassed the annual conference altogether when he announced that the party proposed to directly ballot the membership for endorsement of the pre-election manifesto rather than adopt the conventional and constitutional procedure of consulting its nominally sovereign body. Once again the device of requiring either complete acceptance or rejection was the preferred method for legitimising Blair's leadership.

Though one of the main attractions of OMOV had been to dilute the input of the activist minority which could be safely presumed to favour more radical policies than the leadership, even the more passive members reached by postal ballots could prove troublesome. Certainly the evidence of opinion polls in 1999 suggested that the Labour membership in London would favour Ken Livingstone's candidature for the new mayorship – an outcome which horrified the leadership. Similarly, when the Labour leadership in the devolved Welsh Assembly became an issue, the majority of the party membership supported Rhodri Morgan rather than the Blair-sponsored candidate. But by this time candidate selection was subject to a more rigorous centralisation than anything before witnessed in the party. It is perhaps a measure of the magnitude of the modernising project which the Blair leadership is determined to see through that none of the MEPs who opposed the elimination of Clause IV survived the selection procedure adopted for the elections of 1999 (the closed regional list system) and that a similar process eliminated MPs of the calibre of Dennis Canavan (Falkirk) from the list fielded in Scotland for the first devolved assembly in the same year. These central lists were partly justified as a way of increasing the percentage of female and ethnic minority representatives, but they also seem designed to weed out individuals out of sympathy with the general direction of the party, even though the shrinkage and marginalisation of the leadership's left critics was already far advanced before Blair became leader of the party. The Campaign Group of MPs, for example, associated with the Bennite left, had become ineffectual and lacked new ideas; other sources of dissent had folded up, resigned from the party, had been expelled or 'constructively dismissed'.[45]

Similarly, the distancing of the party leadership from the affiliated trade unions that had begun in the 1980s was taken further. In 1996 the party's individual membership exceeded 300,000 and, in accordance with the decision taken in 1993, the block vote at annual conference fell from 70 to 50 per cent of the total. Trade union sponsorship of MPs was ended in March of the same year by the simple expedient of switching such financial support to local party organisations. (Meanwhile, the declining position of the unions was made apparent by the fact that only 36 per cent of British workers were covered by collective bargaining agreements – a figure that declined to 22 per cent for the private sector in the south east of the country outside London by 1998). Blair also made a determined effort to increase the proportion of party finances which came from wealthy individuals and corporate sponsors. In 1991 such money amounted to 26 per cent of total income; but by 1997 55 per cent of the £24 million pounds raised that year came from individuals and companies, with the trade union share down to 40 per cent. This seems to have created problems normally associated with the Conservative Party. Soon after taking office the Labour government was found to have 'a startlingly close relationship' with lobbyists employing former staffers from the leadership's office – some fifty to sixty of them were found to be working for 'almost every lobbying company' including arms manufacturers and tobacco companies.[46]

Though the prospect of any repetition of rank-and-file initiative in defiance of the party leadership, such as occurred in the 1970s and early 1980s, had been greatly reduced by the membership turnover mentioned above, elaborate, leadership-controlled policy-making procedures were proposed in *Partnership for Power*, a document endorsed by the NEC in 1997. This was undoubtedly adopted with an eye on the management of the annual conference – scene of dramatic debates and rebellions in the 1970s and 1980s. The proposals suggested changing the composition of the thirty-two-person NEC so that, apart from twelve places reserved for women, there would be reserved places for representatives of the government, the PLP, local councillors, MEPs and local party activists. MPs would no longer be eligible to stand in a special constituency section of the NEC – an arrangement that had always secured places for the left of the party even in the 1950s, the heyday of social democratic centralism. The policy-making functions of the NEC would in any case not be revived under the new regime. Instead, a Joint Policy Committee, chaired by the prime minister and equally composed of representatives from the NEC and the government, would act as a 'steering group' for another new body – the National Policy Forum. This would have the task of policy development and would consist of 175 members elected for a two-year term, including fifty-four constituency representatives elected by regional groups of delegates at annual conference. It would establish policy commissions covering broad areas of policy, composed of individuals drawn from the Forum, the NEC and government. These policy commissions would report back to the Forum; the Forum would then present an annual report to the conference. Though the conference would remain nominally sovereign, the Joint Policy Committee and a new Joint Campaigns and Elections Committee would take 'strategic oversight of policy development' and 'strategic responsibility for campaigns and message delivery'.

It is possible that these changes could produce more careful, better informed policy making than was ever possible through the annual conference and the various sub-committees of the NEC. But there is no doubt that the new arrangements are designed to give the professional politicians domination of the process and eliminate the influence of nationally known militants elected directly by the annual conference on to the NEC. The two-year rolling review cycle is also certain to provide filters and mediations against 'extremism'. Policy agendas will be established by the leadership, the substance of policy will be chewed over in detail by small groups and presented publicly only when a show of party unity can be the expected end product.

Ultimately, the Labour Party's history and structure created the conditions of divided authority which so obviously characterised its internal life in the late 1960s, 1970s and 1980s. The affiliated trade unions founded the party and help to explain its federal structure. But for most of the party's history the power of the affiliated unions was actually deployed to maintain the hegemony of the parliamentary leadership. It was only from the late 1960s that the block votes of the trade unions at party conferences and the influence of the trade unions in policy making generally were transformed from being assets of the parliamentary leadership and a precondition of stability into a principal cause of internal strife and electoral embarrassment. Admittedly, as we have already noted, the link with the unions was perceived as a public relations problem by some of the leading revisionists in the late 1950s. But on balance the centre-right of the parliamentary party had more reasons to thank the trade union connection than regret it. It is measure of how much that situation had changed that the party's industrial relations spokesman told journalists in 1996 that the trade union link could be broken in the foreseeable future.[47]

The foregoing discussion shows that changes in the Labour Party since 1983 conform in many ways to a West European-wide trend. Party leaders are increasingly reliant on the mass commercial media and have less use for activists. Readership of the party press has collapsed even in countries where it was significant well into the 1950s, such as Austria, Norway and the Netherlands. Personalised leadership is more pronounced everywhere and policy formation is correspondingly centralised in the leadership circle of a Blair, Craxi, Soares, Papendreou, Mitterrand or González. Factionalism certainly grew in the 1970s but was reduced in the 1980s and 1990s. In Italy, the PSI membership, always feeble after Craxi became leader in 1976, was largely nominal in the years before corruption charges signalled its financial and electoral collapse in 1993. Generally, the party bureaucracy has tended to grow at the centre and the parliamentary leadership is increasingly in control of party headquarters. The party secretariat has expanded in all the countries where state subventions have given the leadership access to financial resources independent of the party membership. This has enabled party leaders to appoint marketing experts, researchers, consultants and advisers who are responsible only to themselves. State finance of parties is a factor in Finland, Denmark, Germany, Norway, Sweden, Austria and Belgium. It is significant for the official opposition in Britain. In many countries account must also be taken of the enormous patronage which governing parties can dispense. In extreme cases such as Italy – where a monocratic structure was created in the PSI under Craxi, coexisting with powerful provincial cliques which had control over such matters as local alliances – the socialists became enmeshed in webs of corruption.

Recruitment in social democratic parties is generally poor among the young and the working class and the membership is ageing, increasingly educated and white collar. The Labour Party's ageing membership suggests that, like the SPD, it has a problem that has not been helped by the tendency of the party to close down its youth organisations in response to their tendency to adopt an oppositional stance and sometimes a Marxist leadership.[48] In Italy the PCI steadily lost members from its 1940s peak and was faced with an ageing cadre and a declining proportion of industrial and agricultural workers in its ranks before its final dissolution. The centralisation of the policy-making process is apt to reinforce the dominance of the elite of professional politicians even in parties which made certain concessions to the aspirations of the membership in the 1980s, such the British Labour Party, the Belgian Socialists and Danish Social Democrats. Apart from the countervailing forces that we have noted – to which the diminishing role of party congresses can be added – the ability of party members as individuals to participate in the election of leaders or reselection of MPs or contribute to rolling policy discussions is not comparable with the empowerment of activists drawing upon their own resources and forms of self-organisation. Such changes can be cosmetic and must be judged the more so as the membership is increasingly atomised, centrally recruited and judged inferior by the parliamentary leadership to other sources of finance, opinion formation and voter mobilisation. Relationships with the unions have also become more distant. In Italy the socialist and communist factions of the trade union federation, the CGIL, were disbanded in the 1990s. In Denmark the role of affiliated unions has been reduced on the party executive and since 1990 payment of the political 'levy' has been voluntary for the individual who is now able to contract out. Corporate trade union affiliation at local level was ended in Sweden in 1990 and Norway in 1992. The unions themselves increasingly judge that too close a relationship can damage their interests. But there can be little doubt that the period since 1973 has strained these relationships and the parties have gone further down the road of service to a disembodied 'public opinion' gleaned from the focus groups.[49] The public has nevertheless grown disenchanted with politicians across Western Europe, not least on the grounds of their corruptability. Perhaps this is related to the growing intimacy of parties with the state[50] – as they strengthen themselves in a variety of ways at this level – as well as their diminishing capacities to represent and connect with civil society.

These trends are far from irreversible. The Labour Party's experience in the years 1964–81 shows how the regime of social democratic centralism that had prevailed since the war broke down as the elites managing the party divided and allowed an activist drive for greater membership participation to challenge the dominance of the parliamentary leadership. This too was mirrored, *mutatis mutandis*, elsewhere. The mass party is necessarily a coalition of different forces which can give the appearance of a 'loosely coupled anarchy'.[51] But appearances can be deceptive and it is a mistake to say, as Losche does, that 'these days, large political parties are essentially decentralised and fragmented service organisations'.[52] A plurality of groups can be institutionalised within their structures, but this does not mean that they exert significant influence. That will depend on a variety of factors, many of them external to the party organisation. All that can be said by way of a generalisation is that the normal configuration of forces within the social democratic parties since the war has enabled parliamentary elites to be the overwhelmingly dominant power, with trade union elites in a supporting role. If the trade union role within social democracy has entered a long decline, however, coalition building within the party may become a more uncertain business for the parliamentary leaderships.

Notes

1 R. Michels, *Political Parties* (New York, Free Press, [1911] 1962).

2 R. H. S. Crossman, *Socialism and the New Despotism* (London, Fabian Society, tract 298, 1958), p. 23.

3 S. Neumann, 'Towards a comparative study of political parties', in S. Neumann (ed.), *Modern Political Parties* (Chicago, IL, University of Chicago Press, 1956), p. 395.

4 O. Kircheimer, 'The transformation of the Western European party system', in J. LaPalombara and M. Weiner (eds), *Political Parties and Political Development* (Princeton, NJ, Princeton University Press, 1966), pp. 178–9.

5 From the introduction to W. E. Paterson and A. H. Thomas (eds), *Social Democratic Parties in Western Europe* (New York, St. Martin's Press, 1977), pp. 16–17.

6 In the Austrian case the unions' tradition of political neutrality has not prevented a major crossover between senior office-holders of the Socialist Trade Union Faction in the works councils and the trade union confederation, the ÖGB, and the SPÖ. Senior officials of the labour associations also made up over 40 per cent of the SPÖ's MPs in the 1970s and still accounted for 38 per cent in 1991. See C. Kunkel and J. Pontusson, 'Corporatism versus social democracy: divergent fortunes of the Austrian and Swedish labour movements', *West European Politics*, 21:2 (1998) 12, and M. Sully, 'The Socialist Party of Austria', in Paterson and Thomas, *Social Democratic Parties in Western Europe*, pp. 223–4.

7 D. Hine, 'Leaders and followers: democracy and manageability in the social democratic parties of Western Europe', in W. E. Paterson and A. H. Thomas (eds), *The Future of Social Democracy: Problems and Prospects of Social Democratic Parties in Western Europe* (Oxford, Clarendon Press, 1986), p. 264.

8 S. B. Wolinetz, 'The Dutch Labour Party', in Paterson and Thomas, *Social Democratic Parties in Western Europe*, p. 352. See also L. Heerma van Voss, 'The Netherlands', in S. Berger and D. Broughton (eds), *The Force of Labour: West European Labour Movement and the Working Class in the Twentieth Century* (Oxford, Berg, 1995), p. 60.

9 See A. J. Taylor, 'Trade unions and the politics of social democratic renewal', *West European Politics*, 16:1 (1993) 133–55, 149.
10 Lord Passfield (Sidney Webb) described the General Council of the TUC as 'pigs' for its obdurate opposition to cuts in pay and unemployment benefit. See R. Skidelsky, *Politicians and the Slump* (Harmondsworth, Pelican, 1970), pp. 414, 405–413.
11 H. Compston, 'Union participation in economic policy making in Scandinavia, 1970–1993', *West European Politics*, 18:1 (1995) 104.
12 K. Heidar, 'The Norwegian Labour Party: social democracy in a periphery of Europe', in Paterson and Thomas, *Social Democratic Parties in Western Europe*, p. 296.
13 H. Bergstrom, 'Sweden's politics and party system at the crossroads', *West European Politics*, 14:3 (1991) 17–18.
14 Stig Malm was the last in this tradition in the early 1980s. See D. Sainsbury, 'Swedish social democracy in transition: the party's record in the 1980s and the challenge of the 1990s', *West European Politics*, 14:3 (1991) 41.
15 See W. E. Paterson, 'The German Social Democratic Party', in Paterson and Thomas, *Social Democratic Parties in Western Europe*, pp. 145–6; H. Compston, 'Union participation in economic policy making in France, Italy, Germany and Britain, 1970–1993', *West European Politics*, 18:3 (1995) 324; A. Martin and G. Ross, 'European trade unions and the economic crisis: perceptions and strategies', in J. Hayward (ed.), *Trade Unions and Politics in Western Europe* (London, Frank Cass, 1980), p. 48.
16 B. Criddle, 'The French Socialist Party', in Paterson and Thomas, *The Future of Social Democracy*, p. 224.
17 See R. Mouriaux, 'The CFDT: from the union of popular forces to the success of social change', in M. Kesselman (ed.), *The French Workers' Movement* (London, Allen and Unwin, 1984), pp. 79–80.
18 Criddle, 'The French Socialist Party', pp. 240–1, note 11.
19 J. Bridgford, *The Politics of French Trade Unionism: Party–Union Relations at the Time of the Union of the Left* (Leicester, Leicester University Press, 1991), pp. 23–4. Bridgford adds (p. 23) that most CFDT members within the PS, according to one survey at the time of the union of the left, belonged to the CERES faction because it was the most left-wing grouping and the one most strongly committed to the alliance with the communists.
20 R. Gillespie, 'The break-up of the "socialist family": party–union relations in Spain', *West European Politics*, 13:1 (1990) 48–9.
21 A. Smith, 'Spain', in Berger and Broughton, *The Force of Labour*, pp. 197–8.
22 K. Heidar, 'Towards party irrelevance? The decline of both conflict and cohesion in the Norwegian Labour Part'y, in D. S. Bell and E. Shaw (eds), *Conflict and Cohesion in the Western European Social Democratic Parties* (London, Frances Pinter, 1994), pp. 101–2.
23 T. Tilton, *The Political Theory of Swedish Social Democracy* (Oxford, Clarendon Press, 1981), p. 246.
24 E. Kolinsky, *Parties, Opposition and Society in West Germany* (London, Croom Helm, 1984), pp. 73–4
25 *Ibid.*, pp. 76–7.
26 S. Berger, 'Germany', in Berger and Broughton, *The Force of Labour*, p. 89.

27 Paterson, 'The German Social Democratic Party', pp. 82, 136.
28 Kolinsky, *Parties, Opposition and Society in West Germany*, pp. 84–5.
29 S. Berger, 'Germany', p. 89.
30 A. J. Taylor, 'Trade unions and the politics of social democratic renewal', pp. 136–7.
31 *Ibid.*, p. 145.
32 See S. Padgett, 'The German Social Democratic Party: between old and New Left', in D. S. Bell and E. Shaw (eds), *Conflict and Cohesion in the Western European Social Democratic Parties* (London, Frances Pinter, 1994), pp. 27–8.
33 See P. van Praag Jr, 'Conflict and cohesion in the Dutch Labour Party', in Bell and Shaw (eds), *Conflict and Cohesion*, pp. 133–9.
34 D. Arter, '"The War of the Roses": conflict and cohesion in the Swedish Social Democratic Party', in Bell and Shaw (eds), *Conflict and Cohesion*, pp. 80–2.
35 Source: G. Voerman, 'Le paradis perdu. Les adherents des partis sociaux – democrats d'Europe occidental, 1945–1995', in M. Lazar (ed.), *Le Gauche en Europe Depuis 1945: Invariants et Mutations du Socialime Européen* (Paris, Presses Universitaires de France, 1996).
36 Bell and Shaw (eds), *Conflict and Cohesion*, p. 174. See the editors' 'Conclusion'.
37 M. A. Sully, *Continuity and Change in Austria: The Eternal Quest for the Third Way* (New York, Columbia University Press, 1982), pp. 205–18, 228–31.
38 Heidar, 'Towards party irrelevance?', p. 106.
39 S. Gillespie, 'Spain', in Bell and Shaw (eds), *Conflict and Cohesion*, p. 64.
40 E. Shaw, *Discipline and Discord in the Labour Party: The Politics of Managerial Control, 1951–87* (Manchester, Manchester University Press, 1988), pp. 298–9, 29–9. Disciplinary measures had to be consonant with the precepts of natural justice and consistent with the Party's rules.
41 R. Heffernan and M. Marqusee, *Defeat From the Jaws of Victory: Inside Kinnock's Labour Party* (London, Verso, 1992), p. 115.
42 P. Seyd and P. Whiteley, *Labour's Grass Roots* (Oxford, Clarendon Press, 1992); see also their 'Dynamics of party activism in Britain: a spiral of demobilisation?', *British Journal of Political Science*, 28:1, 113–38.
43 D. Farnham, 'New Labour, the new unions, and the new labour market', *Parliamentary Affairs*, 49:4 (1996).
44 See *Red Pepper*, February 1996, pp. 22-3.
45 The Communist Party of Great Britain (CPGB) had been able to organise as much as 10 per cent of TUC delegates in the mid-1970s, but was defunct by 1991. Thousands of activists resigned from the Labour Party – 38,000 in 1995 alone. Arthur Scargill led the best-known secession when the Socialist Labour Party was formed in 1996. Militant was in part ejected, in part 'constructively dismissed' by the changing ideological and organisational climate.
46 'Labour's links with lobbyists', *Independent*, 24 March 1998.The party's growing dependence on the finance and goodwill of wealthy individuals was also at the centre of controversy concerning the exemption of Formula One racing from the ban on tobacco advertising and Blair's personal role in Rupert Murdoch's attempt to purchase part of Silvio Berlusconi's media empire in Italy. See 'Blair helped Murdoch media bid', *Guardian*, 24 March 1998.

47 *Guardian*, 13 September 1996. Stephen Byer's made these remarks over dinner while attending the annual conference.

48 See J. Callaghan, 'The background to "entrism": Leninism and the British Labour Party', *Journal of Communist Studies*, December (1986) 380–401.

49 Kitschelt argued that while social democratic parties were not condemned to decline by virtue of socioeconomic change, they were obliged to adapt in the context of the shift to neo-liberalism and post-materialist values – both of which forces he accepted uncritically. Kitschelt saw this adaptation as most efficiacious when leaderships enjoyed 'strategic autonomy', but he imagined that 'new inputs' would continue to get through as long as the same leadership tolerated a heterogeneous, activist membership and a degree of internal conflict. In reality 'strategic autonomy' is buttressed by reliance on 'focus groups' for such 'inputs' as the leadership deems expedient. See H. Kitschelt, *The Transformation of Social Democracy* (Cambridge, Cambridge University Press, 1994), pp. 35–6.

50 See P. Mair, 'Party organisations: from civil society to the state', in P. Mair and O. Katz (eds), *How Parties Organize* (London, Sage, 1994).

51 P. Losche, 'Is the SPD still a labor party? From a "community of solidarity" to a "loosely coupled anarchy", in D. E. Barclay and E. D. Weitz (eds), *Between Reform and Revolution: German Socialism and Communism From 1840 to 1990* (Oxford, Berghahn, 1998), pp. 531–56.

52 *Ibid.*, p. 535.

9

The decline of social democracy?

In the 1950s social democracy could be perceived as the victim of its own success in Britain – if we regard the full-employment, welfare-state consensus of the post-war years as its achievement. By the 1970s, however, this system had allegedly generated growing demands on the state which were reinforced by the irresponsible promises of political parties seeking election. Having raised expectations in this way and strengthened innumerable pressure groups and sectional interests by maintaining corporatist institutions and a culture of state intervention, inflationary tendencies became endemic to the economies concerned. Attempts to fulfil promises in the straitened circumstances of stagflation which prevailed in the 1970s could only lead to more inflation and a transfer of the costs of expenditure to the future. But this was The Future That Did Not Work – one of insatiable demand for welfare benefits, uncontrollable inflation, bureaucratic incompetence, stagnation, rising crime and social conflict.[1] As Alan Wolfe perceptively observed in 1978, 'Having determined why social democratic coalitions have failed, conservative observers and capitalist institutions have begun to operationalize plans to remedy this failure and once more make the world safe for capitalism'.[2]

We could conclude that social democracy, assisted for a while by the US, helped to make capitalism work after 1945; that it was in turn kept purposeful by the long post-war boom; and that it has lost its way during the period since 1970 when the Keynesian mechanisms suffered a prolonged blockage.[3] We could notice the paradox that 'when capitalism appears to be working well – creating jobs and ensuring stable prices – voters often acknowledge their support by casting their lot with leftist and social democratic parties. On the other hand, when recession appears likely and economic restrictions inevitable, conservative, procapitalist parties seem to gain greater support.'[4] Certainly the negative part of this equation holds true for the economically depressed inter-war years and for the recent period since the collapse of the Bretton Woods system. But it is often said that this is more than a conjunctural problem, that 'the point has to be made unequivocally that socialism is dead, and that none of its variants can be revived'.[5] Numerous reasons have been given to support this thesis – more than can be covered here – but those that can be considered most fundamental point to secular trends that transform social structures and the capacities of nation-states to manage their economic affairs. The focus of our discussion is social democracy, on the grounds that parties in this tradition have for many decades represented the principal centres for movement towards a socialist conception of society in the countries of Western Europe.

The charge that these parties had long since abandoned socialism is facile. Self-avowed socialists existed in all of them and even 'revisionists' defined their objectives in terms of equality. When it became apparent in the 1970s that multinational capital flows were undermining domestic macroeconomic policy – the principle instrument of social democratic government – the attempt was made to go beyond Keynesianism in parties such as the French Parti Socialiste and the British Labour Party.[6] Similarly in Sweden, where the Social Democrats enjoyed unbroken rule since 1938 and the most successful reformist model was supposed to prevail, the SAP, far from complacently announcing 'the end of history', embarked on a programme in the early 1970s designed to challenge managerial prerogatives and fight for economic equality. By the early 1980s it is true that the left was everywhere in retreat as neo-liberal policies prevailed internationally and the social democratic impasse seemed to consist of a straight choice between the necessity of austerity, and even repression, in office or watching from opposition while conservative forces deregulated the economy in the interests of market forces. Social democracy, it could be argued, had overly relied on the efficacy of the state both to facilitate and legitimate capital accumulation and was first undone by governmental overload in the 1970s – in circumstances of a growing contradiction between falling growth, low productivity rates, and rising demands for state action – and then faced by a transformation of the class struggle into a battle over public policy.[7] But the resolution of this struggle in favour of a redistribution of power and wealth to corporations and capitalists acting outside the state sector was resisted from within social democracy and continues to be limited to the extent that organised labour fights for an alternative.

It is precisely at this point that the left is said to be fatally weakened by epoch-making changes in the economies of the Western world. Advanced capitalist societies are said to be subject to changing technological and institutional conditions affecting the production and exchange of all goods. Flexible manufacturing systems, new management hierarchies, and the application of information technology to the monitoring of performance are the main characteristics of a post-Fordist[8] conjuncture, alongside the emergence of transnational financial markets and institutions which are increasingly autonomous and detached from investment in goods. Flexible production involves increased subcontracting and new 'lean management' structures that allegedly create autonomous work teams 'empowered' to find more efficient ways of solving specific problems and reaching production targets. 'Downsizing' of middle management, quality circles, 'just-in-time' procurement of parts, and the ability to switch machines and workers to different tasks, are all part of this equation.

For all the assurance with which this grand narrative has been put in the academic and, perhaps more surprisingly, left-activist literature, the whole concept of the 'flexible firm' revolution has been challenged on the grounds of its atypical character.[9] Nobody doubts the rise of non-standard forms of employment but the idea of an organisational revolution in modern business is another matter, though there is little doubt that it has been given credibility by political propaganda emanating from organisations such as New Labour.[10] Even if the change to post-Fordism had been as sweeping as the New Times analysis suggested, however, it is far from self-evident that the labour-market deregulation implemented in the UK in the 1980s was the appropriate policy response, as compared with the regulatory regimes operating in, say, Sweden and Germany, since Britain is a leader in neither education nor training and shows no signs of becoming one. As for the political impact of the growth in non-standard forms of employment, these are likely to vary widely – all types of workers, for example, are better protected in some states (Germany, Sweden) than others (Spain, Britain) – and forces of global competition, just like the new management practices operated by some of the multinationals, have to be 'mediated through the social, political and institutional structures' of different countries, producing different outcomes,[11] rather than overwhelming pressure for conformity to a supposed gold standard such as the US.

The left is nevertheless faced with the continued shrinkage of the blue-collar working class, which typically represents only around 25 per cent of the workforce in Western Europe today. In the advanced industrial societies the proportion of secondary-sector workers peaked decades ago – as early as 1911 in Britain (at 51.6 per cent), as recently as 1962 in France (at 38.1 per cent). It is, on some accounts, evidence of an emerging 'post-industrial society', one that has been 'driven by an unprecedented avalanche of technological innovations'. Contemporary changes amount to an evolutionary step in the development of the 'productive forces' with the paradoxical result that the workers who were supposed to transform the system in the Marxist theory (which gave explanatory primacy to the productive forces) 'today constitute a residual endangered species'.[12] This alone jeopardises the future of left-wing parties according to Przeworski and Sprague who deduce that 'the era of electoral socialism may be over', on the basis of this secular decline of the 'traditional' working class.[13] Zolberg adds that 'the decline of Labour in the United Kingdom, of the Democratic majority in the United States, and the Communist party in Italy and France is attributable in large measure to the basic fact that "blue-collar" workers constitute a declining proportion of national electorates'.[14] The trends are expected to continue with the further decline of manual work in metalworking, steel and coal industries. The growth of employment in menial, low-skilled jobs in the tertiary sector is not expected to compensate for these losses.

Other secular trends corrode social democracy as its natural base, the manual workforce, continues its decline throughout Western Europe.[15] Everywhere employees in the tertiary sector predominate. Andre Gorz bids *Farewell to the Working Class*[16] partly because the shrinkage of the economically active proportion of the population has been common to all OECD states in the recent period, an observation that is said to raise the question of the diminishing significance of the world of work for progressive politics.[17] But the political capacity of organisations dependent on the working class is not just affected by the shrinkage of the blue-collar workforce; it is also adversely affected by the growing internal differentiation of the working class. In some versions of this argument, the working class is the subject of a tripartite division in which a shrinking semi-skilled sector is sandwiched between a growing mass of the unemployed, the unskilled and the casualised on the one hand, and a stratum of relatively prosperous, relatively secure workers on the other.[18] In other accounts Western societies are divided into a comfortable two-thirds, which may or may not form a contented bloc opposed to tax increases,[19] and a poverty-stricken third.[20] If the argument is linked to globalisation, it is possible to explain the enormous growth of income inequalities since 1970 and those still to come, in terms of centrifugal forces in the world economy which create a gilded, cosmopolitan elite at one end of the scale, devoid of national ties and responsibilities, and a residuum at the bottom condemned to a declining standard of living.[21] All these accounts are united in finding evidence of the decay of solidarity, whether it be based on wage dispersion, the extending spread of working conditions and lifestyles, or some combination of these factors. The stress is on the secular, rather than the conjunctural character of these tendencies. Similarly, observers point to the obstacles to collective action arising from long-term trends affecting age and the growing generation gap; or gender and the feminisation of the workforce; or ethnicity and the divisions arising from immigration. Anderson, for example, argues that immigration has 'eroded a culture of solidarity in the working population of most [Western European] nations'.[22]

Some analysts go beyond the thesis of working-class decline to perceive a fundamental dissolution of the 'class mechanism' itself, which they say has become so attenuated as to be unimportant in explaining political behaviour, identity, conflict and sociopolitical cleavage.[23] Inequality, social stratification and capitalism will remain, but classes, which reformed from localised 'communities of fate' to nationalised 'quasi-communities' organised by parties and unions in the late industrial period, have been decomposing since the

1970s. The collapse of corporatist and Fordist arrangements, the dealignment of voting, the appearance of new social movements and their agendas are all manifestations of class dissolution, according to this argument. The 'new politics' is evidence of 'a changing hierarchy of values' and the issues in which they find expression transcend the class-based political loyalties of old. New parties arise and the old parties respond by scaling down or completely abandoning class rhetoric in order to broaden their appeal.[24] As globalisation erodes the national framework of politics, cross-class interest alliances achieve growing significance in recognition of the reconfiguration of collective interests on a regional or skills-based foundation:

> salient political identities are being formed around such highly publicized and politically prominent issues as ethnicity, migration, gender, civil rights, environment, and nuclear energy. These identities are displacing the old class identities as 'generators of political action', at least among the young and educated urbanites. As a consequence, class discourse is no longer prominent and popular. Class language has also been abandoned by political parties, unions, associations, social movements, and academics, especially on the left.[25]

Connections can be made between these trends and the changing patterns of political behaviour in Western Europe. Studies reveal a decline in 'partisan identification' and a rise in the salience of (shifting) issues in determining how the ballot is cast, though the evidence for the decline of class voting is more impressive in the case of the UK than elsewhere in Western Europe.[26] Tax revolts, predicted as a consequence of the emerging fiscal crisis of the state in the 1970s,[27] and sometimes conceptualised as 'the oldest form of class struggle', are now perceived as a brake on social reform and a motor-force for neo-liberalism, even in countries where survey evidence shows demand for improved services.[28]

Our first note of scepticism in relation to these arguments of secular decline might be sounded through the observation that working-class conservatism was often very much stronger in the recent past than the decline thesis implies. Before the Second World War in Britain, for example, the Conservative electoral dominance was founded on majority support among the working class.[29] De Gaulle's political strength in post-war France derived in large measure from the support of the proletariat; as recently as the second ballot of the presidential election of 1965 he secured 45 per cent of the working-class vote against his rival, François Mitterrand.[30] It is also worth noting that the working class was always heterogeneous, fragmented, unevenly unionised – with the unskilled and low-paid particularly poorly represented – and pulled in different directions by rival loyalties. This was true in the very period, 1870–1914, when social democratic parties first emerged across Europe.[31]

It is also apparent that the stability of the blue-collar population varies significantly from one country to another during the period we are concerned with. In France it was stable between 1968 and 1992 and the decline of the peasantry was arguably the most dramatic change in the class structure.[32] In West Germany the twenty years following 1968 did see a decline in both the proportion of manual workers and those engaged in manufacturing (from 48 per cent to around 40 per cent), but the SPD's vote remained fairly stable and it is not possible to say that social change had eroded its future prospects. The proportion of the workforce belonging to West German trade unions increased between 1968 and 1986 (31 per cent to 35 per cent), while church attendance, an important predictor of right-wing voting, fell from 46 per cent to 26 per cent of the population. In 1992, one survey of the evidence concluded that 'the social democrats have the potential to surpass the CDU/CSU as the strongest single party of the Federal Republic'.[33] In Italy the same secularisation process seems to have been at work as in Germany, with attendance at mass falling from 50 per cent of the population in 1968 to 25 per cent in the 1980s. While industrial employment fell, especially in the 1980s, and unions lost members and were increasingly concentrated in both the public sector and sectors subject to secular decline, the significance of social structure and the influence of class-consciousness actually grew in voting behaviour throughout the 1970s, dipping only slightly in the 1980s.[34]

Spain's recent emergence from dictatorship helps to explain some of the wilder fluctuations in party support recorded there since 1976. It has also been affected by profound changes in the social structure which are far more complex than a simple decline in the proportion of blue-collar workers. Spain was able after 1976 to open up to the rest of Europe and self-consciously modernised itself – at the cost of 23 per cent of the workforce unemployed by 1991. At first, much was conditioned by the fear of provoking the fascist right if the pace of reform went too fast. The urban–rural balance continued to change as the peasantry declined; church attendances fell; gender relations changed too. For all this, religion remained more important than class in determining voting behaviour throughout the 1980s. In Sweden, by contrast, where the left was continuously in government from 1932–76 and returned to power for a further nine years after the conservative hiatus of 1976–82, religion has never been an important predictor of voting. Sweden has had high levels of class-based voting unequalled outside of Scandinavia. The proportion of the workforce organised by the trade unions exceeds 80 per cent and the number of women in paid employment is almost the same as men.

Yet industry peaked in importance in the Swedish economy during the 1960s. Since that time services have grown faster. If the prospects of social democracy were simply a function of the size of the blue-collar workforce, Sweden would be one of the places where the left would be in sharpest decline. It is true that 1968 was the last time the SAP received as much as 50 per cent of the vote and that its support fell to 43 per cent in 1976. But the Social Democrats' surprise defeat in 1976 had much to do with the salience of the cross-class issue of nuclear energy in that particular election. When the usual left–right ideological axis re-emerged, as it did in the election issues of 1982, the SAP was returned to power. It is also true that it depended on coalition partners, but this was nothing new. As recently as 1994 the total left vote in Sweden exceeded 56 per cent of the total, if we include the Green Party (MPG), which has been capable of obtaining around 5 per cent of the vote since 1988, and the Left Party (Vp) – the former Communists – with a comparable core support.

If Sweden is a 'post-industrial society' with an increasing proportion of the workforce outside the industrial sector, the SAP's success can only be due to the willingness of a large proportion of the 'new middle class' to vote for the left.[35] But it has been argued that this is only possible when the social democratic programme is diluted. If the working class is a minority in society, according to this particular argument, the social democratic choice is between perpetual electoral defeat and programmatic purity on the one hand, or electoral success and dilution of the programme on the other, as the party reaches out for allies from other classes.[36] In practice, it has been argued, social democracy chooses electoral success, programmatic dilution and inevitable loss of working-class support. We have seen that Przeworski's prediction – which gains at least statistical force by virtue of the narrow definition of the working class utilised, ensuring that it is invariably a minority – cannot explain the policies adopted by social democratic parties in the 1970s. In Britain, Sweden and France a definite left orientation emerged which succeeded in attracting voters; yet neither of these things should have happened in Przeworski's scheme of things.

One has only to go back a short time to find a very different sociological determinism. The victory of the French Socialists in 1981 was in part attributed to long-run 'processes of economic and social change in France ... such factors as movement from the country to the towns and decline in religious attendance, during the more than twenty years of right-wing rule', according to McCarthy. Agricultural workers had shrunk from 28 per cent of the population in 1954 to 9 per cent in 1975, while the decline of the importance of Catholicism in sustaining the right is recorded in voting studies,[37] as well as through such factors as the transformation of the CFDT into a transmission belt for the PS and the growth of a Catholic leftism in the 1970s.[38] Mitterrand's close challenge for the presidency in 1974 (49.3 per cent against Giscard d'Estaing's 50.7 per cent) was read as evidence of a profound shift within the working-class electorate from Gaullism to the left. Ten years earlier the religious beliefs of the voters and the degree to which these beliefs were observed were found to be the best explanations of French voting behaviour.[39] But 'the secularisation of French society took a giant stride in the 1970s', as church attendances continued their fall, and the total left vote increased correspondingly between 1968 and 1981 at each parliamentary election.[40]

Some commentators saw the left as the inevitable beneficiary of this secularisation process on the grounds that the salience of class was bound to increase as religion declined, thus 'releasing to the Left large numbers of those hitherto influenced away from their 'natural' class party'.[41] While it had to be admitted that the irreligious might more commonly support the right in future, the main result of the decay of religion in determining French voting behaviour seemed to be the rediscovery of social inequality, according to R. W. Johnson. In Britain, until the 1970s, the most authoritative voting studies predicted the growth of the Labour vote.[42] When the dealignment trend later became apparent, it was stressed that both major parties were adversely affected by it and the erosion of 'partisan identification' was plausibly attributed to growing public alienation from ideologically similar organisations, neither of which had been able to arrest the country's relative economic decline.[43] After the 1979 general election, the British Election Survey found that on six of the eight contentious issues of the campaign, the Conservative Party was more representative of the views of the electorate ; the spectre was now raised of the conservatisation of the electorate,[44] such was the shift in values apparently recorded against Labour.[45] Just a few years later the same author reported on the persistence of collectivist and socialist values within the electorate.[46] Even more recently we have been treated to surveys that show an increase in class-consciousness in Britain,[47] though these were soon succeeded by the announcement of a new classificatory schema justified in some quarters in terms of the growth of the middle class. I mention these contradictory positions not merely to suggest that a certain scepticism might be in order, but also to remind readers of how recent some of this evidence concerning long-term trends actually is.

Classes were defined in relational terms by both Marx and Weber and their explanatory significance derived from the way these relations were thought to mould the interests and experiences of real people. Paradoxically, we are invited to believe that class is less salient in Western Europe at the very time when large and often bitter class struggles have been resurgent. There was reason to talk about the 'resurgence of class conflict' from the late 1960s[48] when massive strike waves engulfed Sweden, Italy, France and Britain. Estimates of the impact of the large increase in strike activity in Sweden and Denmark between 1979 and 1985 suggest that it added four or five percentage points to the growth in trade union density in those countries – a case, perhaps, of 'intensified class struggle' stimulating 'workers' self-organisation'.[49] We saw that social democratic programmes became more ambitious in the 1970s in Sweden, Britain and France, and an offensive was waged around economic equality, industrial democracy, employee investment funds and public ownership. There was also a new emphasis on the dangerous power of multinational capital in both the Alternative Economic Strategy (Britain) and the Common Programme of the Left (France) and the need for tougher measures to realise the social democratic programme. In Sweden the limits of the social consensus that had prevailed since the war were quickly exposed when a proposal emanating from the blue-collar union confederation, the LO, threatened to collectivise the ownership of firms. The Meidner Plan, as it was known, was received with horror and fierce opposition from business until the Social Democrats watered it down. By that time social democratic legislation had already breached the terms of the 1938 Saltsjobaden agreement to respect managerial prerogatives by challenging them across a broad front. The subsequent offensive of the employers' organisations against centralised collective bargaining and the costs of the welfare state were in part related to the left's radical ambitions. Similarly, the advent of monetarist policies in the 1980s signalled a class offensive against the left and in Britain took the form of widening inequalities and an explicit attempt to eliminate 'socialism'. Class relations were certainly a significant basis for conflict through the 1980s, though it is true that the electoral successes of the right in Britain shifted much socialist discussion to the related questions of how the Conservative agenda achieved hegemony and succeeded in demobilising the left. None of this necessarily denies that class is the basis for collective intervention, though in search of the sources of hegemony non-class factors received increasing emphasis in socialist discussion.

The structural conflict between capital and labour remains an important explanadum, particularly in social and economic policy. The undoubted growth, and increasing heterogeneity of the middle class, does not negate this point. No structured conflict has ever been claimed to exist between the working class and the middle class in socialist theory and the latter is by no means regarded as an automatic ally of capital. On the contrary, increasing numbers of middle-class jobs and lifestyles bear close comparison in some important respects to those of the workers commonly regarded as the left's natural constituency. The growth of insecurity in white-collar employment is an aspect of this.

Class solidarity

As we have mentioned, it is argued that the working class is increasingly heterogeneous in terms of its experiences of work, or the lack of it, as well as against criteria such as income, security, age, gender and origin.[50] At the lowest levels of security and income is a population of the long-term unemployed, the casualised workers and the unskilled generally. Some theorists have argued that this stratum includes, if it is not actually coterminous with, a new underclass of the feckless and criminal. The left has generally rejected this designation as reactionary (though not New Labour), but has noted the functional value of a reserve army of labour to capitalism, both economically and ideologically. The existence of this very lowest stratum disciplines those just above them, warning that resistance to 'flexibility' will result in their demotion to the ranks of the unemployed. At the same time, Conservative politicians (joined on occasions by New Labour) promote the idea that the poor are the authors of their own misfortune, constituting both a parasitic (fiscal) burden on the employed and a threat to their welfare (in the form of crime and immorality as well as a financial drain). The prospects for solidarity between the more prosperous workers and the underclass are accordingly difficult to secure.

In the economic conditions of today, when the stratum of semi-skilled workers above the underclass is shrinking, it is doubly difficult to prevent the working class dividing in two in social, economic and political terms. In some versions of this argument a one-third/two-thirds society has emerged.[51] Galbraith's analysis of US politics, for example, identifies what he calls 'a culture of contentment', producing an electoral alliance between the comfortable and the very rich to exclude the interests of the working class from the political agenda.[52] The large size of the American middle class, and the exceptionally low turnout in US elections, is said to have made this possible. But the defection of the skilled and semi-skilled workers to the Conservatives in Britain in 1979 and 1983 was conceptualised in much the same way. Thompson perceives a '30–50–20 per cent' economy in Britain and sees the political problem as one of forging a new solidarity – persuading the middle 50 per cent to bear the burden of Keynesian redistributory policies at a time of tax resentment, if not tax rebellion.[53] There is probably something in this, but it is not clear what.

Inevitably, periods of rapid economic change characterised by structural adjustments can witness the collapse of centres of established industry. Britain was especially badly hit in the slump of 1979–81; in France the downswing was especially severe in 1980–83; in Germany the reunification process which began in 1990 and the determination to meet the Maastricht criteria for currency convergence made the unemployment problem worse in the mid-1990s. The trend over the whole period since 1970, however, has been to reduce the centres of trade union and left strength, as old heavy industrial sites have declined and replacement jobs have been subject to conditions which obstruct the formation of class solidarity; such as casualisation, part-time work, no-union firms, relocation to small town and greenfield sites.[54] It would be surprising if class remained a stable source of identity, consciousness and action under these circumstances. Some research suggests that it was only a modest predictor of values in the 1980s when measured against various attitude scales, but that very large national variations existed too.[55] One might also expect that the unemployed and insecure low paid – people who suffer cumulative disadvantages affecting their personal welfare – would be more supportive of collectivist institutions and values than the greater proportion of the working population. This seems to be true, but empirical analysis of this problem also reveals the growth of collectivist attitudes among those in relatively secure employment in mid- to late 1980s Britain and suggests that politics, rather than labour-market segmentation, is the most powerful factor in producing such attitudes.[56] Class alliances and alliances between class fractions have to be constructed politically and for electoral purposes at least there seems to be no fundamental obstacle to a blue-collar/white-collar alliance as the evidence of countries such as Sweden show.

Voting trends

Evidence of party decomposition centring on declining voter turnout, increased voter volatility, falling partisan identification and the decreased salience of parties in the everyday lives of voters was noticed in the US by the late 1960s.[57] A decade on and these were said to be 'familiar phenomena to observers throughout the world' and especially relevant to the left because 'the particular class composition that enabled social democratic experiments to take place are decomposing **faster** than other political coalitions, making social democratic parties as a rule the single most vulnerable to possible decomposition'.[58] Why? Because working-class attachment to social democratic parties can no longer be taken for granted, according to Wolfe, who cites the challenge from the left revealed by elections in Norway (1973) and Denmark (1973). Second, because the social democrats are associated with welfare states that represent resented tax burdens, as witness the problems of British Labour (1979), the Danish Social Democrats (1973) and the Democratic Party in the US. Third, because social democratic strategy since 1945 has been to compensate the inequalities generated by the market through housing policies, welfare and public works; when people realised they were not getting ahead of others, reasons Wolfe, the social democrats took the blame.[59] Left voting strength in Britain was said to be concentrated in the social groups, employment sectors and regions that were least dynamic and demographically favoured in 1979 and 1983.[60] But the fragmentation of the class structure which the Conservatives capitalised on in Britain also had sources in the growing fiscal and cultural segmentation of the workforce by age which were also rooted in demography (increased longevity, longer retirement, rising care costs for the elderly) as well as the new 'flexible' economy. Increased social differentiation was said to militate against collectivist provisions with which the left was associated and emotionally involved because the 'one size fits all' approach was obsolete and its specifically redistributive thrust was an electoral loser.

The conservatisation'of the electorate[61] which these trends either signify or portend was also said to be exacerbated in some countries by immigration which had served to erode the culture of solidarity in countries such as France, Italy, Flanders, Austria and Denmark, where the anti-immigrant right has

Table 9.1 *Electoral share of socialist parties in general elections (averages)*

State	*1945–90*	*1945–73*	*1960–73*	*1974–90*	*1980–90*
Austria	45.2	44.2	46.3	47.0	44.6
Belgium	30.2	32.1	30.0	27.2	28.2
Denmark	36.0	37.7	38.7	33.3	32.2
Finland	24.8	24.8	24.0	24.9	25.4
Greece				35.8	42.2
Ireland	11.2	12.4	14.5	9.3	8.7
Italy	16.5	17.6	17.3	14.9	16.4
Holland	29.1	27.7	25.9	31.5	31.0
Norway	42.3	44.2	42.9	38.7	37.4
Spain				38.6	27.2
Portugal				30.6	27.2
Sweden	45.5	46.3	46.8	43.9	44.5
W. Germany	37.3	36.3		38.8	
UK	41.5	46.0	45.1	34.3	29.2
Average	31.2	31.7	31.8	31.5	31.5

Note: Average excludes Greece, Portugal and Spain.

already obtained significant working-class support.[62] Voting alignments were subject to other changes which denied the social democratic left the automatic loyalty it had built up within the working class of Britain and other countries. The process of partisan dealignment found in Britain was said to make class a poor predictor of voting. For all this, however, there is no evidence that the Western European social democratic vote is subject to a secular erosion.

The averages shown in Table 9.1 illustrate perhaps surprising stability in the socialist vote.[63] European electorates appear to be much more stable than one might expect in an age of electoral 'dealignments'. Indeed, Peter Mair observes that the average level of aggregate volatility in the period 1945–89 shows an average shift of less than 9 per cent – in other words a net aggregate stability of 91 per cent.[64] Mair's figures refer to all parties of course and not just socialist parties. They are relevant, however, particularly in view of his finding that there was actually less volatility in the years 1966–89, the period that has been identified as a time of particular electoral turbulence, than there was in the supposed golden age. The years after 1968 were, of course, the period when the New Politics became an issue for political scientists and the 'old left' was allegedly faced with a particular challenge.

Rivals to social democracy

According to this argument the left itself must fragment as the social structure becomes more differentiated. At least two lefts appear – the old, which is blue-collar based and fights for class-related issues, and the new whose most intensely disputed issues 'no longer deal with ownership and control of the means of production'.[65] The new politics of the left is said to be an effect of affluence which promotes individualism and a preoccupation with self-actualisation, both of which are said to undermine hierarchies and collectivism – the preserve of the old left.[66] The electoral breakthrough of *Die Grunen* in March 1983, when it secured 5.6 per cent of the vote and qualified for representation in the *Bundestag*, was one of the signals that the 'new social movements' of the late 1960s were here to stay. These movements – feminist, pacifist, environmentalist – challenge social democracy, so it is said, as well as the right and represent the rise of post-materialist values, a challenge to conventional preoccupations with economic growth and class, as well as bureaucratic hierarchies and statism. Some commentators have concluded from this that the working-class parties 'are now in all likelihood on their way out' and the trade unions are in decline as 'major social forces'.[67] It is a judgement that allows for periods of red-green coalition and admits that the agenda of the new social movements 'can be seen as parts of the socialist programme' which social democracy left unsolved. It also sees that skilful leaders can do what Oskar Lafontaine achieved in the Saar by coopting the new ideas to maintain social democratic electoral power. But it is an analysis that can be content to take 'globalisation' as a given and link the New Politics to an emerging world of decentralised, small-scale firms; as the old Fordism expires, according to this view, the 'old left' politics associated with it becomes redundant.

Such reasoning suggests a major transformation is underway. But there is as yet no evidence for a drama of this magnitude. While it is true that the social democratic parties, like their conservative or Christian democrat rivals, find themselves with a smaller share of the average vote than they obtained in the 1960s, the average net loss of the established parties is only of the order of 11 per cent in the last thirty years, a period during which they have polled an increasing absolute number of votes. Only around 5 per cent of voters support the green parties in Western Europe – not spectacular evidence that societal change must inevitably bring electoral change and new parties.[68] Clearly parties can adapt and survive and the cleavages that structure voting alignments are varied, bearing complex rather than crudely reductionist relationships to social structure. Even if society is changing in the way depicted, it is wrong to assume that politics must change with it. It is perfectly possible, for example, that many of the old left values associated with social democracy will survive the circumstances that gave rise to them and enter into future political alignments. This is indeed what I have argued in chapter four when reviewing evidence from some of the Scandinavian countries and Germany.

Decline of party

Left parties have nevertheless also been subjected to a decline in membership in a number of countries.[69] The surviving membership is predominantly middle aged and not so active as it was. The trend is too widespread for local explanations to be convincing, such as the repeated disappointments arising from the experience of failed governments, or because of restricted opportunities for meaningful participation, as central governments diminish the powers of local governments and party leaders insulate themselves from the influence of the mass organisations. Right-wing parties, moreover, are affected by the same pattern. The left parties not only have difficulty in recruiting youth, however; they cannot persuade the working class to join. Their memberships are predominantly male and middle class. Culturally the significance of the social democratic parties has been diminishing for decades but now 'the stream of specialised working-class publications has nearly dried-up',[70] while the volume of information to which individuals are exposed from non- or anti-socialist forces has reached massive proportions. A strong and active membership is believed to be especially necessary to left-wing parties for just this reason; they can act as opinion leaders in their communities and as ambassadors for the party, to some extent countering the propaganda and values of its opponents. Some research suggests that academics have underestimated their importance in mobilising the vote.[71]

Seyd and Whiteley also argue that party members are the 'selectorate' who determine candidates and, in safe seats, representatives. From this pool future government ministers emerge. They also have powers to 'deselect' or to support their MP against the party centre. They are potential candidates themselves, of course, and a source of ideas – both their own, and those that they pick up from the communities and the neighbourhoods to which they belong. Party parliamentary elites may court public wrath and indifference if they are too cocooned from these sources of information. They may become irrelevant if they fail to modernise their ideas. The decline of party memberships is therefore significant, as is any evidence that we may discover showing that party elites have insulated themselves from such mass influences as remain tied to the party. In Britain during the 1980s socialist activists actually acquired powers, in relation to mandatory selection of MPs and the election of the party leader, that they had never had before. Similar changes occurred in the Danish Social Democratic Party and the Belgian Socialists. Nevertheless, the Labour Party in Britain subsequently introduced a number of changes which, taken together, have recentralised power in the party around the parliamentary leader.[72] If there is a trend in continental Europe it is surely the dependence of parties on state subventions, the diminishing significance of membership subscriptions and the bureaucratic growth of the party centre, which is increasingly dominated by the parliamentary leadership rather than representatives of the mass party.[73]

Decline of trade unionism

A labour and socialist culture was associated with those centres of heavy industry – in engineering, mining, steel, shipbuilding and transport – that have been reduced, especially in the years since 1970. Just as the loss of party members accelerated as unemployment rose,[74] so also did membership of trade unions across Western Europe. In Britain the TUC lost over 5 million members after 1979; in France trade union membership fell from 25 to just 10 per cent of the workforce. Nearly all OECD countries had fewer industrial disputes in the 1980s than the 1970s and union membership rates were generally falling in the 1990s. Attempts have been made to link this latter change to the reorganisation of labour markets, the erosion of class as an organising principle and to the reduced electoral fortunes of social democratic parties.[75] Where union densities were already high – as in Scandinavia[76] – the unions nevertheless successfully expanded membership in the 1980s among public- and service-sector workers. Within the unions, however, the balance of power swung towards white-collar organisations, sometimes provoking policy divisions between the different union confederations, such as in Sweden. In the weakly unionised countries, membership was overly dependent on traditional areas of strength in the shrinking manufacturing sector. Of course, the growth of unemployment and casualised labour beyond the reach of the unions weakens the unions' capacity to speak for the working class, just as the middle-class membership of the social democratic parties finds it difficult to represent the people of the housing schemes. Such trends arguably leave the unrepresented workers vulnerable to apathy or the blandishments of the populist right.[77]

An undoubted trend in some countries since the 1970s has been the tendency to decentralise wage bargaining. This has occurred in Belgium, Denmark, Sweden, Britain and Ireland and to some extent in Germany and France. If decentralisation weakens the authority of union confederations it could be reasoned that their influence on macroeconomic policy making will suffer too, while inter-union rivalry is likely to increase.[78] A key social democratic 'power resource'[79] is thus weakened. But the argument can be made to work the other way too. The removal of social democrats from office in Sweden (1976–82), and in Denmark, Belgium, Britain and the Netherlands for most of the 1980s contributed to the loss of union influence over state policy because 'the decline of social democracy removed unions from the corridors of state power'.[80] The more obvious factor in union decline, however, is unemployment as became clear even in Sweden when the full-employment policy – which had been maintained throughout the 1980s – collapsed in the 1990s. To this could be added evidence that as economies become more open and vulnerable to foreign competition the odds of trade union decline increase.[81] But this is speculative.

Long-term predictions about the unions should be treated with caution. In the early 1960s membership levels were declining and unions looked set to face a crisis of function but between 1968 and 1970 'every country in western Europe apart from Austria and Switzerland ... experienced a major rise in industrial conflict. Consequent on this came a growing political importance, membership growth and a new radicalism at both national and shop-floor levels'.[82] Nevertheless, the recomposition of the workforce will mean that non-manual workers will form a growing proportion of the employed. Crouch predicts that unions will either reflect this change or retain their old sense of direction only by failing to reflect it. If the former occurs, trade union members will either belong to separate confederations, as in Scandinavia, with the professional confederation gradually challenging the dominance of the old social democratic workers, or this process will take place within a single confederation as in Britain or Austria.[83] The more rapid demise of jobs in manufacturing will accelerate this process.

Governments and employers have taken advantage of the forces undermining unions to assist the process by fragmenting industrial relations. In Britain some employers have insisted on single-union agreements, plant-by-plant negotiations to break national agreements and national negotiations. In Germany, Austria and the Netherlands employers have done the same through the works councils. In 1984 the Swedish employers' organisation *Sveriges Arbetsgivarforeningen* broke a fifty-year tradition of centralised bargaining by insisting on company-level negotiations only. The reaction against corporatism occurred either because unions were unable to deliver the requisite levels of acquiescence – as in Denmark, Italy and the UK – or did so only in return for benefits which employers came to regard as inordinately expensive as in Sweden and Germany. This is what 'overloaded government' and '*der Gewerkschaftsstaat*' ('trade union state' – a state run for the benefit of organised labour) was allegedly all about.[84] But the pace of employer-state disenchantment with corporatism obviously varied according to how successful it had been from one country to another; the ferocity of the British Conservative attack on the TUC illustrates this as does, at the other extreme, the cases of Sweden, Austria and Norway. For some proponents of the globalisation thesis, however, an accelerated trend towards globally oriented business threatens the established rights of labour by undermining the state's capacity to guarantee those rights.[85] While the growth of such rights in the past entailed the growth of state regulation, global capital now has the power to evade many state controls and insist on the reduction of others, while states themselves engage in a Dutch auction for inward investments leading to the same results. Unions, meanwhile, lag well behind capital's capacity for transnational action.

There is, nevertheless, evidence that unions are making progress towards transnational action.[86] The more production is actually integrated transnationally, so the argument goes, the more will workers become aware of the need to coordinate with their counterparts overseas. Like anyone else, they are able to use new technologies to achieve this effect, as in the protracted Liverpool dockers' strike.

Crisis of the welfare state

The crisis of social democracy is often said to be synonymous with the crisis of the welfare state, an institution which accounts for between one-fifth and one-third of GDP in all the advanced industrial societies or well over half of all that their states spend. Since the 1970s welfare systems have been put under pressure by the fiscal crisis of the state. This has been exacerbated by the demographic trends referred to above[87] and the appearance of mass unemployment at a time when left politicians in some countries have been induced to think that proposals to increase direct taxes are vote losers. The election results in Denmark in 1973 and 1989–90, and the UK in 1979–87 are often cited as examples of tax revolts, as we have seen.[88] But when, we might ask, were proposals to raise taxes ever vote winners? Resistance to tax rises and new taxes is 'normal' and it has taken abnormal circumstances – notably two world wars – to ratchet up taxes this century. It is hardly surprising that there was resistance to tax increases and support for tax reductions in the recent period of uncertain economic growth alternating with recession. As Mann points out, there is no need to invoke 'postmodernity' or 'globalism' to explain opposition to taxes in a period of stagnant or falling real incomes.[89]

Budgetary constraints also derive, in this period, from contingent problems such as the attempt to meet the Maastricht criteria for monetary union, which involve restrictions on the level of budgetary deficit and national indebtedness. These considerations lay behind austerity programmes in Germany, France and Italy in the mid-1990s. But the principal reason for the retreat of 'tax-and-spend' reformism since 1970 has been the slowing down of growth rates, the rise of unemployment and the identification of inflation as the principal economic evil. In this context, there has been a revival of pre-war arguments against welfare expenditure; high levels of public expenditure, it is said, reduce competitiveness, undermine work motivation, and crowd out economic growth. Indeed, retrenchment is often said to be the order of the day; in Belgium, Germany and Ireland spending fell as a proportion of GDP by virtue of restraint coupled with economic growth. Speculation that sustained cuts in public expenditure programmes might provoke middle-class exit and thus generate the need for even more retrenchment, has entered the discussion. Some commentators perceive a 'profound shift toward a new kind of regime', often on the basis of globalisation, not only in Britain under the Conservative Party, but also in states like Denmark, Sweden, New Zealand and Australia – where left-dominated governments held office in the 1980s.[90]

Once again the ultimate cause of change is held to be 'increased internationalisation' of production and financial flows, acting through the agency of an alliance between workers and capitalists in the 'exposed' competitive sectors of the economy, in conjunction with politicians and bureaucrats worried about fiscal deficits and declining international competitiveness. Such groups identified the state, and particularly the welfare state – which each of them had expanded to absorb the growing numbers of unemployed – as the chief culprit by the early 1980s. This strategy had misfired by abetting wage explosions, unsustainable levels of public and foreign debt, and rising inflation. State bureaucrats also became anxious about 'overload' and a loss of state autonomy as a consequence of the rising expectations of society.[91] In particular, it has been argued that in each of the 'small states in big trouble', such as Denmark and Sweden, reorganisation of welfare involved the decentralisation of operational authority and responsibility for services, coupled with centralisation of control over the volume of spending and the injection of market-like pressures to foster efficiency. Schwartz concludes that economic deregulation and liberalisation in the 1980s assisted the process by which states extricated themselves from the overload problem. The upshot of welfare reforms is allegedly to reinforce individual reliance on the private suppliers of services and reduce the demand for collectively provided services, thus reinforcing the trend for the state to withdraw and leave as much as possible to the market.[92]

But while there is a superficial plausibility in regarding retrenchment policies as the logical corollary of the shrinking power of organised labour in conditions of economic slowdown and jobless growth, welfare states create much larger constituencies than that of the blue-collar working class: 'in many countries today almost half of the electorate receive transfer income from the welfare state', according to Pierson.[93] The level of welfare expenditure is thus not an uncomplicated index of left strength. What is worth noting is that there is no pattern of decline to report – contrary to the expectations encouraged by writers such as Schwartz – only a tendency for the slow starters to catch up (see Table 9.2).

Conservatives have to reckon with a popular support for welfare services that goes well beyond the ranks of organised labour to include all beneficiaries of such programmes as well as those who inspired, created or provided them. Surveys of EU citizens found strong support (two-thirds majorities) for the view that government must maintain social protection even if it means higher taxes, though in the UK and Denmark voters also wanted tax cuts.[94] Taylor-Gooby's survey of decision makers in EU states on welfare expenditure found recognition of the burden represented by taxation, but acknowledgement that it is justified by the services provided. The majority of those interviewed said that they believed the public was prepared to pay.[95]

This seems to be upheld even in the most expensive systems such as those of Scandinavia where the system has arguably 'grown to limits'. Retrenchment has not brought about fundamental change in such countries and the

Table 9.2 *Social protection expenditure as % of GDP, 1970, 1980 and 1991*

	1970	*1980*	*1991*
Belgium	18.7	28.0	26.7
Denmark	19.6	28.7	29.8
France	19.2	25.4	28.7
Germany	21.5	28.7	26.6
Greece	n.a.	12.2	20.7a
Ireland	13.2	21.6	21.3
Italy	17.4	19.4	24.4
Luxembourg	15.9	26.5	27.5
Netherlands	20.8	30.8	32.4
Portugal	n.a.	14.7	19.4
Spain	n.a.	18.1	21.4
UK	15.9	21.5	24.7
EU12	18.0b	24.4	26.0

Note: a – 1989 statistic; b – EU9.
Source: Commission of the European Communities, *Social Protection in Europe* (Brussels, CEC, 1994).

main innovations of the 1970s and 1980s, such as parental leave, have survived the recent cuts in expenditure and remain at more generous levels than they did two decades ago.[96] Social democrats have also had little difficulty in winning business support for those 'supply-side' policies designed to stimulate economic growth by investment in human capital and measures that encourage labour-market flexibility. Presumably this is why there is so much talk about such policies throughout Western Europe, though it is frequently packaged in terms of globalisation. There is little evidence for the contrary thesis of 'social dumping'. A low social wage will not of itself attract investment if a country has inadequate labour productivity, and this depends on a variety of other factors including education and infrastructure. However, these considerations do not prevent business using its greater bargaining power in circumstances of greater capital mobility and weaker trade unionism in order to attack industrial relations systems which offer measures of protection to wages and working conditions.

Nevertheless, Pierson argues that the evidence does not support the proposition that retrenchment is greatest where the left is weakest. The electoral unpopularity of retrenchment policies, moreover, makes cutbacks unlikely except when budgetary crises occur and far from producing a self-reinforcing dynamic of cuts, such programmes provoke support for the welfare system.[97] Measuring retrenchment programmes involves more than examining levels of expenditure, since these can be inflated by unemployment while disguising significant erosion of rights. Pierson focuses on structural shifts in the period

1974–90, involving reliance on means-tested benefits, privatisation programmes, and changes in eligibility rules; any increase in these is taken to represent evidence of retrenchment. His data for Britain, Germany, Sweden and the US 'suggest a surprisingly high level of continuity and stability' in respect of social security transfers as a percentage of GDP, public expenditure as a percentage of nominal GDP, and the percentage of public employees in the workforce. He concludes that 'economic, political, and social pressures have fostered an image of welfare states under siege. Yet if one turns from abstract discussions of social transformation to an examination of actual policy, it becomes difficult to sustain the proposition that these strains have generated fundamental shifts.'[98] Some change in social policy is inevitable over two decades, but incremental modifications do not add up to the radical break that some see in the period since 1973. Nowhere is there evidence of middle-class exit leading to more retrenchment, according to Pierson.

My purpose in this concluding chapter has been to question generalisations concerning the long-term decline of the left. Clearly, the response of social democratic parties to the undoubtedly adverse conditions of existence that have prevailed since the early 1970s has been to retreat from the more ambitious goals associated with these parties. Many have excluded their more radical sections from the policy-making process. The reduced influence of activists and trade unions may have contributed to declining membership, as we have already suggested. It has certainly assisted the process of programmatic adaptation to the new circumstances. In the 1970s worsening economic conditions first brought about a radical programmatic turn in a number of countries. But in most countries in which social democratic governments existed in the late 1970s and 1980s – the UK, Germany, France, Spain, Greece and Portugal – election manifestos were soon forgotten as administrations struggled with stagflation and/or the neo-liberal international turn. A policy convergence has occurred around market-oriented strategies as witnessed in the policies of social democratic governments in Australia, France and New Zealand as well as the programmatic retreat of those exlcuded from power in the same years such as the British and Belgian socialists.

The perceived policy failure which this retreat entailed in the minds of many activists may have undermined collective incentives to participation. But ideological change also enabled these parties to make overtures to voters who rejected socialism and the social democratic vote did not collapse. If the need for heterogeneous support encourages the adoption of heterogeneous values, as several commentators mentioned above have stressed, this may lead in time to the recruitment of significant cohorts who subscribe to the new values, while those disillusioned with the abandonment of traditional policies eventually exit, losing political will or joining other left organisations. If the process is sustained for long enough, development becomes 'path dependent', parties are changed permanently. This may have happened already in Britain. But this is not what has happened in Scandinavia and Germany, where the case for managing capitalism in a social democratic way remains strongly advocated and widely supported.

Modern democracies provide conditions conducive to the creation and maintenance of certain conventional wisdoms. Politicians are vulnerable to the buzz words of the moment (notably 'globalisation' today). When international forces seem to compel governments in specific directions irrespective of local mandates, voters may conclude that left deviations from the preferences of money markets are impractical, and left parties incompetent or worse. Social democratic leaderships reach the conclusion that practical politics excludes attempts to transcend, control and regulate markets. They study focus groups to find the policy prescriptions which voters will support. It is an exaggeration to contrast the supposedly 'full-blooded' socialist policies of yesteryear with the current caution, but there has undoubtedly been a loss of faith in socialist ideas such as planning and a widespread perception that globalisation undermines the old national economic management.

Though the overwhelming majority of those on the left in Western Europe found the state socialism of the communist regimes repellent, the collapse of those regimes in 1989 and the subsequent turn to the market would seem to have reinforced the case against socialism *per se*. One major reason for this was the absence of a popular demand in the East for the democratisation of a system that did, after all, foster welfare, egalitarianism, job security and planning. In other words, it could be read as a rejection of socialism in all its forms. Another reason is that the interventionist state of Western social democracy had already lost legitimacy (to varying degrees, of course) in the 1970s – the right no longer found corporatist arrangements conducive to capital accumulation in certain countries and the New Left in particular had developed its own case against the secrecy, bureaucracy and centralism which obstructed the sort of participatory, decentralised, socialism that it favoured. But while the left alternatives failed, or failed to find administrative expression, the right secured power in Britain just as monetarist policies were adopted in the US and internationally. The Thatcherite polemic against the state drew on arguments developed by the left but in order to undermine the welfare state rather than to upgrade it for modern times. The New Right also developed its own philosophical critique of state planning when the empirical evidence for its inefficacy was at its peak. These are arguably among the reasons for the pervasive 'metaphysical pathos' of pessimism which informs so much discussion of the left's prospects in the period under review. My modest ambition in this chapter has been to challenge this sentimentality by alerting readers to the evidence which contradicts the thesis of secular decline.

Notes

1 S. Brittan, 'The economic contradictions of democracy', *British Journal of Political Science*, 5:April (1975) 129–59; A. King, 'Overload: problems of government in the 1970s', *Political Studies*, 23, June–September (1975) 290–5; G. Sartori, 'Will democracy kill democracy?', *Government and Opposition*, 10, Spring (1975); R. Emmett Tyrell, Jr, *The Future That Does Not Work* (New York, Garden City, 1977).

2 A. Wolfe, 'Has social democracy a future?', *Comparative Politics*, 11, October (1978) 101.

3 See C. S. Maier, 'The politics of productivity: foundations of American international policy after World War Two', *International Organisation*, 31, Autumn (1977) 626.

4 Wolfe, 'Has social democracy a future?', p. 106. This pattern was certainly true of Sweden where social democratic support rose in periods of stable prices and economic growth. See B. Sarlvik, 'Recent electoral trends in Sweden', in K. H. Cerny (ed.), *Sandinavia at the Polls* (Washington, DC, American Enterprise Institute for Public Policy Research, 1977), p. 93.

5 R. Dahrendorf, *Reflections on the Revolution in Europe* (London, Chatto, 1990), p. 38.

6 F. Hirsch, *Alternatives to World Monetary Disorder* (New York, Random House, 1977). The AES in Britain was inspired precisely by the conviction that trends in the internationalisation of capital had made the old Keynesian policies inoperable. See S. Holland, *The Socialist Challenge* (London, Quartet, 1975). Many of the same themes can be found in the Common Programme of the left adopted in 1974 by the PCF and PS.

7 Wolfe, 'Has social democracy a future?', p. 109.

8 Fordism is characterised as a system of mass production of standardised products employing semi-skilled (male) labour which operates under hierarchical (and authoritarian) management structures in big factories obtaining economies of scale. The spread of Japanese management techniques has undoubtedly modified this system by turning the screw of exploitation. Whether it has done much more than this is open to doubt.

9 See A. Pollert, *Farewell to Flexibility?* (Oxford, Blackwell, 1991) and her 'Dismantling flexibility', *Capital and Class*, 34 (1988) 42–75. R. Brenner and M. Glick write that 'the whole notion of Fordism, in both its supply-side and its demand-side aspects is theoretically incoherent and empirically irrelevant …'; see their 'The regulation approach', *New Left Review*, 188 (1991) 113.

10 See the introductory chapters in the White Paper *Fairness at Work* (London, Department of Trade and Industry, 1998), especially ch. 2. More generally, see S. Driver and L. Martell, *New Labour: Politics After Thatcherism* (Cambridge, Polity Press, 1998), pp. 42–3.

11 See C. Cousins, 'Changing regulatory frameworks and non-standard employment: a comparison of Germany, Spain, Sweden and the UK', in A. Felstead and N. Jewson (eds), *Global Trends in Flexible Labour* (London, Macmillan, 1999), pp 100–21.

12 A. R. Zolberg, 'Response: working class dissolution', *International Labour and Working Class History*, 47, Spring (1995) 28.

13 A. Przeworski and J. Sprague, *Paper Stones: A History of Electoral Socialism* (Chicago, IL, University of Chicago Press, 1986), p. 184
14 Zolberg, 'Response', p. 31.
15 P. Anderson, 'Introduction' to P. Anderson and P. Camiller (eds), *Mapping the West European Left* (London, Verso, 1994), p. 12.
16 Gorz argues that the power of the skilled workers has been definitively broken by the spread of computerisation and automation, and the link between the growth of the productive forces and class antagonism has broken too. See A. Gorz, *Farewell to the Working Class* (London, Pluto Press, 1980), pp. 14, 28.
17 Zolberg, 'Response', p. 29.
18 See for example, C. Hakim, 'Trends in the flexible workforce', *Employment Gazette*, November 1987, 549–60. This source estimates that up to one-third of the UK workforce could be regarded as 'flexible' by 1987.
19 J. K. Galbraith sees such an alliance between the rich and the middle class opposed to redistribution in the US. See his *The Culture of Contentment* (London, Penguin, 1992), p. 26.
20 See W. Hutton, *The State We're In* (London, Cape, 1996); and the Communist Party of Great Britain, *Manifesto For New Times* (London, CPGB, 1987).
21 R. Reich, *The Work of Nations* (New York, Vintage, 1992), p. 3. To give Reich his due, he does propose action to deal with this threat to community, such as significant redistribution of income.
22 Anderson, 'Introduction', pp. 13–14.
23 See J. Pakluski and M. Waters, 'The reshaping and dissolution of social class in advanced society', *Theory and Society*, 25:5 (1996) 668. See also T. Nichols Clark and S. M. Lipset, 'Are social classes dying?', *International Sociology*, 6:4 (1991) 397–410.
24 *Ibid.*, p. 678.
25 *Ibid.*, p. 682.
26 For the UK see I. Crewe, B. Sarlvik and J. Alt, 'Partisan dealignment in Britain 1964–1974', *British Journal of Political Science*, 7, (1977) 129–50. The decline of class identification in the voting behaviour of the young is noted for Germany and Italy in M. Franklin, T. Mackie, H. Valen *et al.*, *Electoral Change: Responses to Evolving Social and Attitudinal Structures in Western Countries* (Cambridge, Cambridge University Press, 1992), pp. 201, 253. While 'issues and ideological attitudes are replacing social position as the most important determinants of party choice' in Sweden, this appears to be largely an effect of the increased percentage of the white-collar electorate who vote for left parties – a consequence of what the author ascribes to Sweden's transition to a 'post-industrial society' (pp. 339–61).
27 J. O'Connor, *The Fiscal Crisis of the State* (New York, St. Martin's Press, 1973), pp. 228–31.
28 Such as the UK and Denmark, both of which experienced an electoral shift at least partly motivated by a revolt against the tax burden (in 1979 and 1973 respectively). See P. Taylor-Gooby, 'Paying for welfare: the view from Europe', *Political Quarterly*, 67:2 (1996) 116–26. This report shows widespread popular support for welfare states.
29 R. McKibbin, 'Class and conventional wisdom: the Conservative Party and the

"public" in inter-war Britain', in his *Ideologies of Class* (Oxford, Oxford University Press, 1990), pp. 287–8.

30 R. W. Johnson, *The Long March of the French Left* (London, Macmillan, 1981) p. 85.

31 See, for example, J. Benson, *The Working Class in Britain, 1850–1939* (London, Longman, 1989), pp. 190–8. See also E. J. Hobsbawm, *The Age of Capital, 1848–1875* (London, Abacus, 1977), pp. 262–3, and the same author's *The Age of Empire, 1875–1914* (London, Weidenfeld and Nicolson, 1987), pp. 118–41.

32 See, M. Lewis-Beck and A. Skalaban, 'France', in Franklin *et al.* (eds), *Electoral Change*, pp. 168–9.

33 F. Urban Pappi and P. Mnich, 'Germany' in *ibid.*, p. 204.

34 T. Mackie, R. Mannheimer and G. Sani, 'Italy', in *ibid.*, pp. 243–4, 253.

35 M. Oskarson, 'Sweden', in *ibid.*, p. 350.

36 Przeworski and Sprague, *Paper Stones*, pp. 2–3

37 Lewis-Beck and Skalaban, 'France', pp. 167–79.

38 P. McCarthy (ed.), *The French Socialists in Power, 1981–86* (New York, Greenwood Press, 1987), pp. 1, 15;

39 M. Brule, 'L'Appartenance Religieuse et le Vote du 5 decembre 1965', *Sondages*, 28:2 (1966) 15–19.

40 Johnson, *The Long March of the French Left*, p. 106; the total left vote increased from 40 per cent in 1968, to 45 per cent in 1973, to 49 per cent in 1978, to 57 per cent in 1981. It fell to 43 per cent in 1986.

41 *Ibid.*, p. 111.

42 D. Butler and D. Stokes, *Political Change in Britain* (London, Macmillan, second edition, 1974).

43 I. Budge and I. Crewe, *Party Identification and Beyond* (London, Wiley, 1976), pp. 35, 39.

44 Cited in I. Crewe, 'The Labour Party and the electorate', in D. Kavanagh (ed.), *The Politics of the Labour Party* (London, Allen and Unwin, 1982), pp. 10, 29.

45 I. Crewe, 'Why the Conservatives won', in H. Penniman (ed.), *Britain at the Polls 1979* (London, AEI, 1981).

46 I. Crewe, 'Values: the crusade that failed', in D. Kavanagh and A. Seldon, *The Thatcher Effect: A Decade of Change* (Oxford, Clarendon Press, 1989), pp. 239–50.

47 Gallup discovered that 81 per cent of the population believed there was a class struggle in Britain in 1995, while 76 per cent of its respondents in 1996 agreed with the same proposition. In the 1960s an average of 48 per cent took this view, growing to an average of 60 per cent in the following decade. Cited in K. Moody, *Workers in a Lean World* (London, Verso, 1997), pp. 35–6.

48 See C. Crouch and A. Pizzorno (eds), *The Resurgence of Class Conflict in Western Europe Since 1968* (London, Holmes and Meier, 1979).

49 L. J. Griffin, H. J. McCammon, and C. Botsko, 'The unmaking of a movement? The crisis of U.S. trade unionism in comparative perspective', in M. T. Hallinan, D. M. Klein and J. Glass (eds), *Change in Societal Institutions* (New York, Plenum, 1990), p. 189.

50 S. Berger and M. Piore, *Dualism and Discontinuities in Industrial Societies* (London, Cambridge University Press, 1980).

51 Hutton, *The State We're In*; CPGB, *Manifesto For New Times*.

52 Galbraith, *The Culture of Contentment*.

53 G. Thompson, 'Globalisation and the possibilities for domestic economic policy', *Internationale Politik und Gesellschaft*, 2 (1997) 161–71.

54 For Britain see D. Massey, 'The shape of things to come', in R. Peet (ed.), *International Capitalism and Industrial Restructuring* (Allen and Unwin, 1987), pp. 105–22.

55 E. O. Wright, 'The continuing relevance of class analysis – comments', *Theory and Society*, 25 (1996) 709–10.

56 D. Gallie and C. Vogler, 'Labour market deprivation, welfare and collectivism', *Archives Europeennes De Sociologie*, 31:1 (1990) 81–113.

57 W. D. Burnham, 'The end of American party politics', *Transaction*, December (1969) 20.

58 Wolfe, 'Has social democracy a future?', pp. 113–14.

59 *Ibid.*, p. 121

60 I. Crewe, 'The disturbing truth behind Labour's rout', *Guardian*, 13 June 1983; also see his 'Partisan dealignment ten years on', *West European Politics*, 7 (1984) 195.

61 For Britain see Crewe, 'The Labour Party and the electorate', pp. 11, 38.

62 The point is made by Perry Anderson in his 'Introduction' to Anderson and Camiller, pp. 13–14.

63 W. Merkel, 'The end of social democracy?', in C. Lemke and G. Marks (eds), *The Crisis of Socialism in Western Europe* (London, Duke University Press, 1992), p. 141. See also W. Merkel, *Ende der Sozialdemokratie? Machtressourcen und Regierungspolitik im westeuropaischen* (Frankfurt, Vergleich, 1993).

64 P. Mair, *Party System Change* (Oxford, Clarendon Press, 1997), p. 80.

65 Clark and Lipset, 'Are social classes dying?', p. 403.

66 R. Inglehart, *The Silent Revolution: Changing Values and Political Styles Among Western Publics* (Princeton, NJ, Princeton University Press, 1977); see also his 'The changing structure of political cleavages in Western society', in R. J. Dalton, S. C. Flanagan and P. A. Beck (eds), *Electoral Change in Advanced Industrial Democracies: Realignment or Dealignment?* (Princeton, NJ, Princeton University Press, 1984), pp. 25–69.

67 J. Galtung, 'The green movement: a socio-historical exploration', *International Sociology*, 1:1 (1986) 81, 86, 89, note 13.

68 Mair, *Party System Change*, pp. 82–6.

69 G. Voerman, 'Le paradis perdu. Les adhérents des partis sociaux-démocrates d'Europe occidentale, 1945–1995', in M. Lazar (ed.) *La Gauche en Europe Depuis 1945: Invariants et Mutations du Socialime Européen* (Paris, Presses Universitaires de France, 1995).

70 Zolberg, ' Response', p. 30.

71 P. Seyd and P. Whiteley, *Labour's Grass Roots: The Politics of Party Membership* (Oxford, Clarendon Press, 1992), pp. 174–200.

72 See on this L. Panitch and C. Leys, *The End of Parliamentary Socialism: From New Left to New Labour* (London, Verso, 1997), and E. Shaw, 'Organisational transformation in the Labour Party: the case of candidate selection – some preliminary findings', PSA Conference, Nottingham, 23–24 March 1999.

73 See P. Mair 'Party organisations: from civil society to the state', in P. Mair and O. Katz (eds), *How Parties Organize* (London, Sage, 1994), p. 14.

74 In the decade after 1985 membership fell in the parties of the UK, Austria, France, Sweden, Germany, Finland, Denmark and Norway. See Voerman, 'Le paradis perdu.'
75 B. Western, 'A comparative study of working-class disorganisation: union decline in eighteen advanced capitalist cuntries', *American Sociological Review*, 60, April (1995) 179–201.
76 Partly thanks to the Ghent system of unemployment insurance.
77 C. Crouch, 'The future prospects for trade unions in Western Europe', *Political Quarterly*, 57:1 (1986) 8.
78 Western,'A comparative study of working-class disorganisation', pp. 183–6.
79 See W. Korpi, *The Working Class and Welfare Capitalism* (London, Routledge and Kegan Paul, 1981).
80 Western, 'A comparative study of working-class disorganisation', p. 187.
81 *Ibid.*, pp. 194–5.
82 Crouch, 'The future prospects for trade unions in Western Europe', p. 5
83 *Ibid.*, p. 6.
84 *Ibid.*, p. 10
85 See C. Tilly, 'Globalisation threatens labor's rights', *International Labour and Working Class History*, 47, Spring (1995) 4.
86 A. Breitenfeller, 'Global unionism: a potential player?', *International Labour Review*, 136:4 (1997) 531–55; A. Herod, 'The practice of international labour solidarity and the geography of the global economy', *Economic Geography*, 71:4 (1995) 341–63; K. Moody, 'Towards an international social-movement unionism', *New Left Review*, 225 (1997) 52–72; H. Ramsey, 'Solidarity at last? International trade unionism approaching the millenium', *Economic and Industrial Democracy*, 18:4 (1997) 503–37.
87 Pensions, for example, are predicted to rise to 61 per cent of social expenditure in Germany by 2040 and 40 per cent in the UK and 44 per cent in Sweden. See OECD, *Ageing Populations: The Social Policy Implications* (Paris, OECD, 1988).
88 Taylor-Gooby, 'Paying for welfare', p. 116; N. F. Christiansen, 'Denmark: end of an idyll?', in Anderson and Camiller (eds), *Mapping the West European Left*, p. 90.
89 Cited in L. Weiss, *The Myth of the Powerless State* (Cambridge, Polity Press, 1998), p. 190.
90 H. Schwartz, 'Small states in big trouble: state reorganization in Australia, Denmark, New Zealand, and Sweden in the 1980s', *World Politics*, 46:4 (1994) 528.
91 *Ibid.*, p 537.
92 *Ibid.*, p. 554.
93 P. Pierson, 'The new politics of the welfare state', *World Politics*, 48:2 (1996) 146.
94 Taylor-Gooby, 'Paying for welfare', pp. 117–18, 121.
95 *Ibid.*, pp. 125–6.
96 J. D. Stephens, 'The Scandinavian welfare states: achievements, crisis, and prospects', in G. Esping-Andersen (ed.), *Welfare States in Transition* (London, Sage, 1996), pp. 55–6.
97 Pierson,'The new politics of the welfare state', p. 156.
98 *Ibid.*, p. 173.

Bibliography

Aaronovitch, S., *The Road From Thatcherism: The Alternative Economic Strategy*, London, Lawrence and Wishart, 1981.

Aglietta, M., *Regulation et Crises*, Brussels, Calman-Levy, 1976.

Ahlen, K., 'Sweden introduces employee ownership', *Political Quarterly*, 56:2 (1985).

——, 'Swedish collective bargaining under pressure: inter-union rivalry and incomes policies', *British Journal of Collective Bargaining*, 27:3 (1989).

Albert, M., *Capitalism Against Capitalism*, London, Whurr, 1993.

Almond, G. and Verba, S., *The Civic Culture*, Princeton, NJ, Princeton University Press, 1963.

Amark, K., 'Afterword: Swedish social democracy on a historical threshold', in K. Misgeld, K. Molin and K. Amark (eds), *Creating Social Democracy – A Century of the Social Democratic Party in Sweden*, Philadelphia, PA, Penn State University Press, 1993.

Ambler, J. S., 'French socialism in comparative perspective', in J. S. Ambler (ed.), *The French Socialist Experiment*, Philadelphia, PA, Institute for the Study of Human Issues, 1985.

——, 'Is the French left doomed to fail?', in J. S. Ambler (ed.), *The French Socialist Experiment*, Philadelphia, PA, Institute for the Study of Human Issues, 1985.

Andersen, J. G. and Borklund, T., 'Structural changes and new cleavages: the progress parties in Denmark and Norway', *Acta Sociologica*, 33:3 (1990).

Anderson, P., 'Introduction' to P. Anderson and P. Camiller (eds), *Mapping the West European Left*, London, Verso, 1994.

Anderson, P. and Mann, N., *Safety First: The Making of New Labour*, London, Granta, 1997.

Arendt, H., *Eichmann in Jerusalem*, Harmondsworth, Penguin, 1965.

Armstrong, P., Glyn, A. and Harrison, J., *Capitalism Since World War Two*, London, Fontana, 1984.

Arrighi, G., *The Long Twentieth Century*, London, Verso, 1994.

Arter, D., '"The War of the Roses": conflict and cohesion in the Swedish Social Democratic Party', in D. S. Bell and E. Shaw (eds), *Conflict and Cohesion in the Western European Social Democratic Parties*, London, Frances Pinter, 1994.

Atkins, R., 'Stockholm: Swedes press EU to move against tax havens', *Financial Times*, 28 November 1997.

——, 'Lafontaine links tax to EU budget', *Financial Times*, 17 December 1998.

Atkins, R., Norman, P. and Peston, R., 'Schröder backs Lafontaine', *Financial Times*, 3 December 1998).

Baglioni, G., 'Industrial relations in Europe in the 1980s', in G. Baglioni and C. Crouch (eds) *European Industrial Relations: The Challenge of Flexibility*, London, Sage, 1991.

Baran, P. and Sweezy, P., *Monopoly Capitalism*, New York, Monthly Review Press, 1967.

——, 'Notes on the multinational corporation', *Monthly Review*, 21:5 (1969).

Barkan, J., *Visions of Emancipation: The Italian Workers' Movement Since 1945*, New York, Praeger, 1984.

Barnett, C., *The Audit of War*, London, Macmillan, 1986.

——, *The Lost Victory*, London, Macmillan, 1995.

Barratt Brown, M., *Defending The Welfare State*, Nottingham, Spokesman, 1998.

Barratt Brown, M., Coates, K. and Eaton, J., *An Alternative*, Nottingham, Spokesman, 1975.

Beavis, S., 'It's boom-time for the cynical tendency', *Guardian*, 31 January 1997.

Beer, S. H., *Britain Against Itself*, London, Faber and Faber, 1982.

Bell, D. S., 'The socialists in government', in D. S. Bell and E. Shaw (eds), *The Left in France*, Nottingham, Spokesman, 1983.

Bell, D. S. and Criddle, B., *The French Socialist Party: The Emergence of a Party of Government*, Oxford, Clarendon Press, second edition, 1988.

Bell, D. S. and Shaw, E., 'Conclusion', in D. S. Bell and E. Shaw (eds), *Conflict and Cohesion in the Western European Social Democratic Parties*, London, Frances Pinter, 1994.

Benn, T., *Arguments For Socialism*, London, Cape, 1979.

——, *Arguments for Democracy*, London, Cape, 1980.

Benson, J., *The Working Class in Britain, 1850–1939*, London, Longman, 1989.

Berger, S., 'Liberalism reborn: the new synthesis in France', in J. Howorth and G. Ross (eds), *Contemporary France: A Review of Interdisciplinary Studies*, London, Frances Pinter, 1987.

——, 'Germany', in S. Berger and D. Broughton (eds), *The Force of Labour: West European Labour Movement and the Working Class in the Twentieth Century*, Oxford, Berg, 1995.

Berger, S. and Piore, M., *Dualism and Discontinuities in Industrial Societies*, London, Cambridge University Press, 1980.

Bergstrom, H., 'Sweden's politics and party system at the crossroads', *West European Politics*, 14:3 (1991).

Bernstein, E., *Evolutionary Socialism*, New York, Schocken, [1899] 1961.

Bevan, N., *In Place of Fear*, London, Quartet, [1952] 1978.

Blair, T., *New Britain: My Vision of a Young Country*, London, Fourth Estate, 1996.

Blitz, J., 'Italy seeks to defuse dispute over policy', *Financial Times*, 3 December 1998.

Boggs, C., *The Socialist Tradition: From Crisis to Decline*, London, Routledge, 1995.

Braunthal, G., *The West German Social Democrats, 1969–1982: Profile of a Party in Power*, Boulder, CO, Westview Press, 1983.

——, *The German Social Democrats Since 1969: A Party in Power and Opposition*, Boulder, CO, Westview Press, 1994.

——, 'The perspective from the left', *German Politics and Society*, 34:1 (1995).

——, *Parties and Politics in Modern Germany*, Boulder, CO, Westview Press, 1996.

Breitenfeller, A., 'Global unionism: a potential player?', *International Labour Review*, 136:4 (1997).

Brenner, R., *The Economics of Global Turbulence*, *New Left Review*, special issue, 229 (1998).

Brenner, R. and Glick, M., 'The regulation approach: theory and history', *New Left Review*, 188 (1991).

Bridgford, J., *The Politics of French Trade Unionism: Party–Union Relations at the time of the Union of the Left*, Leicester, Leicester University Press, 1991.

Briggs, A., 'The welfare state in historical perspective', *Archives de Europeenes de Sociologie*, 2 (1961).

Brittan, S., 'The economic contradictions of democracy', *British Journal of Political Science*, 5, April (1975).

——, 'The economic contradictions of democracy', in A. King (ed.), *Why Is Britain Becoming Harder to Govern?*, London, BBC, 1976.

Brook, L., 'Public spending and taxation', in R. Jowell (ed.), *British Social Attitudes*, 13th Report, Aldershot, Dartmouth, 1996.

Brown, B. E., *Socialism of a Different Kind: Reshaping the Left in France*, Westport, CT, Greenwood Press, 1982.

Brown, G., 'Equality – then and now', in D. Leonard (ed.), *Crosland and New Labour*, London, Macmillan, 1999.

Brown, K. D., 'The Labour Party and the unemployment question 1906–1910', *Historical Journal*, 14:3 (1971).

Brule, M., 'L'Appartenance Religieuse et le Vote du 5 decembre 1965', *Sondages*, 28:2 (1966).

Buchan, D., 'Jospin plea over capital flows', *Financial Times*, 12 September 1998.

Budge, I. and Crewe, I., *Party Identification and Beyond*, London, Wiley, 1976.

Burkitt, B. and Whyman, P., 'Public sector reform in Sweden: competition or participation?', *Political Quarterly*, 65:3 (1994).

Burklin, W. P., 'The split between the established and non-established left in Germany', *European Journal of Political Research*, 13 (1985).

Burnham, W. D., 'The end of American party politics', *Transaction*, December (1969).

Butler, D. and Stokes, D., *Political Change in Britain*, London, Macmillan, second edition, 1974.

Callaghan, J., 'The background to "entrism": Leninism and the British Labour Party', *Journal of Communist Studies*, December (1986).

——, *Great Power Complex*, London, Pluto Press, 1997.

Callaghan, J., *Time and Chance*, London, Collins, 1987.

Cambridge Political Economy Group, *Britain's Economic Crisis*, Nottingham, Spokesman, 1975.

Cameron, D. R., 'Exchange rate politics in France, 1981–83: the regime-defining choices of the Mitterrand presidency', in A. Daley (ed.), *The Mitterrand Era: Policy Alternatives and Political Mobilization in France*, London, Macmillan, 1996.

Carney, L. S., 'Globalisation: the final demise of socialism?', *International Journal of Politics, Culture and Society*, 10:1 (1996–7).

Carr, W., 'German social democracy since 1945', in R. Fletcher (ed.), *Bernstein to Brandt: A Short History of German Social Democracy*, London, Edward Arnold, 1987.

Castles, F. 'Scandinavian social democracy: achievements and problems', *West European Politics*, 1978.

——, *The Social Democratic Image of Society*, London, Sage, 1978.

Castles, F. and McKinlay, R. D., 'Does politics matter? An analysis of the public welfare commitment in advanced democratic states', *European Journal of Political Research*, 7:2 (1979).

Chossudovsky, M., *The Globalisation of Poverty: Impacts of IMF and World Bank Reforms*, London, Zed Books 1997.

Christiansen, N. F., 'Denmark: end of an idyll?', in P. Anderson and P. Camiller (eds), *Mapping the West European Left*, London, Verso, 1994.

Clasen, J. and Gould, A., 'Stability and change in welfare states: Germany and Sweden in the 1990s', *Politics and Policy*, 23:3 (1995).

Clogg R., *Parties and Elections in Greece*, London, Hurst, 1987.

Coates, K., 'Unemployed Europe and the struggle for alternatives', *New Left Review*, 227 (1998).

——, 'Europe without frontiers', *New Socialist*, 59, February–March (1989).

Coates, K. and Barratt Brown, M. (eds), *A European Recovery Programme: Restoring Full Employment*, Nottingham, Spokesman, 1993.

Cohen, J. and Rogers, J., '"Reaganism" after Reagan', in L. Panitch and R. Miliband (eds), *The Socialist Register 1988*, London, Merlin, 1988.

Cole, A., 'A house divided: socialism a la francaise', in G. Raymond (ed.), *France During the Socialist Years*, Aldershot, Dartmouth, 1994.

Communist Party of Great Britain, *Manifesto For New Times*, London, CPGB, 1987.

Compston, H., 'Union participation in economic policy making in Scandinavia, 1970–1993', *West European Politics*, 18:1 (1995).

——, 'Union participation in economic policy making in France, Italy, Germany and Britain, 1970-1993', *West European Politics*, 18:3 (1995).

Conference of Socialist Economists, *An Alternative Economic Strategy*, London, CSE Books, 1980.

Cook, R., speech to the Institute for European Affairs, Dublin, 3 November 1997.

Cousins, C., 'Changing regulatory frameworks and non-standard employment: a comparison of Germany, Spain, Sweden, and the UK', in A. Felstead and N. Jewson (eds), *Global Trends in Flexible Labour*, London, Macmillan, 1999.

Coverdale, J. F., *The Political Transformation of Spain after France*, New York, Praeger, 1979.

CPSA/SCPS, *Cuts that Puzzle: The Case Against the Cuts*, London, CPSA/SCPS, 1975.

Crewe, I., 'Why the Conservatives won', in H. Penniman (ed.), *Britain at the Polls 1979*, London, AEI, 1981.

——, 'The Labour Party and the electorate', in D. Kavanagh (ed.), *The Politics of the Labour Party*, London, Allen and Unwin, 1982.

——, 'The disturbing truth behind Labour's rout', *Guardian*, 13 June 1983.

——, 'The electorate: partisan dealignment ten years on', *West European Politics*, 7 (1984).

——, 'Values: the crusade that failed', in D. Kavanagh and A. Seldon, *The Thatcher Effect: A Decade of Change*, Oxford, Clarendon Press, 1989.

Crewe, I., Sarlvik, B. and Alt, J., 'Partisan dealignment in Britain 1964–1974', *British Journal of Political Science*, 7 (1977).

Criddle, B., 'The French Socialist Party', in W. E. Paterson and A. H. Thomas (eds), *The Future of Social Democracy: Problems and Prospects of Social Democratic Parties in Western Europe*, Oxford, Clarendon Press, 1986.

Cripps F., and Ward, T., 'Road to recovery', *New Socialist*, July–August (1982).

——, 'Government policies, European recession and problems of recovery', *Cambridge Journal of Economics*, 1, March (1983).

Crosland, C. A. R., 'The transition from capitalism', in R. H. S. Crossman (ed.), *New Fabian Essays*, London, Turnstile Press, 1952.

——, *The Future of Socialism*, London, Cape, 1956.

——, *The Conservative Enemy: A Programme of Radical Reform for the 1960s*, London, Cape, 1962.

——, *A Social Democratic Britain*, London, Fabian Society, tract 404, 1971.

——, *Socialism Now and Other Essays*, London, Cape, 1974.

Crossman, R. H. S., *Socialism and the New Despotism*, London, Fabian Society, tract 298, 1958.

Crouch, C., 'The future prospects for trade unions in Western Europe', *Political Quarterly*, 57:1 (1986).

——, 'The fate of articulated industrial relations systems', in M. Regini (ed.) *The Future of Labour Movements*, London, Sage, 1992.

——, 'The terms of the neo-liberal consensus', *Political Quarterly*, 4 (1997).

Crouch, C. and Pizzorno, A. (eds), *The Resurgence of Class Conflict in Western Europe Since 1968*, London, Holmes and Meier, 1979.

Crozier, M., Huntingdon, S. and Watanuki, J., *Crisis of Democracy*, New York, New York University Press, 1975.

Dahl, R., *An Introduction to Democratic Theory*, Chicago, IL, University of Chicago Press, 1956.

——, *Who Governs?*, New Haven, CT, Yale University Press, 1961.

——, *Polyarchy*, New Haven, CT, Yale University Press, 1971.

Dahrendorf, R., *Reflections on the Revolution in Europe*, London, Chatto, 1990.

Daly, M. 'Welfare states under pressure: cash benefits in European welfare states over the last ten years', *Journal of European Social Policy*, 7, 2 (1997).

Dell, E., *A Hard Pounding*, Oxford, Oxford University Press, 1991.

Delwaide, J., 'Postmaterialism and politics: the "Schmidt SPD" and the greening of Germany', *German Politics*, 2:2 (1993).

Driver, S. and Martell, L., *New Labour: Politics After Thatcherism*, Cambridge, Polity Press, 1998.

Dubois, P., Durand, C. and Erbes-Seguin, S., 'The contradictions of French trade unionism', in C. Crouch and A. Pizzorno (eds), *The Resurgence of Class Conflict in Western Europe Since 1968, Volume One: National Studies*, London, Macmillan, 1978.

Durbin, E., *New Jerusalems: The Labour Party and the Economics of Democratic Socialism*, London, Routledge and Kegan Paul, 1985.

Dutch Government Press Release, 'White Paper: Taxes in the Twenty-First Century: An Investigation', 11 December 1997.

Dutch Ministry of Economic Affairs, 'Knowledge in action', Ministry of Economic Affairs website, accessed January 1999.

Dutch Ministry of Finance, 'The Dutch Tax Authorities and Foreign Businesses', Dutch Ministry of Finance website.

Dyson, K. H. F., 'The politics of economic management in West Germany', *West European Politics*, 2 (1981).

Economist, 'All mod cons: Tony Blair's economic inheritance', *Economist*, 27 September 1997.

——, 'The vision thing: Tony Blair says his mission is to modernise Britain', *Economist*, 27 September 1997.

Ehrmann, H. W., *French Labor From Popular Front to Liberation*, Oxford, Oxford University Press, 1947.

Elephantis, A., 'PASOK and the elections of 1977', in H. Penniman (ed.), *Greece at the Polls*, London, Hurst, 1987.

Elliott, L. and Kelly, R., 'Labour admits city is needed', *Guardian*, 4 October 1994.

Emmett Tyrell, Jr, R., *The Future That Does Not Work*, New York, Garden City, 1977.

Esping-Andersen, G., 'Social class, social democracy, and the state', *Comparative Politics*, 11 (1978).

——, *Politics Against Markets*, Princeton, NJ, Princeton University Press, 1985.

——, *Three Worlds of Welfare Capitalism*, Cambridge, Cambridge University Press, 1990.

—— (ed.), *Welfare States in Transition*, London, Sage, 1996.

Esser J., 'State, business and trade unions in West Germany after the "Political Wende"', *West European Politics*, 2 (1986).

Eudes, D., *The Kapetanios: Partisans and Civil War in Greece, 1943–49*, London, New Left Books, 1972.

R. Exell, 'Arousing suspicions', *New Times*, 28 February 1998.

Falkner, G. and Talos, E., 'The role of the state within social policy', *West European Politics*, 3 (1994).

Farnham, D., 'New Labour, the new unions, and the new labour market', *Parliamentary Affairs*, 49:4 (1996).

Field, F., *Losing Out: The Emergence of Britain's Underclass*, Oxford, Blackwell, 1989.

Fishman, R. M., 'Rethinking state and regime: Southern Europe's transition to democracy', *World Politics*, 42, 3 (1990).

Fitzmaurice, J., *Austrian Politics and Society Today*, Basingstoke, Macmillan, 1991.

Fox Piven, F., 'Is it global economics or neo-laissez-faire?', *New Left Review*, 213 (1995).

Fox Piven, F. and Cloward, R. A., *The New Class War: Reagan's Attack on the Welfare State and Its Consequences*, New York, Praeger, 1980.

Frank, T. C., 'France: an unforgivable exception', *Le Monde Diplomatique*, April 1998.

Frankland, E. G., 'Federal Republic of Germany: *Die Grünen*', in F. Muller-Rommel (ed.), *New Politics in Western Europe: The Rise and Success of Green Parties and Alternative Lists*, Boulder, CO, Westview Press, 1989.

Franklin, M., Mackie, T., Valen, H. *et al.*, *Electoral Change: Responses to Evolving Social and Attitudinal Structures in Western Countries*, Cambridge, Cambridge University Press, 1992.

French Embassy and Information Service, *News From France*, April 1998.

Friedman, M., *A Programme for Monetary Stability*, New York, Fordham University Press, 1960.

——, *Capitalism and Freedom*, Chicago, IL, University of Chicago Press, 1962.

Friend, J. W., *Seven Years in France*, Boulder, CO, Westview Press, 1989.

Froud, J. *et al.*, 'Stakeholder economy? From utility privatisation to New Labour', *Capital and Class*, 60 (1996).

Fulcher, J., 'The Social Democratic model in Sweden: termination or restoration?', *Political Quarterly*, 65:2 (1994).

Galbraith, J. K., *The Affluent Society*, Harmondsworth, Pelican, 1958.

——, *The Culture of Contentment*, London, Penguin, 1992.

Gallie, D., Penn, R. and Rose, M. (eds), *Trade Unions in Recession*, Oxford, Oxford University Press, 1996.

Gallie, D. and Vogler, C., 'Labour market deprivation, welfare and collectivism', *Archives Europeennes De Sociologie*, 31:1 (1990).

Galtung, J., 'The green movement: a socio-historical exploration', *International Sociology*, 1:1 (1986).

Gamble, A., *Free Economy and Strong State*, London, Macmillan, 1988.

Garner, R., 'How green is Labour?', *Politics Review*, 8:4 (1999).

Garrett, G., *Partisan Politics in the Global Economy*, Cambridge, Cambridge University Press, 1998.

Giddens, A., *The Third Way: The Renewal of Social Democracy*, Cambridge, Polity Press, 1998.

Gilbert, B. B., *British Social Policy, 1914–1939*, London, Batsford 1970.

Gillespie, R., *The Spanish Socialist Party: A History of Factionalism*, Oxford, Clarendon Press, 1989.

——, 'The break-up of the "socialist family": party–union relations in Spain', *West European Politics*, 13:1 (1990).

Glassman, M. 'The siege of the German Social Market', *New Left Review*, 225 (1997).

Glyn, A., 'Social democracy and full employment', *New Left Review*, 211 (1995).

Glyn, A. and Sutcliffe, R., 'Global but leaderless? The new capitalist order', in L. Panitch and R. Miliband (eds), *The Socialist Register 1992*, London, Merlin, 1992.

Gobin, C., 'Taming the unions', *Le Monde Diplomatique*, November 1997.

Gordon, D., 'The global economy', *New Left Review*, 168 (1988).

Gorz, A., *Farewell to the Working Class*, London, Pluto Press, 1980.

Gould, P., *The Unfinished Revolution*, London, Little Brown, 1998.

Graham, G., Parker, A. and Wighton, D., 'Chirac seeks to soothe UK', *Financial Times*, 4 December 1998.

Grant, C., *Delors: The House that Jacques Built*, London, Nicholas Brealey, 1994.

Griffin, L. J., McCammon, H. J. and Botsko, C., 'The unmaking of a movement? The crisis of U.S. trade unionism in comparative perspective', in M. T. Hallinan, D. M. Klein and J. Glass (eds), *Change in Societal Institutions*, New York, Plenum, 1990.

Guardian, 'Blair does the business', *Guardian*, 22 January 1997.

Haerpfer, C., 'Austria: the "United Greens" and the "Alternative List/Green Alternative"', in F. Muller-Rommel (ed.), *New Politics in Western Europe: The Rise and Success of Green Parties and Alternative Lists*, Boulder, CO, Westview Press, 1989.

Hakim, C., 'Trends in the flexible workforce', *Employment Gazette*, November 1987.

Halimi, S., 'Less exceptionalism than meets the eye', in A. Daley (ed.), *The Mitterrand Era: Policy Alternatives and Political Mobilization in France*, London, Macmillan, 1996.

Hall, P., 'Socialism in one country: Mitterrand and the struggle to define a new economic policy in France', in P. Cerny and M. Schain (eds), *Socialism, the State and Public Policy in France*, London, Frances Pinter, 1985.

Hall, S., Massey, D. and Rustin, M., 'Uncomfortable times', *Soundings*, 1, Autumn (1995).

Halsey, A. H., *Change in British Society*, London, Oxford University Press, 1981.

Hamilton, M. B., *Democratic Socialism in Britain and Sweden*, London, Macmillan, 1989.

Hanley, D., *Keeping Left? CERES and the French Socialist Party*, Manchester, Manchester University Press, 1986.

Harris, J., 'Enterprise and the welfare state: a comparative perspective', in T. Gourvish and A. O'Day (eds), *Britain Since 1945*, London, Macmillan, 1991.

Hatch, M. T., 'Corporatism, pluralism and post-industrial politics: nuclear energy in West Germany', *West European Politics*, 1 (1991).

Hatfield, M., *The House the Left Built*, London, Gollancz, 1978.

Hay, J. R., *The Origins of the Liberal Welfare Reforms 1906–1914*, London, Macmillan, 1975.

——, 'Employers and social policy in Britain: the evolution of welfare legislation 1905–1914', *Social History*, 4 (1977).

Hayek, F. A., *The Road to Serfdom*, London, Routledge and Kegan Paul, [1944] 1976.

——, *Law, Legislation, and Liberty: A New Statement of the Liberal Principles of Justice and Political Economy*, London, Routledge and Kegan Paul, one-volume edition, 1982.

Heclo, H. and Madsen, H., *Policy and Politics in Sweden*, Philadelphia, PA, Temple University Press, 1987.

Heerma van Voss, L., 'The Netherlands', in S. Berger and D. Broughton (eds), *The Force of Labour:West European Labour Movement and the Working Class in the Twentieth Century*, Oxford, Berg, 1995.

Heffernan, R., 'Blueprint for a revolution? The politics of the Adam Smith Institute', in M. Kandiah (ed.), *Think Tanks in British Politics Vol. 2*, London, Frank Cass, 1996.

Heffernan, R. and Marqusee, M., *Defeat From the Jaws of Victory: Inside Kinnock's Labour Party*, London, Verso, 1992.

Heidar, K., 'The Norwegian Labour Party: social democracy in a periphery of Europe', in W. E. Paterson and A. H. Thomas (eds), *Social Democratic Parties in Western Europe*, New York, St. Martin's Press, 1977.

——, 'Towards party irrelevance? The decline of both conflict and cohesion in the Norwegian Labour Party', in D. S. Bell and E. Shaw (eds), *Conflict and Cohesion in the Western European Social Democratic Parties*, London, Frances Pinter, 1994.

Helleiner, E., *States and the Reemergence of Global Finance*, Ithaca, NY, Cornell University Press, 1994.

Helm, J. A., 'Codetermination in West Germany', *West European Politics*, 1 (1986).

Herod, A., 'The practice of international labour solidarity and the geography of the global economy', *Economic Geography*, 71:4 (1995).

Hewitt, C. 'The effect of political democracy and social democracy in industrial societies: a cross-national comparison', *American Sociological Review*, xlii:3 (1977).

Hine, D., 'Leaders and followers: democracy and manageability in the social democratic parties of Western Europe', in W. E. Paterson and A. H. Thomas (eds), *The Future of Social Democracy: Problems and Prospects of Social Democratic Parties in Western Europe*, Oxford, Clarendon Press, 1986.

Hirsch, F., *Alternatives to World Monetary Disorder*, New York, Random House, 1977.

Hirst, P. and Thompson, G., *Globalisation in Question*, Cambridge, Polity Press, 1996.

Hobsbawm, E. J., 'Trends in the British labour movement', in E. J. Hobsbawm, *Labouring Men*, London, Weidenfeld and Nicolson, 1968.
——, *The Age of Capital, 1848–1875*, London, Abacus, 1977.
——, 'The face of Labour's future', *Marxism Today*, October (1984).
——, *The Age of Empire, 1875–1914*, London, Weidenfeld and Nicolson, 1987.
Holland, S., *The Socialist Challenge*, London, Quartet, 1975.
——, (ed.), *Out of the Crisis: A Project for European Recovery*, Nottingham, Spokesman, 1983.
——, (ed.), *The European Imperative: Economic and Social Cohesion in the 1990s*, Nottingham, Spokesman, 1993.
Hulsberg, W., *The German Greens: A Social and Political Profile*, London, Verso, 1988.
Humphreys, P., 'Legitimating the communications revolution: governments, parties and trade unions in Britain, France, and West Germany', *West European Politics*, 4 (1986).
Hutton, W., *The State We're In*, London, Cape, 1996.
Hymer, S. and Rowthorn, R., 'Multinational corporations and international oligopoly: the non-American challenge', in C. P. Kindelberger (ed.), *The International Corporation: A Symposium*, Cambridge, MA, MIT Press, 1970.
Inglehart, R., *The Silent Revolution: Changing Values and Political Styles Among Western Publics*, Princeton, NJ, Princeton University Press, 1977.
——, 'Value change in industrial societies', *American Political Science Review*, 81:4 (1987).
——, 'The changing structure of political cleavages in Western Society', in R. J. Dalton, S. C. Flanagan and P. A. Beck (eds), *Electoral Change in Advanced Industrial Democracies: Realignment or Dealignment?* Princeton, NJ, Princeton University Press, 1984.
Inglehart, R. and Andeweg, R. B., 'Change in Dutch political culture: a silent or a silenced revolution?', *West European Politics*, 3 (1993).
Jacques, M., 'New Europeans', *Guardian*, 7 July 1997.
Jagland, T., 'Speech to the Socialist International Council', DNA website, 1998, accessed January 1999.
Jay, D., *The Socialist Case*, London, Faber and Faber, 1937.
——, *Socialism in the New Society*, London, Longmans, 1962.
Jay, P., 'How inflations threatens', *The Times*, 1 July 1974.
——, *Employment, Inflation and Politics*, London, Institute of Economic Affairs, 1976.
Johnson, B., 'Herr Blair takes a bow, but cannot take the credit', *Daily Telegraph*, 19 June 1996.
Johnson, R. W., *The Long March of the French Left*, London, Macmillan, 1981.
Joppke, C. and Markovits, A. S., 'Green politics in the New Germany', *Dissent*, Spring (1994).
Kalecki, M., 'Political aspects of full employment', in M. Kalecki, *Selected Essays on the Dynamics of the Capitalist Economy, 1933–70*, London, Cambridge University Press, 1971.
Keegan, W., 'Deep depression and severe weather warning for the Tories', *Observer*, 7 January 1996.
Kesselman, M., 'Prospects for democratic socialism in advanced capitalism: class struggle and compromise in Sweden and France', *Politics and Society*, 11:4 (1982).

——, 'Lyrical illusions or a socialism of governance: whither French socialism?', in R. Miliband and J. Saville (eds), *The Socialist Register 1985*, London, Merlin, 1986.

Kettle, M., 'Labour's bright new dawn ends at Dover', *Guardian*, 21 June 1997.

——, 'The next step: a blueprint for New Labour's world role', *Guardian*, 7 February 1998.

King, A., 'Overload: problems of government in the 1970s', *Political Studies*, 23, June–September (1975).

——, 'The problem of overload', in A. King, *Why Is Britain Becoming Harder To Govern?*, London, BBC, 1976.

Kircheimer, O., 'The transformation of the Western European party system', in J. LaPalombara and M. Weiner (eds), *Political Parties and Political Development*, Princeton, NJ, Princeton University Press, 1966.

Kitschelt, H., *The Transformation of Social Democracy*, Cambridge, Cambridge University Press, 1994.

——, 'Austrian and Swedish social democrats in crisis: party strategy and organisation in corporatist regimes', *Comparative Political Studies*, 27:1 (1994).

Kohl, J., 'Trends and problems in postwar public expenditure development in Western Europe and North America', in P. Flora and A. J. Heidenheimer (eds), *The Development of Welfare States in Europe and North America*, New Brunswick, NJ, Transaction Publishers, 1981.

Kolinsky, E., *Parties, Opposition and Society in West Germany*, London, Croom Helm, 1984.

——, 'Political culture change and party organisation: the SPD and the second "Frauleinwunder"', in J. Gaffney and E. Kolinsky (eds), *Political Culture in France and Germany*, London, Macmillan, 1991.

Korpi, W., *The Working Class in Welfare Capitalism*, London, Routledge and Kegan Paul, 1978.

Kosonen, P., 'From collectivism to individualism in the welfare state?', *Acta Sociologica*, 30:3/4 (1990).

Krugman, P., 'The myth of Asia's miracle', *Foreign Affairs*, November–December (1994).

——, *Peddling Prosperity*, New York, Norton, 1994.

Kuhnle, S., 'Political reconstruction of the European welfare states: a critical review of recent debates', in H. Cavanna (ed.), *Challenges to the Welfare State: Internal and External Dynamics for Change*, Cheltenham, Edward Elgar, 1998.

Kunkel, C. and Pontusson, J., 'Corporatism versus social democracy: divergent fortunes of the Austrian and Swedish labour movements', *West European Politics*, 21:2 (1998).

Labour Party [Norway], *Statement of Principles and Action Programme*, Oslo, DNA, 1996.

Labour Party, *Labour's Programme 1973*, London, Labour Party, 1973.

——, *Britain Will Win*, London, Labour Party, 1987.

——, *Social Justice and Economic Efficiency*, London, Labour Party, 1988.

——, *Meet The Challenge, Make the Change*, London, Labour Party, 1989.

——, *Labour's Better Way for the 1990s*, London, Labour Party, 1991.

——, *Looking to the Future*, London, Labour Party, 1991.

——, *Made in Britain*, London, Labour Party, 1991.

——, *Modern Manufacturing Strength*, London, Labour Party, 1991.

——, *It's Time To Get Britain Working Again*, London, Labour Party, 1992.
——, *Labour's Campaign For Recovery*, London, Labour Party, 1992.
——, *Opportunity Britain*, London, Labour Party, 1992.
——, *Rebuilding the Economy*, London, Labour Party, 1994.
——, *A New Economic Future For Britain*, London, Labour Party, 1995.
——, *Building Prosperity – Flexibility, Efficiency and Fairness at Work*, London, Labour Party, 1996.
——, *New Labour: New Life for Britain*, London, Labour Party, 1996.
——, *Vision For Growth*, London, Labour Party, 1996.
——, *Labour's Business Manifesto: Equipping Britain For the Future*, London, Labour Party, 1997.
——, *New Labour: Because Britain Deserves Better*, London, Labour Party, 1997.
Lafontaine, O., *Globalisation and International Cooperation*, Bonn, SPD, 1996.
——, 'The future of German Social Democracy', *New Left Review*, 227 (1998).
——, 'Globalisation and international cooperation – social democratic policy in an age of globalisation', in D. Dettke (ed.), *The Challenge of Globalisation for Germany's Social Democracy: A Policy Agenda for the 21st Century*, Oxford, Berghahn, 1998.
Lash, S., 'The end of neo-corporatism? The breakdown of centralised bargaining in Sweden', *British Journal of Industrial Relations*, 23:2 (1985).
Lauber, V., *The Political Economy of France: From Pompidou to Mitterrand*, London, Praeger, 1983.
Laughland, J., *The Death of Politics: France Under Mitterrand*, London, Michael Joseph, 1994.
Lawson, R. 'Germany: maintaining the middle way', in V. George and P. Taylor-Gooby (eds), *European Welfare Policy: Squaring the Circle*, London, Macmillan, 1996.
Leaman, J., 'Central banking and the crisis of social democracy – a comparative analysis of British and German views', *German Politics*, 3 (1995).
Lecher, W., 'The current state of the trade unions in the EU member states: Britain', in W. Lecher (ed.), *Trade Unions in the European Union: A Handbook*, London, Lawrence and Wishart, 1994.
Lewin, L., *Ideology and Strategy: A Century of Swedish Politics*, Cambridge, Cambridge University Press, 1988.
Lewis-Beck, M. and Skalaban, A., 'France', in M. Franklin *et al.* (eds), *Electoral Change: Responses to Evolving Social and Attitudinal Structures in Western Countries*, Cambridge, Cambridge University Press, 1992.
Liebman, M., 'Reformism yesterday and social democracy today', in R. Miliband and J. Saville (eds.), *The Socialist Register 1985*, London, Merlin, 1986.
Linton, M., *The Swedish Road to Socialism*, London, Fabian Society, tract 503, 1985.
Lipietz, A., *The Globalisation of the General Crisis of Fordism*, Paris, Cepremap, 1984.
Lipset, S. M., 'The changing class structure and contemporary European politics', in S. Graubard (ed.), *A New Europe?*, Boston, MA, Houghton Mifflin, 1964.
Lipsey, D. 'Do we really want more spending?', in R. Jowell (ed.), *British Social Attitudes*, 11th Report, Aldershot, Dartmouth, 1994.
Livingstone, K., 'Reassembling the left', *Chartist*, 115, May–June (1987).
Loney, M., *The Politics of Greed*, London, Pluto Press, 1986.
Losche, P., 'Is the SPD still a labor party? From a "community of solidarity" to a "loosely coupled anarchy"', in D. E. Barclay and E. D. Weitz (eds), *Between Reform and*

Revolution: German Socialism and Communism From 1840 to 1990, Oxford, Berghahn, 1998.

Lowe, R., 'The erosion of state intervention in Britain 1917–24', *Economic History Review*, 31 (1978).

Lyrintzis, C., 'Political parties in post-Junta Greece', in H. Penniman (ed), *Greece at the Polls*, Washington, DC, Duke University Press, 1981.

Mackie, T., Mannheimer, R. and Sani, G., 'Italy', in M. Franklin *et al.* (eds.), *Electoral Change: Responses to Evolving Social and Attitudinal Structures in Western Countries*, Cambridge, Cambridge University Press, 1992.

Maclean, M., 'Introduction', in M. Maclean (ed.), *The Mitterrand Years: Legacy and Evaluation*, Basingstoke, Macmillan 1998.

MacShane, D., *French Lessons For Labour*, London, Fabian Society, 1986.

Maier, C. S., 'The politics of productivity: foundations of American international policy after World War Two', *International Organisation*, 31, Autumn (1977).

Mair, P., 'Party organisations: from civil society to the state', in P. Mair and O. Katz (eds), *How Parties Organize*, London, Sage, 1994.

——, *Party System Change*, Oxford, Clarendon Press, 1997.

Mandel, E., *Europe versus America*, London, New Left Books, [1968] 1970.

——, *Late Capitalism*, London, New Left Books, 1975.

Mann, M., 'As the twentieth century ages', *New Left Review*, 214 (1995).

Marklund, S., 'Welfare state policies in the tripolar class model of Scandinavia', *Politics and Society*, 16:4 (1988).

Markovits, A. S., 'The West German left in a changing Europe', in C. Lemke and G. Marks (eds), *The Crisis of Socialism in Europe*, London, Duke University Press, 1992.

Markovits, A. S. and Gorski, P. S., *The German Left: Red, Green and Beyond*, Cambridge, Polity Press, 1993.

Marquand, D., 'After euphoria: the dilemmas of New Labour', *Political Quarterly*, 4 (1997).

Marshall, T. H., *Citizenship and Social Class and Other Essays*, London, Cambridge University Press, 1950.

Martin, A. and Ross, G., 'European trade unions and the economic crisis: perceptions and strategies', in J. Hayward (ed.), *Trade Unions and Politics in Western Europe*, London, Frank Cass, 1980.

Martin, D., *Bringing Common Sense to the Common Market*, London, Fabian Society, tract 512, 1988.

Marwick, A., 'The Labour Party and the welfare state in Britain 1900–1948', *American Historical Review*, 73:2 (1967).

Massey, D., 'The shape of things to come', in R. Peet (ed.), *International Capitalism and Industrial Restructuring*, London, Allen and Unwin, 1987.

Matthews, R. C. O., 'Why has Britain had full employment since the war?', *Economic Journal*, 78:3 (1968).

Mauroy, P., 'Draft of speech to SI Council', 18 May 1998, DNA website, accessed January 1999.

McCarthy, P. (ed.), *The French Socialists in Power, 1981–86*, New York, Greenwood Press, 1987.

McCormick, J., 'Apprenticeship for governing: an assessment of French socialism in power', in H. Machin and V. Wright (eds), *Economic Policy Under the Mitterrand Presidency, 1991–1984*, London, Frances Pinter, 1985.

McKibbin, R., 'Class and conventional wisdom: the Conservative Party and the "public" in inter-war Britain', in R. McKibbin, *Ideologies of Class*, Oxford, Oxford University Press, 1991.

——, 'The "social psychology" of unemployment in inter-war Britain', in R. McKibbin, *Ideologies of Class*, Oxford, Oxford University Press, 1990.

Meidner, R., *Employee Investment Funds*, London, Allen and Unwin, 1978.

——, 'Why did the Swedish model fail?', in R. Miliband and L. Panitch (eds), *The Socialist Register 1993*, London, Merlin, 1993.

Merkel, W., 'After the golden age: is social democracy doomed to decline?', in C. Lemke and G. Marks (eds), *The Crisis of Socialism in Western Europe*, London, Duke University Press, 1992.

——, *Ende der Sozialdemokratie? Machtressourcen und Regierungspolitik im westeuropaischen*, Frankfurt, Vergleich, 1993.

Merkle, P., 'The SPD after Brandt: problems of integration in a changing urban society', *West European Politics*, 11:1 (1991).

Meyer, T., 'The transformation of German social democracy', in D. Sassoon (ed.), *The Rise and Success of Green Parties and Alternative Lists*, London, I. B. Tauris, 1997.

Michels, R., *Political Parties*, New York, Free Press, [1911] 1962.

Minkin, L., *The Labour Party Conference*, London, Allen Lane, 1978.

——, *The Contentious Alliance: Trade Unions and the Labour Party*, Edinburgh, Edinburgh University Press, 1991.

Moody, K. 'Reagan, the business agenda and the collapse of Labour', in L. Panitch and R. Miliband (eds), *The Socialist Register 1987*, London, Merlin, 1987.

——, 'Towards an international social-movement unionism', *New Left Review*, 225 (1997).

——, *Workers in a Lean World*, London, Verso, 1997.

Moss, B. H., 'Economic and monetary union and the social divide in France', *Contemporary European History*, 7:2 (1998).

Mouriaux, R., 'The CFDT: from the union of popular forces to the success of social change', in M. Kesselman (ed.), *The French Workers' Movement*, London, Allen and Unwin, 1984.

Muller, C., 'The Institute of Economic Affairs: undermining the post-war consensus', *Contemporary British History*, 10:1 (1996).

Myrdal, G., *Beyond The Welfare State*, New York, Bantam, [1960] 1967.

Navarro, V., 'The decline of Spanish social democracy, 1982–1996', in L. Panitch and C. Leys (eds.), *The Socialist Register 1997*, London, Merlin, 1997.

Nay, C., *The Black and the Red: Francois Mitterrand, The Story of an Ambition*, London, Sheridan, 1984.

Neumann, S., 'Towards a comparative study of political parties', in S. Neumann (ed.), *Modern Political Parties*, Chicago, IL, University of Chicago Press, 1956.

New Democratic Party, Resolution from the 18th Federal Convention at Regina, Saskatchewan, 11–13 April 1997.

Nichols Clark, T. and Lipset, S. M., 'Are social classes dying?', *International Sociology*, 6:4 (1991).

Northcutt, W., *Mitterrand*, London, Holmes and Meier, 1992.

Observer, editorial, 29 November 1998.

O'Connor, J., *The Fiscal Crisis of the State*, New York, St. Martin's Press, 1973.

OECD, *Ageing Populations: The Social Policy Implications*, Paris, OECD, 1988.

Offe, C., *Contradictions of the Welfare State*, London, Hutchinson, 1984.

——, 'New social movements: challenging the boundaries of institutional politics', *Social Research*, 52:4 (1985).

Olsen, G. M., *The Struggle for Economic Democracy in Sweden*, London, Avebury, 1992.

Olson, M., *The Logic of Collective Action: Public Goods and the Theory of Groups*, Cambridge, MA, Harvard University Press, 1965.

——, *The Rise and Decline of Nations*, New Haven, CT, Yale University Press, 1982.

Orlow, D., 'German social democracy and European unification, 1945 to 1955', in D. E. Barclay and E. D. Weitz, *Between Reform and Revolution: German Socialism and Communism from 1840 to 1990*, Oxford, Berghahn, 1998.

Oskarson, M., 'Sweden', in M. Franklin *et al.* (eds), *Electoral Change: Responses to Evolving Social and Attitudinal Structures in Western Countries*, Cambridge, Cambridge University Press, 1992.

Padgett S., 'The West German Social Democrats in opposition, 1982–86', *West European Politics*, 4 (1987).

——, 'The German Social Democrats: a redefinition of social democracy or Bad Godesberg Mark 2', *West European Politics*, 1 (1993).

——, 'The German Social Democratic Party: between old and New Left', in D. S. Bell and E. Shaw (eds), *Conflict and Cohesion in the Western European Social Democratic Parties*, London, Frances Pinter, 1994.

Pagoulatos G., 'Governing in a constrained enviroment: policy-making in the Greek banking deregulation and privatisation reform', *West European Politics*, October (1996).

Pakluski, J. and Waters, M., 'The reshaping and dissolution of social class in advanced society', *Theory and Society*, 25:5 (1996).

Parkin, F., *Middle Class Radicalism*, Manchester, Manchester University Press, 1968.

Partij van de Arbeid, *Platform of Principles*, trans. J. Rudge, Amsterdam, PvdA, n.d.

Paterson, W. E., 'The German Social Democratic Party', in W. E. Patterson and A. H. Thomas (eds), *The Future of Social Democracy: Problems and Prospects of Social Democratic Parties in Western Europe*, Oxford, Clarendon Press, 1986.

——, 'The German Social Democratic Party', in W. E. Paterson and A. H. Thomas (eds), *Social Democratic Parties in Western Europe*, New York, St. Martin's Press, 1977.

Panitch, L. and Leys, C., *The End of Parliamentary Socialism: From New Left to New Labour*, London, Verso, 1997.

Panitch, L. and Miliband R., 'The new world order and the socialist agenda', in L. Panitch and R. Miliband (eds), *The Socialist Register 1992*, London, Merlin, 1992.

PES, Press release, June 1997, PES website, accessed January 1999.

——, 'Creating an orderly framework for the world economy: towards a more efficient, stable, and fair global financial and monetary system', PES website, accessed January 1999.

PES-ECOFIN-Group, 'The new European way – economic reform in the framework of EMU', 12 October 1998, PES website, accessed January 1999.

Peston, R., 'Brown plans Anglo-German working party', *Financial Times*, 19 November 1998.

Peston, R. and Studemann, F., 'UK plays down chance of veto over European Tax on savings', *Financial Times*, 10 December 1998.
Pierson, P., 'The new politics of the welfare state', *World Politics*, 48:2 (1996).
Pollert, A., 'Dismantling flexibility', *Capital and Class*, 34 (1988).
——, *Farewell to Flexibility*, Oxford, Blackwell, 1991.
Pontusson, J., 'Radicalisation and retreat in Swedish Social Democracy', *New Left Review*, 165 (1987).
——, *The Limits of Social Democracy*, Ithaca, NY, Cornell University Press, 1992.
Preston, P., *Franco*, London, Fontana, 1995.
——, *The Politics of Revenge: Fascism and the Military in Twentieth Century Spain*, London, Routledge, 1995.
Prowe, D., 'Ordnungsmacht and Mitbestimmung', in D. E. Barclay and E. D. Weitz (eds), *Between Reform and Revolution: German Socialism and Communism from 1840 to 1990*, Oxford, Berghahn, 1998.
Pryke, R., *Though Cowards Flinch: An Alternative Economic Strategy*, London, MacGibbon and Kee, 1967.
Pryor, F. L., *Public Expenditures in Communist and Capitalist Nations*, London, Macmillan, 1968.
Przeworski, A. and J. Sprague, *Paper Stones: A History of Electoral Socialism*, Chicago, IL, University of Chicago Press, 1986.
Ramonet, I., 'Europe under the Bundesbank', *Le Monde Diplomatique*, July 1997.
Ramsey, H., 'Solidarity at last? International trade unionism approaching the millenium', *Economic and Industrial Democracy*, 18:4 (1997).
Ramsay, R., *Prawn Cocktail Party: The Hidden Power Behind New Labour*, London, Vision, 1998.
Red Pepper, February 1996.
Rehn, G. and Viklund, B., 'Changes in the Swedish model', in G. Baglioni and C. Crouch (eds), *European Industrial Relations: The Challenge of Flexibility*, London, Sage, 1991.
Reich, R., *The Work of Nations*, New York, Vintage, 1992.
Riddell, P., 'Blair plays new economy card to trump Tory appeal', *The Times*, 5 January 1996.
——, 'Opening a doorway to the past', *The Times*, 2 June 1997.
Rimlinger, G. V,. 'Welfare policy and economic development: a comparative historical perspective', *Journal of Economic History*, 26 (1966).
——, *Welfare Policy and Industrialization in Europe, America and Russia*, New York, Wiley, 1971.
Robinson, M., *The Greening of British Party Politics*, Manchester, Manchester University Press, 1992.
Rhodes, M., 'Globalisation and West European welfare states: a critical review of recent debates', *Journal of European Social Policy*, 6;4 (1996).
Rose, R. and Page, E. C., 'Action in adversity: responses to unemployment in Britain and Germany', *West European Politics*, 4 (1990).
Ross, G., *Jacques Delors and European Integration*, Cambridge, Polity Press, 1995.
——, 'The limits of political economy: Mitterrand and the crisis of the French left', in A. Daley (ed.), *The Mitterrand Era: Policy Alternatives and Political Mobilization in France*, Basingstoke, Macmillan, 1996.

Ross, G. and Jenson, J., 'Political pluralism and economic policy', in J. S. Ambler (ed.), *The French Socialist Experiment*, Philadelphia, PA, Institute for the Study of Human Issues, 1985.

Ross, G., Hoffman, S., Malzacher, S. (eds), *The Mitterand Experiment*, Cambridge, Polity Press, 1987.

Rothstein, B., 'Marxism, institutional analysis, and working-class power: the Swedish case', *Politics and Society*, 18:3 (1990).

Rowthorn, B., *Capitalism, Conflict and Inflation*, London, Lawrence and Wishart, 1981.

——, 'The politics of the Alternative Economic Strategy', *Marxism Today*, January (1981).

—— 'Europe ... or bust', *New Socialist*, May–June (1982).

Ruggie, J., 'International regimes, transactions and change: embedded liberalism in the postwar economic order', *International Organisation*, 36 (1982).

Ruigrok, W. and van Tulder, R., *The Logic of International Restructuring*, London, Routledge, 1995.

Sainsbury, D., 'Scandinavian party politics re-examined', *West European Politics*, 1 (1984).

——, 'Swedish social democracy in transition: the party's record in the 1980s and the challenge of the 1990's', *West European Politics*, 14:3 (1991).

——, 'Swedish social democracy and the legacy of continuous reform', *West European Politics*, 16:1 (1993).

SAP, *The Swedish Social Democratic Party Programme*, adopted by the 31st party congress, 1990, translated by Roger Tanner, Stockholm, Tryckeri AB, 1992.

——, 'Stepping into the year 2000: the congress of the future, Sundsvall 1997: policy guidelines adopted by the party congress', SAP, n.d.

Sarlvik, B., 'Recent electoral trends in Sweden', in K. H. Cerny (ed.), *Sandinavia at the Polls*, Washington, DC, American Enterprise Institute for Public Policy Research, 1977.

Sartori, G., 'Will democracy kill democracy?', *Government and Opposition*, 10, Spring (1975).

Sassoon, D., (ed.) *The Italian Communists Speak for Themselves*, Nottingham, Spokesman, 1978.

——, *One Hundred Years of Socialism: The West European Left in the Twentieth Century*, London, I. B. Tauris, 1996.

Saville, J., 'The welfare state: an historical appraisal', *New Reasoner*, 3, Winter (1957–8).

Scammell, W. M., *The International Economy Since 1945*, London, Macmillan, 1980.

Scase R., *Social Democracy in a Capitalist Society*, London, Croom Helm, 1977.

Scharf, T., 'Red-green coalitions at local level in Hesse', in E. Kolinsky (ed.), *The Greens in West Germany: Organisation and Policy-Making*, Oxford, Berg, 1989.

Scharpf, F. W., *Crisis and Choice in European Social Democracy*, Ithaca, NY, Cornell University Press, 1987.

Scheuch, E. K., *Wird Die Bundesrepublik Unregierbar?*, Cologne, Arbeitgeberverband der Metallindustrie, 1976.

Schissler, H., 'Social democratic gender politics', in D. E. Barclay and E. D. Weitz (eds), *Between Reform and Revolution: German Socialism and Communism From 1840 to 1990*, Oxford, Berghahn, 1998.

Schwarz, H., 'Small states in big trouble: state reorganization in Australia, Denmark, New Denmark and Sweden in the 1980s', *World Politics*, 46:4 (1994).

Schwartz, H.-P., *Konrad Adenauer: Volume One: From the German Empire to the Federal Republic, 1876–1952*, Oxford, Berghahn, 1995.

Schweitzer, C. C., Karsten, D. *et al.* (eds), *Politics and Government in the Federal Republic of Germany: Basic Documents*, Leamington Spa, Berg, 1984.

Schweitzer Monatshefte, symposium, Wird Die Schweiz Unregeirbar? (Is Switzerland Ungovernable?), April 1975.

Scruton, R., *The Meaning of Conservatism*, London, Macmillan, 1980.

Searle, G. R., *The Quest For National Efficiency*, Berkeley and Los Angeles, CA, University of California Press, 1971.

Semmel, B., *Imperialism and Social Reform*, London, Allen and Unwin, 1960.

Servan-Schreiber, J.-J., *The American Challenge*, Harmondsworth, Penguin, 1969.

Seyd, P. and Whiteley, P., *Labour's Grass Roots: The Politics of Party Membership*, Oxford, Clarendon Press, 1992.

——, 'Dynamics of party activism in Britain: a spiral of demobilisation?', *British Journal of Political Science*, 28, (19XX).

Share, D., *The Making of Spanish Democracy*, New York, Praeger, 1986.

Shaw, E., *Discipline and Discord in the Labour Party: The Politics of Managerial Control, 1951–87*, Manchester, Manchester University Press, 1988.

——, *The Labour Party Since 1979: Crisis and Transformation*, London, Routledge, 1994.

——, 'Organisational transformation in the Labour Party: the case of candidate selection – some preliminary findings', PSA Conference, Nottingham, 23–24 March 1999.

Shonfield, A., *Modern Capitalism: The Changing Balance of Public and Private Power*, London, Oxford University Press, 1965.

Singer, D., *Is Socialism Doomed?*, Oxford, Oxford University Press, 1988.

Skidelsky, R., *Politicians and the Slump*, Harmondsworth, Pelican, 1970.

Smith, A., 'Spain', in S. Berger and D. Broughton (eds), *The Force of Labour: West European Labour Movement and the Working Class in the Twentieth Century*, Oxford, Berg, 1995.

Smith, J., 'The ideology of family and community: New Labour abandons the welfare state', in L. Panitch and C. Leys (eds), *The Socialist Register 1997*, London, Merlin, 1997.

Social Democratic Party, *Common Future, Common Goals*, Copenhagen, Social Democratic Party, 1996.

Socialist International Council, 'To regulate globalisation and to globalise regulation', agreed in Geneva, 23–24 November 1998, Socialist International website, accessed January 1999.

Spretnak, B. and Capra, F., *Green Politics*, London, Paladin, 1985.

SPD, *The Basic Policy Programme of the Social Democratic Party of Germany*, Bonn, SPD, 1990.

——, 'Globalisation and sustainable development', adopted by SPD Hanover conference, 2–4 December 1997, SPD website, accessed January 1999.

——, 'Europe: a united continent of peace, welfare and social security', adopted by SPD Hanover conference, 2–4 December 1997, SPD website, accessed January 1999.

——, 'Work, innovation, and justice, SPD manifesto 1988', adopted at Leipzig, 17 April 1998, SPD website, accessed January 1999.

SPÖ, *The New Programme of the Austrian Socialist Party (SPÖ)*, Vienna, SPÖ, 1978.

Standing, G., *Unemployment and Labour Market Flexibility: the UK*, Geneva, ILO, 1986.

Stedman-Jones, G., *Outcast London*, Harmondsworth, Peregrine, 1976.

Stephens, J. D., 'The Scandinavian welfare states: achievements, crisis, and prospects', in G. Esping-Andersen (ed.), *Welfare States in Transition*, London, Sage, 1996.

Story, J., 'The Federal Republic – a conservative revisionist', *West European Politics*, 2 (1981).

Strange, S., *International Monetary Relations*, London, Oxford University Press, 1976.

——, *Casino Capitalism*, Manchester, Manchester University Press, 1997.

Strauss-Kahn, D., 'Six of the best', *Financial Times*, 16 April 1998.

——, 'Speech at the Forum Paris Europlace, New York', 17 April 1998.

Streeck, W., 'German capitalism', in C. Crouch and W. Streeck (eds), *The Political Economy of Modern Capitalism*, London, Sage, 1997.

Sully, M., 'The Socialist Party of Austria', in W. E. Paterson and A. H. Thomas (eds), *Social Democratic Parties in Western Europe*, New York, St. Martin's Press, 1977.

——, *Continuity and Change in Austria: The Eternal Quest for the Third Way*, New York, Columbia University Press, 1982.

——, 'Austrian social democracy', in W. E. Paterson and A. H. Thomas (eds), *The Future of Social Democracy: Problems and Prospects of Social Democratic Parties in Western Europe*, Oxford, Clarendon Press, 1986.

——, 'The 1995 Austrian election: winter of discontent', *West European Politics*, 3 (1995).

Swenson, P., *Fair Shares: Union Pay and Politics in Sweden and West Germany*, Ithaca, NY, Cornell University Press, 1989.

——, 'Bringing capital back in, or social democracy reconsidered', *World Politics*, 43:4 (1991).

Taylor, A. J., 'Trade unions and the politics of Social Democratic renewal', *West European Politics*, 16:1 (1993).

Taylor-Gooby, P., 'Comfortable, marginal and excluded' in R. Jowell (ed,), *British Social Attitudes*, 12th Report, Aldershot, Dartmouth, 1995.

——, 'Paying for welfare: the view from Europe', *Political Quarterly*, 67:2 (1996).

Teague, P., 'The Alternative Economic Strategy: a time to go European', *Capital and Class*, 26 (1985).

——, *The European Community: The Social Dimension*, London, Kogan Page, 1989.

Thelen, K. A., *Union of Parts: Labor Politics in Post-War Germany*, Ithaca, NY, Cornell University Press, 1991.

Therborn G. and Roebroek J., 'The irreversible welfare state: its recent maturation, its encounter with the economic crisis and its future prospects', *International Journal of Health Studies*, 16:3 (1986).

Thorpe, A., *A History of the Labour Party*, London, Macmillan, 1997.

Thompson, D., *Democracy in France Since 1870*, Oxford, Oxford University Press, fifth edition, 1969.

Thompson, G., 'Globalisation and the possibilities for domestic economic policy', *Internationale Politik und Gesellschaft*, 2 (1997).

Tilly, C., 'Globalisation threatens labor's rights', *International Labour and Working Class History*, 47, Spring (1995).

Tilton, T., 'Why don't the Swedish social democrats nationalize industry?', *Scandinavian Studies*, 59 (1987).

——, *The Political Theory of Swedish Social Democracy*, Oxford, Clarendon Press, 1990.

Torfing, J., 'Workfare with welfare: recent reforms of the Danish welfare state', *Journal of European Social Policy*, 9:1 (1999).

Townsend, P., 'Persuasion and conformity: an assessment of the Borrie Report on social justice', *New Left Review*, 213 (1995).

Traynor, I. and Walker, D., 'Analysis: social democracy: pretty in pink', *Guardian*, 15 September 1998.

Tromp, B., 'Party strategies and system change in the Netherlands', *West European Politics*, 4 (1989).

Tufte, R., 'Political parties, social class, and economic policy preferences', *Government and Opposition*, 14:1 (1979).

Upham, M., *Trade Unions and Employers' Organisations of the World*, Harlow, Longman, second edition, 1993.

Urban Pappi, F. and Mnich, P. .'Germany', in M. Franklin *et al.* (eds), *Electoral Change: Responses to Evolving Social and Attitudinal Structures in Western Countries*, Cambridge, Cambridge University Press, 1992.

Uri, P. (ed.), *Les Investissements etrangers en Europe*, Paris, Editions Dunod, 1967.

Vandenbroucke, F., *Globalisation, Inequality and Social Democracy*, London, IPPR, 1998.

Van der Pilj, K., *The Making of a Transatlantic Ruling Class*, London, Verso, 1984.

——, 'The sovereignty of capital impaired: social forces and codes of conduct for multinational corporations', in H. Overbeek (ed.) *Restructuring Hegemony in the Global Political Economy: The Rise of Transnational Neo-liberalism in the 1980s*, London, Routledge, 1993.

Van der Wee, H., *Prosperity and Upheaval: The World Economy 1945–1980*, Harmondsworth, Pelican, 1987.

Van der Wurff, R., 'Neo-liberalism in Germany?', in H. Overbeek (ed.), *Restructuring Hegemony in the Global Political Economy: The Rise of Transnational Neo-liberalism in the 1980s*, London, Routledge, 1993.

Van Praag, Jr, P., 'Conflict and cohesion in the Dutch Labour Party', in D. S. Bell and E. Shaw (eds), *Conflict and Cohesion in the Western European Social Democratic Parties*, London, Frances Pinter, 1994.

Veron, R. 'Multinational enterprise and national sovereignty', *Harvard Business Review*, March–April (1967).

Vidal, D. 'Uncertainty over the welfare state: miracle or mirage in the Netherlands?', *Le Monde Diplomatique*, July 1997.

Visser, J. 'Traditions and transitions in industrial relations: a European view', in J. V. Ruysseveldt (ed.), *Industrial Relations in Europe: Traditions and Transitions*, London, Sage, 1996.

Voerman, G., 'Le paradis perdu: les adherents des partis sociaux-democrates d'Europe occidentale, 1945–1995', in M. Lazar (ed.), *Le Gauche en Europe Depuis 1945: Invariants et Mutations du Socialime Européen*, Paris, Presses Universitaires de France, 1996.

Vogel, D. 'Why businessmen distrust their state', *British Journal of Political Science*, 8:1 (1978).

Wass, D. 'The changing problems of economic management', *Economic Trends*, 293 (1978).

Webber, D., 'Combatting and acquiescing in unemployment? Crisis management in Sweden and West Germany', *West European Politics*, 1 (1983).

Wedgwood Benn, A., *The New Politics: A Socialist Reconnaissance*, London, Fabian Society, 1970.

Weiss, L., *The Myth of the Powerless State*, Cambridge, Polity Press, 1998.

Western, B., 'A comparative study of working-class disorganisation: union decline in eighteen advanced capitalist countries', *American Sociological Review*, 60, April (1995).

White, D. S., 'Reconsidering European socialism', *Journal of Contemporary History*, 16 (1981).

Winch, D., *Economics and Policy*, London, Hodder and Stoughton, 1969.

Winter, J. M. (ed.), *War and Economic Development*, London, Cambridge University Press, 1975.

Wolfe, A., 'Has social democracy a future?', *Comparative Politics*, 11, October (1978).

Wolinetz, S. B., 'The Dutch Labour Party', in W. E. Paterson and A. H. Thomas (eds), *Social Democratic Parties in Western Europe*, New York, St. Martin's Press, 1977.

——, 'Socio-economic bargaining in the Netherlands: redefining the post-war policy coalition', *West European Politics*, 1 (1989).

Woodward, C., 'Reality of social reform: from laissez-faire to the welfare state', *Yale Law Journal*, 72 (1962).

Wright, E. O., 'The continuing relevance of class analysis – comments', *Theory and Society*, 25 (1996).

Young, H., *The Iron Lady: A Biography of Margaret Thatcher*, New York, Noonday Press, 1989.

Zolberg, A. R., 'Response: working class dissolution', *International Labour and Working Class History*, 47, Spring (1995).

Index

Note: 'n' after a page reference indicates a note number on that page.